You Rejoice My Heart

Kemal Yalçın

translated by Paul Bessemer

Gomidas Institute
London

ISBN 978-1-909382-80-0

Second Edition

© Kemal Yalçın, 2024. All rights reserved.

For more information please contact:
Gomidas Institute
42 Blythe Rd.
London W14 0HA
Web: *www.gomidas.org*
Email: *info@gomidas.org*

Original dedication in Turkish edition

To Meline, with my sincere love and profound respect....

TABLE OF CONTENTS

About the Author — ix
Map showing principal locations in *You Rejoice My Heart* — x
Preface to the Second Turkish Edition — xi

Part One: It never occurred to me to ask
Meline, the Turkish language Teachers' instructor — 3
Meline is ill — 12
"We've escaped death" — 22

Part Two: On the road
The start of the journey — 31
Looking for Armenians in Amasya — 36
Madam Safiye - My heart did what it pleased — 45
The Sivas train — 57
The time of the Deportation — 60
Do You Know What a Place Looks Like After a Fire? — 65
In Taşova — 70
An accounting on the way to Erbaa — 75
Snow and thunderstorms in the mountains of Erzurum — 79
Mustafali from Denizli — 82
The things I heard in Aşkale — 84
Baba Yusuf of Aşkale — 89
How do you get to Ani? — 93
Spring never came to Ani before you did — 99
Ohan Özant of Amasya and Vahram Karabent of Merzifon — 108
Ohan Özant from Amasya — 111
Vahram Karabent of Merzifon — 117
The calamity didn't spare the Greeks, either… — 124
Despite everything, we survived… — 129

Part Three: Meline's world
I saw my own prejudices when I loved you… — 137
The past that made Meline who she is — 142
Meline, the concierge's daughter — 148

The Capital Tax	152
"Don't let the girl end up a blind chicken!"	153
Kirkor Ceyhan	155
"I'm from Zara, I've always looked for Zara…"	155
The only way to escape death	160
The past years in Zara	165
"I lived through the calamity of September 6-7, 1955"	170
"I should pack up and go to a more peaceful country!"	172
"I've always looked for Zara…"	176
"If I've been able to make it this far…."	179
Meline's Hunger Strike	183
"Come, Meline: you'll go on with life even without your father!"	186
"I saw a pair of eyes! It's all over!"	188
"There's one more chance"	189
Madam Kalustyan's crime	190
Crossroads	191
Who really was the person behind that bewitching pair of eyes?	196

Part Four: Kegham İşkol's students and friends

Is that how May is in Istanbul these days?	203
Zakarya from Kayseri	209
"How did this happen?"	211
In the schoolyard of the Şişli Karagözyan Orphanage	215
The things my father told me…	219
A man seeking his village	222
"Why didn't I look into my own past?"	226
Jale of Şebinkarahisar	232
The marriage of a Turk and an Armenian	235
The power of love	238
The reasons for hatred of the Armenians	244
Master Sarkis of Karaman: "We shouldn't have let him beat the priest…"	250
"We married in order to put an end to this poverty!"	255
The calamity they call the "Deportation"	256
You must endure what fate brings to you	269
"I am going to send my children to school, no matter what!"	275
We were called "infidel soldiers"	277

Moving to İstanbul	281
The night of September 6-7, 1955	283
What's the reason for this century-long hostility?	289
"I've never been a nationalilst"	292
Since I've grown old, I've started to look for traces of my childhood	293
"We shouldn't have let him beat the priest…"	295

Part Five: Crypto-Armenians

The Armenian Haci İbrahim from Kâhta	303
"My father's prayers"	305
"The things that befell my father…"	307
"We were all living alone, in fear…"	310
Others of "our kind" in Kâhta	312
Those things that Veli Dede experienced	314
They snatched my mother and took her away'	318
The Armenian disease	322
"Attack the infidel quarter!"	327
"Milla Çelebi roused me from my slumber"	330
Red mark in their identity cards	333
"Fear, always the fear!"	335
Sultan Bakırcıgil: "Infidel ants!"	336
"We don't have anything to laugh about"	338
My father's moods	341
The bitterness of having to hide one's origins	345

Part Six: "See what happens to a young man when he goes abroad"

The years abroad	351
"Give me your hand, Paris"	352
"Like a fish out of water"	354
"I have to find a job and start working"	356
"My right to live is finally recognized"	356
The dictionary of Armenian mythology	359
"There's one other possibility, but it, too, might mean death"	360
Black earth under the snow	361

Part Seven: My heart laughs with you

Kegham's grave	367
"Our religions are different, our God is the same"	368

"My heart laughs with you" 369
A final note 371

Appendix
Responses to *You Rejoice My Heart* (Turkish edition) 375
Destruction of first Turkish edition of *You Rejoice My Heart* 391

ILLUSTRATIONS
Safiye of Amasya 68
Baba Yusuf of Aşkale 92
Sourp Asdvadzadzin Cathedral and the mosque of Minuchihr in Ani 98
Ohan Özant of Amasya 110
Vahram Karabent of Merzifon 118
Kirkor Ceyhan of Zara 158
Zakarya of Ekrek (Kayseri) 205
Master Sarkis of Karaman 296

ABOUT THE AUTHOR

Kemal Yalçın was born in the Honaz sub-district of Turkey's Denizli Province in 1952. After finishing primary school he went to the Gönen Teacher Training School in İsparta.

In 1973 he graduated from the Çapa Advanced Teachers' College in Istanbul and the Philosophy Department of Istanbul University's Faculty of Literature. After that, he taught philosophy at the Kaman Lycée in Kırşehir and the Kabataş Lycée in Istanbul.

During the years 1975-1976 he served on the General Executive Committee (*Genel Yönetim Kurulu*) of the Universal Education and Instruction Employees Unity and Solidarity Committee (*TÖB-DER*).

He worked in journalism and publishing in the years 1978-1980.

In 1981 he came to Germany, where, since 1989, he has worked as a Turkish instructor in Bochum.

His works include:

Sürgün Gülleri ('Roses of Exile', poetry)

Geç Kalan Bahar ('The Late Spring', poetry)

Emanet Çeyiz ('The Security Trousseau', novel)

Bilim Tuktusu ('Passion for Knowledge', autobiography)

Barış Sıcağı ('The Warmth of Peace', poetry)

Sınıfta Çiçek Zor Açar ('Flowers Don't Bloom Easily in the Classroom', recollections, stories)

Almanya'da Türkçe Anadil Eğitimi ('Turkish Mother-tongue Education in Germany', study)

He has received the following prizes:

1991 – First Prize, poetry; Petrol-İş Award

1996 – First Prize, poetry; Cologne Multicultural Society Award

1998 – Novel of the year, Turkish Culture Ministry

1998 – Abdi İpekçi Special Prize for Friendship and Peace

1998 – Turkey-Greece Communications Prize

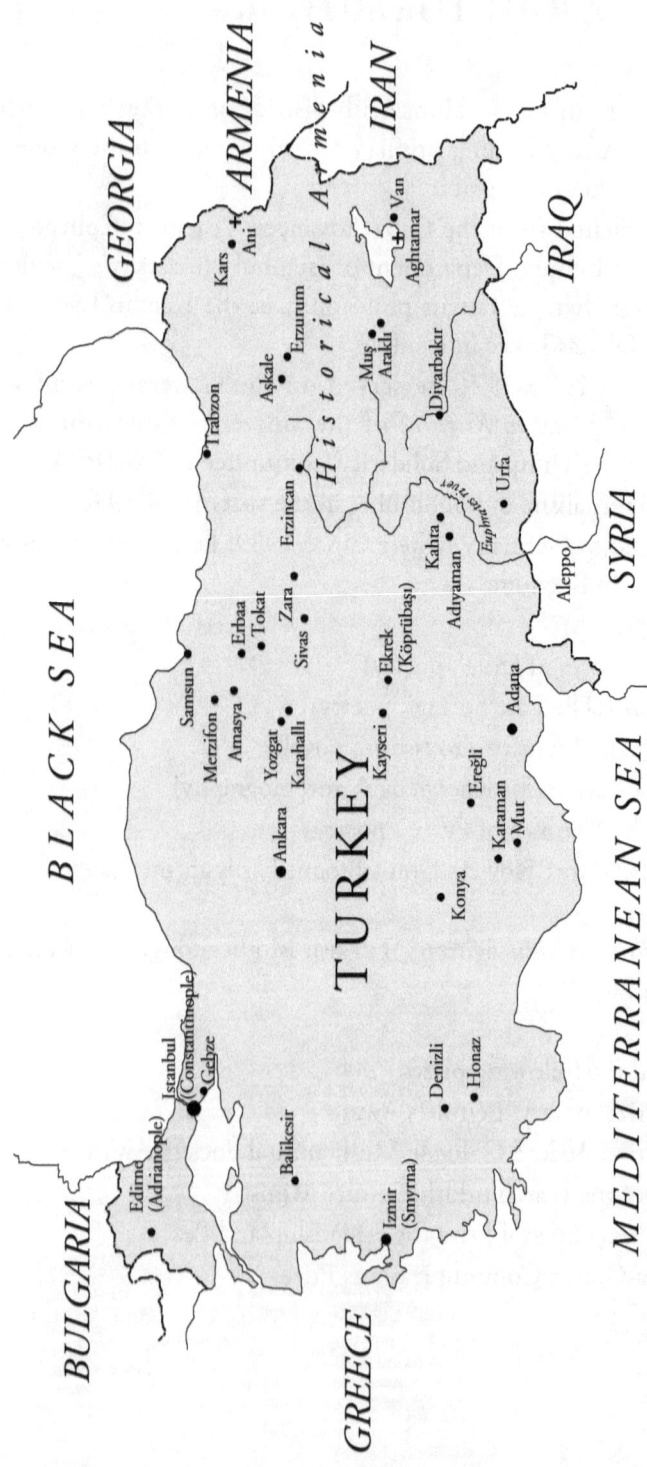

Map showing principal locations mentioned in *You Rejoice My Heart*

PREFACE TO THE SECOND TURKISH EDITION, 2003

In accordance with a publishing contract that I signed in Turkey with Doğan Book Publishing, 3,000 copies of *You Rejoice My Heart* were ordered and printed up in December, 2000. They were to be distributed on January 15, 2001. However, on January 12, the responsible director of the printing house communicated the following message to me: "Because of a warning from on high, we won't be able to distribute your book at present! We are going to wait until a more propitious time!"

I waited for a whole year. Countless times I asked when my book was to be distributed. The answer I repeatedly received was: "We can't publish your book at present! The political situation in Turkey is not right!" Finally, I decided to have my book published in Germany, paying for the publishing expenses out of my own pocket.

When it first appeared, *You Rejoice My Heart* received great attention. I received letters and telephone calls from places throughout the globe. You can read a selection of these in the appendix of this edition.

I went to the headquarters of the publishers on August 17, 2002 in order to discuss the status of my book. The company directors told me: "Haven't you heard? We had *You Rejoice My Heart* destroyed!" and then they showed me the "Destruction Order"[*] that had been signed by Istanbul's 13th Notary Public. Without asking me, without informing me in advance, and without any official inquiry against either myself or my book, all of the printed copies of this title had been destroyed in a paper shredder on June 21, 2002 and in the presence of Istanbul's 13th Notary Public (A copy of the "Destruction Order" that was later sent to me is also found in the appendix of this edition).

In a letter jointly signed by the publishing company's board of directors, they defended their decision, saying: "By destroying this book, we believe that we have prevented a new, black stain upon our country that could occur through a new case being opened [against it in the court of public opinion]."

During periods in which democratic rights, and the freedoms of thought and expression are being trampled under foot in Turkey—particularly after

---

[*] The Turkish, *İmha Tutanağı*, actually means something more like a 'statement' or 'decision' of destruction.

the military coup of September 12, 1980—a great many books, newspapers and magazines have been destroyed or condemned to the flames; a great many writers, intellectuals and artists have been tried and punished for the "crime" of free expression. But for a publishing house to voluntarily destroy with its own hands a book that it had itself printed and published, and in the presence of an official notary public... This was unheard of! The slogans "Democracy is coming!", "Restrictions on freedom of thought are being lifted!" are often claimed here, but if that's so, these reforms are coming at a snail's pace; sometimes it seems that we've barely progressed!

What a shame that the political order in Turkey remains such that publishers can be intimidated enough to destroy their own books, that creative freedoms remain blocked. What a shame for all that creative effort that has been wasted!

The destruction of books, the restriction of freedom of thought, and the punishment of those persons who speak truth and lift the veil off society's taboo subjects: nothing will be achieved by all this. Those who actually believe that they are accomplishing something by this are not only deceiving themselves—they're also deceiving the society in which they live. What's more, they are bringing shame to Turkey.

I am publishing this second edition in Germany in the hope that Turks, Armenians, Kurds, Syriac Christians[*] and all other peoples will get to intimately know and understand one another, that ties of friendship between them will be revived, that a culture of peace will eventually develop within Turkish society, and that the disgraceful actions by humanity and the great sufferings of the past century will never be forgotten nor experienced again. I convey my thanks and gratitude to all of the readers and friends who have lent me their assistance.

Kemal Yalçın
Bochum, March 1, 2003

---

[*] Members of the Syrian Orthodox Church, known in the United States as Chaldean or Assyrian Christians.

You Rejoice My Heart

Part One

It Never Occurred to Me to Ask

Meline, the Turkish language teachers' instructor

The coolness of autumn had arrived… It had started to rain the previous evening, but the rain had stopped again sometime during the night. That morning, as I first ventured out of my house, I was bathed and refreshed by the stunning brightness of the day. A bird was singing in the tree in the courtyard. I looked up into the magnificent, cloudless blue heavens above. My inner contentment seemed matched by that of my surroundings.

Today was the first session of the professional development course organized by the Culture Ministry of the Province of North Rhine/Westfalia for Turkish language instructors working in the province's unified middle school district. It was a Tuesday in October. The year was 1992.

The place where our course was being held was the Anne Frank Comprehensive School in Dortmund. We would be meeting in classroom number 105. I didn't recognize a single one of the other teachers who I met in the corridor. Of the other Turkish instructors whom I met, the first ones were Şükrü and Naziye. Inside the classroom, the desks were arranged like a horseshoe. I sat two desks from the window, to the right of instructor's desk. I sat with my back to the window so that I wouldn't be distracted by having the sun in my eyes. That way, I would be better able to see the faces of those persons facing me, as they would be lit up by the light streaming in through the window. Naziye sat to my left, Şükrü to my right.

At exactly 9:00 a.m. two women and one man entered the room. They sat down, side by side, at the long teacher's desk in front of the chalk board. The face of the woman who sat nearest me looked clouded. She had a sour expression. The gentleman who sat on the far side of the desk was fat, with completely disheveled hair and a head that looked like it arose directly from his body, without the aid of a neck; his checkered shirt was in need of a good ironing; his face looked tired, his eyes, somewhat bloodshot, as if from too much reading.

As for the woman sitting in the middle… My God! What a beauty! She had a face that was positively radiant… Her two eyes sparkled like the sun… every part of her looked in its place and perfectly coordinated with all the other parts, from the color of her shoes to the very strands of her hair!

Those hazel-colored eyes with the hint of green said, "Hello, friends!" Her voice was like the spring, her gaze, like a bouquet of flowers!

I replied "Hello!" and took the freshest, most colorful flowers of that gaze and gave them an immediate place in my heart.

"Today we begin the third of our courses, which have been going on for four years now in Düsseldorf and Dortmund" she began. "As you know, each course lasts for two years. Throughout the course your school will excuse you from your teaching duties on every second Tuesday. On those days we'll study here, together. One week, we'll work with your group, the next week, with the Düsseldorf group. Once a year the two groups will come together at the Institute for the Development of Curriculum and Textbooks in Soest, and there we'll hold a weekend seminar. Now let's introduce ourselves. I'll begin with myself. My name is Meline. I teach English and Turkish at a school in Düsseldorf. I'm from Istanbul. My German friends Johannes and Rozwita and myself will be directing this course."

Then, beginning on the left side, all of the participants introduced themselves, one by one. Altogether there were seventeen teachers. All of us had taught in Turkey, some for three years, some for five, others much longer. We had all begun teaching in Germany at different times. Almost half of us had left Turkey and come here after the September 12, 1980 military coup. Ali and myself had not been able to visit Turkey for twelve years. Ali had published five books.

One of the participants, when his turn came, said, "My name is İbrahim. I graduated from the Philosophy Department of the Teacher Training Academy in Çapa." As soon as he said that, I looked intently at his face.

"I'm also from Çapa," I said. "Aren't you our very own İbrahim?"

We embraced. Suddenly, I was engulfed in the memories of those bloody clashes and struggles that had occurred in Çapa. İbrahim had been three classes above me... He had been one of the main leaders in the clashes. He was one of the vocal and ardent militants.

At the academy, each of the departments had a clearly designated work room. We called them "study rooms." The study room of the philosophy students was directly above the marble staired entry of the main, ceramic tiled school building. The students who were studying mathematics, physics and Turkology were a mixed bunch, but the philosophy students were leftists to a man. İbrahim was like our big brother. İbrahim gave the first lessons in "Dialectic and Historical Materialism" to the new students.

Many years had passed since then. For years, we had had no information on each other's whereabouts. The events of the time had dispersed us all, the storms had swept us up and buffeted us from one place to another. Wherever the gusts of fortune had deposited us, we had to grab a foothold and attempt to begin our lives again. And now, twenty-two years later, we sat together again in the same course, beginning our first lesson.

Seeing İbrahim again had brought back memories of Çapa. And again I was transported back to Istanbul....

In my mind, I entered the grey, scowling iron door of the Çapa Teacher Training Academy. I walked silently along the tree-lined path to the garden in the back. The Yellow Dormitory! There it is! My ears are ringing with the sounds... The sun has gone down. It's as if the world has gone black!

I'm in the dormitory at the head of the stairs, next to the girls' dormitory. It's about ten at night... All of my dorm mates are stretched out on their bunks. Above me, on his upper bunk, is Hüseyin Aslantaş. He's reciting poems by Nâzim. Not from a book, but from memory. Now he's reciting "Tahir and Zühre," but he's not doing a very good job of it. He experiences it as if he himself was Tahir. A voice from the corner of the dormitory calls out "Once more!" So Hüseyin once again transforms into Tahir and gushes forth! Hüseyin has fallen in love that day! He went to his beloved and spilled his heart to her. But the girl rejected his overtures.... That night we all became intoxicated with Hüseyin's love. Time flowed by like water. It was long past "lights out" time.

I went down to the laundry room on the bottom floor. I was going to wash my socks. Soaping and scrubbing, I washed my socks in the cold water.... Suddenly, from the upper floor comes the sound of gunfire! Three shots—or was it five? Quick! There's no time! My soapy socks in one hand, wearing only my pajamas, I bolt headlong into the middle courtyard garden... There's no one else there but me... It's pitch black. Did someone shut off the lights? I can see dark shapes next to the garden path: are they people or just trees? But there's none of our friends, no one from our dormitory! The doors of the school have been locked. I'm disoriented. I turn and go back the way I came.... I climb the stairs to the top floor and walk the entire length of the long, narrow, dark corridor. There's no one in sight, neither mouse nor man! I reach the dormitory room: there, in front of the door to our room, Hüseyin is lying stretched out on the floor, his right arm extended over his head, his left arm, hidden behind his back...

"Hüseyin!" I yell, "Hüseyin! They've shot Hüseeeyyin!"

But it won't open! The door won't open!

I look at Hüseyin. There's a pool of blood forming around the left side of his head... I want to pull his head out of the pool of blood. I reach out my left hand to Hüseyin... I want to cradle his head, but as I do so, my fingers come in contact with something hot and soft—it's Hüseyin's brain! Raw and exposed and mixed with the bone fragments of his shattered skull! I gasp and reflexively retract my arm, as if my fingers had touched burning hot needles!

"Hüseyin! Hüseyin is dead! Open the door!"

The door opens, most of those inside are in pajamas and barefoot... there's much confusion and shouting.

"Pick him up! Pick him up! We've got to get him to the hospital! He's still alive! Hüseyin's still alive! He'll survive!"

I don't know who said what—who had the strength at that moment? Was it Hizir[*] who came to our aid at that moment of need?

But how were we going to pick him up and carry him to the hospital? The exits had all been locked. There was no concierge, no teacher and no key! We took him down and through the huge iron entrance door. Once we were on the street we took Hüseyin to the Çapa Hospital, running all the way...

"They've shot Hüseeeyyin! They've shot Hüseeeyyin!"

There's no one about, no one to ask, "Who shot him?" I'm crying as I run with Hüseyin. The sound of my own voice echoes off the high walls of Çapa. There's no one around to even say, "Don't weep!" The only voice I hear is my own...

Hüseyin lived for three more days.

It was the month of February. We bore his flag-draped coffin on our shoulders, and brought it before the Atatürk and Youth Memorial in the

---

[*] Literally, the Turkish transliteration of the Arabic word "Green," *Hızır*, or "The Green Man," who is a popular figure in the folk mythology of Anatolia and the Levant. He is reputed to be immortal and who comes to the aid of those in distress.

main building of Istanbul University. We placed it on the catafalque. His mother fell upon his coffin and wouldn't be separated from it…

"My son!" she wailed, "My son! Would that they had shot me instead of you, my son!"

Afterward, we took Hüseyin's body as far as Sirkeci, followed by a procession of thirty thousand students and youth. His body was then taken aboard an automobile ferry. After a wait, the ship's whistle let out a long, mournful howl, and we accompanied Hüseyin as he embarked on his last journey…. In a small village in the Kangal District of the province of Sivas, we labored through the snow to return him to the frozen, black earth.

Now I'm crying within—but where am I? The fingers of my left hand are tingling again, burning with the sensory memory of Hüseyin's shattered skull and brains… But I'm now in the Anne Frank Comprehensive School: Naziye is on one side of me, Şükrü is on the other…

Meline and I make eye contact. Her hazel eyes look at me and ask, "Hey now! What's up with you? Are you still with us?" And with my eyes I answer, "They shot Hüseyin, Meline! Hüseyin from Sivas! They shot him in Çapa, on the day he fell in love! My fingertips are burning!"

On her green blouse there are tiny white flowers… so tiny, so white….

At one point we have a break. İbrahim and I get together and relive those past days in Çapa. We recall Hüseyin Aslantaş and grow sad. He had been a brilliant youth with a promising future, like a young, healthy sapling.

What did we talk about that day? What recollections had we brought up? I can no longer remember a thing…

Our course progressed. We increasingly came to realize just how much we had been molded and formed by the objectives and principles of our Turkish "national education." We found ourselves unsuited to the German system of education and pedagogy. The purpose of this course was to bridge the gap and bring our thinking in line with the German system.

I learned to be a teacher all over again. There was no "national education" as such in Germany, just education. We translated into Turkish the German Constitution, the principles and objectives of the country's educational system, as well as its statutes and curriculum.

Again and again, we stressed the importance of mother-tongue education and the fact that in a multi-cultural and multi-national society like Germany, such education was a fundamental right.

We discussed the need to tolerate different cultures and national identities, the various frictions between Turkish and German students and ways to resolve these.

We learned to approach the national differences between the students and various cultural identities with tolerance when we prepared curriculums and lesson plans and discussed and debated subjects in the classroom. We vowed to prevent the other students from oppressing the Kurdish and Alevi[*] students, who were usually a minority in our classes.

Our first joint weekend seminar was held at Soest in March. We thirty-five Turkish language teachers who attended the seminar discussed and debated the problems at our schools and the ways in which these could be resolved.

On Saturday evening, we held a party for ourselves. It was an evening of music and song. Sometimes together, sometimes alone, we played and sang songs from all corners of Turkey, from Aegean melodies to folk songs from the Black Sea region, from long, rambling *uzun havas*[†] to popular songs of Istanbul.

That evening, Meline sang songs of Istanbul in the "Nihavend" *makam*.[‡] I had never heard any song that came so directly from the heart, from deep inside as did her song. Was she singing or praying? And her voice: it seemed at times to be diving deep into the waters of the Bosphorus and then emerging back to the surface; at other times it seemed to be burning with

---

[*] The Alevi are a Shi'ite sect with some syncretistic characteristics who make up approximately 20% of the population of Turkey, and who were historically concentrated particularly in Central and Eastern Anatolia. Not to be confused with the "Alawi" sect of Syria, (who are known as "Nusayri"s in Turkey). Because of the long standing religious and political mistrust (and in some cases, out and out hatred) shown them by much of the Sunni population and a history of discrimination and persecution by the Ottoman regime, the Alevi have been ardent supporters of the secular Turkish Republic and hold a prominent place in the country's military, cultural and commercial elites.

[†] Literally "long air," these are lengthy Anatolian melodies which lack a set rhythmic pattern.

[‡] A melodic creation characteristic of classical Turkish (and much Middle Eastern) music, one which determines the starting and ending tones, among other things. The word *nihavent* refers to a *makam* characteristic of, or originating in, the Iranian city of Nahavend.

the ache of a deep, deep wound. There was something in it beyond the reach of my understanding, some wisdom, some hidden thing…

She was happy. She lit up the night with her laughter. I approached her.

"Meline," I asked her, "were you singing a song? or a lamentation? or were you saying a prayer?"

She smiled.

"Hey now, mister," she said playfully, "don't touch the wounds of my heart! Leave it be, and let's sing a couple more songs when our voices recover! But you also sang *İzmir'in kavakları* (The Poplars of Izmir) and *Karadır kaşların* (Black Are Your Eyebrows) a little differently!" Our eyes then met. I don't know what she saw in my eyes at that moment. I looked in those hazel-colored eyes of hers. From within those Istanbul songs of hers a turquoise blue water had flowed. From her songs, I had felt some hidden sorrow of Meline's. But I didn't know what it was.

Afterward, we all began to dance. Meline led us in a *çiftetelli* folk dance. There was no exaggeration or artificiality in Meline. She flowed and moved like clear, limpid water. But it wasn't exactly a *çiftetelli* she was dancing, it was something different.… In her movements there were hints or traces of a religious dance.… What was the reason for this? Again, I couldn't grasp it. I didn't understand, and that intrigued me all the more.…

During the second year of the course, the classes passed with studying and exploring epics, poems, parables, jokes and fables. We looked at examples of Turkish, Uygur, Arabic, German and Japanese parables, and sometimes we'd look at the different versions of the same fable as told by different peoples, in different regions.

We conducted a comparative study of the different versions of the parable of the Patient Stone. We discussed and debated various methods of approaching it in class. The Patient Stone was the parable on which we spent the most time. I really loved this parable. Meline was a great help in allowing me to comprehend the inner essence of the parable. The fundamental tragedy in the Patient Stone is not that the stone splits after having experienced injustice; it's that the committing of injustice is the reason that the stone splits.

We completed our two-year course in July, 1994 and received our certificates of completion. Then, we all went out for a "goodbye supper." By then we had grown comfortable with one another. In our brief time together we had learned that Johannes was a linguistics expert, that he hardly had the time to look after himself because of his thirst for knowledge, because of how he overworked himself. His profound and thorough knowledge of Turkish, Arabic, French and Ottoman constantly amazed us. During the learning process, every time one of us committed an error, he would elicit peals of laughter from us when he would say, with his thick voice, "*Ayva!*" ("Quince!") instead of "*Ayvayı yedik!*" ("We've eaten the quince!" *i.e.*, "Now we're done for!"). The sound of "*Ayva!*" still rings in my ears today.

But my main joy was in getting to know Meline. The more I knew her the more I loved her. A very warm friendship developed between us. So much so that I was very sad when the course finally came to an end. No more would I be able to see Meline twice a month, something that I had come to eagerly look forward to during the intervening periods.

"After the summer vacation, we simply have to meet again, Meline," I told her.

"Goodness, we're going to see each other before then!" she replied, bursting into that special laughter all her own.

Meline invited Johannes and myself to dinner at her house on Monday, September 26, 1994. It was the first time I had seen her house. Her husband Dieter was not there that evening. He had shown the tact and delicacy of going to his mother's that evening so that we would be able to speak Turkish freely among ourselves.

Meline's house was well-organized and immaculately clean. There were expensive carpets and *kilim*-type throw rugs on the floors and hanging from the walls. Beside them were also old black-and-white photographs of Istanbul's Beyoğlu district, precious glazed ceramics and tiles from İznik and Kütahya… and books, hundreds of books…

The evening was done according to her custom: she took photographs of those guests visiting her house for the first time, and these were placed in her guestbook, beside the thoughts and impressions written down by the guests.

"I've already prepared all the food" Meline said, "but I want to take your picture before we eat. I'd be very pleased if you would write your feelings in our guest book."

So she took photographs of us. Then Johannes wrote his impressions. Now it was my turn.

"Meline," I said, "your invitation has made me very happy. Be well. I will write that which comes into my head, but first, I want to ask you a very important question."

"Ask away, sir!" she said. "Let's hear this important question!"

"Meline, God bless you. Thank you so much. I want to sincerely thank you, Johannes and Rozwita. You exposed us to examples of German, Turkish, French—even Chinese poetry; we studied all manner of stories and sagas; we even got to study Japanese, Turkish, Uygur, as well as German parables... But why didn't you ever give us any examples of Armenian parables, Armenian folk tales, Armenian poems?"

Meline looked like she'd been struck. Her noble face constricted and tensed. Even her voice changed. Then with a voice that came from deep within her being, stressing every syllable, she replied:

"Mister! The questions you ask! I've waited six years for that question. Over that time I've taught as many as one hundred and fifty teachers. Not a single one has ever come up and said 'Meline, you're Armenian. You have your own parables, folk tales, and poems in your own language. To be sure, tell us Uygur parables, but also recite us a poem in Armenian. Give us an example of an Armenian folk tale.' How could I tell one if no one ever asked! How could I tell an Armenian parable when at the beginning of our course, one of the participants—their name isn't important—complained about me to the Province's Culture Ministry, saying, 'How can an Armenian teach Turkish to Turkish teachers?' When I was recounting the Japanese parable, I so wanted to tell an Armenian one as well, but I couldn't do it. Would our class have been able to stand for it were I to tell one? If you were me, would you have told one? I waited for six years—but did a single one of our Turkish-as-a-mother-tongue teachers ever say, 'You're an Armenian! You've got your own mother tongue!?' Not one."

And I, too, had been one of those who had never said a thing. It had never occurred to me to ask whether or not Meline, an Armenian whom I loved—an Armenian teacher whom I loved—and who had captured my heart from the first time I saw her, had her own mother tongue....

Where had this shortcoming in me come from? Even as I had sat there, defending the right of everyone in the world to learn their mother tongue—even the right of everyone in the world to have a mother tongue, how could I have overlooked the mother tongue of my Armenian teacher from Istanbul? How could I have forgotten? Why had I been unable to feel what another person feels? Why hadn't I been able to see through their eyes?

I cursed myself for my insensitivity!

Meline is ill

Meline's words became a permanent nagging ache inside me. I wrote a poem in her guest book. It was only through poetry that I was able to express what I was feeling at that moment.

I waited six years for one of yours to come up and say, "You're Armenian. Do you have your own mother tongue?"

I couldn't get Meline's words out of my mind. Her state at that moment, the way her face looked... I kept seeing them before my eyes. I had been affected by her from the first time I saw her; I placed the "bouquet" of one of her glances in a cherished place in my heart. The flowers of this bouquet never wilted. And now, just a few words from her had irreversibly changed my world. They had stirred up the leaven of my very being; they were an unexpected breeze, rustling the dry branches of my soul, a breath of fresh air that blew the curtain over my consciousness and allowed a bright light to shine on certain areas of it for the first time.

After this, I began to feel even closer to Meline, I began to love her more. My feelings of friendship began to warm and grow into something else...

When we didn't see each other in person, we would talk and greet each other by telephone, or by sending cards or letters. I wanted to get to know Meline, to understand her better.

"Who are you?" I'd ask her. "Tell me more!"

She'd laugh and go on.

"I'm Meline. I'm from Istanbul. An Armenian in my own way... What are you going to do with it afterward?"

"Meline, my dear, I don't just want to know what you are: I want to know who you are. Tell me a little about yourself!

"Oh, leave me be! Go find those Greek girls that you researched earlier. Go and give them the trousseaus that their grandfather had put away for them. I was very moved by the story of the Minoğlu girls. You ought to leave everything else and continue to write about them."

What we mostly spoke about were my hunt for traces of the Minoğlu daughters.... The older folks I had met in Greece and Turkey during the course of these searches had recounted the events that they had experienced between the years 1919 and 1925…

I had heard about the bitter events that the Armenians had experienced from the Greeks who had been forced to emigrate from Anatolia, and from the Turkish refugees who had been forced to leave Greece. They were like brief, isolated scenes from a long film. The old refugees had also spoken of the existence of old Armenian women in the areas of Amasya, Taşova and Erbaa who had survived by converting to Islam and marrying Turks.

I would inform Meline, sometimes by phone, other times by card, of the things I heard and learned from the refugees. When we would get together every two or three months I would show her the photographs I had taken. I would excitedly explain the things I had heard about the Armenians.

Meline would listen, and listen…. I'd look in her eyes: sometimes those turquoise waters that seemed to flow out of her songs of Istanbul would be calm and transparent, other times they would grow turbid and troubled, and still others, they would flow in counter currents and eddies. Her face radiated light, but sometimes the sun in her eyes would cloud over. She would laugh, but her laughter would contain within it the faint echoes of mourning and wailing from somewhere deep inside her, from a place that I didn't know, that I wasn't capable of understanding. When she spoke it was as if it wasn't just a single voice speaking, but rather a whole chorus of voices speaking with every single word that came out of her mouth. Every note of the songs she sang was like a drop in the ocean of memories that she bore inside her. But this ocean was uncharted water for me. I didn't know it; I could only sense its presence.

Each time we spoke on the phone, each time we met, Meline would ask about the Minoğlu daughters.

"What have you done since the last time we spoke?" she would say, interrogating me. "How much have you written?"

"With all of the written assignments, classes and school matters, I haven't been able to find the time to do any writing or thinking," I would say apologetically.

"Leave all that, Kemal! This isn't a subject that you can afford to wait another day, my dear!"

She continually pushed me and encouraged me. She inspired me to write.

At one point I finally said, "That's it! I've written all that I'm going to write!" and brought the saga of Sophia and Eleni's trousseaus to an end. I gathered up my file and brought it to her. She hugged me and congratulated me. I was so thrilled… I was happy… On that day Meline was as full of hope and enthusiasm as a pink almond blossom heralding the onset of spring. The water in her eyes, the radiance in her face was clear and calm, like a blossom-covered tree branch.

That day, as soon as I entered the door of her house, my eyes immediately fell upon the carpet that lay upon the floor. I didn't dare step on it. I hesitated…

"Meline! How beautiful this is!"

"I found it at a carpet seller's in Cologne. I liked it from the moment I saw it. It's an old Armenian carpet. It must have been woven in the area around Erzurum, Kars and Van. They don't make any more like these. There aren't any more Armenians left to weave them… I know an Armenian carpet when I see one! I didn't even haggle with the owner. I just counted out the money, bought it, and took it home."

"How do you know whether or not a particular carpet is an Armenian one?"

"From the cross and from the fox motifs in the middle or some place on it… the crosses can be placed in various places on the carpet. But there can only be one fox motif. They used to place different animal and flower motifs on Armenian carpets. The Armenian cross was always placed with great care and attention. Sometimes it's hidden. Those who understand these things know how and where to look for them…. Fear is even hiding in the knots, the colors and the motifs of the carpet."

The carpet had numerous shades of red, yellow, green and blue. The more I looked, the more excited I became. Looking at it, a person would suppose their self to be somewhere in the fields of Anatolia… It was silent, mysterious… it seemed to contain both hope and sorrow, side by side, inextricably woven into one another…

"Meline," I said, "I can't bear to step on this carpet!"

"Step, dear! *Step*!" she said, exhorting me. "The carpet that you speak of was made to be walked on."

But still, I hesitated. I skirted it and sat down at the table.

That day I spoke with Meline about a name for the book.

"How about 'The Last Witnesses'?" I suggested. "What about 'My Neighbor's Trousseau'?"

"Slow down, Kemal my dear! First let me read the draft. In the meantime, we'll both think about it a bit. It has to be a name that reflects the book's contents and its main idea."

It was less than a week after that when Meline called me, excited:

"I've got it, Kemal! I've got it. The name of the book has to be 'The Security Trousseau.'"

"Meline, that's perfect!"

And in that way, Meline found a name for my book.

In the meantime, summer vacation arrived. I was in Turkey during the month of July. I had missed my country. I had missed Honaz, its vineyards and its gardens. After we got to Denizli, we drove straight to our garden, even before going to the house.

There I spent some time by my mother's side. Ever since my father had passed away, my poor mother had loved the garden more and more. It wasn't easy; the place where our garden stood had belonged to some Greeks who were expelled from Honaz in 1920. The things they would say if they could—both the land and its former owners! When its owners left, the trees and fields were left without anyone to tend them. These lush and verdant gardens were left burnt and shriveled from a lack of water. The land then passed from one owner to another.

But land is like a delicate, loving and faithful woman. You can understand it from its language, from its condition. You have to love it like your very soul. You can't allow it to dry up. The land around Honaz is stony, sandy and full of rocks. It can't be left unwatered. You have to remain faithful to the land. You can't simply pass it off from one hand to the next. Whatever you plant here will grow—even people! But you have to know how to plant....

So my beautiful Greek gardens passed from hand to hand, they saw one owner after another. The vineyards withered and reverted to simply bare mountainsides, the gardens went to seed and simply became empty fields.

In 1950, my father purchased this land from a man named Mustafa, the son of Boncuklu Bekir. I wasn't around yet. My mother, my father and my brothers embraced this land and invested their hearts in it. They cleared out the stones from the fields with their bare hands. Then they planted row after row of cherry, peach and other fruit trees. I came into the world during the first year that the cherries bore fruit. I first opened my eyes to a branch full of fruit. I came into this life on this earth, in this garden, on this mountainside.

During those days, we would move to the garden during the summers. My mother would spread out our beds on the ground of the terrace. I would sleep between my mother and father. It would be as if I was covering myself with the vast grayish blue blanket of the starry heavens. The stars in the heavens didn't bother me, but the shooting stars did. I'd get scared and hug my mother tightly. My father used to tell parables and old epic tales. They were like a lullaby for me. When I'd awake the following morning the sun would already be up, and I'd find myself on the edge of the mattress....

But for my mother, the garden and the earth in which it was planted had a very different meaning... Ever since my father had died, my dear mother would speak with the trees and flowers that they had planted together. She'd take a stick in her hand and hold it like a baton and go wandering through the garden, stopping at every tree, inspecting every fruit.

She had reserved two Napoleon cherry trees for me, saying, "My son should eat from these when he comes!"

After it had been newly turned, the earth was like a thick, coarse mattress... it was warm. Out on the hillside terrace I would take off my socks and shoes and when I walked it would almost burn my bare feet with its heat.

I would go with my mother to the Napoleon cherries in the lower section of the garden. Over time, the trees had become heavy-laden with fruit. There were so many that would fall that we'd be ankle-deep in them.

"What a waste, mother!" I exclaimed. "I'm only going to eat a couple of handfuls of these cherries!"

"You've got a right to eat from this garden too, my son! You helped clear out the rocks, you helped to water it. You used to climb up and eat the fruits from the very tops of all the trees. Your father would say, "Eat from the lower branches!" but you would go up to the very top. I would say to your father, "Leave the child be, he's working hard; let him eat from the best!" Then we'd argue, saying, 'Not from the bottom! Not from the top!' Ha! That was a lie... Go now, up to the top. It's your custom. Eat your fill!"

Ah, my mother! I hugged her and kissed her. Her perspiration and the camphor she used still smelled like musk. It had always smelled like that during my childhood.

"C'mon, mother: whip out one of 'em and let me nurse!" I said, teasing her. That made her laugh and laugh.... She looked young again!

"O ho! My son, you nursed until age four. You'd play and play until you got hungry, and then you'd come running and nurse. In order to wean you, I finally had to smear tar on my breast and stick black sheeps' wool to it so that you would become disgusted. But you came running as usual, took off the wool and threw it on the ground and nursed, despite the tar on my breast... You'll never grow up, my son!"

I kissed her again and wished her a long life!

"Come on, now. Up you go! Eat as many of the cherries as you want and put a few in the basket, too. Those can be eaten at home."

I ate to my heart's delight and gave some to my mother. I filled up the basket, too. The snow-capped peak of Honaz Mountain was hidden behind the clouds. From the top of the cherry tree I could see the fruit trees that my father had planted, row after row, from one edge of our land to the next, from one border to the other.

When my father would plow with his oxen out here during the daytime, or when watering it at night, he would generally sing folk songs. There were two I remember hearing very frequently:

Ham meyveyi kopardılar dalından	They plucked the fruit, unripe, from the branch
Beni ayırdılar nazlı yarımdan	They separated me from my delicate beloved
Demedim mi nazlı yarım ben sana	Did I not say to you, my delicate love?
Sık muhabbet tez ayrılık getirir.	Close friendship quickly brings separation.

He'd always let out a sigh of "Ahh!" when he finished this. Then he'd pause a little and start again.

Söğüdün yaprağı dal arasında	[Like] the willow's leaves, amid its branches
Güzeli severler bağ arasında	Lovers of beauty, amid the vineyard [rows]
Üç beş güzel bir araya gelmiş de	A handful of beauties came together
Benim sevdiceğim yok arasında	But the one I love is not among them

Who knows how many times I heard these songs when he was planting and tending to these trees, when he was plowing and watering this land. The songs had worked their way into the very earth itself. Nowhere else could I find cherries, apricots and peaches that tasted like the ones here. I could never find my father's folksongs in the cherries grown in some other place, in the earth of another place. Maybe it was like that for everybody. Maybe the Greeks who had been the first owners of this land had also continually sought the taste of the cherries that they had first grown here. When I ate these cherries and apricots, it was as if I could hear my father's voice.

With the basket in one arm, and my mother in the other, we walked. "Didn't father create a great atmosphere, mother?" I said to her.

"Oh, my son! May he rest in peace. Your father loved women very much; he created a very nice mood around him, too. The vineyards and gardens still mourned, they long for those songs that I had begun to sing. No matter what a person was doing, when they heard them their hearts would skip a beat.... These gardens and vineyards didn't become the flower-filled paradises they are just from plowing and watering; they also got there because of your father's songs. May God be merciful unto him. His time here came and went; everything passes in this world!"

We reached the house. The grapes dangling from the arbors were not yet ripe. My nieces and nephews, and their parents, my old siblings and their spouses all came running with their families. They welcomed me, and I kissed their hands, while the little ones kissed mine. We practically gushed with joy; we had missed each other so much. Everyone who had heard had come. There wasn't enough space on the veranda for everyone.

Before I knew it, my six-week trip to Turkey had passed. My son and I again returned to Germany.

I called Meline. She wasn't there.

"She still hasn't returned from vacation," I was told.

A week later, I tried again. Still no luck.

"She's supposed to be back any time…"

I tried many more times, but not a peep from Meline. My concern grew. She should have called… Had something happened to her? No, that's impossible, I told myself. But I wasn't convinced.

By then it was already the end of September. One night, very late, I called again. Her husband Dieter answered.

"Good evening Dieter!" I said. "I'm sorry for disturbing you at such a late hour. I wasn't able to reach you during the daytime. I'd like to speak with Meline…."

"Good evening," Dieter replied. "Don't worry about the hour. I'd let you speak to Meline, but she's not here!"

"Not there? What happened?"

"She's ill! Very ill, in fact!"

"Is there a telephone at the hospital? Can I speak with her?"

"Unfortunately, no. She's too sick to be able to speak on the phone. But if you want, you can write to her. I'll give you the address…."

My God! How could she have become so ill? What did she have? My house began to constrict on me—the whole world began to close in on me!

I sat down and quickly wrote Meline a card:

Dear Meline,
Get well soon! I only now learned from Dieter that you were ill. What do you have? I'm beside myself with worry. I'd like to see you if it's possible.
The world is only beautiful and meaningful when you're in it.
Kemal

Two days later, the reply came:

Dear Kemal,
I'm very, very ill. I don't even have the strength to pick up the telephone. Please forgive me, but I can't even talk with you in my present state. Later on, after I get better, we'll speak. Take care,
With Love,
Meline

It was a card designed with a motif of yellow flowers, written with great care, and placed inside a thin envelope. It was simple and sober, like Meline herself.

Her card had helped to soothe my nerves, but I was still concerned. I couldn't even imagine Meline in a state where she couldn't even pick up the phone.

I couldn't speak with her? Fine. But not to visit? No way! What did these doctors know about what ails her, about what she needed to get well?

The next day, my classes were over at 1:20 p.m. I shopped for and found a wide-mouthed, shallow, handled basket. I then went to a Turkish market and bought pomegranates, grapes, quince, pears, walnuts, black figs, the most beautiful vegetables I could find and chestnuts. I bought a bouquet of spring blooms from the florist…

I wrapped the chestnuts in aluminum foil and roasted them on the electric range. Then I wrapped them well before they cooled in order to retain their smell. I arranged the fruits in the basket and covered the mouth of the basket with the flowers. I wrote Meline a note on a card decorated with İzmit tile motifs and placed it in an embroidered handkerchief.

> *Dear Meline,*
> *Nothing could be farther from my mind than to disturb you. I'm not going to come and visit you until you tell me 'Come!' But please accept these fruits. I know what ails you. You're not sick. If you can't eat the pomegranates, then have them squeeze them for you and drink the juice. If you can't eat the other fruit, the quince, then smell them. They are better than medicine.*
> *Without you, Meline my dear, the flowers are orphaned and lonely! Hang on, Meline! You're strong. You'll not just pick up the telephone: you'll lift the entire world! You will get better. May it be soon!*

I located the hospital where Meline was being treated. It was near Düsseldort Airport. I found out the department and room number from the hospital's information booth: third floor, room 311. Being very careful not to let Meline see me, I entered the nurses' station at the entrance to the corridor.

"Excuse me. Could you please take this basket to a Miss Meline in room 311? She's very ill. She said she wouldn't be able to speak with me. Please give her my greetings. I'll wait here for you."

"There's no need to excuse yourself. I'd be happy to take it. You just wait here."

Meline's room was three doors down. If I just walked ten steps in that direction I could see her face. But that was impossible. She'd told me "Don't come at present. I'm not well" in her letter. I thought about this as I waited in the nurses' station. It couldn't have been more than two minutes before I heard her voice.

"Kemal! Kemal!"

I looked and she was coming down the corridor. I practically jumped toward her.

"Meline! Dear Meline!"

We embraced. I felt like she disappeared in my arms. She had withered away to almost nothing.

"And just where do you think you're going without coming to see me?"

"I wanted to see you, but you…"

"You've come this far; to the very door of the room I'm in!"

"But I didn't want to disturb…"

"Disturb? What are you talking about? Come, let's go back to my room!"

I felt like the world was mine again. Meline's husband Dieter was there. As soon as the nurse had set down the basket, Meline had sprung out of bed. Now she excused herself and got back into bed."

"You see what shape I'm in, Kemal!"

"May you recover speedily. What do you have? What happened to you?"

"I've returned from being on the edge of death. I underwent three difficult operations, one after the other." A month from now I'm going to have a fourth. The situation is not as you knew it. But, God be praised, we've been saved from the jaws of death!"

"Now wait a second, Meline, my dear. What's going to happen to you if these bad things continue like this? Look! I've brought you some fruit from Turkey."

"Thank you so, so much! But I can't eat any of them right now!"

"Here, have some pomegranate; they give you strength!"

"I can't even have one seed of them!"

"Then drink some of the juice!"

"I can't even drink anything, dear. Not a drop!"

"Well, if you can't eat them, you should at least smell them! Even the smell will do you good!"

So she smelled the quince, the pomegranate and the *bostangüzeli*. The chestnuts had already cooled down by then, but she took a couple and peeled them, smelled them, and gave them to her husband.

"I can't eat them" she said. "Here, you have some before they get cold."

Dieter and I ate some of the chestnuts while Meline picked out the nuts and fruits she wanted and smelled them. Ignoring her illness, Meline asked me all about the things I'd seen and experienced on my summer vacation, on 'The Security Trousseau.'

I told her all about the cherries, apricots and peaches in our garden, and about the strolls I took there with my mother. We laughed and made each other laugh. I didn't want to tire her out so I told her that I should go already. Although I said "Don't get up!", she wouldn't listen. She accompanied me to the end of the corridor.

"Meline, my dear: Let the patient stone be the one that cracks, not you!"

"Don't worry, Kemal. God is great. Don't bury me yet! After all the calamities and hardships that I've overcome so far, don't you think I'll be able to get through this one too?"

Meline had really been reduced down to next to nothing. But she hadn't lost any of her hope. I had come here to encourage her, but it was she who was encouraging me!

"I'm going to have one more dangerous operation. But I'm not even worried about the outcome. I've already had to lie here for days without budging. I didn't even have the strength to lift my arm. But all that time my brain was working. My mind and my memory have been in good order. I thought about Meline, and I went over my whole life, and thought about all those things that have made me what I am. I've asked myself: What is it that's eating at me? What is it that has put me into this state?"

"And what is it, Meline? What is it that's eating at you?"

"Well, I've resolved a lot of things in my head. I've become calmer. I'm still not well, but I'm already stronger!"

"What is it that has darkened your bright world, Meline?"

"Now's not the time for that… Another day, when you come back. There's so much to tell!"

"We've escaped death"

When I opened up the window blinds in the morning, I was dazzled by the white glare that greeted me. The first snow of the year had fallen overnight. The world outside was blanketed in white. Even the weeping willow which greeted me when I opened the windows was engulfed in white. The air, which had suddenly grown cold, had left a covering of frost on the trees.

It was Sunday. How wonderful! No school today! I pulled the dining table that faced the wall over in front of the window and prepared my breakfast. Outside, it was snowy and cold. I sat inside, drinking my tea and conversing with the willow. When it snows, I can't stay still. I dressed quickly and went out into the street. My neighbors were already shoveling the snow in front of their houses. The scrape of their shovels drowned out the barely audible whisper of the falling snow... I turned off into the little grove near my house. Behind me, the raucous chorus of snow shovels continued unabated.

Have you ever heard the sound of snow falling or melting? There are all sorts of different snows: flurries, light powders, sleet... I love to hear the gentle patter or plip-plop of a soft snow falling on different objects. There's a type of snow that falls ever-so-gently on the leaves, the branches, the brambles, the grasses... Each snowflake makes a different sound depending upon what it lands; there are countless variations....

I learned to differentiate the different snow sounds and types from my grandfather. During my childhood, I used to sit with my grandfather and stare out the window of his room at the awesome, steep and tall Kocakale fortress, which rose up from the earth as if the earth itself was raising its head heavenward. My grandfather would take me in his lap and tell me about the changing face of Kocakale which differed from season to season. I no longer remember how it looked in the summer time. What I especially remember were the images of Kocakale in the spring and winter time. When my eyes followed Kocakale up the mountain, it seemed to be shooting straight toward the clouds... Then, it would reach them and disappear in the mist-shrouded mountain. Then I would get scared and curl up in my grandfather's lap.

When we were in elementary school, my friends and I would run straight into the fog that would come rolling over the old cemetery and Kurudere. We'd fall and get back up, fall and get up... I wanted to catch the clouds, seize hold of the thick billowing fog, but every time I drew near, they would disappear and I would fail in my mission!

Now, a lifetime of years and a thousand miles away, the fog was rolling onto those portions of the forest path that led up into the hills, at the end of the Western Boulevard of Wattenscheid. Some places had already disappeared. I couldn't contain myself any longer. I had to run and catch the clouds again! I shouted as loudly as I could. I had to make my voice echo off the rocks... But there were no rocks, no valleys here off which to bounce my voice! I stopped and listened to the gentle sound of the snow falling. Then, amid the soft pitter-patter of the snow, from very deep within me, from somewhere far, far off within my memory, came the voice of Emrah:

İncecikten bir kar yağar	The snow falls gently
Tozar elif elif diye	It scatters its [white dust] here and there
Deli gönül abdal olmuş	The wild heart grows blind and confused
Gezer elif elif diye...	Wandering here and there

I returned home accompanied by Emrah.

I called Meline... It was our first conversation since my visit to the hospital.

"Where have you been, Kemal my dear? What sort of paradise is it that's so good that nobody's seen you or even been able to reach you by phone? I tried to call you several times, but you were never there... I was going to try again today, for a heart-to-heart talk. And now you called...."

The tone of her voice was bright. Her laughter came in waves, like the contentment of a blossom-laden branch swaying gently in a clear, gentle spring breeze. Outside, a fine snow was falling.

"Get well, Meline! How long since you got out of the hospital?"

"Thank you, Kemal. God is great, we've escaped death. I'm doing really well. I got home from the hospital ten days ago. I'm continuing my treatment at home. As soon as I get myself together, I'm going to return to school, to my classes. I really miss the kids. I have to work for six more months before I can retire."

"There's a gentle snow falling here!"

"Here too. I wanted to walk around in it, but I've got to watch out for myself. I can't afford to get chilled. Let me just get through this winter... Every day there's more that we need to talk about."

"Take care of yourself, Meline!"

"You too!"

After an entire year's worth of treatment, after three major operations, one after the other, Meline did get better. She had escaped death! Her health and her strength returned.

Her illness had begun with very bad pains. At first she tried to ride them out, thinking that they would pass, but when they didn't, she finally went to the doctor. After examining her and running her through some tests, the doctors gave their diagnosis: inflammation of the abdomen. Without any delay or elaboration, they sent her directly to a good hospital that treated such conditions. There, they put her through some more exams and tests, the conclusion of which was an immediate operation. It went very well, but while she was undergoing subsequent treatment, her intestines ruptured as a result of complications. She was immediately taken for a second operation. It was a very dangerous procedure, but she got through this one in good order, as well. However, as a result of the operation she was very weak; she didn't even have the strength to hold a telephone receiver. Even so, she never lost hope. She acted decisively and systematically against what ailed her. She never gave in to the pains and the illness. Her husband Dieter was always by her side.

I kept trying to understand the reasons for Meline's illness. I tried to identify with Meline, saying, "There are some unsatisfied longings within you that are making you ill." It was with this idea in mind that I had brought her the fruit basket. But what were those longings that had made Meline take to her bed and were slowly eating her away to nothing? Why everyone who suffered such longing become bedridden like Meline? I had no idea....

After she returned to health, Meline returned to teaching English and Turkish and the Düsseldorf Gymnasium. She completed the necessary paperwork and other obligations for retirement, and went into retirement after that. We spoke frequently by phone at that time. When I didn't hear her voice for two weeks, it felt like two months.

For Meline, just because she had stopped working didn't mean sitting around at home all day. On the contrary, retirement became a very special period in her life. Her love of learning was as vital as ever. Now that she was retired, she was going to complete her degree in the history that so fascinated her, but for which she had never had the time to complete. She made a decision: she completed the necessary documents and enrolled in the History Department of Essen University.

Even over the phone I could feel the joy and happiness from the waves of her voice, as she informed me of the good news of her enrollment.

"Kemal," she said, "I enrolled in the university today!" I'm going to start to study history! I want to relearn the history that we learned in Turkey from elementary school through university, but this time through the eyes of the Europeans."

The months of winter and then spring came and went. At the end of June, Meline and I met at Essen University. I was taking a seminar in the Department of Turkish Instruction on "The Interpretation of Parables and Epics in Turkish Courses in the Middle East." Meline had just gotten out of the Turkish course she was teaching in the same department. When we had been discussing the time and place where we would meet, she had mentioned that her class at the university on Thursday was over at 6:00 p.m., the same time that my course was over. That was good for both of us!

This was the first time that I saw Meline since she had left the hospital. We had really missed one another. When I saw her, she was wearing summer clothes. We embraced one another. She looked to be well. She had gained weight, and her general mood and characteristic joyfulness had all returned. Her face was even more beautiful, more radiant now than it had been that first moment I saw her at the course in Dortmund.

"My dear Meline! How wonderful you look. Your eyes and your face are positively radiant. May it remain that way!"

"Thank you very much. Like I told you, while I was undergoing treatment at the hospital, I didn't even have the strength to pick up the phone. But my mind was active. I thought long and hard about all of those things in the past, all those things I experienced that had made me who I am, that had made us who we were. I healed the wounds that were inside my body, and I also brought to the light of day those dark, unclear places in my spirit. I made peace with myself... You understand: I washed myself clean, I illuminated my own internal world."

"How are your history lessons going?"

"Kemal, my dear, I'm attending classes regularly. During those thirty years that I taught school I did a little study, but in dribs and drabs. Now I'm going to finish it. We're studying Ottoman history. I'm taking a seminar called 'Ottoman Society in Tourism and Travel literature.' It's very interesting."

"Meline, my dear. I'm not going to ask you how you're doing. I'm not going to say to you 'Get well!' In an earlier time there was a Meline hidden underneath all the straw... Her face was always smiling, but her insides were weeping. She couldn't explain her pain to anyone. One day she fell ill. She was gravely sick and without any strength... Once in the world she had had a beautiful mother and an understanding father. They heard that one of their daughters had fallen ill while she was abroad.... so they alit on the wind and flew until they arrived at their daughter's side. Her mother asked her, 'What's wrong, my daughter?'

"Her father asked, 'What do you have, my princess?' But their daughter could not speak. They took their daughter to their side and began to walk.

They walked over hill and dale, until they finally reached a spring that was the source of all rivers, one that filled all the world's oceans. There their daughter opened her eyes and reached out her hand. The girl's mother stroked her daughter's face with her hands, and gave her some of the water to drink. Their daughter's face started to smile and her tongue was loosened…."

Meline laughed long at this. But I kept on with my fable without pausing… She interrupted me:

"Alright, already! I'll tell you everything; *everything*! What beautiful fable is this?"

"For the past three weeks I've been going over the Patient Stone parable that you taught us with the teaching candidates. We finished it today. Meline, what was it that finally split you, the Patient Stone?"

"I concede, my dear. I'll tell you everything, but only on one condition!"

"I accept all the conditions that you set!"

"Not so fast. First, listen to what they are, and think about it…."

"I've already done a lot of thinking until now!"

"Look, Kemal: this is a difficult task. My condition isn't easy…"

"So be it. Even if it kills me!"

"Watch what you say!"

"If it's that bad, let me know what it is!"

"I'll tell you, but listen well. You were going to go to Turkey this summer vacation. You have to go and find those old Armenian women that you heard still lived in the regions of Amasya and Erbaa from the owners of 'The Security Trousseau' that you sought out. The ones who survived by converting to Islam and marrying Muslim men. You have to go and speak with them. After that, you have to go to Erzurum and Aşkale. From there you have to go through Kars and see Ani. After Kars, you have to go on to Van. You'll take the ferry to Aghtamar Island in lake Van. From there, come back to Istanbul. You need to ask around. Find these old Armenians. Speak to them for as long as you can… Afterward, come back and we'll speak. That's my condition. It's difficult; it's a hard matter… But first go and see; then understand me!"

Part Two

On the Road

The start of the journey

It had been ten days since I had arrived in Honaz from Germany. We had all kissed and hugged and caught up on the time we were apart. Now, we were working on the land. We gathered sour cherries. The apricots were heavy-laden with fruit this year; it seemed as if there were more fruit than leaves, even. The branches were straining under their bounty. We gathered up all the ripe apricots. That lightened their load a bit. The trees seemed to recover, as their branches again returned to their positions. The pears, bending over almost to the point of being horizontal, and the early peaches seemed to be gesturing to people, saying, "Come, eat my fruit!"

The taste of fruit plucked straight from the tree was different. The taste of fruits and vegetables was sweetened by the hoeing one did around them, by watering and by the beads of sweat from those tending to them, drops which slowly but surely penetrated their roots.

I grew tired. I had to rest after struggling with the earth. It was our turn to irrigate the gardens. After evening fell Cuvar came to the house and told us: "You guys will take the water after Afero, the son of Mevlüt the immigrant. He'll finish watering in the mid-afternoon."

The following day, toward mid-afternoon, my older brother İsmet, his sons Oktay and Özgür, my son Şafak and I, and my older sister Ayşe all loaded onto the tractor trailer and began the journey to the garden. If we began to take water to the garden at five in the afternoon, we would be finished about five the next morning. We would have to irrigate the garden all night long and into the morning. Night watering was difficult work. But it was our turn. We took out our flashlights, lanterns and warm jackets.

When we arrived, Afero was flooding the plum trees.

"*Kalimera Afero!*" I shouted, "*Ti kanis!*"

"*Kalimera Kemal! Kala!*" he replied.

"Don't work too hard! Here, have some of these peaches! Cool off a bit!"

"Welcome! Brother Kemal, come and stay here! Enough already with Germany!"

Afero was a childhood friend of mine. His father, his mother and all of his uncles had come from Greece during the 1924 Turkish-Greek population exchange,* from the village of Vranşno in the Grevena district of the Province of Salonica (Thessaloniki). Afero's mother tongue was Greek. His relatives hadn't known a single word of Turkish when they arrived. When we were young he taught me some Greek. Now I regret not having learned more.

He had come alone to water.

"Here, give me that shovel already!" I told him. "I'll look after the water and you go eat some peaches. Go and cool off a bit."

He squatted in the shade of one of the plum trees and ate the peaches I had given him. Then, he lit himself a cigarette and we drifted back to the old days.

"You went and visited the places we're from: Grevena, Vraşno. My mother and father died without ever seeing those places again. I want to go and see them; I want to see the village where my mother and father used to live, I want to see their house, the mountains and the stones of their youth."

"Go and see them if you can, Afero!"

He finished his cigarette and flicked the butt into the water. "Thanks. Be well" he said taking back the shovel.

He finished his watering after another half an hour. He closed off the sluice of the irrigation canal. The water entered our garden, gradually finding its way into the deep cracks and fissures in the dried out earth, bubbling and gurgling its way down as it slowly filled them.

"Okay, then!" Afero exclaimed. "Take it easy. I'm going home and it's off to work with you!"

The water flowed copiously. It was practically waist-deep. We were flooding the garden. We began from the dried stubble of the broad bean plants. The ground had been parched from lack of water. A small bit of the water sunk into the ground and disappeared, but most of it wasn't being absorbed yet. Toward evening, Ayşe's son Nevruz came up with a wagon containing his grandmother, his uncle Ali İhsan, and our sisters-in-law, Pembe and Sultan. My sister-in-law Sultan had brought supper.

---

* The exchange, or *Mübâdele* as it is known in Turkish, was agreed upon during the Peace Treaty between the new Republic of Turkey and the various allies, signed at Lausanne in July, 1923. The terms of the exchange went into effect on January 1, 1924.

"Take it easy! Come, let's eat dinner together before it gets cold. Channel the water into two or three different channels. It will continue to flow on its own."

They set the garden table that was on the terrace. My mother called us all to the table, "Hurry, now! Come and eat!"

Food tasted different out in the garden. And the taste of food eaten in my father's hearth, with the whole family, had a different taste than that. In such a wonderful atmosphere, even a chili pepper tastes sweet.

"Make the water flow all through the garden," my mother said. "Let the trees drink their fill. Let it reach down to your father's spirit! Ahhhh, how your father loved the water, the earth. Ah, this passing world! He too, passed in his time!"

The water worked its way to all corners of the garden floor, and down the slope to the cherry trees in front… as if it were looking for my father.

My older brother İsmet sensed that something was up. Over dinner he had changed the direction of the conversation and, turning to me, asked:

"Hey, Kemal, my brother. Is it true that, God willing, you're heading out after tomorrow?"

I had told him and my mother about Meline. I had told them that I was going to go to Amasya and look for Armenians, and that I would go to Erzurum, Aşkale, Kars and Ani after that. İsmet was worried.

"You know to be careful not to let anything happen to you, little brother!" he said. "Look, it's not for nothing that you weren't allowed to enter the country for thirteen long years. Thank goodness, you've been able to come and go freely without fear or any calamity for the last three years. But please, don't mix yourself up in these matters. I know that those things you said are true. You're right, but…"

My sister Ayşe, who was a biology teacher, was also concerned. You could hear it in her tone of voice and see it in the color of her face.

But my brother İsmet wanted the question of my going to look for Armenians to be brought out and discussed before my mother and the rest of the family. From our previous conversations I had understood that he wanted to dissuade me from going.

"Let's finish with the watering tonight. I'm traveling to Ankara by car tomorrow evening. From there I'm going on to Amasya…"

My mother, Pembe, and Ali İhsan were all hearing about my trip for the first time. Nevruz, Oktay, Özgür and Şafak had heard us when we had spoken about it the day before with my elder brother.

My mother said:

"What are you going there for? What business do you have there?"

Pembe said:

"You only come once a year, Kemal. And then you don't stay here when you're here! We're not tired of you yet! Come and relax; You should remain here, you'll be tired after all that irrigating and hoeing! But now you say you're going to Amasya! Where's that, anyway? Is it far? But don't let anything else happen to you! I couldn't stand it."

My other sister-in-law Sultan said:

"You should think long and hard about it, Kemal…. You know best, but…. What business do you have there?"

Ali İhsan then broke in:

"My brother, don't stick your nose in just any place! Once when you did this in the past, you said 'We're going to save the country!', but the fact is, you barely managed to save yourself. You had to go into exile for thirteen years. I tell you, I couldn't take any more of having to miss you while you're in exile!"

My mother couldn't restrain her curiosity for another moment:

"Enough, now. Tell us what there is over there that you're going to see. What business do you have there?"

"Oktay," I said to my older brother, "This looks like it's going to take a while. Go, quickly, and redirect the water channels and then come back. This matter is getting bigger."

My sister Ayşe then said:

"You're right, brother. If I had been one of those teachers, it would have never occurred to me to ask either. I'm curious about Meline. I've never met her but I already love her as if I had! It's by not asking that we've come to this state. If it were up to me, though, I'd tell you not to go this year. Let things in the East calm down a bit. Then go."

My son Şafak then pressed his claim:

"Dad, didn't you promise me when we were still in Germany that you'd take me to the sea?"

Nevruz then cast his vote:

"Good for you, Şafak! Let's go to the sea! To the sea!"

But my mother then broke in with:

"Be still now, Şafak! And you keep out of it, Nevruz! Now, where are this Meline's mother and father? Are her relatives from Amasya? They expelled our Greek neighbors. They lost. What happened to the Armenians? You went all the way to Greece looking for those Minoğlu descendants, who you found there. Did you do a bad thing by giving back these girls their dowries so many years later?"

"Mother, those were Greeks. These are Armenians," İsmet reminded her.

"And aren't the Armenians also God's servants?" my mother replied. "Aren't they human beings? When we were staying with my Aşan, who teaches in Tokat, I would often get really bad headaches, sharp pains like someone was sticking a knife in my head. They were so bad, I could hardly stand them. We went to the doctor, but that didn't help. One evening we went with our landlord Gülizar Hanım to an old Armenian woman. She was a very clean woman, with a radiant face. She didn't have anyone left and was all alone. She wouldn't light a single candle at night. She didn't even light one when we came. The Turks had killed her husband a long time ago. May no one have to suffer such loneliness! She said: 'I can't sit here in the light on earth while my husband is lying under the ground in darkness!' After that she took out a thick book with black covers and began to read. I don't know what she read, but it was sort of like our book. She read and read... 'Kiss it three times!' she finally said. I kissed it. My headache stopped right away, as if someone had cut it out with a knife. After that day I never had those pains again. I wanted to give her money, but she wouldn't take it. Later on I brought her a little *tarhane** and some tomato paste.

Your father had told you 'Go find the Minoğlu girls!' and sent you off to Greece. May he rest in peace! If he were still alive now, he would again tell you 'Go and find them!' So go, my son, go! Go find that old Armenian woman in Tokat if she's still alive. Go tell her 'Thank you. You made my mother's headaches go away!' and send her my greetings. May she receive it!"

Ahh! My mother! My wise and knowing, camphor-smelling mother! I hugged her and kissed her.

"You say 'Go! Find the old Armenian woman in Tokat and send her my greetings!'... Well, that's enough for me! Be well, mother! Be well, all of

---

* Dried yoghurt used as a base for soups and some sauces in Turkey.

you! I know that you're all concerned for me. But I've made a promise to Meline. After tomorrow I'm setting out."

After that, things calmed down around the table. A cool evening breeze began to blow. The leaves of all the trees on the terrace, the mulberries, the figs, the yellow-red peaches, and of the cherries, the roses and four-o'clocks, the dahlias, the mint, the herbs and brambles all began to flutter and smile.

The others at the table then began to speak, one after the other:

"You know best, Kemal my brother!"

"You know best, uncle!"

"Watch out for yourself, little brother!"

"Take me along with you, father!"

"Nothing ventured, nothing gained!"

"But be careful who you talk to. Don't just speak with anyone!"

"Thank you, everyone. May you all be well. Don't worry! Come on now, off to work! The water reached the foot of the garden. Nevruz, take your grandmother, you cousins and your uncle Ali İhsan home."

Pembe said:

"Let's take Şafak with us, too!"

"No, Pembe," I said. "My son should learn how to irrigate the garden at night. Anyway, there's also a new moon tonight. He should see that!"

So we bid our farewells to those going back to the house. İsmet pulled some of the embers from the shrub roots and put them in front of the hearth. He then laid two of the dried roots from the largest tree in the hearth. He and Şafak then brought some of the dried brush from the pile and threw it in. The fire roared with its new meal, and threw its flames high into the sky. From the tops of these huge, writhing tongues of flame, sparks jumped forth and flew skyward. The colors of the flowers, leaves and branches facing these brilliant crimson flames changed into a myriad of hues. The flames were reflected in the torrents of water, appearing to dance on their surface before being extinguished in its blackness. Those places not illuminated by the fire were graced by the fireflies, who flitted around like little dancing droplets of light.

Combining with the sounds of the buzzing and flying insects, the silhouettes of the trees and their branches danced in the light of the blaze, continually morphing from one monstrous shape to another. And that night, the earth of the garden drank its fill of water, fire and stars.

Looking for Armenians in Amasya

On the morning of July 11, 1998, I stepped out of the bus onto the tarmac of the Amasya inter-city bus station. I got off near the Tamimi Monument. From the Government Bridge, I stared into the waters of the Yeşilırmak river. The huge, bending leaves and branches of the immense plane trees in the Herkiz Garden Park were drinking from the waters of the river; the river's currents danced with the drooping silent branches of the trees.

I settled in a hotel. I wanted to sleep off the weariness of the long overnight bus ride. I awoke around noon time. The entire way I had thought long and hard about what I was going to do, about where and with whom I should begin my work: I was going to find Master Ali.

Three years earlier, when I had been looking for still surviving persons who had undergone the population exchange, I had made the acquaintance of Ali, the master carpenter, who had helped me with all the means at his disposal. I would explain my problem to him and ask for his ideas on how we could solve it. If I was unable to find Master Ali, I would request help from the other refugees and "immigrants" that I had met three years ago. But no matter what, I was determined that I would find those Armenian women who had survived by marrying Turks, the ones in Amasya, in Erbaa, in Tokat whose existence I had learned of from the old refugees.

Master Ali's shop was in the stone caravansary known as "Taşhan." Every part of Amasya, and especially the old part of Amasya known as the "inner city," as well as the banks of the Yeşilırmak, all were full of the old handiwork of the Ottomans, and of Greeks and Armenians. In the saddle of the steep rock out of the top of which rose the fortress of Amasya were the magnificent "King's Graves."

Taşhan was built in the fifteenth century. Who was the architect? Of which nation did he come? Who was the master builder whose hands had embellished the beautiful stones of the arched entrance gate and inner courtyard, whose hands had carved and engraved the stones and iron as delicately as if they had been a silk handkerchief? I had no idea. On the building's inscription, only the name of the pasha who had ordered its construction was mentioned. But of the names of those who had labored building and ornamenting the edifice there was no trace.

As I entered, I looked one more time as I entered Taşhan's majestic entrance gate. How this beautiful stonework had been ruined by neglect and ignorance of its worth! The filth was ankle deep! If those who had built this caravansary or had ordered it built were to suddenly arise and come here, what would they have to say to us, I wonder?

Taşhan's inner courtyard was a small patch of light in the midst of all this disorder, filth and neglect. And in the middle of the courtyard, directly across from the entrance gate, grew a plane tree.

When I arrived at his shop, Master Ali was immersed in his work. I said "Hello!" He responded in a sincerely friendly manner, and then he looked up at me.

"Ho hoo! What's this?!? Welcome!"

Wiping his hands onto his apron in order to remove the sawdust, he came over and we hugged like lifelong friends.

"Welcome and welcome again! Here, you can put down your bag on the bench. Please, sit down!" And then, turning to the tea boy: "Run, boy. Go tell the tea seller that you want two fresh teas." He then returned to me. "So, let's see: is it a fair or foul wind that has blown you back to these parts?"

"A fair one, Master Ali. A fair one!" I replied. We've got no business with the foul! So, how have you been since we last spoke?"

"Thank you and be well. Let's say I've been well. I no longer enjoy my work like I used to... but I'm trying to keep things running."

"Did you get the photographs I sent?"

"I did. Thank you very much. And may the hand that took them remain strong. Please forgive me that I wasn't able to write you a few lines back."

At that point the teas arrived. We drank them while Ali's apprentice nailed together a window frame. We found it impossible to speak amid the sounds of the hammer and saw, so Master Ali said:

"Come, let's go and sit in the shade of the plane tree. We can speak more easily there."

It was cooler under the tree's shadow, and we were able to speak to one another there, now that he was out of earshot of his apprentice. It wasn't for an apprentice to know everything that his master did. He didn't need to be a party to every one of the master's discussions....

"Master Ali," I began, "I've got a problem. I've come here because I need your help."

"I swear, sir, anything that is in my power to do, consider it done!"

"I heard that there are some old Armenian women who survived in Amasya and the surrounding villages by marrying Turks. I want to speak with these women. Do you know anything about such women? Have you ever heard of such a thing? How would I go about finding them?"

He placed his right hand on his chin and thought for a bit:

I've heard a great deal about them. Until about fifteen years ago, there even used to be some Armenians in Amasya. Nowadays, though, there's no one left. Some died, some moved to Istanbul. There were some Armenians around Erbaa and Tokat. Sometimes, during the time that the Armenians were being expelled, some Turks took beautiful Armenian women or girls for themselves. Some became second wives, others servants, and still others became concubines. Some of the Armenians became Muslims in order to survive. I heard about one of these who they used to call "Hüseyin, the infidel's son." His mother was an Armenian. Her name doesn't come to mind right now…

Who should we ask? Where should we look? Sir, this matter isn't like the Greek one. You can't go up to just anyone and ask. You can't go just anywhere to look for them. Let's say, for instance, that you find one. Do you think he'll trust you enough to speak with you? Remember: these people have been rescued from the jaws of death. Fear has worked its way into their very bones! Once I used to have a couple of Armenian customers. They weren't *dönme*s (converts) or anything like that. But they were always hesitant to talk. Being a 'convert' is much harder. You've got no one of your own family around. Can you imagine what it's like, not to have a single branch of your family to cling to in the entire world? But let's forget about that for a minute. Do you know what it means to be an Armenian or an Alevî in Amasya?

Let's see… who… who… Ha! I've got it! There's such a woman in the village of my neighbor, the one whose shop is over in the corner there. Let's stay calm now and go ask him without getting him upset.

Then, with a light, cheery voice as if he wasn't at all concerned, Master Ali called out:

"Hey, tinsmith! You've been polishing that copper without letup since morning! You'll work yourself to death. Come, sit with us and cool off a bit!"

The tinsmith responded as if he'd been expecting to be summoned. Without the slightest show of reluctance, he stopped his work, washed his hands and came over where we were sitting. His hands had been stained black from the copper pots. He looked at Master Ali with an inquisitive glace that seemed to say, "Who's this?"

"He came here three years before," Master Ali responded. "This is the gentleman who took and sent me those photographs that I showed you."

"Welcome!" the tinsmith said. "I'd shake your hand, but mine is full of soot." He was a big man, with a healthy paunch pushing out his dirty, torn shirt and leaning over the belt of his drooping pants.

I held out my hand:

"Please, don't apologize!" I said. "It's hard work being a tinsmith. You definitely earn your keep. 'Let your hands be black, not your reputation!'" I said and shook his sooty hand. I didn't get a very good impression from this man, though.

He pulled up a stool and sat down next to Ali.

"What are you drinking?" Ali asked him. "You're hot. Have something cool to drink!"

"Make it an *ayran*!"*

"Boy!" Ali called out. "Run and get an ayran for the tinsmith! Make sure it's cold. And two teas for us. Order something for yourself as well."

Master Ali knew the tinsmith's temperament and moods well. Instead of broaching the subject right away, he took the long way...

"So, tinsmith, your business is doing fine these days. The old adage is right that says, everyone should do the work that they like, and the labor of a good man is also good!

At this the tinsmith relaxed his guard a bit. It was clear that he enjoyed the flattery. The *ayran* and the teas arrived. The tinsmith downed his *ayran* in one gulp.

"Tinsmith," Ali began, "did that old Armenian woman in your village die?"

"No, she's still alive, and fit as a fiddle!"

"What was her name?"

"I don't actually know that family very well. Her name is Safiye, or something like that."

The tinsmith then grew suspicious. He shifted on his stool:

"Master Ali, what are you going to do with this Armenian woman? What business do you have with the Armenians?"

Sensing the tinsmith's unease, Ali reverted back to flattery and tried to lighten up the conversation:

---

* A very popular refreshment throughout the Middle East, it is made by churning together yoghurt, salt and water.

"My mother died. I want her for my father!"

At that the tinsmith laughed long and hard, his big belly dancing up and down, and Ali then saw his opening:

"This gentleman is a dear, dear friend of mine. He's come here to do research. He would like to find some old Armenians to speak with."

The ayran that he had downed in one gulp was still cold in his stomach. He lightly turned, and, looking directly at me, looked me over from head to foot.

"Is that so?" he said. "Well, then, let me think about it. I've got a lot of work right now. We'll speak again two or three hours from now," and with that, he got up and withdrew. Master Ali watched him silently, following him with his eyes until he reached his shop. Then he turned his head toward me:

"This looks like it's going to be a difficult matter. But we don't have any choice. We'll wait a few more hours. You go stroll around a bit. Let me go home and eat, and then I'll be back again later."

I returned to the shop at two and said hello to Master Ali.

"Our friend the tinsmith has closed up his shop and left for the day. He didn't leave any messages for us. We have to play the game. Let's go to the coffee house. If he's not there, we'll go around to all of the other places he might be."

With that, he took off his apron and hung it on the peg. We left the shop with him leading the way.

"My son," he said to his apprentice, "some people are going to come for this table. Give it to them. If anyone asks about me, tell them I'll be back after an hour."

Ali seemed disappointed. He said to himself:

"This man didn't close up his shop at this hour of the day in order to go play games. Come, let's hope for the best!"

We found the tinsmith, sitting and playing cards at an old coffeehouse that seemed to be covered in a thick film of cigarette soot and the smell of nicotine.

"Peace upon you, gentlemen!" Master Ali said.

"And upon you peace, Master Ali!" they replied. "Come, sit down and have a tea!"

"I left my store under the care of my apprentice."

The tinsmith didn't even raise his head to look at us. He kept his glance firmly on his cards.

"Master Ali," he said, "Don't mix me up in these matters! Don't bring trouble into my life. I didn't hear anything, I didn't see anything, I don't know anything!" and with that he threw down his cards on the table in a manner that was clearly meant to be understood as "I'm done with you! Get lost!"

Not a single one of those playing cards or watching them looked me in the face. "Well, then. Carry on with your game!" we said and, seeing no reason to drag out the matter, we left the coffeehouse.

Master Ali was crestfallen.

"I spit in your face!" he cursed at the tinsmith who wasn't present. "You ought to be ashamed of yourself! He acts as if we were going to rob someone! What's wrong with these people?"

We went back to his shop, with Ali speaking most of the way, sometimes to me, sometimes to the tinsmith.

"Sir, you've come all the way here from God knows how far. These are good works you do. But we're going to have to do it ourselves. I've got a relative who's a taxi driver. Let me call him. You haggle with him over the price. It's about ten kilometers to the village we're going to go. Don't give him more than two million lira.[*] Let's go and ask. Some good God-fearing person who knows about these matters will find us."

What wonderful people one can find in this world, in this Anatolia of ours! There are those who are afraid of their own shadows, and others, like Master Ali, who will drop everything they are doing and bend over backwards to give you all the help they can!

Five or ten minutes later there was a taxi waiting for us in front of the Taşhan. Master Ali leaned over and asked the driver:

"We're going to Yassıçal and back again. How much money do you want for that?"

"Give whatever you want, Ali my brother!"

"We'll give two million. Is that enough?"

"What? Am I going to haggle with you? God bless you, master!"

---

[*] This amount is not a figure of speech or a joke. During the 1980s and 1990s, inflation in Turkey regularly ran at nearly 100% per annum. The amount stated by Ali would have been around US $10-15.00 at the time.

Before we left, Master Ali gave instructions to his apprentice. Then we got in the taxi and were off, traveling through the lush greenery of the Yeşilırmak valley until we reached the village of Yassıçal. The whole trip took less than half an hour. The first thing that Ali did was to knock on the door of a person from whom he used to purchase cypress wood. He asked the woman who came out into the courtyard where her father was. She replied that he was out in the fields.

"We were looking for someone from this village. Her name is 'Safiye' or something like that…. Do you know which house she lives in?"

"Grandma Safiye lives in that house up the street there," the woman said, pointing. "She was there yesterday. If she's not there now she's probably out in her garden."

"Well, would you look at that! All we had to do was mention some trace, some name, some village and we found her house!"

We were going to find her, alright. Or somebody, anyway. Master Ali's eyes grew moist. Stroking his long whiskers with satisfaction, he said, smilingly:

"We were lucky. We didn't come in vain!"

The taxi struggled to get up the steep dirt path. We stopped before the house that the woman in the courtyard had described. Ali called out. The young women with covered heads sitting on the swing ushered us in through the gate. They were happy-faced, healthy-looking people. Master Ali did all the talking:

"We've come to speak with Madam Safiye. Is she here?"

"My grandmother is in the garden. They're gathering peaches. If you're in a hurry, we can run and call her…."

"We are. I had to close up my carpentry shop to come. The gentleman here has some business. If it's far away we can all go in the taxi."

So we all went and came back together in the taxi.

Madam Safiye came up to us with a basket full of peaches. She had a radiant face and her white hair peeked out from under the edges of a white band. She welcomed all of us. Master Ali introduced me to her. I took out my book *The Security Trousseau* from my bag.

"I came to these parts three years before in order to speak with some of those persons who had come from Greece during the population exchange. I went to Greece twice, as well. While I was there I spoke with Anatolian Greeks from Amasya and Taşova. I wrote and published this book about it. This is my book here. What I would like to do now is to speak with Armenians who survived by marrying Turks. I'm meeting you now for the first time only thanks to the help I received from Master Ali. I realize that this is the first time you've ever seen me, and that you may not wish to speak with me. I would be very happy if you would, though. I've come all the way from Germany to Denizli, and from Denizli to here."

Madam Safiye looked at my book, running her eyes over the cover and over the pictures inside. Then she gave it to her daughters and granddaughters, who passed it from hand to hand, looking at it in turn. But there was a stillness, a hesitation, and a doubt-filled hesitation in Madam Safiye and the others. They were right in being suspicious.

"I don't know very much," Madam Safiye finally said. "First, have some of the peaches that I brought. I only now picked them. My son with his wife and children are out picking more right now. Daughter, go put on some tea. And bring some ayran. If you're hungry don't hesitate to say something!"

We ate some of the peaches; the tea came after that and we drank it. The house was built in a deep valley, on the slope facing the sun. Across from the house was a pine-covered mountain. There were fruit orchards aligned in neat rows at the base of the valley. There was abundant water. The sound of its bubbling and gurgling echoed off the walls of the deep ravine. Apart from a small flock of clouds, the heavens above were a beautiful turquoise blue. It was a bright, peaceful world here. And it was impossible that the people who lived in such a peaceful world could be bad.

The best thing to do was to send Ali back to Amasya with the taxi. That way I could remain and speak to them privately.

"Master Ali," I said. "It looks like this is going to take a long time. You've got your own work to do. Thank you so much for your help! I'll never forget the good turn you've done me."

I then took him off to the side and said:

"Here, take this five million lira. Give what you want to the taxi driver, keep the rest for yourself. I've kept you from your work. I'm sorry."

After they left, everyone seemed to be more relaxed. Even their voices changed. Madam Safiye untied the band over her head and retied it. She studied my face as best she could without being obvious. She seemed to be looking for some trace, some sign. With the voice of a tender, calm, self-confident woman who had seen much, experienced much, and had preserved her clear conscience, she said:

"My son, do you have any Armenian in you?"

"No, ma'am. I'm Turkish."

"So where did you get the idea to come and ask us? I'm seventy years old. Until today, no Turk has ever come out and asked us about what we were, or what we remember."

I then told her all about Meline, about her saying, "I've waited six years!" and about Meline's condition for speaking with me.

"She waited for six years," Safiye observed, "but I've waited for seventy! No one has ever asked. You've thought about this rightly. And you've taken a good path. Where is this Meline from?"

"From Istanbul."

"I understand her. Where are her mother and father from?"

"I'm not sure. I didn't ask."

Good question! Where *were* Meline's parents from? Were they also from Istanbul? Yet one more question to ask her when I got back.

"And what would you like to learn from me? What shall I tell you?" Madam Safiye asked.

"If you please, I would like you to tell me about Madam Safiye's life, her mother, her father, and the things she's seen and heard."

Madam Safiye

My heart did what it pleased

Anyway, I was born in 1931.... I'm sixty-seven years old now. I was born in Amasya. I'm a native of Amasya. My father was a saddle maker. My mother was a housewife. She was an Armenian, of course. Her name was Zeytimya. My father's name was Nishan.

I went to school when I was seven years old. I passed through the first, second and third grades with the grade of 'good.' But in fourth grade, I only went for fifteen days. There was a big earthquake after that. That would have been 1939. And I fell ill, too. Boy, was I scared!

After the earthquake, my father didn't send me back to school anymore. So against my will, I was taken out of fourth grade. I stayed at home doing nothing for a whole year. After that my mother sent me to learn dressmaking. One and a half years later, I graduated with honors and a certificate in dressmaking.

Our house was very close to that of my husband's family. Because of that we noticed one another and fell in love. My husband's name is Mustafa. He was already married and had a child. No matter how much he wanted me, my parents wouldn't give me to him for all the money in the world. He was both a Turk and married. During those days, the Armenians wouldn't give one of their own to a Turk, to a Muslim. Before me, only two other Armenian girls had gone to marry Turks. But they ran off and eloped, without the consent of their parents. One ran off with a soldier. The other Armenian girl was my teacher. She ran off with the army cashier. He was an old guy from Çanakkale. He took my teacher off with him to Çanakkale. His parents were very old and sick. They finally died. A few years later, her husband passed away as well. As she didn't have anyone else in Çanakkale, she decided to come back here. That was the year that a big flood hit Amasya. Her mother, her father, and all her siblings were carried off by the flood, but they didn't die. They survived. But she herself was injured. They took her to the hospital. At the hospital she got to know an Armenian man. Later on they got married. The years passed by quickly. As the years passed by, she lived her life, with all its loves, passions and sorrows, as if it were never going to end. But my teacher, the beauty named Vartanush, has been buried now for a long time.

What was I saying? Oh, yes. I fell in love with Mustafa. And he was crazy about me, too. His military service came up. But before he went off to the army we found a way to speak to one another:

'I really want you' he told me. 'Will you wait for me until I'm back from military service?'

'So help me God, I'll wait for you!' I told him. At that time I wasn't thinking clearly at all. I couldn't keep these three words inside, they just came out of my mouth without thinking. All of a sudden I felt like I was burning up. Mustafa took my hand. It felt like it was made of fire.

Mustafa was a brave and honorable man. The entire world was arrayed against him. But even if all of Amasya came to prevail upon me, I wouldn't be given to another.

His military service seemed to go on forever. Days passed by; then it was months. I had promised him that I would wait. One hopeful suitor after another came and left disappointed. All of those who came were Armenian. But I had given my heart to Mustafa. I had given him my hand. My heart refused to even consider another.

Naturally, my mother wanted to give me to one, my father to another.... The one that my father wanted for me my mother disapproved of. And my father said 'No' to my mother's choice.

As for me, I told them from my heart:

'It doesn't matter what you say. Nothing's going to come of all this. No matter what happens, I'm going to Mustafa!'

When a person falls in love they can't always see clearly. They lose all their fear, even of death! They'll do whatever it takes just to find a way to be with their beloved. I was consumed with my love for Mustafa. I would get dressed and wander the streets!

As I said, one suitor after another came and went. They all asked for my hand, but I didn't want to go to any of them. I told them all 'No!' My parents never gave up.

'If you didn't like that one,' they'd say, 'Go marry this one!' I resisted, though. I would lie awake at night thinking. I couldn't sleep. As soon as I'd chase one out of my head, another thought would seize me.

I saw that it wasn't going to be possible. Should I send word to Mustafa? If I said 'Come!' he still wouldn't be able to. I finally told Mustafa's mother:

'My desire [for Mustafa] keeps growing. They are going to send me off to Istanbul. I don't want to go. Let Mustafa come and take me, or I'll come myself to your house!'

After that, Mustafa's father, his wife and everyone else found out about us.

My father-in-law was a very sensitive man. He understood the situation and figured out a way. He went and spoke with a judge whom he knew and sought advice. He explained the situation to him and asked:

'The girl wants of her own volition to flee to our place. Can we be punished for that in the future?'

'Nothing can happen to you, as long as the girl keeps her word. She shouldn't become afraid and lose heart.'

We sent messages back and forth. Neither my mother nor my father had any idea as to what was going on.

One evening I fled to Mustafa's house in Yassıçal village. The moon rose over the mountain like a big porcelain plate.... The moonlight shone down on the hills and the hollows of the big rocks. I could hear night birds singing in the distance. From the valley below I could hear the splashing and gurgling of the waters of the Yeşilırmak river, echoing off the valley walls. I glanced at the moon. It was as big and bright as the sun! Even now, at this age, I've never again seen a full moon so big and bright as it was on that night. Did I run? Or was I flying? I don't know. How did I manage to get down the stairs of my parents' house? How did I manage to open the front gate without anyone hearing me? I don't know. It was as if the gate opened of its own accord, as if the stone path rolled out before me like a meadow of green grass.

Mustafa himself was still in the army, but his father and mother had taken the necessary measures. They were ready to grab whatever came by, even a flying bird.

When I stepped through the front gate of their house I prayed to God:

'Thank goodness! I've made it to Mustafa's front door... I've passed through the door from which they can't take me back!'

They looked for me high and low.... My Lord! It seemed like all of Amasya was up in arms... They pressured my father-in-law greatly. But his family ferreted me away and hid me first in one place, then another. Six months passed. Mustafa was given leave. I felt on top of the world! All of the beautiful things that I experienced then made up for having had to run away and for all the pain I had suffered.

But life's one thing, the law's another. What did the law understand of my love for Mustafa? The gendarmerie raided our house. They came and took me, claiming that I was too young to get married, and brought me back to my father's house. It was so hard to be returned, under the gendarmes' custody, to the house from which I'd fled.

The days passed like molasses. The dark nights closed in on me, making it hard for me to breathe. My soul felt caged in. I felt like I was suffocating! I wasn't able to see Mustafa again. While he was down dealing with the gendarmerie, the police and the ministry, his leave ran out. He went back to the army, but he did it leaving something undone!

As for me, they took me and put me under house confinement in Boğazbağı. I remained at my older sister's house. She had already been promised in marriage. His name was Hayganush...

We had a Turkish neighbor in Boğazbağı. Her name was Pakize. Aunt Pakize had a daughter by the name of Gülizar. She was the same age as my older sister.

While I was there they wouldn't let me meet or speak with anybody. They wouldn't even let me leave the house and garden. I grew bored. I felt like I was going to burst! It was a summer day; there was no escape from the heat. I'd go inside the house, come back out again. I looked for something to do in the garden in front of the house. I drew some water from the well and wet the area in front of the house, and swept and mopped it. I watered the flowers. My elder sister was also bored. Together, we found something to do. Toward evening, little gusts of breeze began blowing in from the straits. Somehow, the way it cooled my insides, I started thinking of Mustafa. I got goose bumps, and the hairs on my neck stood up. It felt as if the breeze was blowing in and out of my veins. I began to tremble. I broke out into a sweat. I felt like Mustafa was coming...

Sometimes, we spoke through the front gate with the Turkish woman who was our neighbor. Gülizar would come to our place, too. Sometimes, my sister would go to her place. Only I wasn't allowed to go anywhere. Not from fear, but because my father had forbidden it!

One day, during midmorning, I was washing the front courtyard. My sister was sitting on the steps. Our neighbor came up to our house and said:

'Girls, you're bored. Come, we're going to pick apricots and peaches!'

We really were bored stiff. So my sister and I went off to pick fruit. My older sister sat under a sour cherry tree and talked and laughed with Gülizar. Meanwhile, Aunt Pakize sidled up to me and we began picking cherries together. After a while she shot me a glance:

'Girl,' she said, 'I've got good news for you!' and showed me a piece of paper in her hand. Out of both joy and terror, my heart jumped into my mouth. I looked up and saw that Gülizar and my sister were coming straight toward us. But Madam Pekize was a very experienced and crafty woman:

'Girls,' she said to them, 'Yadigâr, Hayganush! Be quick. Go climb up that tree and fill these baskets! We'll gather up the other ones from the branches we can reach down here!'

They took the baskets in their hands and unhesitatingly began clambering up the tree. They started to laugh and play while they were picking the fruit. Aunt Pakize came over to me and pressed the letter into my hand without letting anyone else see it.

My hand felt like it was on fire! I wanted to tear it open and read it right then and there! But Aunt Pakize just smiled and stroked my back, saying:

'Zaruhi, my girl, pick the cherries slowly... What's your rush?'

I understood what she was trying to tell me.

I understood her meaning, but try telling that to my heart! I still felt like I was going to explode from curiosity and excitement. I began to walk away, to go for a stroll.

What would happen if my older sister saw me? Would Aunt Pakize's husband, Uncle Şevket, notice what was going on? Uncle Şevket was a different type altogether. He'd snatch the letter from out of my hand and give me a good shellacking!

'I've got to find a way to go back to the house,' I told myself. But while this was happening, Şevket's voice rang out.

'Aunt Pakize,' I said, 'Uncle Şevket is calling from down by the river, but I can't make out what he's saying. Do you think he's calling us?'

'I can't understand either, Zaruhi, my dear. Hurry over there and see what he wants!'

I wanted to go, but I hesitated. 'Let my sister or Gülizar go!' I said. But Aunt Pakize smiled and said, 'They're up in the tree. You're already down here. Hurry, girl. Run!'

I ran straight for the bottom of the garden. Uncle Şevket was sitting in the shade of the trees on the side of the road closest to the river.

'What can I do for you, Uncle Şevket? We were picking cherries and we thought we heard your voice, but we couldn't make out what you were saying.'

'Are you picking fruit, too, Zaruhi? Be well. Tell your Aunt Pakize that she should fill the baskets and bring what she's collected since morning. I want to take them to Amasya before evening.'

'I'll tell her' I said and turned around to head back. I walked between the trees on the river bank. In an instant I'd taken the letter out of my pocket and began reading. It was from Mustafa's father:

Zaruhi, my daughter,
They've taken you back. But don't believe those things that are said! Don't despair. If you come to Amasya I'll bring you [back to our house]. We'll be all around you [protecting you]. No one will be able to touch a hair on your head. Keep your spirits up and your mouth closed! Write your answer!

I felt on top of the world again! I felt like I was floating above the ground. I carefully placed the letter in a secret place and came back quickly to Aunt Pakize, where I told her what Uncle Şevket had said.

'Come, girls! That's enough for today! Thanks for all your help, Hayganush and Zaruhi!' she said. 'We'll bring the baskets. You go on back home. Look out. Your father's coming… He's going to be angry at all of us!'

We returned to the house. We drew some water from the well and washed ourselves and cooled off with the ice cold water. Then we went in and lay down. My sister fell asleep immediately. I was somewhat tired, too, but I couldn't sleep. I slowly got up and went into the other room. I took out the letter that I had hidden in my bosom and read it one more time. It gave me strength and confidence. My hands, my feet—my whole body felt rejuvenated.

I hid the letter inside the house and then went and lay down next to my sister. I fell asleep and slept until the evening.

My mind kept racing. How could I get a reply to Mustafa's father? How could I get back to Amasya as soon as possible? Then the thought came to me: Why couldn't I tell the person who brought me the letter about its contents?

The next day in the afternoon I took the letter out without letting my sister know. I had discovered a way: I went to Aunt Pakize. She was washing her laundry, hanging up the wet pieces and taking down that which was already dry. I went to her quietly. I snuck up behind her and put my hands over her eyes.

'You little mischief maker! What's your problem now?'

She was all alone. I went and sat down beside her. 'Aunt Pakize, I want to tell you something, but you can't ever tell anyone from my family!'

'You sweet girl, would I say a thing? Come, say what you want!'

'Thank you so much! The letter you gave me yesterday has given me hope. Mustafa's father wrote it.'

'Well, now, let's read it and see! What does he say? What does he want from you?'

So I took the letter out and read it.

'My daughter, how are you? Are you well? I'm behind you. Don't worry. Don't cry.' After that, I started to make up things. 'My daughter, I'll be with you with twelve armed men. Not even a bird or snake will be able to get through. There's no reason to cry! Whatever happens, don't give up or think that the thing's over. In a very short while I'm going to come and get you!'

That was the only lie I ever told in my life.

Neither Aunt Pakize, nor her daughter Gülizar, nor Uncle Şevket could read or write. I would always read things for them when they asked me to….

Aunt Pakize believed what she'd heard, and now she grew very afraid. She was terrified, in fact.

'Oh no!' she exclaimed, 'They're going to kill one of my people! This is a disaster! I swear, girl, you're leaving here at once… It's safer in Amasya… There's a narrow inlet to the valley here. They could kill someone here, day or night, and nobody would ever know. But the city is the city. There's the police, guards, soldiers… '

In making up part of the letter, it had actually been my goal to scare her. And it had worked! But Aunt Pakize couldn't just come out and say: 'We're scared. We don't want to be involved in any calamity. Go away!' So instead, because she knew my father's temperament, she decided instead to find some means of humiliating him, so that he would be forced to go.

The next morning my father was busy making a screen safe. In those days, there weren't any ice boxes, so people would put their food in one of these cabinets, which had screen on all four sides. My father had put one together that morning. All that was left to do was to run the wires through it. Because she knew this, Aunt Pakize went and told him in a very snide voice:

'Nishan, you still haven't finished the screen safe you've been working on all morning? It's already ten and you still haven't run the wire through!'

My father turned beet red. I know my father. He does really fine work. He had been a famous saddle maker for years… There was no one better in Amasya. He was that famous and that talented saddle maker. You could tell the harnesses that he had made by the workmanship, the embroidery and the color. He even put little bells on his saddles that were attached to the horse collar. The harnesses that my father sewed were easily identifiable by the color of the embroidery and the sound of the bells. The packhorses that wore the harnesses that were my father's handiwork looked better, and their owners were happy.

My father's workshop was in the Pirinççiler Çarşi (Brassmakers' Market). I never left his side when I was young. When I began to grow older, I would try to help him. That made my father happy, and he would stroke my head, saying:

'My daughter, one day you'll sew things for people; for young girls and women, not for horses and pack animals. My daughter will grow up to be a seamstress!'

I remember things very well from those days. Nobody would have scoffed at the work my father did. My childhood was largely spent in his workshop, and I never heard anyone else say to my father, 'What sort of work is this, Master Nishan? You're not working very well. It's ten o'clock and you still haven't finished!'

After I ran away, he couldn't even look strangers in the face, and he would get angry at everything because of his sorrow. Aunt Pakize's words had greatly distressed my father. The color of his face changed from one shade to another…. I understood my father's temperament; I could understand what was passing through his mind and his heart from the expressions on his face…

He was angry at me. Even when I was in the room he would act as if I wasn't there. That evening he told my mother:

'We've been here too long. Madam Pakize came in today and said such-and-such. What she's trying to tell me is 'Go!' We can't remain here any longer. Pack up everything. We should already go tomorrow morning.' Then he gave me a look that said, 'These things are happening to us because of you!'

I hung my head and left the room without uttering a sound. I went out to one corner of our huge terrace and gazed at the stars for a while. Maybe Mustafa was also looking at the stars right now, I thought to myself... Something stirred inside me then. I listened to the voice of my heart. Then I began to cry.

The next morning my mother went to Aunt Pakize and said:

'We're going to leave already, Aunt Pakize. Thank you and be well! Please forgive us, we've inconvenienced you!'

'Inconvenienced me? Nonsense!' replied Aunt Pakize. 'What's your hurry?'

We'd packed our things already. My father had already set off for Amasya.

'I'll wait for you on the road,' he'd said. 'If some transportation comes I'll try to stop it and send word to you.'

We did what my father said. We waited... Noon came and went, then the afternoon... Still, no word...

Toward evening, my father began to despair... 'The entire day went by without a single car coming by' he complained when he finally came back.

'What's your rush?' Aunt Pakize said. 'The station agent is our relative, and tomorrow he's got an appointment in Amasya. We'll all go to Amasya with him!'

And so we were forced to stay with Aunt Pakize for one more night. The next morning we all went to our house in Amasya across from the veterinary building.

Her relative's appointment was in the afternoon. Everybody got ready to go out.

Aunt Pakize said to my mother, 'Why don't you come too? Let's bring your daughters as well. A person needs to get out every once in a while.'

'Impossible!' my mother answered. 'I brought them here so that nothing bad would happen to us. But now it's just not possible...'

My mother was afraid that they would kidnap me again at the appointment or somewhere on the way there. In the end, they went and we stayed at the house.

Our house was separated from that of Mustafa's family by just one house. In those days, the house gates leading onto the street were very big. They would lock them.

I heard a voice from Mustafa's house. I listened intently, and there it was again: the voice of Mustafa's father. That meant they were home. Since it was harvest time, they should have been in the village. The fact that they were in the house was a sign of something in the works.... My brain was racing... What did they have planned? I couldn't sit still from all the excitement and curiosity.

I went out to the courtyard with the pretext of going to do some washing. It was also possible to do the wash on the roof. But I would wash in the private courtyard. I looked around... I wanted them to see me. I watched the house of Mustafa's family.

I would stand up from the washing now and then, hoping that they would see me. My mother-in-law looked over at me. She was trying to tell me something... I couldn't understand. I was mad with anticipation!

I continued to wash the clothes, but there was no water left for rinsing. We didn't have running water or a fountain in our house. Not every house in Amasya had one in those days; and even those that did have one, the water didn't always flow. But there were two fountains in every district of Amasya that constantly flowed.

Ever since I'd run away my mother no longer let me go out into the street to take water from the fountain.

My mother and I were at loggerheads in those days. We didn't say a word to each other if it wasn't necessary.

'There's no more water!' I told her.

'Don't go. I'll go and get some!' she replied.

When my mother went to get water, she'd usually lock the outer gate to the street, keeping us inside. She took the key with her. Both she and my father were still terrified that they would come and kidnap their daughter again. So they took preventive measures... The previous evening I had eavesdropped on my parents when they had spoken. They were going to send me to Istanbul with one of their acquaintances the day after tomorrow.... My whole world was collapsing.

After my mother left I found a pencil and paper and quickly wrote:

My father is going to send me to Istanbul tomorrow morning. Do whatever you have to! Find some way! If you can't find a way [to come and get me] I will escape to your place tonight!

My father-in-law was watching our house. When he saw that my mother had gone to the fountain for water, he went out on the balcony of their house. We made eye contact... I showed him the paper upon which I had written.... I made a sign with my hand like I was writing.

My mother-in-law thought I was asking for a blank piece of paper. She quickly sent one of her daughters to the side courtyard with some paper. I grabbed the young girl and told her:

'Look, girl, I don't want paper. Quick! Take this letter and give it to your father. Tell him to read it quickly and give me a reply!'

Thank God, there was a long line at the fountain. By the time my mother returned, my father-in-law had managed to get a reply back to me through his daughter:

My daughter,
We heard that you would be coming home. We left the harvest and came here in order that we wouldn't be leaving you all alone. Do what you will. Find some opportunity. Leave and come here! Don't hesitate or look back!

I waited until the night, making plans in my head.

Finally, the time came. I don't know whether it was the air in Boğazbağ or the water from the fountain, but my sister took ill. We had to stay up with her nights because of her malarial fevers. I couldn't take a step without waking her up. My sister was absolutely against my going to marry a man who was already with wife and child—especially if he was a Muslim and a Turk. During those times it was very unusual for an Armenian girl to marry a Turk. Only two other girls had done so; one had run off with an army officer, the other with a health official.

Toward midnight my sister's fever watch began. I went to the bathroom in order to have a quick look around. I looked and saw that my father-in-law was dozing on the terrace of the house. He was waiting for me...

Meanwhile, my sister's fever was returning; she was bathed in sweat; then she fainted and fell asleep.

I quickly got up. I bundled up my clothing and things. In fact, I had already packed up everything during the day.... Then I quietly and softly went downstairs. My parents locked the front gate every night. Maybe they had forgotten that night... it was unlocked when I got there. I opened it without making a sound and snuck out into the street. My father-in-law had left the front gate and the one to the terrace unlocked. He had prepared the way for me... I pushed open the gate with the tips of my fingers and went inside.

Mustafa's father was leaning against one of the posts of the terrace. He had fallen asleep.

'Father! Father!' I said, but he didn't hear me.

'Father! Father!' I said a little louder. 'I'm here! I've come!'

He woke with a start and looked at me dazedly:

'Are you here, my daughter?'

'I've come, father!'

Immediately, he got up and prepared everything...

'Come, girl. Let's go right away! I sent the women and children away this evening. I've been waiting for you here!'

Silently we descended the stairs. We opened the huge front gate without a sound and went out into the street. He didn't even close it behind us so that it wouldn't make any noise. We didn't say a word until we reached the end of the street. After we'd turn the corner, he told me where we were going:

'My daughter, don't be angry or offended. I'm sending you to the family of our relative Deniz in Bostanlık, They've got some grown daughters of their own. They'll protect you and won't leave you alone. While you're staying there I will either send my wife or Mustafa's first wife Güllü. They'll tell you what to do next.'

We drove all night and arrived at the house of Deniz's family toward morning. We pressed on the door of their house. We knocked and knocked, but no one opened the door. But somehow, all our knocking and shouting succeeded in finally waking them up. They opened the door...

Mustafa's father explained the situation to them and they quickly ushered us inside.

'Come in! Come in!' they said. 'Congratulations, my girl! Don't be afraid. We won't let them take you back, no matter who comes!'

Deniz's wife came and took my arm and encouraged me.

'Come, sit down, my dear. That's how things are sometimes. You did well! Congratulations! Don't be afraid!'

After that he woke up her daughters.

'Daughter, go quickly and make up the attic room where we raise silk worms. Lay out a bed for our girl. She's tired. She should lie down and rest.'

In that time, they used to raise silk worms in Amasya. They would keep them in the attic. The two daughters, tall and slender like cypress trees and one more beautiful that the next, went and did what their father had commanded. Then they called me upstairs. Both of the girls were older than me. They encouraged me:

'You did well.... You're listening to your heart! May God bring this to a successful conclusion! Don't be afraid. We're here with you. Let's wait until morning and see how things are. Now, go and lie down and rest... Afterward we'll speak plenty...'

What wonderful girls they were! May God grant them their heart's desire. And may God spare them the calamities that he has visited upon me...

I lay down. My eyes were sore and burning from a lack of sleep, but still I couldn't fall asleep. I kept going over everything that had happened, and everything that might yet happen.... Despite what they'd said, I felt totally alone at that moment... If Mustafa had been at my side, if he had been the one who had smuggled me out of Amasya, I wouldn't have been afraid at all!

The Sivas train

While I lay there, dreaming of Mustafa, the train from Sivas passed by on the tracks near the house. It was a very long train...

'Oh Lord!' I said within myself, 'If only Mustafa were on that train... If only Mustafa would come and save me! If Mustafa came, I would be safe from the gendarmes, from the courts. It's not hard to flee; what's hard for a person is to be caught.

'Oh Lord!' I continued to think. 'If only that train would stop and Mustafa would get out of it, if only my mother's family doesn't come to take me back... If only I could get away from all of them...'

I prayed and pleaded to God. All the while, the sound of the train was in my ears. Was it slowing down? Was that its whistle that I heard? Was it going to stop? Had it stopped already? But in fact it hadn't stopped. It continued moving until it was long gone....

'Oh Lord, you are Great!' I prayed. But the quiet of the early morning returned once more....

My heart jumped... I got up and sat in my bed... It was not yet dawn... I lay back down again.... 'If only Mustafa were here by my side... If he were here, and I was rescued!' Wishing and hoping, I fell back asleep.

Suddenly, there was a knock—someone was knocking on the front door! Was I dreaming? My eyes were open... Someone was knocking, and more and more impatiently... Was it the gendarmes? The watchmen? Had they found me already? Not another time before the judge! They had me surrounded. All of Amasya had come after me! The knocking persisted; 'Open up!' someone said. That voice! Could it be?

It sounded like his voice… but that was impossible! Or was it?... Oh Lord, what should I do?

'Open up, come on, sis! It's me, Mustafa!'

Mustafa? My Mustafa! Oh Lord, you truly are Great!

I jumped up and ran to the door. My heart was pounding so hard I thought I would die! But I wasn't thinking. It didn't occur to me to run downstairs and open the door for him.

Now someone was banging on the door of my room. But my hands and feet wouldn't move… it didn't occur to me to go and open it…. I had locked the door from the inside…

'Girl! Open the door! It's me, Mustafa!'

'Open the door, Zaruhi! I'm here! Mustafa's here!'

I turned the key in the lock… and the door opened… There was Mustafa, standing before me! Oh Lord! How Mustafa embraced me! How he hugged me tightly!

I was so happy! So happy!... I cried so… How I cried!

'Zaruhi, what's wrong with you? Why are you crying? Stop, don't cry!'

'Let me cry… You've come, and I'm crying out of joy!'

I've come to this age. I was married for forty-six years… I loved him very much, and he loved me very much… I'll never forget that morning, though! Every time I think about it, even now, I get goose bumps once again!

'I could die right now and be happy!' I said to myself. That had made my running away worthwhile…

When I finally came to myself, I asked him:

'How did you get here? How did you manage it? Did you run away from the army?'

'No, no, Zaruhi!' he said. 'I learned everything from Recep, the son of Topal Mehmet, from our village, when he went on leave. He told me about the first time you ran away, and how you were caught fifteen days later and how they returned you to your father; he told me everything. I felt like the entire Mutki gendarmerie station had collapsed on my head! 'Oh no!' I said, 'If they give Zaruhi back to her father I'll never find her again! Her father will sneak her off somewhere far away!' I was on duty that day and I stood there and thought with my weapon in my hand. The sergeant came over to me and said:

'Mustafa! I've got good news!'

'Ask what you will, Sir, and I'll do it!' I said.

'Your leave permit has arrived! Congratulations! Go on, take it!'

I was so full of confidence… so happy! I immediately snatched the paper from his hand and came running. I went straight home, without even changing into civilian clothing. I arrived in Amasya and went straight to the house, but there wasn't anyone there. All I heard was shouting and crying from your house… I didn't understand what had happened. At about the time of the morning call to prayer, I went to the house of my relative Mustafa Işık and knocked on his door. He informed me that you had fled and were being hidden here!'

Mustafa was a tailor. He had sewn clothes for judges, police officers, commissioners and watchmen. He was very well-respected.

'You stay here today,' he said. 'I'll let my father know that I've arrived. After that I'll go to the police station and let them know.'

Things got easier now that Mustafa had arrived.

Toward evening, Mustafa's first wife Güllü and his mother came and took me to the village.

Mustafa had been given a full month's leave. After six weeks, they sent out a warrant for him. He went and turned himself in. He had a trial, and they gave me three months in jail and him six months. I was still under-age. 'I abducted her' he said, in order to lighten my sentence. Because of me, he had to sit in jail for five months.

I became pregnant with our daughter. I had just turned sixteen. We called her Türkan.

Mustafa was in the army for four whole years. Finally, he was released and came home. By then, I was nineteen years old. Both of us worked as tailors. We worked at home and in the shop.

There was a person named Haci Efendi, who was the big man of our village. He was very well loved and respected, both in the village and in Amasya. His word was like the law. It was at the time of the elections for a village headman.

'Come,' he said, 'Let's make Mustafa the village headman. If anyone can make our village progress and develop it's him.'

They came and asked Mustafa to run. Mustafa then asked me what I thought.

'If I become headman of the village,' he asked, 'will you come to the village to live?'

'Wherever you are, that's where I'll be,' I told him.

He won the election, and after that he served as village head for seventeen years. We married when I was fifteen years old. We were married for forty-six years. I got along well with his first wife Güllü. Mustafa passed away in 1992. God rest his soul. He was a good man. He was an Alevî, I'm a Christian. He was Turkish, I'm Armenian. He was raised as a Turk, while I grew up as an Armenian until age fifteen. In those days there wasn't a church or anything like that in Amasya. They destroyed them all during the 'deportation'* and afterward.

I already told you that my father was a saddle maker. All of his friends and acquaintances were Turks, Muslims. He didn't know anything about church or religion. All he knew was that we were Armenians and that our religion was different. What religion we did practice we would do at home. We didn't let a lot of people know about it. Even so, we were so afraid! In reality, there were still about fifty or sixty Armenian households in Amasya in those days. But there wasn't any church, school or anything like that for the Armenians. They were all older folks. Now, there's no more Armenians there at all.

Mustafa never broke my heart. And I never regretted having run away. He never interfered with my religion, nor with my name.

'You believe what you believe,' he'd say. I love you, and you love me. That's what's important.'

It was my mother-in-law who changed my name. Safiye was the name of her daughter-in-law who died. 'My daughter, from now on let your name be Safiye!' she said to me. Until age fifteen my name was Zaruhi. In Armenian, *zaruhi* means elegant, pretty, or pleasant.

My mother had had a little sister by the name of Zaruhi. She was very beautiful and had also been a seamstress, and my mother had loved her very much. She died or was killed in that disaster we call the 'Deportation,' along with her mother and father, and all of her other siblings. From that great big family, only my mother survived. When I was born, my mother decided to name me after my dead aunt.

The time of the deportation

My mother's name was Zeytimya; my father's name was Nishan.

My mother.... my mother.... she had brown eyes and brown hair.... She was very quiet. She used to cook the most wonderful dishes. In my mother's family there were six sisters, including her. She didn't have any

---

* Throughout the book, the Armenians interviewed tend to use the word *Sevkiyet* (dispatching, sending) for the expulsions and ensuing massacre of the Armenian population of Anatolia as a result of the Deportation Order (*Tehcir Kanunu*) issued by the Unionist Ottoman government during World War One. For clarity's sake, I have translated it as "deportation" or "The Deportation/s," depending on the context.

brothers... Those things that happened during the Deportation....

At that point Safiye Güner dried her tears with the ends of the white, embroidered scarf on her head. I saw that the eyes of her daughters and granddaughters, who had until then sat silently and respectfully listening to her, were also filled with tears. Safiye Güner sat there for a period, not saying a word.... Her gaze and mind had drifted off, down along the Yeşilırmak river valley, among the pine trees on the river bank before her house. She was silent. Where was she? What places was she revisiting? She seemed like one searching for people far, far away. Safiye Güner, who had recounted the story of her flight, of her marriage and her husband, had now disappeared, gone somewhere else. In her place, sitting before us now was Zaruhi, the little Armenian girl who loved her mother very much. Maybe she was looking for the long dead aunt who was her namesake....

None of us broke the silence. No one even stirred or made a peep....

Time flowed by, like a gust of wind blowing down the hills and through the valley, like the waters flowing through the river.

After a time, Safiye herself broke her silence. She motioned to her daughters and granddaughters:

"These ones here: what do they know about the military mobilization? About the deportations? What do they know about what it is to be an Armenian? Until today, I've never told anyone about those bitter days, about that calamity... about how my mother was left all alone with no one in the world. They don't know a thing about any of this!"

"She never told us anything!" one of them said, confirming Safiye's claim.

"We heard the story of her running away very often" another added.

"She loved my father very much!"

"My mother Safiye managed to adapt herself wherever she went. She's very understanding and wise. I love Grandmother Safiye more than my own mother!"

"She brought a newness to our village. She sewed the trousseaus for all the brides here."

"That's the first time I ever heard the name Zaruhi!"

"She never told us about her relatives, or about my aunts!"

"Come on, tell us about my great grandfather and grandmother!"

"Why did your mother end up all alone?"

"Grandmother, what's that 'Deportation' that you mentioned?"

When Safiye began to speak once again, her voice changed. Now, every word that came out of her mouth was bathed in heartache, in grief, in tears.

Before the deportations came in 1915, my mother's father had been a craftsman. He had built a factory. An engineer by the name of Kopdok arrived from Germany. We worked together with this German engineer. Together, he and my father built the factory. The German engineer only had one son. As for my mother's family, they had six daughters. One day, Kopdok said to my father:

'Look, my friend. I only have one son, and you have six daughters. Come, give one of your daughters to my son. Let me take responsibility for her. Let it be your choice, let it be your decision. But let us make it clear.'

So my grandfather gave my mother to the German engineer for his son. The German was very rich. The house in which my mother lived was very close to the Kopdoks' house. My mother was already spending most of her time in the Germans' house.

Before the Deportation, there were many Armenians in Amasya.

Then came the Deportation. They came and rounded up all the Armenians and took them away.... My mother's father, her mother and all her sisters were sent away on the Deportation.

Because my mother was registered under the German's name, they neither looked for her nor asked about her. Those who were sent away never came back. You couldn't ask what had happened to them and they never found out a thing. She never heard another thing about her father or mother.

My mother didn't tell me very much when I was young, before I married Mustafa. Maybe she didn't want to reopen her wounds. Even I never told every thing I knew and had heard to my children. A person doesn't want their children to grow up with hatred, doesn't want to discourage their children or burden them down with all this; a person doesn't want their children to be weighted down with these problems.

I can still remember some of the things that my mother told me.... Her youngest sister was an excellent seamstress. She used to sew all the bridal gowns and trousseaus. She named me after her sister.

I became a seamstress, like my namesake. My mother sent me off to learn dressmaking. When I first came to the village, all the women and girls wore the _üçetek_ dress.[*] I taught them to dress according to the latest

---

[*] Literally "three skirts," it is a type of peasant dress worn over a _shalvar_ (baggy trousers).

fashion. This is an Alevî village. The Alevîs are people who are generally receptive to novelty and change. My husband would cut out pattern from the fabric and I would sew the pieces. I used to sew bridal trousseaus, just like my namesake aunt. I'd make them out of velvet and bright, shiny fabrics. I didn't even take money from most of them. In any case, I had raised half of them. I loved them like my own daughters.

My mother always hoped for news of her family. She would ask anybody and everybody she met. She never knew where all the members of her family went to. 'I never found out, all those long years, whether they were still alive or if they had died' she used to tell me. 'If I knew that they were alive, I would even have gone to the other end of the world in order to find them"

Sometimes I would ask her:

'Mother, where are my grandfather and grandmother? Where are all my aunts and uncles? Where are all your family?'

Children are curious. They want to know everything. They ask questions. My mother would tell me a little bit.

'They took them all away during the Deportation and lost them,' she would tell me.

Sometimes, a person just wishes that they at least had tombstones for their relatives, for their grandparents and great grandparents. But it's not only my grandparents and great grandparents, there are thousands of people who don't even have a grave where they were buried...

In this great big world, neither my mother nor my father had any family members who survived. There was only one rich Armenian from among my father's relatives who survived. He and his family later moved to Istanbul, and then to Paris. There wasn't anyone else to even look for or ask about their relatives.

But hey now, it wasn't just us! There were probably many, many people who were caught up in the storm and blown to the other side of the world and were out there looking for, asking about and curious about their relatives who survived, about the places where they were born and raised.

My son İlhan had a truck. He used to transport many different goods to Iran. Once he met a man in Iran who said to him 'Please take me to Amasya! I've got to see it. I'm certain that I have relatives there. I should see them.'

He was an Armenian. When had the storm blown him to Iran, during the Deportation? Or afterward? He had become very rich in Iran; he had much money and property, but he still wanted to know about his relatives in Amasya. My son gave him our address. But he never came.

My mother survived because of the German engineer Kopdok.

It was on a Saturday… My mother used to go to the *hamam** on Saturdays. She was going to go on that day, too. She told the son of the German in whose house she lived, 'I'm going to the *hamam*.'

Meanwhile, the German's son had seen that the Deportation was underway. He saw the Armenians being rounded up and sent away. But because my mother had been outside the city, in their house in the vineyard, she didn't know that they were rounding up the Armenians.

The German's brother, because he didn't want my mother to be upset, told her 'Don't go to the hamam this week. Go next week instead!' And that's how my mother was saved from death.

My grandfather was very rich. But nothing at all remains of either his property or of the German's.

My mother's wedding was as much of an adventure as mine was.

It was the year right before the Deportation that my father asked for my mother's hand in marriage. But my father's father drove a spring-loaded carriage. Her parents wouldn't give her to him. 'He's just a carriage driver' they said. Instead they gave her to an Armenian cobbler. My father was very offended by this. 'God willing, she'll be mine in the end!' he said.

By some coincidence, this cobbler and my father served together in the army at that time. My father did seven whole years of military service. He had a commanding officer who was of the rank of captain. He really loved my father and protected him because my father was able to do anything. Because of this, the captain protected my father, and didn't send him off to his death.

They murdered my mother's first husband while he was doing his military service. My mother was left a widow with a child.

A short while later, her mother- and father-in-law were sent off and deported.

When my father returned from his military service he asked for my mother's hand in marriage again. She accepted his proposal and they married.

But because of their fear and their sorrow, they didn't have any children. During those years, they used to gather all the orphaned Armenian children they found in the towns, on the roads and in the countryside and bring them before the municipality in Amasya. Anyone who wanted could take the children they liked and adopt them.

My father told my mother:

---

* The Turkish bath, the bathhouse

'Woman, we don't have any children of our own. And it doesn't look like we're going to have any at this rate. Let's go down to the municipality and find a boy we like from among the Armenian orphans and take him as a son. We'll get to experience the love of a child and also save an Armenian child. We'll be doing a good deed in God's sight.'

My mother agreed with what my father had said, so they went down to the municipality together. They entered the building and there was a whole row of children! While they were looking for a child, a young girl came running up to them shouting 'Mother! Mother!' and threw herself around my mother. Apparently, she had thought that it was her mother...

So my mother looked my father in the eye. Taking a girl child wasn't exactly what they'd planned back at home.

'Let it be so!' my father said. 'This girl thinks you're her mother. She came running up to you and hugged you. Let's take her.'

So they took this orphaned girl and signed all the paperwork to officially adopt her. She had been found and brought to the municipality the previous Wednesday. She was Armenian. They gave her the name Fikriye.

A few years after they adopted this Armenian girl, God gave my mother a boy child. After that, my second older brother was born, then my older sister, then me...

When my older sister Fikriye grew up they gave her to a master builder who built the Amasya Hospital. But Fikriye didn't have any children. Her husband fell ill and died. All his possessions went to my sister Fikriye.... But her sister-in-law didn't want to give them to her....

She hired a lawyer to see to their inheritance claims. The lawyer was a widower. My sister Fikriye really liked him. They got married and Fikriye gave birth to a son and a daughter. The boy died, but the girl is still alive. She lives in Germany right now.

Do you know what a place looks like after a fire?

These are hard things to talk about! If you think about all the things that happened to us, you can't believe how we managed to make it till now.... Do you know what a place looks like after a fire? A house will burn down and be reduced to ashes and charcoal, all the flowers become scorched and die.... Even the people and other living things that you've protected become scattered to the winds. The families and children who escape the fire become dispersed, scattered all over. The smell of fire, the fear.... it's years before they go away....

Have you ever seen a forest fire? How the green pine trees and shrubs burn? How the earth itself splits open? How the pine cones go crazy and explode? You can hear them in the darkness, these pine cones that set themselves on fire in trying to escape from the blaze... In trying to escape they just end up spreading the fire.... Afterward, there are only a few trees, a few shrubs and pine trees still standing where the fire was, blackened and burnt.... It takes a long, long time for mountains that have burnt to become green again. Even when things do start to grow on them again, it's not like it was before.... The springs dry up, the waters stop running... It takes a lot of work to make burnt places grow and flourish again.... It takes patience, it takes love....

You can't underestimate a rock.... you can't just assume a tree will grow... The rock grows angry at the one who splits it.... the tree resents the one who burnt it... Have you ever seen a tree, or a house or even ground that's weeping? Like a huge tree that's been struck by lightning? It's still alive, but its leaves and branches don't look happy to live; even years later, the flowers and blossoms that grow on it look pale and lifeless... the earth, trees, even people lose their productiveness, their ability to be fertile....

There are some people who become angry and hateful, others who become fearful. And there are those who become both hateful and fearful. Those are the ones you have to watch out for. Sometimes, there's one in the village who sets fire to the harvest of someone he hates, just to cause him harm. He only wants to burn the crops of his enemy, but then a wind or a storm appears and the fire jumps from one field to the next. Before you know it, the entire harvest, the entire village has been engulfed in flames.... The person who lights the fire ends up within it. That's how these things work! They say that a fire only burns the place it touches (i.e. a calamity only really affects its victim). That's true. In a place that burns, there are both good things and bad things. The snake burns along with the gazelle. But a human conflagration is like nothing else in the world. There are those who like to make other people suffer, who cause them great harm and grief, but in fact they are only harming their own humanity, destroying or poisoning the humanity of which both they and the other person are a part. The smoke from a fire makes everyone choke. The smoke from a fire affects everyone and everything around it: people, animals, things living and dead. It poisons them....

We are like the survivors of a great fire.... The new shoots and branches of our hearts have been scorched in the blaze. The flowers inside our new buds, the fruit on our branches have been hit by the frost.... I think about my mother... I think to myself about my older sister Fikriye.... For some reason I've started to think about them very often in these last months.... They were without children for many long years.... There are so many Armenian women who haven't been able to have children.... So many Armenian men whose line has dried up.... So many young Armenian brides who have been eaten up and finished off by their sorrows and pains.

The warmth of my parents' home that I experienced until age fifteen is still very alive inside me.

I ran off to Mustafa when I was fifteen. My mother and father were furious at me and very hurt. What mother wants her daughter to run off and elope? Afterward we made our peace. And my mother and father never scorned me or berated me, saying, 'Where did you think you were running off to? Is this appropriate for us?' After I changed my name they even called me Safiye.

But my older sister was furious at me. 'Girl, if you were going to run off with a Turk, why didn't you at least run off with the station chief who wanted you, instead of a man who already had a wife and child?'

But that's how the heart is! And I never regretted having run off...

When I was a child my father was very devoted to me, while my mother adored my older sister. She'd get angry at my father, saying: 'You give that girl so much attention! You shouldn't give so much attention to your daughter. One day you're going to suffer on account of this girl!'

As I said, my father was a very happy and jolly, fun-loving person. He was well-respected and well-liked by those around him. I also liked my father very much. He wouldn't sit at home with my mother; he'd always be fussing around at his leather workshop, and I'd be going about with him.

One time, I was doing just that, hanging around at my father's shop, and he was taking the measurements for horse harnesses. 'Father, father!' I said, coming quickly up to his side. The horse bit me on the arm and threw me down. I don't know what happened. I fainted. He snatched me up and brought me straightaway to the hospital. They revived me. They bandaged my arm. Over time it got better, but the bite mark still remained.

I wasn't much use when I was young. I couldn't sit still in one place for long. I loved to ride horses. When I was a child I fell from a horse and hurt my foot. I got over that, too.

Safiye or Amasya

In the end, I went to the *hoja* (Muslim teacher). He looked at my stars and said, 'Please, don't go to high places! We cannot know your fate, but your death will be from falling from a tree!'

After that, I was very careful. I didn't go climbing trees very much after that. Thank god, I'm still healthy. What he said hasn't come to pass, God willing!

At that point, one of her granddaughters said, as if revealing a secret, "My grandmother has another side she's not telling you about. So I'll tell it. My grandmother writes very beautiful folk songs."

Safiye Hanım laughed, childlike:

"Hey now, don't spill all the beans here!" And then she continued, as if she didn't mind telling this side of herself after all:

I used to sing very beautifully when I was young. I knew a lot of songs. Most of them were melancholy things, sad folk songs and the like. There was one called 'I was a Foot Soldier.' I used to sing it a lot. Then there was one 'The Water is Trickling, Trickling.' The one I sang the most, though, was 'Foreign Lands.' It's a very old, sad folk song. I learned it from my mother. She used to sing it. It went something like this:

Yad eller aldı beni	To foreign lands they took me
Taşlara çaldı beni	Onto the stones they cast me
Yardan ayırdı felek	Separated from my beloved, was my fate
Gurbete saldı beni	Into exile they sent me
Yol verin geçeyim dumanlı dağlar	Show me the way that I may pass, O shrouded mountains
Dağların ardında nazlı yar ağlar	Beyond the mountains, my delicate beloved sits and weeps
Düştüm bulunmaz derde	She is not here, and I am in torment
Nerde sevdiğim nerde	Where is the one I loved, Where is he?
Yol uzun gurbet acı	The way is long, the exile bitter
Dağlar var ara yerde	There are mountains, separating us
Yol verin geçeyim dumanlı dağlar	Show me the way that I may pass, O shrouded mountains
Dağların ardında nazlı yar ağlar	Beyond the mountains, my gentle beloved sits and weeps

There's lot's more to it... but now that I'm old I can't remember it all so well.

I turn around and look at myself and what I was.... So many years, what years! Is that what they call fate? I don't know. I never experienced anything bad from my husband. I remember him very fondly and respectfully. I've never had even a pinch of misfortune in the village, not even with my children.

I've been very happy in life.

By then the hour was well past noon. I thanked Safiye Hanım, her children and her grandchildren. I wanted to ask their leave to depart.

"I'm not going to send you away hungry!" she exclaimed. "You came all this way up to now. You asked me—Zaruhi... First have a couple bites, then you can go!"

What generous and good-hearted people there are in this world.

I did what she asked, and when I departed, it was as if we had been lifelong friends.

I put my pack on my back and began walking and thinking. I had heard these things that Safiye Güler had said for the first time. They had thrown me into confusion. How had these things happened? Why? For what purpose? My head was full of questions but few answers. I was going to take the road to Amasya, and from there go to Taşova by *dolmuş* (minibus service). It was getting close to evening. The mouth of the Yassıçal river valley, which opened onto the Yeşilırmak valley, gradually broadened and turned into a plain. There were cherries, peach orchards, grapevines, vegetables... a bounty wherever one looked. It looked as if there wasn't an inch of ground here that hadn't been cultivated. The air was still hot, and I was sweating a lot. I could feel beads of perspiration trickling down my back. But in my ear I could still hear the voice of Safiye Hanım and the things she had said. Who knew what else I would see and hear? My curiosity was growing like the Yeşilırmak itself. It took me to the Black Sea, to the Mediterranean, even as far as the ocean....

In Taşova

The sun was just setting as I arrived in Taşova. I got out of the *dolmuş* and headed for the shop of Engin, whom I had got to know three years earlier.

I had called him from Amasya to tell him I was coming and he was expecting me.

"My friend, I told Sedat the teacher that you were coming. He's an immigrant, like us. His parents, his family, his whole clan came from Kaylar near Thessaloniki. He's a good person. I gave him the copy of *The Assurance Dowry* that you sent me. He really liked it. He ordered sixty more copies from Istanbul. He went from street to street, coffee house to coffee house selling them. He's the head of the teachers' union. He's waiting for you down at the union office."

I got to know the teacher Sedat. From the first time I met him, I got the impression that this was a sincere, honest person. Engin had to return to work, saying: "I closed up my shop and came. I'm all alone [at the shop]. You two go stroll around and talk. Come see me in the evening."

Sedat and I hit it off like old friends. He spoke of his work for the union, of Taşova, of the condition of the teachers.

"Engin said that you brought a bunch of copies of my book and sold them. Thank you!" I told him.

"There's not a single person in Taşova who hasn't read *The Assurance Dowry*," he said. "I even found myself in the book. I learned things that I've never heard from anyone. May God give you strength. Come, let me show you around a bit!"

He locked the union branch office and we walked the streets, talking, talking.... We came to a coffee house that was full of people playing games and speaking loudly. As we sat down, the sound of the drink glasses and backgammon pieces being slammed down drowned out the voices of the people.

Sedat took my arm and addressing the others at the coffee house said:

"Friends, I'd like your attention for just one minute. I've brought you the author of *The Assurance Dowry*!"

Immediately, the drinkers, the backgammon players, the card players, all stopped what they were doing. Those who were talking fell silent. A middle-aged man who had been sitting in the back corner of the coffee house spoke first: "Welcome!" Then, as if they had been waiting for his cue, the others began to welcome me in turn. One man sitting two tables away who was older than me arose and approached me.

"You wrote about my father! God bless you!" he said, and took my hand with the intent of kissing it.

"No, not like that!" I said, and shook his hand instead.

A teenager who had been playing backgammon closed up the board and came over.

"The things you wrote were just like what happened in the village of my grandparents and great-grandparents! May your hand never fail!" he said and we embraced.

One of the dice players said, "You wrote about the things that all the immigrants suffered. May your hands remain strong and healthy!"

I shook hands with the coffee house patrons one by one. That was one of the most beautiful moments of my life. The inhabitants of Taşova gave me strength. I was very happy.

My original intention had been to spend one night, and then to continue on my way, but the people there would not let me go.

I asked Sedat whether or not there were any elderly Armenians left in Taşova. I told him about my conversations with Safiye Güler. He was intrigued.

"There were a few Greek women and their children who remained in Taşova and the surrounding villages. Some of their children are still alive. But whether there are Armenians or not I don't know. Tomorrow we'll go and ask the old folks and have them spread the word of what you're looking for. But this is a subject that is fraught with disaster and misfortune. There are those who get immediately bent out of shape at the mention of the word 'Armenian.' There are a lot of Greeks in the villages around Taşova. There were Armenians in Amasya, Erbaa and Tokat. But now there's no more trace of either Armenians or Greeks. The fortune hunters have even dug up the foundations of the churches themselves. They didn't leave hide nor hair."

Sedat's wife Hürriyet was from Adıyaman. I stayed in their house. In the evening she spoke to me for quite some time of what she'd heard about the Armenians in the Adıyaman, Antep and Maraş regions. While recounting some of the stories she did so as if she was going to cry. The things that I heard here where at least as great as those things that Safiye Güner had told me.

So the next day Sedat and I sought traces of any Greek or Armenian until the evening. "There's some in the village of Hacibey," they said. We hopped in Engin's car which he had for his store and passed through Ferizdağ and Kızöldüren villages. It wasn't an Armenian, but rather the traces of a Greek woman that we found. An old person who had known her told her story at great length. She had gone crazy because of the great bitterness and debasements she had suffered, and had died while chained up in the stable.

There were also a number of persons with monikers like "Zeynep the infidel," "Memet the infidel" and "Mustafa the convert (*dönme*)." But despite our effort, we failed to find a single trace of these people.

We sat in the park on the bank of the Yeşilırmak in order to rest a bit. The river flowed quickly in that area. While we were drinking our tea, I told Sedat and his friends that I was going to Erzurum, Aşkale, Kars, Ani and Van in order to look for traces of Armenians. Everyone expressed their concerns.

"Please, be careful! The thing with the Armenians is not like the one with the Greeks."

"Where you're going is a war zone. The law doesn't apply out there!"

"You'd do better not to go! But if you do go, at least go after things have calmed down!"

"Please be careful, even about where you walk. Watch out where you step!"

"Don't just talk to anybody about the Armenian matters. Please, be careful!"

I thanked them all for thinking about me, and then they accompanied me to the bus station where I purchased a ticket to Erzurum.

On the evening of July 13 Sedat, Zülfikâr and four elderly immigrants came and saw me off with wishes of good luck. There were still another forty minutes before my bus was to depart: we were early. The old immigrants told me of their recollections, their fathers, their grandfathers, the elders of their community.

"Ah, our Salonica! Ah, our Kaylar!" they would say, passing away.

"My father went back to the earth saying, 'take me back to Greece, let me see my village!'"

One of those who was quietly listening to their stories and who noticed that they were dressed differently suddenly broke into the conversation:

"Sir, when you came three years ago, did you know what would happen to you?"

No one expected such a question, and all looked at him with surprise.

"I don't know!"

"Of course you don't! You didn't even notice!"

"Sedat had earlier asked me with surprise, 'What are you?'"

"That you were followed!"

"By whom? And do you know from where?"

"I'm a security guard at the bank. When you came to Taşova three years back didn't you ask the bus station attendant who was yelling Taşova! Taşova! 'How do I get to Ferizdağ?'"

"Yes, I did ask!"

"From that moment on the civil police put a tail on you! They followed your every step in Taşova!"

I didn't give in to disappointment. I tried to understand his purpose. From inside me an evil voice said, "Give it up. Don't go to Aşkale or to Ani. I'm telling you not to go. This man is trying to tell you something. You've been followed for two days. The tinsmith informed on you!"

"They're not suspicious of you because you're seeking the immigrants and deportees" he continued, "nor because you inquired about mountain villages like Ferizdağ. They're following you because you said 'I went to Greece and spoke to the Greeks that came from these parts.'"

"Then they suspect me in vain!"

It felt as if our entire pleasant conversation had now been irreparably infected with suspicion and fear. In its place, an ill wind of silence blew.

Sedat's suspicion was mixed with excitement. His face tensed up.

"There's another fifteen minutes until the bus arrives. If you need to, you should go to the bathroom now. It's in the back of the station."

I understood what he was trying to tell me.

"It's a good idea for me to go now" I replied, standing up. Sedat came up behind me and took my arm. He was concerned…

"Master Kemal, I'm suspicious of this whole matter. Come, abandon your plans for going to Aşkale and Ani!"

His words gradually increased the volume of the devilish voice inside me. My mind was racing with all of these thoughts. I can't give it up, Sedat. It's impossible. It's already too late. The bus is just about here!"

"Fine. Get on the bus. But get off at Erbaa!"

"That's impossible!"

"No, it's not!"

An accounting on the way to Erbaa

The bus from Istanbul to Erzurum came to a stop in front of the bus company office. The ticket seller had made the announcement "Last call for Erzurum!"

Saying goodbye to each of those who had accompanied me to the station, I got on the bus. Thinking that they wouldn't stop those traveling to Erzurum, I found my way back to seat number thirty-six and sat down. The driver drove the bus slowly over the Yeşilırmak Bridge and got onto the main road. Turning off the cabin lights, he continually accelerated until he was up to speed, and we were on our way.

The inside of the bus was enshrouded in darkness. The passengers were all asleep or trying to fall asleep. The road was rough and pocked with potholes that hadn't been repaired. The wheels ran through them at high speed, making the bus heave and rock like a horse cart.

I had a window seat, and I rested my head against the glass, staring out into the darkness. Outside was a pitch blackness, interrupted only occasionally by individual lights off in the distance.

I closed my eyes. There was still a struggle going on inside my head. It wasn't the bus throwing me around—it was the battle in my head that was buffeting the bus!

"Don't go! Turn back! You were followed the last time you came; two days and you weren't even aware from where they were following you?"

"Depart from my presence!"

"Can you give up on this love? You'll go to Erzurum and Kars, and someone will inform on you. They'll extinguish you without a trace. You won't even sense it!"

"Turn away from your path!"

"You won't even know what hit you! This Armenian question, it isn't like the Greek thing!"

"My son, isn't the Armenian a servant of God, too? Please give my greetings to the old Armenian woman in Tokat who made my headache go away! Go, my son, be on your way!"

"If you're not going to think about yourself, then think about your son. Think about the boy!"

"One of those orphaned children who had been standing in front of the government mansion in Amasya might have been my own son!"

The bus windows rattled the whole way.... Rocking and lurching, the bus made its way into the belly of the night. My mind flashed like lightning, racing between time and timelessness, between myself and that which was not me.

They opened their mouths in order to eliminate me, in order to stop the course of the Yeşilırmak, in whose current I was caught up... For a time I felt my own loneliness. My foot got caught on a thought that was stuck inside my head; I felt myself on the verge of falling....

A warm hand grabbed my arm. I looked, it was the woman with the black lab coat! That black lab coat-clad woman whose loving, warm smile lit up my insides—It was as if I was taken back to that day, so many years ago!

That day!

On that day we were sitting in the large lecture hall in the Philosophy Department of Istanbul University's Faculty of Literature. Our course, Man's Place in the Cosmos, was being taught by Professor Takiyettin Mengüsoğlu. I was looking for a place in the cosmos for myself.... As the class was coming to an end, suddenly it felt like the stone walls of the building began to quake... We could hear a dull roar—was it coming from inside the building or from outside?

I quickly passed down the long, dark corridor. The roar was coming from outside, at the entrance to the building. I descended the stairs at a run. The roar turned into a thundering from the heavens, and it was coming from the side of Vezneciler Avenue. It echoed and resounded through Hergele Square, with its high roof and white marble tiles. From there I could finally understand what this mighty tumult was saying: "Government, resign! Youth, gather round!"

As soon as I exited the main gate onto Vezneciler Avenue I saw it: women with lab coats, men with blue work overalls... some were carrying branches with leaves still on them, others crowbars, or enormous wrenches... some had their hands clenched in fists... people marching arm in arm... people. A wave of people so vast that Vezneciler Avenue couldn't contain it.

There was no time to think! I embraced the wave; the wave embraced me! It was June 16, 1970... a day when the asphalt was soft from the heat... the human wave flowed toward Beyazit... without breaking... without dispersing...

From the front, the sound of thunder; a sound like the roaring of the heavens came in wave after wave. My voice was a part of this roar, like those of the men and women beside me...

And when there was a pause, the sound of a fearful grinding from behind us... a frightful sound of steel.

"What is that?" I asked no one in particular.

One of the workers, a black-mustached fellow with blue overalls who was holding a tire iron in one hand answered: "That's the grinding of tank treads and the sounds of their engines. We've already broken through three of their barricades!"

Just then, a new sound broke forth like thunder: peoples' voices coming like waves, drowning out the rumbling of the tank treads....

We passed Beyazit Square.

The sidewalks were full of people who had come out to watch.

We reached the gate of the vast *Kapalı Çarşı* (Covered Bazaar).... A young woman worker shouted, "Everyone over here!"

The onlookers stared with rapt attention at the human wave that flowed past them: leather-aproned cobblers' apprentices, hesitant, thoughtful... Some stepped forward to answer the call; others drew back.

"If you don't march now, you'll never march!" a worker with blue overalls shouted in encouragement. The noise of the tanks came in waves from behind us.

Thousands of feet, hearts, heads, minds, eyes—all directed toward the Sultan Ahmet District to the East... The human wave continued, pouring down Divan Way, past Yerebatan Sarayı toward Çağaoğlu. Wave after wave flowed ever onward. As if it was a wall of water. Somehow, the cries of the women drowned out the shouts of the men!

"Government, resign! Government, resign!"

We were directly in front of the building of the Retired Persons Union. There was a tank, looking to stem the human tide advancing toward it!

One of the women with the black lab coats threw herself down in front of the tank's treads, shouting, "Go ahead! Grind me up!"

We were all pressing up, chest level, against the tank. Time seemed to drag; every moment seemed like a year... Hundreds of hands reached for and grasped the treads. The woman kept yelling, "Go ahead! Grind me up!"

I dug my hands so hard into the steel treads that it broke my fingernails. I didn't want the woman in the black apron to be hurt!

"Is it going to pass?"

"It's going to pass so that it doesn't run over the woman!"

I saw that my fingernails had dug into the steel treads.

A moment of hesitation. And then, that hand that had clung onto the treads took hold of the woman and brought her back to her feet.

The woman banged her fists on the tank's hull, "Go ahead! Do it! Grind me up!"

The gushing human wave broke through the barrier at that point, overrunning the tank and submerging it under a torrent of people…. We poured down the incline from Çağaoğlu toward Eminönü….

Whenever I feel myself in straits, whenever I feel myself alone, I think of that woman in the black lab coat, as if she were Hızır, and it gives me strength and hope.

She stroked my head, asking, "So, Kemal, didn't we have a soul when we threw ourselves in front of that tank?" I could feel her heartbeat in those warm hands of hers.

And now, here, in this bus that was hurtling into the darkness toward Erbaa, as I lay reeling from the loneliness of my mission, she came to me and held my arm.

"Go forward!," she urged me.

I was delighted. I felt strengthened against the darkness that was pressing in on me…. Even though I was surrounded by darkness, a sun rose within me.

I saw Meline far off in the distance. But she couldn't see me.

The Erzurum-bound bus was quickly nearing Erbaa. Little Kemal was coming at a run, barefoot, from Honaz…. he had watered the tomatoes until the evening hours… As if he was seated before me… Totally obedient… He opens his mouth, but he doesn't utter a single word… I look him in the face and we come eye to eye…. He slowly lays his head on my lap… I take my right arm and place it around him….I slowly stroke his head… The dried sweat has turned his hair stiff…. I smell his head: the smell of perspiration… He remains asleep as I stroke his hair…

Afterward…

Afterward, the Kemal that loves Meline appears before me….

"If you turn around… if you go back on your promise to my sweet Meline… I'll never be able to look her in the face again!"

Afterward, the pen with which I write comes alive between the fingers of my right hand.

"If you would just surrender to the fears that are plaguing you on your journey" it says, "you'll never write another thing! Don't even bother picking me up! You might as well just break me in half and throw me away into the darkness!"

After that, the fingers of my left hand begin to tingle. I feel the bones, sunk like needles into the shattered skull of Hüseyin Aslantaş… It's soft and warm! There is Hüseyin: lain out in front of the dormitory door, but the door won't open!

The bus to Erzurum comes to a stop before the station in Erbaa.

Through the window of the bus I can see the fruit lined up in the fruit stand adjacent to the bus company office. I wake up little Kemal. I stroke his head and take his hand. We are greeted by cool air as we descend down the rear door. The redness of the enormous peaches glows under the light of the sixty-watt bulb dangling from the roof of the fruit stand. I buy two peaches and wash them in the fountain at the corner. I give one to Little Kemal, one to Big Kemal. They eat… Little Kemal sees cookies in the shop window. "Buy it for me," he says. I do so and give them to him. He opens the package and begins munching a few.

The passengers traveling to Erzurum get back on as the bus gets ready to depart. "Everyone aboard!"

I take Little Kemal by the hand. We get back on the bus through the rear door.

"Come on, then. Let's go! We're continuing to the end of the journey!"

Snow and thunderstorms in the mountains of Erzurum…

It was a warm day in Erzincan. The bus stopped at a gas station. Soldiers got on to check identity cards. They took maybe ten young men off the bus.

"What for?" I asked.

"Soldiers who were returning without permission," someone told me. "After this they would go back to their stations by military means."

The mountains were completely devoid of trees. On the mountaintops, there were patches of snow stretching out among the passes and cliffs….

Mountains, hills, after that a river containing little water. Then, a plain stretching out, from one end of the mountains to the other, as far as the eye could see.... This was a very different country than the one from which I had come!

At around nine o'clock we pulled into the Erzurum bus terminal. I took a taxi to the Erzurum Teachers' Hostel where I found a bed and attempted to shake off the weariness of a long and confusing night's journey.

Today I would go to Aşkale. Tomorrow, Ani...

The teachers' hostel was newly built, a tall, magnificent looking building. Toward noon, the air began to warm up a bit. I asked Information about where to find the Tourist Information Bureau. They instructed me.

It wasn't far and I decided to walk. It was quiet. Not a soul in sight. There was a little room on the right side of the entrance... One side of the wall was full of little box shelves... There wasn't anyone there. When I called, someone did appear. They looked like they had just woken up from their sleep. We said hello.

"I'm going to Ani," I said. "Do you have any brochures regarding Ani?"

"Where's Ani?"

"Ani, in [the Province of] Kars!"

"I don't know! Which brochure do you want?"

He went into the information booth. Most of the shelf boxes were empty. The faded colors, the way they were scattered and spread among the different boxes, and the general disorder gave some indication as to just how long it had been since someone had actually disturbed them. He pressed two of them into my hand.

"These are the only ones we have!" he said.

One was the German-language brochure printed by the Culture Ministry, "Eastern and Southeastern Turkey," the other a brochure in English about Ephesus.

I thanked him and departed. The condition of the place made it clear that asking anything further would be of no use.

I returned to the teachers' hostel. There I sat down and read the brochure on Eastern and Southeastern Turkey. The cover photograph was of a brilliant, colorful *kilim*, or Turkish throw-rug: red, yellow, turquoise, green, black and orange-colored motifs. Two young women, clad in crocus-yellow clothing were laughing and playing against a background of turquoise skies.

My eyes smiled at the joyfulness of the colors.

The first and second pages of the brochure had photographs of the massive carved stone heads on Mount Nemrut. On the third page, under the heading "From Erzincan to Doğubeyazit," there was a half page discussing Erzincan, Erzurum, Kars, Ağri and Doğubeyazit.

The mosques, the citadels, the *hans*, or caravan inns... It told of when they had been built, by whom and in what kingdom or state. It was also mentioned that there were churches in these cities. On page four there was also a large photograph with the caption "Kars: The Disciples Museum." In the section on Kars, it mentioned that the Disciples' Museum (*Apostelkirche*) had been built in the tenth century, and stressed that it was a historical site worthy of visiting. But to which nation had it belonged or why, there was nothing.

Aha! There it was: "Ani: A city that has been around since the Middle Ages, it is located on the Silk Road, forty-two kilometers from Kars on the Soviet border. It contains magnificent citadels and the ruins of numerous churches and mosques." But who lived in those cities during those times? Who built those citadels? The churches? So many unanswered questions...

But first, we'd have to go to Aşkale.

Aşkale was a town which had become associated with the infamous "Capital Tax" of 1943. It was the place where the government had established labor camps to send the Greek, Armenian and Jewish citizens who were unable to pay the Capital Tax as assessed. There they were forced to "work off" their tax debt.

That much I knew. But was it correct? Had forced labor camps actually be set up in Turkey? How had such things happened?

I was going to go to Aşkale and find traces or remains of these forced labor camps, and living witnesses, as well. I just couldn't believe it.... On the one hand, you accept with open arms the Jewish academics, scientists and artists fleeing from Nazi Germany; on the other, you gather up the Jews, Armenians and Greeks who are your own citizens and ship them off to labor camps claiming they didn't pay their taxes!

Had these things actually happened? I would go and see with my own eyes, hear with my own ears. But how must I go about doing this?

Mustafali from Denizli

How would I go about doing this business? I could just jump in a *dolmuş* and go there. But whom would I speak with? This was a topic that you couldn't talk about with just anybody.... It was a sensitive issue about which I couldn't just ask everyone I met....

I left the teachers' hostel. My mind was preoccupied, turning over and over again the questions I had about Aşkale and how I would find out more. I walked straight down the broad avenue, looking in the shop windows. One sign in particular caught my eye: "Denteks." In the display window were tablecloths, towels, trousseau items: all products of Denizli.... I entered the narrow door of the shop. Sitting at the table was a young man whom I didn't know from Adam. Using my best Denizli accent, I said:

"So, that's what it's come to? Big ol' Denizli wasn't enough for you, so you had to up and go to Erzurum?"

Smiling, he stood up.

"Come, brother, come!" he said, extending his hand. We exchanged greetings.

"It doesn't matter where you go these days, the 'Denizlian's have already got there and taken over! Just look at that! *Gahbecik*s come and open shops even here! It's clear—you can even tell the roosters from Denizli! He wasn't kidding, our Özay Gönlüm, when he said it. What a wonderful, beautiful shop you have here!"

Then we started to speak in a Denizli accent... First we asked each other our names, then I remembered.

"I'm Kemal. I'm from Honaz."

"My name's Mustafali. I'm from Bekilli. I sound like someone from Bekilli. I finished university here. I'm a graduate of the Department of English. I met a local girl and got married. I became a Gariköylü."

"One who becomes a Gariköylü becomes precious. Look how well you're doing, brother!"

"Kemal, my brother, during my student years I'd bring towels from Denizli and handiwork from Buldan and sell them. Slowly but surely, I was able to finish school that way. Now I'm teaching here. But teaching doesn't pay the bills. The shop brings in a few more coins, may it bring a blessing! Without that it would be very difficult to get by, even though my wife works too."

"But you're your own man, Mustafali! You're not dependent upon others!"

"Thank God for that!"

"That makes you the happiest man in the world, my friend!"

"Kemal, my friend: what are you drinking? Forgive me for having immersed you in this conversation without first asking."

"No need to apologize, my friend. We're two people from the same place, meeting in Erzurum, of all places. Of course we're going to lose ourselves in conversation!"

We drank our tea and got to know each other more or less. Mustafali didn't seem like a bad man—a little obsessed with money, maybe, but curious. He sort of had the air of having been a sufi. He wallowed in the flattery I dished out. When he received praise he got down off his high horse a little. But how should I broach the subject of Aşkale?

I told him about being a teacher in Germany, about the things that I wrote, about my desire to travel around these parts. I took out a copy of *The Assurance Dowry* from my backpack and showed him. He was pleased. He then listed, one by one, all of the places worth seeing in Erzurum, the mosques, the medreses, etc.

"Be well, Mustafali, my friend. I'm going to go see Erzurum, Aşkale and Ani."

"Kemal, my friend, there's nothing worth seeing in Aşkale. I go there all the time. I've got a friend there. But as for Ani, I have no idea. Where is that exactly?"

"It's in Kars. It's a historical site."

"I swear, I've never heard of it, Kemal!"

"Then let's go there together! You'll go and see it on my account! But first I wan't to go see Aşkale."

"My friend, you won't find anything but loads of soldiers there!"

It was time to broach the subject. It would be best to lay my cards on the table.

"Mustafali, I don't want to visit historical sites in Aşkale, I want to see something else. Have you ever heard of something called the 'Capital Tax?'"

"Never heard of it!"

"Look, compatriot, there was a law that came out in 1942 called the 'Capital Tax.' Because of this law Jews, Armenians and Greeks were demanded to pay a tax that they wouldn't be able to pay. Those who didn't were sent to Aşkale and forced to work."

"Is that true?"

"If it's true or not, I'm not fully sure myself. I'd like to think it's not! But that's what I've heard. I'd like to go to Aşkale and find out whether or not it's true, and to look for some trace or evidence of the camps."

"Now you've got *me* curious… It's amazing: as many times as I've gone to Aşkale, I've never heard a single thing about any 'Capital Tax' or any other kind of tax!"

But now that I had raised the matter and we were talking about it openly, I asked:

"Mustafali, is it better to go to Aşkale by *dolmuş* or by taxi? How much would it be to go by taxi do you think?"

"Somewhere between five and six million lira."

"Mustafali, let me give you the money that I can. You'll both get to see for yourself, and to hear with your own ears whether it's true or not. But there's one other thing: I should tell you now that this whole business is a little dangerous, because I don't want you to say later on that I didn't tell you! I'll give you ten million, not five. We'll go to Aşkale. If there's time, we'll also tour Pasinler and Hasankale."

"Be well, my friend. You've come all the way from Denizli to do research. How could I leave you on your own? And it's a good thing you're doing, too! I told you I had a teacher friend there. Let's look him up, first of all. He'll help us."

"If that's the way it is, Mustafali, then what are we waiting for? Let's go!"

He left the shop in the hands of his assistant, saying we'd be back before evening. Then we headed out the door in the direction of the taxi stand.

The things I heard in Aşkale

When we arrived in Aşkale, we went straight to the house of Ergün the teacher. To our good fortune, he was home at the time. Mustafali introduced us and acquainted him with our purpose. He told Ergün that I was gathering information about the history of Aşkale, and asked if there was anyone in the area with whom we could speak about the subject. It was clear to me that Mustafali was trying to be cautious. He didn't even mention the words "Capital Tax."

After thinking a bit, Ergün said:

"If anyone would know about this, it would be the district culture minister. He's done a whole lot of research about the history of Aşkale and Erzurum. He wrote a book, but he hasn't been able to publish it yet."

I would have liked to say "It might be better if we didn't mix the district culture minister in this matter," but at that point I couldn't: the arrow had already left the bow. Mustafali was brimming over with pride at having expedited the matter. He was grinning from ear to ear. There was no need to take the car, because the building of the Culture Ministry Directorate was close by, less than a five minute walk.

Mustafali locked his car and left his Denizli accent back at Ergün's. He even changed his gait, clasping his hands behind his back. Afterward, he put his left hand in his pocket. He pulled up his pants before entering the door of the three-story building housing the Directorate of the Culture Ministry. He straightened himself up and made himself neat and orderly.

The director knew Ergün and received us graciously. The buttons of his checked suit were all closed, even with the summer heat. His face was taut, the hairs of his mustache fine. The looks he gave us were somewhat haughty and suspicious. His speech, too, was haughty and blustering.

He immediately called his errand boy and sent him out to fetch tea for us. "Why did you get here so late this morning?" he asked the tea boy in a scolding tone so as to put his power and position on display for us.

Ergün directed the conversation toward our subject at hand. He told the director that I had come in order to gather information on Aşkale, and that, since Ergün knew that the director himself was the most knowledgeable person on the subject, he had brought me here.

"Well, then" he began, "Of course, I've not only done in-depth historical research on Aşkale, but on Erzurum as well!" and leaned back in his director's chair. He opened the buttons of his jacket and spoke:

"I should first give you a little information about Erzurum. Erzurum is a very old city. From the religious point of view, it occupies a special place. It played a very important role not only in the Seljuk and Ottoman Empires, but in the Republican period as well. Many important persons have come from Erzurum. The people of Erzurum and of Aşkale have been one hundred percent Turkish throughout history! As you've probably heard already, a little before dawn terrorists killed the head of a village and four of its other inhabitants in a village near Aşkale. What a shame that they haven't yet been able to uproot the traitors. But they will. There aren't any Kurds at all in Erzurum or Aşkale. Only pure-blooded Turks!"

The director went on, and I could see that Mustafali's smile had disappeared. His shoulders sunk. I was racking my brains trying to think how we could get out of there. Although I shouldn't have said it, I did anyway.

"I thank you for your extensive knowledge, Mr. Director. I would like to ask you some things on the basis of your research. Do you know about any connection between Aşkale and the Capital Tax? In your opinion, is it true that non-Muslims came here in 1942?"

In one moment his gaze hardened. He furrowed his brows and placed his hands on the desk.

"There was never any such thing!" he exclaimed. "These claims are the scheming of the Armenian traitors!" And then he fell silent. He looked at my face with great suspicion. We would have to leave without another word.

"Again, I thank you for the information you've given us. You've enlightened me. May you be well!"

We hit the stairs and descended quickly, without looking back and without speaking. Mustafali marched at a brisk pace, never daring to look back. He didn't open his mouth until we had rounded the corner. Once he was convinced that he was securely out of the director's sight and earshot, he put his face close to mine and said in a trembling, fearful voice: "Kemal, my friend, now I understand the problem. We went to the wrong address. Let's get out of here!"

"Don't be afraid, my brother," I said, trying to calm him down. "First, let's sit down and have something to eat. Let's go have some coffee or tea. After that we'll think about what to do next."

The streets of Aşkale were full of soldiers. "If it wasn't for the soldiers, Aşkale would starve!" Ergün said. Mustafali modified this a bit, saying: "If it wasn't for the soldiers and university students, Erzurum would starve!"

I agreed with both of them. There weren't any factories whatsoever, and there was hardly any honest work. But there was plenty of coffee. What else were people supposed to do? The coffee houses were full to the point of spilling out into the streets. People young and old were occupying the short-legged thatched stools.

I didn't want to leave Aşkale empty handed, but what should I do? This wasn't a matter for directors or teachers. For whatever reason the minds of those who had studied the matter had been corrupted. I should go ask the old folk. I wondered what they would have to say.

"Mustafali, my brother," I said, "you shouldn't be involved with me right now. You can take a walk or sit here silently if you'd like. But I'm going to talk with the older people in the coffee house!"

"OK, my friend, go talk. I'm going to sit beside you. I won't speak. But I'm very curious myself. I'd also like to know what the old folks have to say."

I spied a group of old men sitting under the coffee house awning and approached them. I greeted them and they each, in their turn, returned my greetings.

"Please, sir!" they said, gesturing for me to sit down. I pulled up the stool and sat.

"So, where are you from?" one of the others asked. "Are you a soldier?"

"No, just traveling around, seeing what I can," I replied.

At that point Mustafali and Ergün came up behind me and sat down. Again, greetings were exchanged.

"These are my teacher friends" I said, introducing them, "Mustafa Bey teaches in Erzurum, Ergün is a teacher right here in Aşkale."

One portly old man lightly lifted the brim of his hat and spoke:

"What did you come here to see, sir? You can go anywhere to see mountains, rocks, hills and valleys…"

"Aşkale's fame is known throughout the world" I answered. "Why is that?"

"It sounds as if you're not telling us everything you want to say, eh?"

"I asked why Aşkale is so famous. Nothing more, nothing less."

"Sir, you're asking us questions to which you already know the answer—or should! Aşkale *is* famous. It was a place of exile and deportation."

There were five of them and three of us. Together we looked like quite a crowd. And so tea was ordered…

When the word "*sürgün*" (exile, deportation) was mentioned, they laughed a little among themselves. One tall, thin-faced fellow spoke next:

"Do you know what the 'Capital Tax' was? It came out during İnönü's time. They gathered up and brought here all the rich Armenians, Jews and Greeks during the winter of 1942. They made them shovel the twelve-foot-high snow on Kop Mountain. These were Istanbul gentlemen who'd never held a pick or shovel in their lives! I was a tailor at that time. They would hide their money in the collars and hems of their greatcoats. They'd receive their wages and come to me to hide it for them. Afterward they'd have me sew it up. They were good people. Refined people. You'd break 'em just by looking at 'em!"

"They turned our coffeehouse into a dormitory. They'd lay out their beds and lie down, one next to the other. They'd get up in the morning and form themselves into a line. Then they'd hand out picks and shovels and march them off quickly to break ice and shovel snow. There was a sergeant at their head and he was no nonsense! These were people who lived in İzmir and İstanbul: when had they ever experienced the deadly cold of some place like Aşkale? They arrived here with low cut shoes. The poor creatures' hands and feet froze from the cold. I actually saw their frozen fingers fall off with my own eyes!"

"They also cleaned out our stable and made it into a dormitory" said the oldest of the bunch. "They suffered greatly from hunger. I sold bread to those hungry men!" he concluded.

Mustafali's eyes were rapt with attention as he listened. He didn't say a thing. Ergün simply looked stunned, nodding in agreement with the things that were said. Maybe he'd heard such things before. There wasn't anything new in those things he heard, but I was hearing them for the first time. I wanted to jog their memories a bit:

"Fine," I said, "but couldn't they have complained to someone? Were there any who ran away?"

"Who could they have complained to!? Where would they run to in the middle of cold winter!? In the mountains around Erzurum, you'd either freeze to death or be eaten by wolves!"

One old man in a visored cap, whose face didn't show a trace of evil and who had until then listened silently to all that was said now spoke up:

"I ate these people's bread. People shouldn't be so cruel to one another. Through actions like these they've dragged the name of Aşkale through the mud. An old man... maybe sixty... in the middle of winter, they gave him a pickaxe. 'Get to it! Break those rocks! Clear that road!' they'd order. But this man didn't know how to use a pickaxe. He didn't even have the strength to lift it above his head! They'd make them work even to the point of killing them! That's a sin! If a man's a Christian, then he's a Christian!

Doesn't he have a God too? If you're going to punish someone, put him in prison. But breaking up the ice, shoveling in twelve feet of snow? Is that not inhuman?"

"Look," I said, "this is the first time I'm hearing these things. I want to write them down. Can I record your conversation?"

At that the mood of the place changed immediately. One of the fellows stood up and said: "Sir, don't bring disaster upon our heads! This matter isn't something run-of-the-mill! I saw fingers fall off with my own eyes! But I can't put that on tape. At my age I can't afford to go to court. Forgive me, if you will."

Another one said: "You get us to talk and then you'll go. You'll write it all down. But we'll remain here. If tomorrow they come and put us under guard, are you going to come and save us?"

Baba Yusuf of Aşkale

One by one, four of the old men stood and departed. In the end, only one of them remained.

"I ate their bread, sir! It's a shame what happened to those men! Everyone knows what was done to them. There's not a soul in Aşkale who doesn't know. But they won't open their mouths out of fear. We've all been silent, haven't said a word. We've made it until now in that way. But how long should we remain silent? We don't have much longer to live. We may be gone tomorrow. What you'd like to know, ask! Turn on your tape recorder, take a picture of me. Even write down my name!"

But sitting out on the street, recording someone's voice would draw a great deal of attention. So we went inside the coffeehouse. Compared with the area outside it, the room was rather quiet and empty. Ergün and Mustafali also came inside. I pressed the 'record' button and he began:

> They call me 'Baba Yusuf.' The train came to Aşkale in 1938. I saw the train at that time. In the winter of 1942, however, some, maybe as many as three hundred non-Muslims: Armenians, Jews, Greeks, were brought here. They were gathered and brought here from Istanbul and Izmir, from the big cities.
>
> At that time I was seventeen or eighteen years old. These men who were brought were old men. They stayed in the coffeehouses, in the houses, in the hotels… At that time Aşkale was just a little village. There was no way of housing three hundred persons. They turned the stables and coffeehouses into dormitories. They'd burn cow dung and anything

else they could find to keep warm. The boarders paid from month to month. They were in a pretty bad state. They weren't up to the climate here. It was really cold. They were forced to work continually. They remained as much as five months.

There were sergeants in charge of them. Every morning they would line them up and divide them into work teams.

They were put to work shoveling snow on Kop Mountain and in Kop Pass. That's all they did.

Those who weren't up to clearing the snow, or who weren't in a condition to do physical work, gave us money. We'd work in their places. I also did this. I earned much of my livelihood from these persons—Write this down! Let the whole nation know!

There were a whole lot of shortages at that time. Aşkale and its surrounding towns weren't able to collect the sixty thousand lira for their share of the road tax. Each household had to pay six lira. But those who couldn't scrounge together six lira had to go out and work on the roads. That was a lot of money at the time. A cow only cost three or four lira at that time. I bought three cows for eight lira.

These men came when there was this shortage. They were all non-Muslims. 'Who brought you here?' I'd ask, 'What did you do?', 'You're a Turkish citizen, aren't you?', 'Don't you have people who are looking for you and asking about you?' The person for whom I worked was an old Armenian fellow. He had come from Istanbul. He was a very humane person. He explained it to me: 'We're Turkish citizens, just like you! Our only difference is that we're Christian. The state demanded a lot of taxes. We couldn't pay, so the state gathered us up and brought us here!'

'When will we be freed?' they'd ask themselves in self-pity, 'Will we be able to return without paying?' They all missed their children and grandchildren. They loved me like I was their own son.

These men suffered great oppression. They were in a terrible state. They couldn't adapt to the cold of Aşkale. We made shoes from rawhide and stuffed grass and straw into them before putting them on so that our feet wouldn't freeze. But they were city folk. In their entire lives they'd never even seen rawhide shoes—much less rawhide shoes stuffed with straw! Just imagine it: they came here with low-cut shoes! How could they possibly stand the snow and ice of Aşkale and Kop Mountain in those shoes? Their feet froze. Some of them had their fingers cut off because of frostbite. There weren't a lot of people who came and asked about them. Almost half of those who came suffered greatly. They froze, some got ill. In that way totally healthy men were broken and died.

The old man whose bread I ate couldn't take it. He fell ill. One morning, when I came to take up his position, they told me, 'He kicked the bucket!' I was very sorry. I had loved him a lot, and he loved me, too. He was a good man. That's how the time went. Now, whenever I pass by one of those places where they stayed, I can still see them in my mind's eye. That's my fate. That's how Aşkale is.

Until now, no one has ever come and asked about those days. There are people who knew everything, saw everything. Most of them are long since dead and buried. Most of those who are still alive are too afraid to talk about it. You saw that with your own eyes just a short while back. I was also afraid for years and years. I was afraid, always afraid, but what came of it? Did things turn out alright? I'm not long for this world. I see those old men before my eyes all the time.... Sometimes I even dream about them... Now that I've told you, I feel a little more at ease. I earned my daily bread from these people. I broke ice and shoveled snow for them. They were people so frail that you'd break 'em just by looking at 'em. That's what I wanted to tell you; take my photograph, write down my name. The whole nation should know these things...

I wrote down his name; I took his photograph; I recorded his voice.

Be well, Baba Yusuf! Be very, very well, Baba Yusuf, who is faithful, righteous and humane!

We thanked Ergün and we left Aşkale without delay.

On the ride back Mustafali behaved as if he'd lost the ability to speak. For most of the journey he didn't say a word. Only as we neared Erzurum did he open his mouth.

"Take this money," I said proffering it. "It can't possibly measure up to the help you've given me, but take it for the gas, at least!"

"I won't take it, my friend! I've grown a little today. I've been living here in Erzurum for years, I've gone to Aşkale dozens of times. But I've never heard anything like what I heard today!"

Before setting out he hadn't taken the money I had promised him. And now I was only able to put it in his pocket by force.

What wonderful people there are in this Erzurum, this Aşkale.... People like Mustafali, like Baba Yusuf.

Baba Yusuf of Ashkale

How do you get to Ani?

I arose at five in the morning. It was Wednesday, the fifteenth of July, 1998. I was planning to arrive in Kars when it was still early and then go to Ani. I would return to Erzurum on the last bus that evening.

Unfortunately, the information that I had received the day before turned out to be incorrect. The first bus to Kars only left at 7:30 a.m. I waited for two hours in the Eruzum bus station. I watched all of those on the nightshift waking up.

My bus traveled to Kars over Pasinler, Horasan and Sarıkamış. For a long stretch of the journey it followed the Aras river. For me the Aras didn't live up to its reputation. There was very little water in it.

The Pasinler Plain was completely flat. It stretched from one set of bare mountains to another. The fields had begun to yellow. The leaves of the new potato plants had already begun to spread out and cover them. The new cabbages had sprouted up.

Pasinler looked like a rather large village. It looked neglected, withdrawn into itself.

Horasan was no different from Pasinler... It had a great reputation... but there were no factories, no production.

When we arrived in Sarıkamış the scent of the pines was pervasive, filling the lungs of all the travelers. After the utterly barren mountains, hills and plains, the deep green pine forests covering the mountains of Sarıkamış were maddeningly beautiful. How could it be so beautiful?

Sarıkamış: The military base at the entrance to the city. Sarıkamış in all its greatness!

Sarıkamış: the place where Enver Paşa sacrificed one hundred thousand soldiers in the winter of 1915.

Kars. "Elevation: 1750 m. Population: 74,000" it had said on the sign as we entered.

Entering the city, the first thing to catch the eye was the sugar and cement factories. The plain upon which Kars sat was broad, flat and without a single tree poking its head above the skyline. The mountains looked more like hills... and utterly barren.

There wasn't a single tree to be seen in the villages, either. My goodness! Didn't people even plant a tree in front of their houses here?!

The crops on the Kars plain were a little bit greener than those in Pasinler. The grasses were being harvested in the meadows. All along the sides of the road, in the fields, on the hills were thousands of bee hives. When we arrived I asked the old man sitting next to me about them. He told me that the scent of the grasses growing in the plain, in the mountains and even between the rocks attracted the bees. Honey from Kars was famed for its medicinal value. It was a remedy against all ailments.

At ten o'clock I was already in the outskirts of Kars. I then took a *dolmuş* to the city center. I didn't have much time. I would have to quickly find the Kars Tourism Directorate.

Asking everyone along the way, I was finally guided to the building, which I entered. It was a historical, two-story stone edifice. The whiteness of the marble in the broad entrance hall served to cheer up those who entered. The high ceiling was done with delicate craftsmanship. I ascended the rounded stairs and, knocking on the second-floor door upon which was written "Tourist Information Office," I was ushered in. Inside the office there were desks, each of which was occupied.... Because of the large size of all the desks, there was hardly any room for the people to stand up, much less move around freely.

"Hmm... Now which one should I ask?" I thought to myself. I approached the desk next to the window and greeted the person manning it.

"Sir, I would like some information about Ani. Can I get a brochure about the place?"

He shot me a sharp look. Then his face tensed up and his countenance clouded over:

"I don't have any information about Ani! There's nothing in Turkish on Ani!"

"How can that be, sir?" I replied. "This is Kars, isn't it? And isn't this the Tourist Information Office? And isn't Ani in the Province of Kars? If not here, then where could I find such a brochure? If you don't know about Ani, who would?"

He screwed up his face and mouth in a way that said "So, who's this cocky young fellow?" and said:

"And who do you think you are? I told you there are no brochures in Turkish! I don't have any information on Ani!"

"I came from Germany. I want to travel around and see my country. I heard about Ani and I asked for information about it from you because you're the information office."

At this point, the other employees, who had been busy with their own affairs, all raised their heads and turned toward me with piercing gazes. The one at the desk opposite said "What is it you want, sir?"

"I just want information and brochures on Ani."

"Who are you?"

"I came from Germany."

"Take out your identity card! Take these two forms and fill them out!" the director said. There aren't any brochures about Ani in Turkish! Do you understand? Take the brochures about Eastern Anatolia that are in English, French and German!"

I took out my identity card and showed him. He took it and examined it, looking at me and then at the photograph on my card. I filled out the two forms that he had given me: name, surname, place of birth, date of birth, mother's name, father's name, date of arrival, etc. When I finished filling in the blank spaces on the form I signed it.

"Here you go, sir."

"You have to take them to the Security Directorate and have them verified. Afterward, you go to the Kars Museum and buy a ticket. Ani is about forty-five kilometers from here. There's no *dolmuş* or bus service. You'll have to go by taxi!"

I thanked him for the information and departed. Asking for directions on the way I arrived at the Security Directorate. The policeman guarding the entrance accepted my greeting with grace. I took a deep breath. Man, oh man! What was with those people in the Tourist Information Office?

"Officer sir, I'm going to visit Ani. The Tourist Information Office sent me here to have my documents certified."

"Fine. Give me your identity card and your completed documents."

"Here you are."

"Aha! You're from Denizli?"

"Yes. I'm from Honaz!"

"We're neighbors! I'm from Dinarlı. I know Denizli well, but unfortunately I've never had the chance to visit Honaz."

Well, what do you know? This was my lucky day. He stamped my documents without delay and signed.

"Here you go, neighbor. Do you know how to get to Ani? Do you know what kind of place it is?"

"No."

Ani is a God-forsaken place. They built a road, but there's no transportation to there. You're going to have to take a private taxi. Make sure you negotiate well. They generally start off asking for fifteen million lira. Start at five million. Get the best price you can, but no matter what, don't pay more than ten million. And take food and water with you. It'll be hot, and the facilities are minimal. But be very careful! It's a military area. It's right on the Russian border. Now, take these documents and go to the Kars Museum, go in and buy yourself a ticket!"

"Where's the museum?"

"It's all the way on the other side of Kars. It's a long, hard walk. Better to take a taxi. You can get there by taxi. It's on the way to Ani, in any case. But make sure you haggle with the driver like I told you—and be careful in Ani! Don't forget what your neighbor from Dinarlı told you!"

I followed his instructions. Sure enough, the driver wanted fifteen million. I suggested five million and he laughed. "Are you trying to make a fool of me, pal?" In the end, we settled on ten million.

As soon as I got in the taxi he began to ask: Where had I come from? Where was I going? What was my business? etc., etc. I was on my toes. I tried to redirect the conversation by countering his questions with my own. He'd worked in Istanbul for years driving a *dolmuş*. In the end, he got tired of his job in Istanbul and had returned to Kars. In addition, his father was all alone here, so it seemed like a good idea. He bought a taxi, but the work in Kars wasn't very plentiful. He was having a hard time making ends meet. He was talkative and had swarthy features. He looked Kurdish.

We arrived at the museum and went in together. There wasn't a soul in sight. Finally, a sluggish fellow who looked like he resented even the act of walking arrived.

"Sir, I would like some information on Ani. Could you give me a brochure? And I need one ticket, please…"

The unenthusiastic man answered in a manner that made it seem like each word spoken was an enormous effort for him:

"I don't know nothing about no Ani."

"This is Kars, right? Isn't this the Kars Museum?" I said, on the verge of exploding from irritation. Was this my beloved homeland? I continued: "Well, can I speak to the museum director?"

"Not here!"

"Why not? Is his shift over?"

"He had some other matters to attend to. He left!"

At that point the driver took my arm and said with a calming voice, "Please, my friend. Buy the ticket and let's be on our way. We're running late."

When we got back in the taxi he explained the situation to me:

"My friend, this is Kars! It's different here. You can't smart off to just anybody. You asked for the museum director, but he's not at the museum. His son owns a shop in the market and he works there. He stops by the museum maybe once a week. You're right to be upset, but who are you going to complain to? What does that gatekeeper know about Ani?"

I looked out the window of the taxi. The plain of Kars was a broad, endless swath of green. I followed the police officer from Dinarlı's instructions. I went into a store and bought two bottles of water and a couple of kilos of apricots. The fruit was more beautiful than any I'd ever seen. They were as big as peaches, and of a color between white and yellow, like silk. They had been grown on the Iğdır Plain. What a wonderful country! Fruitful and blessed. My Anatolia and its people. People who both created and cursed…

At a checkpoint some ten kilometers from Ani we were stopped by two soldiers. They were checking identity cards. They asked where we were going, and when we would be returning. I produced one of the authorized entry forms. He made us get out of the car and did a thorough search of the vehicle.

"Have a pleasant journey. Go cautiously!" he said, pointing the way with the barrel of his gun.

We passed villages, and hilly lands. In every place, the earth was completely barren. The villages looked like they were from another world, the houses as if they were from the stone age, with low stone walls of sun-dried brick and earthen roofs. On the sides of the houses were piles of manure as high as the roof. And upon those earthen roofs—television antennas as large copper trays…. The only part of the house that was larger were the piles of manure.

"We've arrived in Ani," the driver said. This was the village of Ovacık.

The walls of Ani rose silently and majestically against the stunning turquoise heavens, presiding over the surrounding ruin and despair. The buildings of Ovacık, whose style made it unclear whether they were houses, graves, or merely piles of stone, came right up to the base of the huge walls.

(Above, foreground) Sourp Asdvadzadzin (Holy Mother of God) cathedral in Ani, built in the 10th century. *(Above background)* Sourp Prgitch (Holy Redeemer) from the 11th century.

(Above foreground) The mosque of Minuchihr in Ani was built by the Kurdish Shaddadid dynasty that ruled this region after the 11th century. *(Above foreground)* Sourp Asdvadzadzin (Holy Mother of God) cathedral

Spring never came to Ani before you did.

The heat of July was roasting the surrounding environment. All around, there wasn't a single tree standing inside the village. On the plain, with its sparse vegetation, the green plants had yellowed almost as soon as they emerged. Everywhere, there was dust and dirt. The road to Ani had been recently paved. The fine gravel had not yet adhered to the sides of the asphalt.

Jafer the taxi driver brought many tourists here and showed them around. He knew how and from where to enter the sites, and at which hours one could tour them. He wasn't just a taxi driver, he was an experienced tour guide.

"My friend, it's long past twelve. It'll take more than two days to see all of the ruins in Ani. If you want to return to Erzurum today you'll have to hurry. The last bus for Erzurum leaves at five. If you calculate an hour for the return trip, that leaves you only three hours to stroll around Ani.

Before all else, I should warn you: it's forbidden to take photographs in Ani. Better that you hear it from me than from the soldiers. Things here aren't like in Istanbul. It's very strict! There's no complaining, no arguing. Alright, let's go! Let's take the water and the apricots."

I did what Jafer told me, except that I took my camera with me, despite his instructions.

The walls of Ani became larger and grander as we approached. The stone wall in which the main entrance gate was found was still standing. There was a stylized cross motif out of red stone that was embedded in the front of the castle. It announced to all who came to Ani "This is a Christian city. Welcome to a Christian city of the East!"

As soon as we entered the narrow, blue-painted gate made of iron grating, we encountered ten soldiers. The fortress there was very interesting. It wasn't a single wall, but rather formed two parallel walls. The clubhouse at the entrance had been made between these two stone walls. The soldiers were sitting in the shade of the inner stone wall, their weapons propped up against the wall.

Apart from the soldiers, there was a civilian ticket seller waiting in the shadow of the club entrance. When they saw us, the ticket seller and several of the soldiers got to their feet. We exchanged greetings, and Jafer and I showed the entrance tickets we had purchased in the Kars Museum.

One soldier, his weapon in hand, approached us.

"Welcome," he said. "There are some rules for strolling around here:
One: It is forbidden to take pictures!
Two: It is forbidden to make movies!
Three: It is forbidden to leave the sightseeing route!
Four: It is forbidden to enter the Arapçay Stream!
Five: A soldier will lead you around. It is forbidden to disobey the things which the soldier says!"

I thanked him for the instructions and said:

"You're roasting out here. You're getting dehydrated. I'll observe the things you said to the letter, don't worry. But first, each of you take a couple of these beautiful apricots. I'm sorry there's not more. If I had known how many of you there were I would have purchased more. Here, wet your whistles; 'The sweeter the meal, the sweeter the speech,' no?"

Jafer held out the paper sack to each of the soldiers. Each one took of the apricots and thanked him.

"O.K.," I said, "you've given your warnings and went down the rules with us. Fine and good, but if any of you know anything, can you tell me about the history of these ruins, of what we thought would be the city of Ani?"

"Hey now, my friend; we're only soldiers! Our job is simply to wait and guard the place. What do we know about history? You see what people have built here, how big a city they established..."

"But who built Ani? Do you know what peoples founded it?"

"We don't know. Nobody told us!"

But I wasn't ready to give up yet.

"Hey, Mr. Ticket Seller!" I said, "Give us a little information on the ruins that you sell tickets for!"

"What do I know?" he replied. "I just sell the tickets!"

"Alright, then. Do you have any books, brochures, or anything written or illustrations here that tell about Ani?"

The soldier who had told us the rules said "I've got something, but it's in German."

"Alright: German it is!" I said, thanking him. "Do you speak German?"

"Yes, I'm an *Almancı*."[*]

"Me too. Which city?"

---

[*] *Almancı* Turkish for a Turk who works/lives in Germany; a guest worker, *Gastarbeiter*.

"Stuttgart."

"You're kidding! How did you fall from Stuttgart to here?"

"Don't ask! It's a long story. I'm not the only one from Germany here. My friend here is from Dortmund!"

"Really? I'm from Bochum! We're practically neighbors!"

The soldier from Dortmund stood up and out of the shade of the wall approached me. We shook hands. The one from Stuttgart then took out a seven-page photocopy and a German-language tour guide from the cabinet and handed them to me. The first of the photocopied pages had a roughly sketched diagram of Ani. On the next page the text began. I skimmed the title page: "Ani: Stadt der 1001 Kirchen" ("Ani: City of 1,001 Churches") by Jean-Michel Thierry.

On the last page, the source upon which the author had based his text was written by hand "Armenien-Wiederentdeckung einer alten Kulturlandschaft" (Armenia: The rediscovery of an ancient land and culture).

"A German tourist gaven me both the book and the photocopies a couple of months back," the soldier said. "I looked through it, but my German isn't great. I didn't understand a lot. Here, you can sit down and read it at your leisure."

I sat on the stool to which he had gestured. The explanations in the German tour book were also brief. I quickly read both explanations—If only I had properly prepared myself for this trip while I was in Germany! If only I'd collected enough material on Ani! When Meline had said "Go and see for yourself!" I had imagined Ani as an abandoned city in which people had lived even as late as eighty or ninety years ago. It's streets were made of marble, its houses, out of stone. Even their entrances had two or three marble steps each! The things that had been planted on the streets had long since died. It was like the places I had seen in Ephesus and Şirince…. I had been wrong… It was as if I had been imagining another place entirely….

I began to read the German explanations:

"Ani is the City of 1001 Churches… Here there are incomparable works which show the particular characteristics of the Golden Age of Armenian history…. Ani was built as the capital of Armenia in 961 A.D. by the kindhearted and merciful King Ashot III… At the beginning of the 11th century there were some ten thousand dwellings in Ani and more than

100,000 Armenians living there... Ani was the commercial and cultural capital of that age... The Silk Road passed through Ani... It sits at 1,400 meters above sea level, on a flat, triangular plateau where the Arpaçay river and the Bostandere Valley meet... Ani's wealth during this time made it the target of many of its aggressive neighbors... In order to secure the safety of his capital, King Ashot III had the city's first walls constructed....

His successor, Smbat II, had more walls built on the narrow part of the triangular plateau that is connected with the ground below. These walls are still standing today... King Smbat II gathered unto him architects, master craftsmen and commanders in order to reinforce the defenses on this weaker side of the city's defenses; he looked for a system of defense that would render ineffective the siege weapons of that age, such as mangonels, ballistas and catapults.... finally, in 989 A.D. he had two walls built, parallel to one another, in the narrow area into which no siege machines could be set up....

During the 11th century, the principal enemy of the Kingdom of Armenia was the Byzantine Empire, it's neighbor which had brought all of Anatolia under its rule... Ani and the Kingdom of Armenia's long period of peace and tranquility finally came to an end with a series of Byzantine assaults. Ani was conquered and brought under Byzantine control by Emperor Constantine IX (Monomachus)....

It was in this period, in which the wars and hostilities between the Armenian Kingdom and Byzantine Empire reached their peak, that the Turkic tribes began to enter Anatolia. Byzantine control of Ani was ended by the Seljuk Turks in 1064... Ani then passed into Seljuk control. During the Battle of Manzikert in 1071 the army of the Seljuk bey Alparslan defeated the Byzantine forces. With this defeat, the Byzantines' control of Anatolia began to weaken and recede... Under the Muslim Seljuks, Ani now came under Islamic control.

The first mosque in Anatolia was built in Ani... The main church was turned into a mosque. The Seljuks built a palace there.... Seljuk sovereignty over Ani was ended in the 12th century by the Kingdom of Georgia, which then took it over... The city was conquered and sacked by the Mongols in 1236.... After this, Ani began to decline in size and importance... It was destroyed in 1319 by a massive earthquake... Although subsequently rebuilt, it never regained its former glory and prosperity... Over time, it ceased to be a place of settlement...."

"That's enough preparatory information for now," I told the soldier. "Thank you and be well! If you hadn't given me this book and the photocopies, I would have wandered around in this heat without understanding a thing!" I then got on my feet.

Jafer said to me "I've strolled around Ani a great deal. I don't really feel like seeing it again in this heat. You, go walk around and see what you want. We should leave for Kars at 4:00 p.m. at the very latest."

The soldier from Stuttgart said: "My friend, leave your camera here. I told you it was forbidden to take pictures."

"I should keep my camera by my side, because I'm going to put this book and the photocopies in the case. My notebook and pens are in my case. In any case, one of you will always be with me. I won't take photos."

"I'll guide you around. We'll speak a little German."

He slung his weapon over his shoulder and went before me. The space between two large stones was now the path leading to the ruins of Ani. With the soldier from Stuttgart in front and me trailing behind we went about thirty meters and turned right. We came upon a vaulted entrance gate like a seven meter-long tunnel leading into the thick, inner stone wall. As soon as we entered, the Stuttgart soldier suddenly turned his weapon on me:

"Take out your camera!" he ordered. "Take as many photographs as you can!"

I was shocked and confused by what I was now experiencing. The barrel of his gun was pointed toward my stomach.

"Don't joke around, neighbor of mine from Stuttgart! Don't do it! Don't bring any trouble upon me!"

"Bring trouble upon you? Ha! I'm on you! The gun's in my hand. You're in a forbidden military zone. I give the orders here!"

"I don't want to take any photographs!"

"You're going to take them! You've come all the way from Germany, from Bochum! You can't go back without taking pictures!"

Was he joking or was he serious? I looked in his face and peered in his eyes. We were looking in each others' eyes.... My thoughts were racing... If I took photos, would he report me? Would I get into a big mess over this? My God! We'd had our share of disasters in the past... I was smiling and speaking gently, as if he was joking, but it must have been clear that I was terrified! I could hear the trembling in my own voice.... I felt a cold sweat on my body... What should I do? If I could just get out from this tunnel... Then, a thought flashed through my mind. I abandoned my Turkish and switched to German:

"*Mein Freund! Bitte nicht! Mache keine Scherze!*" ("Please, my friend. Don't joke with me so!")

A smile began to spread across his face.

"*Kein Angst, keine Angst! Spaß... Spaß!*" ("Don't be afraid, don't fear! It's a joke... a joke!")

He lowered the barrel of his rifle and laughed loudly. I began to laugh, too....

"*Spaß... Spaß!*" I repeated, "You scared me silly!"

He retreated from before me and the tone of his voice changed. He put his hand on my shoulder warmly and sincerely, as if we were friends. This Ani of a thousand and one churches stretched out from the arch of the tunnel gate as far as the hills before us.

We began to walk side by side down the designated sightseeing path. In order make conversation I asked him: "So, what wind blew you from Stuttgart all the way to here? Where's your family? Are they still in Germany?"

"Don't ask, my friend!" he said. "A person experiences all sorts of things through his life. In Stuttgart I shot up the local PKK branch office. I got in fights. They arrested me and threw me in prison. Have you ever seen a German prison? Even God Himself wouldn't put someone in there! I got mixed up with drugs while I was inside. Then I got out, but I started dealing drugs as well as taking them. Like a grasshopper, I hopped my way out of trouble once or twice, but the third time I didn't quite get away. They arrested me again. I got five years in prison. As soon as they released me the police had me deported and put me on a Turkish Airlines flight. I stepped out at the airport in Yeşilköy[*] and was taken by the police. I had evaded military service. My hearing was brief: they stuck me straight in the "foreigners' unit." That's been my fate. It's been six months since I arrived here. I finally got some good sense, but it's too late now. I'm forbidden from reentering Germany!"

If I had touched him he would have cried. His voice began to tremble. The person who just moments before had pointed a gun barrel at my gut was gone, and in his place was a man-child who thirsted for even a drop of

---

[*] The Atatürk International Airport, the main airport serving Istanbul.

pity…. He leaned his head ever-so-gently against his right shoulder, from which hung his weapon. We began walking slowly down the narrow tourist path, talking all the while.

"Don't despair. If your mother and father help out maybe you can go back. What's your name?"

"Nizamettin. I'm originally from Kırşehir. But I no longer have either a mother or a father left! After I went to prison and got mixed up with drugs they disowned me. They were the ones who encouraged me to shoot up the PKK office, but now they won't even give me the time of day. I had an Italian girlfriend before I went to prison. She was the most honest and loyal friend I ever had. She didn't leave me when I went to prison. My own family, my brothers and sisters and my parents didn't even come once; only the girl came by herself to visit. She gave me money. I got out of prison and was deported. She followed me as far as Istanbul. She tried hard to help me. She's been my only friend in my life. I felt bad for her. I wrote her letters saying, "I'm never coming back. Don't ruin your life on my behalf. Look out for yourself.""

He fell silent… Slowly he began to sob silently…

"Don't despair, Nizamettin! That's life, sometimes. Don't look to the past: look to the future! Are you still taking drugs?"

"Absolutely not! May others be so lucky!"

"Look, this might have been a very good thing! Otherwise you could have already been dead and gone from drugs! You should be thankful that you've saved your own neck from that disaster! If you want, give me your father's address. I'll give you my address in Bochum. When I get back to Germany I'll call your father. He's still your dad. Your mom's still your mom. Maybe…"

"No, my friend. No!" he said, cutting me off. "You shouldn't know my father… I've erased him from my life, too!"

As we spoke, we reached a sign that said "Silk Road." There wasn't anyone in sight. The magnificently blue Arapçay river flowed through the foot of the steep river valley. Both sides were flanked with sharp rocks. The sound of the flowing water echoed off the rocks. The churches, which had seen and survived all of the calamities, all of the earthquakes, now stood, on the flat, grass-covered ground. Then we came before a church whose exterior was covered with frescoes and carved stones resting right against the side of the Arpaçay Valley.

"My friend," Nizamettin said, "take out your camera and take as many pictures as you can! Don't be afraid. I'm right here by you."

There was nothing suspicious-sounding, no hint of treachery in his voice. I did as he said.

"Don't despair!" I said to Nizamettin when we parted, "These days will pass! You'll marry and build a life for yourself here in Turkey." I thanked him for all his understanding and help.

I didn't want to stir around his deep pain and suffering too much, so we continued to stroll and take pictures together. In Ani there were still some stone walls, churches, monasteries, palaces, mansions and one mosque standing. The regular houses and dwellings had all long since turned to rubble and earth. All of the buildings were made from a stone the color of volcanic brick.

"The Minuçihr Mosque was the first mosque built in Anatolia," the tour book had said. "It's architectural characteristics resemble those of churches. It has an eight-sided minaret." The book also said that it had been constructed during the years when Ani was under the rule of a Kurdish emirate.

The Minuçihr Mosque had been built right against the steep wall of the Arpaçay river Valley. We entered the mosque. The air was incredibly cool. A breeze blew through it in gusts. Through a window in one of the walls I could see the Arpaçay, the İpekyolu (Silk Road) Bridge spanning it, and the country of Armenia on the other side. When it was built, this bridge had been one of the largest of its age. Before it was destroyed by an earthquake, its main span had a width of thirty meters. Now, only two stumps remained, one in Armenia, one in Turkey. How the days passed and the wheels of fortune turned! One day, the excavations in Ani would be completed. The thousand and one churches, now buried beneath the earth, would once again appear within the city's walls. The churches, the mosque, the monasteries would spill over with tourists... the day would come when the İpekyolu Bridge would be rebuilt and would be a bridge of peace between Armenia and Turkey....

Time had been passing as fast as the waters of the Arpaçay. It was already four o'clock. I had taken 72 still photographs. Making our way back around, we came again to the tunnel-like entrance gate. Nizamettin repeated my earlier words, "My friend, you scared me silly!" and laughed. Spending the last hours in lengthy conversation had calmed him down a bit. The fear and suspicion that I had had of him three hours earlier were now gone.

"Do you have any more money?" I asked. "Is there someone who gives you pocket money?"

He bent slightly and his countenance took on a strange expression.

"Please, don't misunderstand," I said, "Here, take this money!"

"No way!" he said categorically refusing to take it.

"C'mon, take it!" I urged. "You're not going to shoot up another office or buy drugs! It's given as a sincere thanks to the Nizamettin who got smart and gave up drugs!"

"I'm still not taking it!"

"If you don't take it, I'm going to take the weapon in your hand and stick it in your gut like you did to me and put in your pocket by force!"

But no matter what I said, he still wouldn't accept it. Finally, I did stuff it in his pocket.

When we got back to the soldiers' clubhouse at the entrance, Jafer the taxi driver said with some irritation, "We're late, my friend. We've got to go!"

"We'll go presently, Jafer!" I said, calming him. "I'm getting used to this place. Tell me, is there a grocery in this village?"

"There is!"

"Go quickly and buy the biggest watermelon you can manage. We're burning up out here. Let's all eat together and cool off a bit."

Jafer went and returned, cradling an enormous melon.

"Nizamettin, detach your bayonet and cut the melon!" I said.

Everyone got a slice. Watermelon had never tasted as sweet as the one I ate that day in Ani. Now, whenever I think of Ani, I'm reminded of Nizamettin's joke, the coolness of the watermelon we ate and the loneliness of the cross on one of the old walls.

At the last checkpoint no one asked about the 72 exposures in my camera. I silently thanked Nizamettin once more for his honesty and understanding. The entire trip back, until we reached the bus terminal in Kars, I thought of him: This human puzzle… the things that passed through the mind of a thirty-year-old person…. People were like roses with thorns! "You can escape the serpent by first stroking it" my grandfather had often said. It was the same way with the rose. Otherwise you'd cut up your fingers on the thorns.

I just made the last bus to Erzurum. When I finally arrived at the teachers' hostel I was overcome with the weariness of the day's exertions.

Meline had said, "Go to Van; go see Aghtamar Island!" Although I had promised that I would, I couldn't see going from Erzurum to Van by bus. The next day I flew to Istanbul. From the window of the airplane I gazed out and viewed Anatolia: there were patches of greenery here and there... but from 8,000 meters, the face of the country looked as if it had been scratched and gouged. And Istanbul itself looked as if all its greenery had been devoured by the red clay of the city's roofing tiles.

I was going to go to the address that Safiye Güner had given me in Amasya, in order to meet her sister's husband, Ohan Özant. I called him from the airport and explained the situation. He invited me to come to his house the following day at noon. In the meantime I had the photographs that I had taken in Amasya, Erzurum and Ani hastily developed. And the next day, at the hour upon which we had agreed, I knocked on Ohan Özant's door....

Ohan Özant of Amasya and Vahram Karabent of Merzifon

Ohan Özant appeared at the door with a smiling face and a sweet, soft voice and ushered me in. We introduced ourselves. Also present were his daughter and two grandchildren. His was still in deep mourning. He told me so before I could ask. He had lost his wife three months back. Although the house was tidy and well-organized, he said, "Ever since my wife has been gone my house has lost its taste and orderliness!" He was grieving. His daughters and grandchildren were with him from morning to night. Even so, he hadn't been able to adjust to the emptiness that he felt in his wife's absence.

We sat on the balcony overlooking the train tracks. I slowly and more fully explained the things that I had only mentioned briefly by phone the day before. I told them how I had found them, where I had come from, my intentions, my objectives and what I did for a living. I showed them some pictures of Safiye Güner, her children and grandchildren.

"I've already been informed of all this!" he said. The previous evening he had phoned Amasya and spoken with Safiye. She had been very pleased with my visit.

Ohan Bey's granddaughter made coffee and brought it. I briefly told of my travels to Amasya, Aşkale and Ani.

"Aşkale… Aşkale…" he repeated, sighing, "Aşkale that extinguished my family's hearth!" He'd heard of Ani, but never gone. I showed him some pictures. Silently I thanked Nizamettin again and again in my mind.

Ohan's grandchildren went to the Armenian Lycée. They were two of the most beautiful young girls I had ever seen…. From the neck of each one of them hung a large cross. Someone had written derogatory graffiti against Armenians on the walls of the school. They explained all sorrowfully.

"Turkey is our country. We were born in Istanbul and we grew up here. Why do they bother us? Do we mix in *their* faith, in *their* religion? As long as they're going to call for the Shari'a, and maintain their Sufi orders, as long as they're going to act like Turkey is only a country of Muslims, we're going to hang crosses around our necks."

Ohan Özant recounted his memories of his years in Amasya. He spoke of his father's death. His face appeared to lose its years when he recalled his mother, his voice took on a childlike tone.

"I'm looking for people who experienced the 'Deportation,' whose memories are still intact" I explained. "I would like to speak with you. Do you think you could help me?"

"You should have come here ten or fifteen years ago! There were many. But back then not a single Turk ever knocked on my door. You are the first. But you're late. Everyone has since passed away. We're about the only ones left. I'll have to do some thinking, some asking around. Come back around six o'clock."

I took some more photographs from his balcony. I then thanked him and departed.

When I returned five hours later the house was full of people.

Ohan Özant welcomed me and said, "We've found some of the living history you were seeking. This is Vahram Karabent. He's ninety-three years old!"

At Ohan's description of him as "living history" Vahram Karabent laughed a great deal… He was like a giant plane tree, full of grandeur and still in possession of his strength.

"Please forgive me," Ohan said, "I sent you away hungry at lunch! It's the loneliness and old age. I wasn't able to make the proper preparations. My

Ohan Özant, Amasya

daughter has prepared some food. Please, let's eat supper first. After that we can speak as long as we wish."

During dinner, Vahram Karabent spoke very little. I had the impression that he was observing me, checking me out. Ohan Özant spoke like an old acquaintance, trying to prod Vahram Karabent to speak, trying to get him to loosen his tongue.

After we finished dinner we moved to the salon. Coffee was brought. Vahram Karabent was seated in the main corner of the salon. Ohan Özant sat next to him. His daughters and grandchildren sat before us. They listened to the conversation attentively and respectfully.

Ohan Özant from Amasya

"My name is Ohan Özant" he began, opening the floodgates of his memory. "I was born in 1915. I was still in swaddling clothes at the time of the Deportation." He stood and paced before us. As we followed his movements, the apartment was deadly still. The world had stopped on its axis and was looking us in the face.

While I was still in diapers we went as far as Kangal, in Sivas Province. In Kangal, an individual called 'Kangallı Asim' received us respectfully. He had built carriages together with my uncle. We remained in Kangal for three years.

When the fires of the Deportations finally burnt themselves out, we returned to Amasya. My aunt's husband, Elikesik Mikail Ağa had become a Muslim during the Deportations because he was an artisan. They didn't send him away. In fact, he did good business in Amasya. He took us under his protection.

I never saw my father again. His name was Dikran. He came from Vezirköprü. My mother's name was Hayganush. My mother's side came from Eğin, a district of Sivas Province.

I had two names. One was 'Ohan' or 'Ohannes,' the other 'İhsan.' Our neighbor Hasan Kaynar gave me the name İhsan. It was the name of his eldest son.

My uncle had been an attorney in Amasya. He had an office there. He did really good business there. He owned a great deal of property and possessions in Vezirköprü. He even owned a *han* (commercial center) in Havza called 'Suluhan,' and two plots of land. My father finished the lycée—they called it a 'Sultaniye' back then—and then became a manufacturer in Amasya. His wealth was well-established.

According to what my mother used to say, her father came from Eğin to Amasya and found work there. He eventually became established.

After marrying and setting up a household, he wanted to bring the rest of his family from Eğin to Amasya.

On the day he came to Eğin to get his family there was an attack and looting of the Armenian community there that lasted for a whole hour. Even as the looting was going on, an order came from Istanbul: *Başı beylik, malı yağma* ("The lives belong to the ruler, the property to the looters')—In other words, "Don't kill them, but you can take their property!"

My maternal grandfather was born, according to the Islamic hijrî dating, in the year 1308 (1893?). My mother was still a child. She never had a daughter to be married. The massacre in Eğin happened twenty years before the 1915 Deportations, in 1895."

Vahram Karabent then spoke up:

When there was the attack against the Armenians in Eğin, there were similar events also in Merzifon, where we lived. It was on a Friday... Before the disturbances they went through and marked the houses.

'The Armenians have armed themselves! They're going to attack the mosque!' they would say to incite the people, 'What are you waiting for?' With that the blood began to flow in the marketplace of Merzifon... The massacre lasted for a full hour... Those Armenians who had shops in the bazaar were killed and their goods were looted. My mother was only two years old at the time. Add it up: my mother was only twenty years old when he died. When she died she was in her ninetieth year. That means that the massacre of Armenians in Merzifon happened already in the 1890s....

Ohan Özant then continued his account where he had left off:

They killed my grandfather in the Eğin massacre. As soon as the situation calmed down my grandmother took her two daughters and came straight to Amasya and moved into the house that my grandfather had purchased there. She worked hard to make a living from the business that he had established.

His oldest daughter—my aunt—was already fully grown by then. She gave her to Elikesik Mikail. Elikesik Mikail was a very well-to-do man. He took my mother and grandmother under his protection.

A short while later, my mother and father got married. Elikesik Mikail Ağa arranged and paid for the wedding.

During the general mobilization, they took my father into the military. Then I was born. Then it was 1915. My father was a corporal in the army, but even so, they also subjected him to deportation. He left and that was the last we ever saw of him. He never came back!

Afterward, my mother searched for years for some trace of my father. She even submitted a request to the army saying, 'My husband died in Erzurum while in the army. Give me his salary!' They gave her this reply. Here, have a look:

'Your husband passed away of natural causes in Derbent Bağları in (the province of) Amasya during deportation. You may not receive the (widows and) orphans' pension.'

In fact, he was actually killed in the mountain pass known as 'Derbent Bağları.'

Ohan Özant's recollections reminded Vahram Karabent of an important event. "Such a calamity also came upon me," he said, and began to tell his tale:

I was on very good terms with the officers, civilian officials and such in Merzifon. We used to go hunting together. It would have been the year 1965.... One day, we went to hunt in the Amasya Pass in a pickup truck. There were four civilians: two teachers, Hasan and Hüseyin Beys... an old official from the Public Registration Office... and myself. All the others were army officers. Recai Bey, the official from the PRO sat in front of me, just like you are, in the bed of the truck. I was holding a really good double-barrel shotgun. When we came to the pass that you called Derbent Bogazları he said to me:

'You see that valley? That one there?'

'Yes,' I told him. 'What about it? What's there?'

'In that valley you're looking at we slaughtered some four or five hundred infidels!'

Suddenly, I knew exactly what he was talking about. My nerves were on edge, and my entire body began to tremble. I grabbed the gun that was in my lap and pressed it against his chest:

'Among those you slaughtered were my sisters, my aunts and uncles, my grandfather and other relatives, you murderer!'

The others didn't give me a chance to act. Hasan Bey, the teacher, quickly pushed the gun barrel away. If he hadn't, as God is my witness, I would have shot him. No, they didn't give me the chance, but I began to say whatever came into my mouth. I didn't spare him or his commanders.

That pretty much spoiled the mood of the whole hunting party. We all fell silent and the mood became chilly.

As soon as those in the driver's compartment saw us they pulled over. The captain quickly hopped out of the truck and asked, 'What's up? Why the grim faces?'

I explained to him what happened. He was furious with the PRO official and publicly disgraced him.

'Yes, these things actually happened! The government of the time was very weak. One blow led to another. One killing led to another. The Armenians were blamed for it and bore the brunt of the violence!'

And in this way, one utterance led to another. One memory spurred the recollection of another. As Vahram Karabent now paused to take a breath, Ohan Özant again commenced to open and recite, one by one, the remaining pages of his life and personality:

> I grew up without a father. Elikesik Mikail Ağa took the place of my father, however. I don't recall those days so well, but I have some recollections—if I haven't just imagined them.
>
> We were very cramped there at Elikesik Mikail's house. He had four sons and one daughter. He loved me and treated me like his own son, though. We ate very well, God rest his soul! May he rest in peace!
>
> Elikesik Mikail Ağa had much property. He had almost one hundred silos. When harvest time came, the merchants would buy barley, wheat, oats, rye and corn and fill up the silos. Then, when the time came they would sell them.
>
> Elikesik Mikail Ağa would sell these silos for what was in the money of that day about three thousand lira. He bought his own share for his two oldest boys. Because the other two sons were still too young, the state would confiscate their share. It was during all this time of buying and selling that Elikesik Mikail Ağa died. I don't remember his death or even his malady that well, but I can remember the years after his death.
>
> We were living in Samsun when the Greeks were subjected to the (1924) population exchange. I remember those days well, because Elikesik Mikail Ağa's third son, whose name was Akil, went to Greece with his Greek friend. We had been traveling around. When we came back to the house we found a note that read:
>
>> *Mother, please don't be worried. I went to Greece with my friend. I'm in Greece.*
>
> After that, my aunt said, 'Let's go and be with my children.' But we weren't able to leave. A while later, Mikail Ağa's two younger children went to France. My aunt, my mother and I were left all alone.
>
> My mother said, 'Let's go live with your uncle. He'll protect us and watch out for us.' So we went to Amasya. The Ottoman Empire had been defeated in the World War. The French, the Greeks, the Italians and the British all occupied various parts of Turkey. The British came

to Amasya. They hung their flags from the Government Mansion. We were living in Amasya in those years. Mustafa Kemal was active then. The country was at war.

When the British came to Amasya they made an announcement that 'Those Armenians who had married Turks and thereby remained in Amasya should, if they weren't happy, come and get divorced. These people will be sent to England and America. Those who had had property and possessions before 1915 should petition for it. We will ensure that their property is returned.'

My mother went and petitioned the British. With their help she got back twenty *donums* of land, two vineyards and the locations of our four shops which had burned down in the great fire that broke out in Amasya in 1915, the year that I was born.

My mother later sold one of the four locations which had fallen to her share of the one hundred and fifty donums of land in the village, so that we could get by. My uncle was a simple *simit** seller. He was impoverished.

With the money that she received for the property, my mother purchased a 1925 model Ford taxi with wooden wheels. She hired a driver and put him to work. She made good money, too. But one day the driver was caught smuggling *raki*.† The Tobacco Regime Administration of the time confiscated our taxi. We couldn't get it back. But we had acquired a taste for taxi work, so my mother purchased another one. It ran unceasingly for five or six months, but the driver ran off with this one, too. At that time there wasn't a lot of traffic on the roads like there is now. They called the neighboring provinces and appealed to the gendarmerie, but no luck: they couldn't locate it. We were very upset. I was nineteen years old at the time.

In 1923 I went to the Armenian church school for about three months. One day they came and destroyed both the church and the school. We were left without any school. Our teacher explained to us what had happened: in those days, there was a man by the name of Hakki Paşa whose word was law in Amasya. He came late the previous evening and ordered the sturdiest wall of the church destroyed. Afterward, he issued a ruling, saying, 'There's a danger of collapse. It's dangerous. The building must be torn down!' So with this decision, they

---

* A sesame bread ring ubiquitous in Turkey.

† "Arak," an anise-flavored alcoholic beverage popular throughout the Mediterranean.

leveled our completely sound church and school right before our eyes. Then they threw us out.

After the Armenian school was destroyed I went to the Turkish school. I wasn't able to learn to read and write Armenian there. I learned Armenian by listening.

Time passed, but when I was in the second grade I had to leave school because we were having difficulties getting by. I was apprenticed to a cobbler. Over time I became a journeyman. Then I went to the army. When I got back from the army I met my wife. It was fate. We got married.

The state confiscated the property of those Armenians who had been deported. My uncle's two-hundred-and-fifty donums of land came to light later when the people from the cadastral survey came to the village. Although he struggled hard, we weren't able to get even an inch of it back. Instead they gave it to the deportees who came from Greece.

My mother managed to salvage her own property with the help of the British. When we sold it and bought something else we ended up owning one-hundred-and-fifty donums in the Kanalköprü district of Amasya. We had a vineyard on the banks of the Yeşilırmak river. We gave it over to a farm manager. He was hungry and ambitious. In 1948 the state built an irrigation canal. That brought water to the district where our land was. It's value went up. Each donum was worth a gold lira.

We got by for forty years renting it out to the manager. The manager got on with the Turks as if they were his brothers. They still call me to come to Amasya. When they see me they say, 'Brother, why don't you come and eat some of our bland soup?'

One after the other, the Armenians in Amasya all migrated to Istanbul or abroad. Eventually, no one was left in Amasya but us. At that point, we too sold our goods and property and came to Istanbul. With the money we got from the sale of the land we purchased a shop in Feriköy and lived on the income we got from it.

I've got two sons and two daughters. They're all married. I've got two grandchildren. They're also married. And with that we've come to the present. My wife died from a heart attack. I'm now eighty-three years old. I often think back on my life. What have I learned?

Here I've given a short account of my life. I came into the world amid fire, destruction, disaster and death. I was rescued from death by Asim from Kangal, may God bless him! I owe him my life!

I'd like to say a few things to people, be they Greeks, Armenians, Turks, or Jews—to all people! I've though about this all my life. I've taught it to my children and grandchildren: Don't think yourself better than others. Be humble and you will be loved.

Muslims: don't discriminate against non-Muslims. If there's real love and affection between us, if we behave toward one another like brothers, if we look at each other as equals, things will turn out better.

I've got a few words for the Turks—especially for those who attempt to discriminate against others. Don't discriminate against others because of their religion. Turkey belongs to all of us. Don't destroy Turkey! My childhood was passed in poverty, fear and unhappiness. We had to struggle hard to get by, we earned our living by the sweat of our brows. We earned everything we got. We managed to get ourselves a little rest and prosperity. I want to end my life peacefully. Don't disrupt our tranquility!

Well, that's all from me. Vahram has lived longer and seen more than I have. He's ten years older than I. He's ninety-three years old. Together, we've lived one hundred and ninety-three years. He's told us a lot in the past. Listen to him now and let him tell you about his life.

With that, Ohan Özant finished speaking. We all turned toward Vahram Karabent. The things he told us seemed like a great epic, but his stories were of the true events that he himself had experienced.

Vahram Karabent appeared strong and healthy for his age. His eyes were clear and bright, his face radiant. He spoke very slowly and thoughtfully, carefully choosing his words. His mind and his memory were amazingly sharp.

"Can you take my picture?" he asked and smiled.

"Write down my name, take my picture! Has the world ever been saved by being afraid? I'm here now, but I might not be here tomorrow. What do I have left that can be taken away? What do you get by remaining silent?"

Those in the room now shifted in their seats and made themselves comfortable. The younger people drew a little closer to him. They opened their eyes, their ears and their minds and began to listen....

Vahram Karabent of Merzifon

I'm Vahram Karabent. I don't exactly know my date-of-birth, but I'm ninety-three years old now. I was born in Merzifon in 1905. I was born

Vahram Karabent of Merzifon

and raised in Merzifon. My mother and father were also inhabitants of Merzifon.

I was ten years old at the time of the Deportation. I remember it very well. I can still see those awful days before my eyes as if it were today. The shouting of the people, their wailing all still echo in my ears.

The first thing they did was to go house to house gathering up all the prominent Armenians, all the males and all those who were educated. First it was the attorneys, the merchants... Those who had heard something in advance, those who perceived what was happening: they disappeared or hid. 'Those who become Muslims will remain here!' they announced. Some of the people did convert right there and they remained. In particular, the artisans and master craftsmen who could be of benefit were left behind.

My father had five brothers. They brought six males from one household. My grandfather, my father and four of his brothers... my four uncles... They made them sound off, then plucked them out and marched them off. Where to? Why? We didn't know.... Not a single one of those who left came back.... My father and mother were twenty-five years old when they took my father away. She was left a widow...

Then they gathered up the women, the young girls, the new brides and the widows who were left behind and marched them off. On the way, the young brides, the girls and the women whom they fancied were taken away to a field. They killed the men. The children were left behind in the town square. Those of substance took home the children they liked and raised them like their own.

So there were many children who remained behind and survived. When the whole calamity finally came to an end, the British and Americans came. They gathered up the orphaned children. Those who were in Merzifon they put under their protection in Merzifon College. Afterward they took them somewhere else.

They found my uncle's daughter safe and sound. They took her too. When they separated them, she was sent to America. She grew up there. She married an Armenian who, like her, had come from Anatolia and was rescued from death. Years later they sought us out and found us. In 1980, I went to America and met with her. She told me of all the things that happened to them. I heard from her about all the calamities that befell them on the way.

My uncle had two sons and two daughters. One of the girls survived; 'My brothers died of thirst!' she told me sobbingly.

The government issued a decree: they were to be loaded onto ox- and horse-drawn carts. Whole families, women and children were taken...

Some of them would kill the men somewhere along the way... those who wanted, took the women and girls off somewhere else.... In this state, broken and beaten down, they marched all the way to the Syrian desert....

Only I, my mother and my brother survived. My grandfather, my father and four of my uncles perished.... Oh, Lord! So much separation... so much forced separation!

O.K., I've told you that already... Now, where was I? At that time the Sultan was still the ruler. The Sultan issued an imperial decree saying, 'Those who become Muslims will remain!' Whether you were Armenian or Greek Orthodox, if you were willing to change your religion and become a Muslim, you would be saved. Those who refused to do so were rounded up and moved.... The government encouraged artisans and tradesmen who had necessary skills to adopt Islam and be saved. There were those who were saved in that way.

We survived because of my grandmother. We changed our religion and survived. My father, my grandfather, my brothers and my uncles refused to convert to Islam. 'If you don't convert you'll die!' they told them.

Before the Deportation there were some three hundred Armenian households in Merzifon. Add it up: at five persons per household, that's fifteen hundred people!

The Armenians were gathered together and marched off. All of Merzifon was full of the fear of death; the entire area was awash with shouting and wailing....

Our Turkish neighbors were also gripped with fear. They were afraid to give us any assistance and said, 'It'll bring disaster upon us. Please, don't get us into trouble!'

The fear of death settled over every place. The penalty for protecting or hiding Armenians was death!

Despite this, there were here and there some upright decent Turks who helped to greater or lesser degrees. Some tried to encourage us saying, 'Don't be afraid! Nothing's going to happen. Go into your houses and lock your doors!'

The Greeks who lived in Merzifon and the surrounding area saw what was happening and understood our situation. There was nothing hidden or secret about it. The Armenians were being sent off to their deaths right before their eyes. But no one could do a thing to help. The Greeks didn't offer any help—they couldn't! They didn't get involved at all, because the penalty for protecting or hiding an Armenian who was to be sent off was death. Turks or Greeks, it didn't matter. People followed the old saying, 'As long as it doesn't bite me, I don't care if the snake lives for a thousand years!' and looked after their own skin.

I remember it well. It was after the days of the Deportation, when all the men were taken away from their homes and gathered together to be taken away. It was a day of great confusion. I saw it as a child. I was very small, but I remember everything. I could see and understand everything that was going on. We became Muslims and were saved from the Deportation. But our fear remained. There was still fear... lots of fear. I don't know if it was because I was still a child or if it was because of the great fear that I felt all around me, but there have only been one or two other times in my life that I've been as afraid as that.

What was the weather like on the day they took my father, grandfather and uncles away? What season was it? I can't remember. But I can still clearly see in my mind like it was yesterday, the way they tore my father from my mother's arms. I still see it in my dreams. I'm more than ninety now, but I still dream about those days.

After my father and his relatives went, we became Muslims, but what was a Muslim child supposed to act like? I had gone to church until that time. I tried to understand it with my child's mind. It seemed to me that my father, my grandfather, my maternal and paternal uncles all got deported because we had become Muslims. I was angry at myself, ashamed of myself, and when I'd hear the Muslim call to prayer I'd take out my cross and expected that my father would suddenly show up.

A child couldn't understand these things. My mother had been left alone at a young age. There were some good people around, upright Turks and Muslims, but lots of lowly dogs, as well. I guarded our door closely, no one could get close to my mother. I also protected my little brother and did what a big brother is supposed to do for him.

It was during those days that the report came: 'Women! We're going to take you where your deported husbands are. Get ready!'

We had Turkish neighbors with whom we got on well and spoke regularly. When they saw us getting prepared they asked: 'What on earth are you doing? What's all this preparation for?'

'Such-and-such news report arrived. We are selling our possessions and going to our husbands' the women said.

'Wise up! Don't just pick up and go without stopping and thinking. In fact, you shouldn't even take a step out of your door—Don't even let yourself be seen around! If you go, you're done for! Those that leave don't return!'

Somehow, we had been taken in. People who are in straits grasp for any stray hope they find.... God bless them for warning us! If our

Turkish neighbors hadn't warned us, we would have been led off to some place from which we never would have returned!

"That's how it was in Amasya, too" Ohan Özant interjected at that point. "My neighbor, Hasan Kaynar, the one who gave me my Turkish name, he was a respectable individual who did a lot to protect the Armenians. He even saved some members of my family. He himself was a Turk. 'Don't believe the announcements promising that they'll send you to your husbands. Don't be ignorant! You can't go to where your husbands are. Don't even come outside! Hide yourselves as well as you can! Otherwise, you'll go thinking you're going to see your husbands, but the place they take you isn't one from which you can return!'"

Vahram Karabent asked for a glass of water. His soul refreshed, he let out a deep "Ahhh." "What was I saying?" he said, ready to begin again, "Where were we?" Then, he began again:

The Deportation period lasted for an entire year. Some died, others went away. Only later some of them came back. They told of the things that had happened to them. Compared to what they had suffered, our hardships had been nothing! How can people—fathers, mothers, children, women, girls, men—how can they endure such suffering, such oppression, such fear? It's unbelievable what happened.... but it's true....

Not everyone who was deported was taken to the same place.... not everybody suffered the same fate.... Everyone suffered greatly, but they suffered different things, in different ways... The person who was of strong constitution remained healthy, the weak ones perished! Those who didn't die survived. Some passed away, others didn't. If those who passed away had a brother, father or mother, the surviving family members felt much more of a need to carry on and survive.

I was only a child at the time, but even now, if I was asked, I could show you all the places where there were Armenian quarters in Merzifon, and the places where Armenian houses were. I could even draw you a map.

The houses that were left without owners were looted by the local Turkish population. Some carried off the possessions they found in the houses, others even jimmied the doors or windows and carried them off. We couldn't say a thing. What I mean is that it just wasn't possible. Who would you complain to? We used to play in the empty, ruined structures.

A little while later, the Muslim deportees from the population exchange with Greece arrived. Atatürk gave them the lands and houses of the Armenians.

Our church and school lasted a couple of years after the Deportation. But those who looted the houses had, for some reason, left the church and the school untouched.

Those who survived the Deportation eventually returned; along with those who had converted to Islam and remained behind; they began to rebuild their lives again.

Of all the Armenian property and possessions it was said 'It's subject to the Deportation [Law]' and confiscated. Then it was turned over to the state treasury. Their property was gone for good.

We grew up as orphans. I remember my father and my grandfather very well. They were very well-to-do men.

My grandfather's father had come from Persia. He purchased a very fruitful farm of 3,200 donums that was located between Merzifon and Amasya. They wouldn't even have given us back a spoonful of dirt from this farm, even if our lives depended on it! That's a long story. I should tell it afterward.

Where were we? Oh yes... Some died, some returned, and we who survived began to rebuild our lives. We had lost everything. We were forced to start from scratch.

I already said this. We saved our lives by changing our religion from Christianity to Islam. But I didn't understand then if this meant being saved or being ruined. This sense of resentment and regret never left me. Because my father and my grandfather didn't change their religion or faith they disappeared—died, even. We—my mother, my brother and I—did change our religion so that we would live.

You can't know what 'conversion' and being a convert really means, the incomprehensible bitterness and difficulty of it that lasts as long as you live. It's just as bad if you actually believe the new faith or if you don't!

The people in Merzifon, our Turkish neighbors, knew that we were converts. It's difficult being a convert. The average Muslim doesn't observe all the requirements of his religion, but they expect the convert to observe all of the injunctions to a tee. They follow you around, they monitor your behavior.

We were free to do what we wanted when we were at home, but outside the home, we had to be very careful. When it was Ramazan, we had to get up for the pre-dawn meal, light lights and act like we were observing the fast. Afterward, we would pull out our crosses and say our own prayers.

We were obliged to do this until 1918. After that, the Ottoman State had been defeated in the World War. Those who wished could revert to their former religion. They even reopend some churches.

The calamity didn't spare the Greeks, either...

Even as they were saying that things would be getting back to normal, the war began again. This time they began to attack the Greeks and subject them to things similar to what had been done to us. Ultimately, the calamity that had befallen us also befell the Greeks some five years later.

Here, take a look at the scar on my arm! Do you know where and how I received this wound? I'll tell you!

The year was 1920. I was fifteen years old. The calamity that had come upon the Armenians had passed, they said, but now Topal Osman's gangs of brigands made their appearance in the regions around the Black Sea. They struck against the Greeks and murdered them.

I remember it exactly how it happened. It was a Saturday. The Topal Osman gang came to Merzifon with the intention of carrying out a raid against the Greeks. But there weren't that many Greeks left in Merzifon. And those who were there weren't rich.

At that time, some of the looters who were already in Merzifon incited Topal Osman's men against the Armenians, some of whom had become Muslims. They wanted, by means of Topal Osman's gang, to wipe out all the Armenians, both those who had remained Christian and those who had converted to Islam. What they were really after was their property.

So at this urging, Topal Osman's men began to attack the houses of the Armenians. A deathly fear gripped the Armenian quarter. What could we do? Whom could we go to?

My aunt's husband, Nuri Bey, had been a postal worker in Amasya. Three months before he had been transferred to Merzifon. We set him and his family up in one of the abandoned Armenian houses. When all this was happening my mother remembered Nuri Bey. We felt sure of him because he was a government official.

Terrified and cowering the whole way, my mother, her mother, my little brother and I went to the house of our relative Nuri Bey. His wife didn't want to take us in, saying, 'They'll carry me off because of you!' Even though she was very afraid, she eventually opened the door and allowed us to come in. But we were clearly unwelcome. We couldn't stay.

Evening came and Nuri Bey came home after having finished his shift. When he arrived he was shaking with fright. 'The whole world's ablaze!' he said, frantically pacing, 'Merzifon is burning! Merzifon is burning!'

Then Nuri Bey's wife said, 'Get going! We're going to experience a disaster because of you!' Our daughter slapped her on the mouth, and said, 'You're an Armenian, too, aren't you? Aren't you the daughter of Armenians? How can you say 'Get going!' to your own relatives?'

She was stuck to the core. Fear sometimes makes people forget their own relatives, even their parents and siblings. My late mother then said, 'This is God's will. Let's go and leave here. What shall be, shall be!'

With that, we left… but there was nowhere we could go other than back to our house! We arrived back home and tried to think about where we could go. If only we could get to Amasya, we thought, we could go to our relatives there! At the time that my father and his family was deported, he made a belt of gold to wear secretly under our clothes with the intention of bringing it along with them. In the end, they couldn't take it with them. My mother now took it from the place where it was hidden. She wrapped it around my waist. She explained to me very precisely how I should behave with it. She encouraged me.

'Come on, let's hope for the best!' she said as we left the house. I was the oldest male in the house, so I walked ahead of them some twenty or thirty meters. I acted as a scout for my mother, grandmother, and little brother, having a look around before they got there. When we reached the back of the school, we immediately came to a crossroads at the bottom of the street; there my way was blocked by two gang members and the Laz[*] who was a neighborhood watchman. I was seized by Topal Osman's men.

'So, boy, are you a Turk or an infidel?' they demanded.

'I'm Turkish! I'm a Muslim!' I protested.

The watchman then spoke up: 'That son-of-a-whore is an infidel's child! How long have you been a Turk?' he demanded, and then gave me two hard slaps to the face.

'Seize him! I know this one. He's an infidel offspring!'

---

[*] A people who live in the northeastern part of Turkey and speak a language similar to Georgian. They have traditionally had a reputation as being warlike and hot-tempered.

One of the brigands took out his bayonet and was going to kill me. I raised my arm to block the blow, and his knife went straight into my arm. While I was struggling to save myself, the gold belt around my waist came undone. Somehow it got wrapped around the brigand's hand. They took it.

'Stop all that!' the leader said, 'He's getting away! Go catch him and kill him!'

I had escaped with my life and fled… but the brigand had wounded me badly on the arm. It was bleeding badly. But I managed to evade them and make it home. My mother and relatives had also fled to our house when they saw what was happening to me. My mother was waiting for me at the door, full of worry. She quickly brought me inside.

I began to cry: 'Our gold is gone! They took our gold!'

'Shush! Don't cry!' she said, 'Let it go! We've got another sack full!'

She bandaged the wound on my arm. But the scar from the wound still remains. That's my souvenir from those days!

We passed the evening in the house. By now we'd given up on the idea of going to Amasya—or anywhere, for that matter! The roads were all controlled by the brigands, even the Armenian quarter was surrounded.

The next day our neighbor Hermine saw us. She took us in. Her daughter, who was a seamstress, was sewing a shirt or something for one of the brigands… That evening, when he came to pick up the shirt he saw us: 'If you're still here this evening, they'll destroy you! Come, let me take you some place safe!' he said. We were helpless. We trusted him. He was one of the good ones, apparently. He did us no evil. He brought us to a Greek school. The school was actually a little house. We looked inside and saw that there were already some fifty or sixty women and children waiting together inside the house.

'At least we're all together' we said. 'It's safer here that way!'

While we waited there, fearing for what might come, two gang members arrived. They held a headscarf-sized cloth in their hands and announced:

'Whoever has money on them, take it out and put it here! No one better try to hide it from us! After this we're going to search the place, and if we find money on anyone, we're going to kill them!'

My mother took the gold she had on her and threw it on the cloth. But Ohannes' aged mother said: 'You poor girl! Do you think they'll spare us just because you gave them gold?'

My mother was a brave woman. She implored the brigands, saying, 'My son, you've taken everything we had on us. Look upon these children: they're hungry, destitute and in miserable shape! Leave us be and let us go home! In such a time, a person forgives and worries himself with his property. He doesn't feel hunger or fear! Not a thing!... He's become rich!'

The brigands took the money and the gold and left. It was time for the evening prayer. The gang members who were watching us began to give orders: 'Get down!' So we did. 'Form two lines!' So we did. 'Let's see how you march!' And so we walked.

We passed the Armenian church and walked straight toward the big French school... When we finally entered, we saw that it held maybe two hundred children, and men and women of all ages. Everyone they found, they brought here....

Now and then they came and threatened us: 'We'll leave those alone who give money! Those who have money in their houses, let them show us where!'

As if the houses were bursting with money... But the people would be deceived; they'd go and not return. The brigands would take the money and then kill them...

The next morning, they set the school on fire all around us. We were burning!... Even the floor became too hot to stand on.... We'd stand on one foot at a time, and then switch feet. I straddled the window sill, one foot inside the building, one foot outside, like I was riding a horse.

I wanted to jump out and flee, but my mother grabbed me.

'Where are you going to run to, if you jump?' she said, 'Where will you go? They've surrounded the place. There are soldiers and civilians patrolling with guns and bayonets everywhere. They're going to watch us burn!'

There are some storms that are so strong that they pull trees out by their roots! The fire spread. It spread quickly over the entire Armenian quarter.

And then, exactly at that time, the government doctor Ahmet Efendi—God bless him!—came running, his hat in his hand, shouting at everyone he saw on the street: 'What sort of unconscionable act is this?! What sort of ungodliness is this?! In what scripture is it written that you should burn people alive?! Isn't this cruel barbarism?! Leave these people be!'

The armed brigands who were posted before the door of the French school yielded and he passed between them. Then he opened the door...

As soon as the door was opened, the people, abandoning their possessions where they were, clawed at each other in their attempt to get out any way they could, even hurling themselves out of doors and windows....

It wasn't more than five minutes after we had gotten out that the entire, huge edifice collapsed. If Ahmet Efendi had not come and we had remained inside for five more minutes, we would have all burned to death. God, in His mercy, had intervened!

They took us from there to the barracks. We slept there for two nights. They gathered up all of the bodies of those who had died.

But in the meantime, the wealthiest quarter of Merzifon, with its beautiful wooden houses, had been turned into a raging inferno and reduced entirely to ashes. The entire Armenian quarter as far as the *hamam* (public bathhouse) was destroyed. Our house had been below the hamam. The hamam had blocked the fire. That was the only thing that kept our house from going up in smoke too.

One week after the gangs had withdrawn they returned again to our house.

How many people had these bands of brigands killed or wounded? I don't know. In those days there wasn't any government presence that would protect people or put out fires, or even keep track of the dead and wounded.

When they came back to our house one week later, the door of our house was opened up wide like the door to a *han*. Because whatever they found in a house they took—even the toilet brush—and carted it off.

They didn't leave a thing in our house. Afterward, we borrowed a broom from our neighbors and cleaned up all the garbage they left in the house. That's the condition they left our house in.

We had had one cabinet in the basement. They had wanted to take that, too, but they couldn't get it though the door.

When human being sink so low, when they are overcome with rancor, they become no better than monsters. Dogs don't bite other dogs, serpents won't bite other serpents, but human beings can find reasons to eat each other or burn each other alive. They'll drink the blood of the neighbors who they've been friendly to for forty years! When people are overcome with anger, nothing can stop them, not God, not morality…

But we survived those days. God bless Ahmet Efendi! It was because of him that we escaped death.

But life goes on… That's how it is with people… Food, drink. Some die, others don't. My mother remained a widow for twenty-five years. From the time I was ten years old I grew up without a father, amid all sorts of hardships and disasters. We didn't have a cent to our names, no possessions or property. They didn't give us back one inch of my grandfather's 3,200-donum farm.

My mother, who didn't have any education or know anything about the outside world, went to work in a carpet weaving shop. She began to weave *kilims** day and night. From the time I was thirteen or fourteen I began to work, too, to try and help us get by.

During that time they started to deport the Greeks. After the raids and attacks by Topal Osman's gangs, the Greeks who lived in the area began to disappear.

The expulsion of the Greeks wasn't exactly like the Armenian Deportation, but still, expulsion is expulsion. May no one ever have to go through it! We couldn't do a thing to help the Greeks. We had no means with which to do anything for them. And we were scared. We were hopeless and alone. It was like the whole world was against us.

There were a lot of Greeks in the region of Amasya, in Samsun and on the Black Sea coast. And the Greeks didn't submit meekly like the Armenians had. They also formed armed bands. They armed themselves and fled to the mountains. They defended themselves up there. If they hadn't taken up arms to defend themselves, not a single one of them would have survived. It wasn't like in 1915. The Greeks were strong. They fought.

Some of the Greeks died, others were killed. Those who had caïques or boats fled to Russia. Others fled to Greece or were sent there.

But the enormity of the disaster that befell the Armenians can't be compared to that of the Greeks. Only a very few of the Armenians managed to survive... no more than one or two from any family or line. But those things that happened to the Greeks can still be seen as comparable in some ways to the calamity that befell the Armenians. During their darks days, most Greek families or lines lost one or two members.

Despite everything, we survived...

What was I saying? Oh yes, the pain of relocation was great...

In the year 1927, I managed to get a travel document so that I could go to Samsun. In those days Armenians weren't allowed to travel freely from place to place.

I found work in Samsun. I worked for three years in a blacksmith's shop that belonged to a carpenter who employed ninety-five people. At the end of that three year period there were only thirteen of us left who

---

* The traditional Turkish throw-rug.

hadn't been weeded out. They gave me compliments, saying, 'You've worked here for three years, and we haven't seen any bad work, yet!'

Two days after I returned from Samsun, my grandmother died.

I returned to Samsun, where I learned carpentry. I opened my own carpentry workshop in 1931. My mother remained alone. There's a little district of Merzifon called Hacıköy. I married an Armenian girl from a village there. That was in 1932. Twenty days after we were married I paid the *bedel** and entered the military. I served for six months.

I told you that my grandfather had had a 3,200-donum farm. After the Deportation some four or five people from Merzifon took it for themselves. I knew the people who took our property. The ones who absconded with it were prominent, wealthy persons and *ağa*s.† The state only gave 250 donums of it to the Muslims who arrived from Greece.

I began to make efforts to get back my grandfather's property. I spent all my earnings on attorneys. I went to the Land Registry Office and looked up the documents. The Land Registry officials had, through some sort of trickery, split up a part of my grandfather's land among themselves.

We still had the vineyard. I had to buy back our own property from the man who had taken hold of it. But, in the end, I understood that this was a process that had no end. I gave up on the attorneys and the courts. Our property had become the property of whoever had cast eyes upon it...

Some of those who had taken our property came to grief, others were deported. Ill-gotten gains always bring misfortune. I approached one of these persons and said, 'Look, you took our property. You know it and I know it. There are two other persons, and they've both been deported. God preserved me for this. I will die after having seen them be deported!'

There was nothing left of my parents' property and possessions. Everything I had, had been earned with the sweat of my brow. Thank God, I had never received anything I didn't deserve!

We had gotten back on our feet somewhat, and we had children. They took me back into mandatory conscription in 1938. 'No matter

---

* The *bedel-i askeriye* was a military exemption fee, traditionally reserved for the non-Muslim minorities and wealthier Turks. This tax gave the payer either a complete exemption from or a reduction of their period of military conscription.

† Literally "lord' or "master," it traditionally refers to large landowners or provincial notables.

how hard, we'll get through it,' I said. First they sent me to training camp in Balıkesir, after that, to Amasya. There was bread rationing.

That was during İnönü's time. The mandatory conscription ended. Just when I thought I would be able to go back to my work and my civilian life, another disaster was visited upon us. The Capital Tax Law came out in 1942. The law applied to everyone with any means. But it was only imposed on the Armenians, Greeks, Jews and Dönmes*—all the non-Muslims. The Capital Tax people came for their property even while they were serving in the army. Whereas they might tell an Armenian to pay five hundred lira, his Muslim neighbor would only be told to pay five *kuruş*.† There was an enormous inequality in the way this tax was imposed. And you had no right to appeal the tax amount that they decided you owed. Those who couldn't pay the tax were sent to Aşkale, near Erzurum.

When the Capital Tax came out, I was doing military service for a second time. The Capital Tax officials wrote to me, too. I had a Turkish friend by the name of Cemal Bey. He was a college graduate and a member of the Municipal Council. He complained, saying, 'You're going to assess us with the Capital Tax, so that we might help them? That's scandalous! A man gets told to pay the Capital Tax while he's serving in the military? Unheard of!'

And it was because of Cemal Bey that I managed to avoid paying the Capital Tax or going to Aşkale. My friend Cemal Bey was a decent man. May he be well!

So we got through the Capital Tax calamity, too. Then I got back to putting my life in order. The only time I've had it easy in my entire life was during the period of the Menderes Government.‡

---

* Literally, "converts," here it refers to the descendants of those Jews who in the late 17th century had followed the messianic pretender Sabbatai Sevi and, like him, converted to Islam while secretly maintaining their own heretical Jewish practices. Although the sect's members largely abandoned it and assimilated into Turkish society in the first half of the 20th century, they are still not fully accepted as true Muslims by many Turks. During the implementation of the Capital Tax, they were assessed a tax rate twice as high as that of other Muslims, while non-Muslims were assessed at up to ten times that of Muslims.

† One hundredth of a lira.

‡ The Democrat Party of Adnan Menderes ruled in Turkey between 1950 and 1960, when it was overthrown by a military coup.

But the Armenians kept leaving, one at a time, to Istanbul, to America, to Canada, to France. In particular it was the young ones who went abroad.

I have one son and three daughters from my first wife. My son and one daughter went to Canada. Nowadays, no matter where you go in the world you can find Armenians. I've even got some cousins in Egypt.

I and my wife remained alone as the last Armenians in Merzifon. Along with those who came from the villages, over time all our old friends and companions disappeared. There was no longer that closeness and trust between people. Even though I didn't really want to, after there was no one else left for me in Merzifon, no neighbors, no acquaintances, I too moved to Istanbul.

As long as there were five or ten Armenian households left in Merzifon, you couldn't have gotten me to come to Istanbul, even if you would have paved the entire way with gold! But being all alone was unbearable. A person feels safer among his own kind… with his wife and friends.

My first wife passed away after we came to Istanbul. I lived alone for two years after that. It was impossible. I remarried, and now I live with my second wife.

I was born in 1905. I'm almost one hundred years old. Now that I've gotten so old, I've started to think back more and more on the old days.

I've lived ninety-three years…. but it's like a dream. I still don't understand anything from this life that I've lived…. What's the point of living after life has lost all its savor.

They often ask me, 'What have you learned from life? What can you tell us?' I say to them, 'Always live together like brothers. Don't think evil of one another!'

I've suffered a lot of hardship and bitterness. I've been so close to death sometimes that I could taste it. Many times I've barely escaped it. There are still those who hate Armenians, who try to divide Muslims and Armenians from one another. They should leave us in peace for a while!

We suffered, but I hope that at least our children won't suffer. There are still those who try to incite people against one another. This is the most crucial thing right now. Many people, because of their ignorance, believe these things. The fact is, God created all of us. Neither the Armenians, nor the Gypsies, the Greeks, or the Jews or anyone else are different. All of humanity is one… When a child is born, he's neither a Christian nor a Muslim. Whatever his parents may be, that's what he'll become. God creates people as one. It's people themselves who make the distinctions. To all those young people, to everyone who asks me, I give the same advice, 'Always love one another! Love is what makes us human!'

After listening to Vahram Karabent and Ohan Özant, I thanked them and left their apartment. It was a hot Istanbul evening. I strolled down to the Bakırköy shore. The sidewalks and streets were spilling over with so many people. I found myself a quiet corner in which to sit down, and I sat there, gazing out into the Sea of Marmara. The moon was out, and its reflection bathed in the glowing waters of Istanbul.

What had I actually heard that day? How could such things actually have happened? What sort of things did the history books say, and what had Vahram Karabent said?... My curiosity had grown as I listened to him and Ohan Özant tell of their lives; I felt a tremendous love and warmth for Meline, who had set me to this task, and for my mother, who had said, "Go and see what you find! If you're in Tokat, send my greetings to the radiant-faced Armenian woman who calmed my headaches!" The sea breeze blew my thoughts and feelings toward Honaz, and toward Meline, who had studied Armenian literature at an Armenian monastery in Venice. I listened for the sound of the breeze on the sparkling, moon glow-drenched water. The tinny-sounding rippling of the waves could not calm my heart.

I managed to reach my mother from the phone booth, and I paid her my respects.

"It was so great that you sent me off to those places. You wouldn't believe the things I've seen, the things I've heard! I'm going back tomorrow. Don't worry, mom!"

After that, I dialed Meline's number in Venice; it felt as if I was ringing her doorbell. She was amazed to hear my voice.

"I was on the road for a whole week," I told her. "Meline, my dear: Except for going to Van and Aghtamar Island, I fulfilled the conditions you set out for me. I'm so glad that you placed these conditions. I'm so glad I've gotten to know you and love you. Without you, I never would have been able to look for and find Zaruhi, or Ani, or Vahram Karabent."

Meline's voice was as bright and sunny as her eyes. But that evening, the smell of seaweed in those underwater passages of Venice infused the adorable melody of her voice.

I repeated Vahram Karabent's last words to me. She was delighted. That made me happy.

"We've got so much to talk about, so much to say to one another. Let's get together as soon as we get back to Germany!"

What Vahram Karabent had said that evening were practically the last words he ever spoke, but it was only a full three months later, in Germany, that I found that out. Ohan Özant's granddaughter Linda informed me of his passing.

His words, "Always love one another. Love is what makes us human!" continued to ring in my ears, to echo in my mind.

May you rest in peace, Vahram Karabent of Merzifon!

Part Three

Meline's World

I saw my own prejudices when I loved you...

Summer vacation had been spent running from one end of Anatolia to the other. I hadn't been able to stay very long in Honaz. I hadn't had the time to make good on the promise to my son that we would go to the sea. He went with his mother and aunt.... We returned to Germany together. I asked for his forgiveness.

"I'll take you to the beach for two weeks next summer!" I vowed.

"Father, you'll just have something else to do!" he replied with some irritation.

Schools in the province of North Rhine-Westphalia began in the middle of August. In teaching, every school year was a new beginning....

The second a person took his first step through the school doors after summer vacation, they caught a whiff of that "school odor." I began the 1998 school year with "scent of school" in my nose, in my brain. The month of August passed with handing out syllabi, distributing books, and the planning of units.

From my house, I called Meline. She wasn't at home. One week later I called again. Still not there. I began to grow concerned. In place of hearing her voice, I received a card from her:

My Dear Kemal,
I know that you're worried. I'm writing to you in order to dispel that worry. I'm doing very well... We are still in Venice. We're going to return at the end of September. Love and kisses!

I called as soon as I received it. During the summer we had spoken to one another about what we'd seen and experienced. The climate in Venice was doing Meline good. Her voice was fresh and animated, like on those evening parties which were livened up by sparkling smiles and laughter. I felt as if I could see her healthy face through the tone of her voice. So much so that I felt no need to even enquire about her health. Such a question would remind her of the grave illness she had experienced. As long as there was no need to do so, we wouldn't ask about each other's health, or remind one another of the illness.

Finally, we decided to meet at her house on the evening of Sunday, the fifteenth of November. After that we would go out to eat.

I was feeling great relief, like a student who had finished his assignment, and anticipation at the prospect of seeing Meline.

On the appointed day, I purchased a bouquet of flowers in colors that Meline loved. I also wrapped the pink printed and embroidered headscarves that I had liked and purchased from the bazaar in Denizli last summer.

My heart was leaping with joy when I knocked on her door.

I had missed her. I hugged Meline warmly and lovingly.... There was no trace of illness to be seen on her. The Meline that I was holding was the Meline from that very first day of the class in Dortmund, the one that I had plucked from her branch and had protectively placed in my heart. My eyes were moist with joy.

She placed the flowers that I had brought into a blue vase that she set on the table, which was covered with a tablecloth that was the handiwork from Buldan.

"Do you know this covering?" she asked, upon seeing my recognition.

"Don't I know the table covering that I brought you?"

For my sake she had covered the table with the cloth from Buldan. What a gracious and tactful person this Meline was! The pink of the flowers complemented the gold-colored narcissus motifs of the tablecloth.

Located tastefully on the wall behind the table were ceramic plates from Kütahya. On the side of the bookshelf hung old black-and-white photographs of Istanbul and Istiklal Caddesi (Independence Avenue).

"Afterward, we'll go to a Chinese restaurant. But first let's sit for a bit," she said. "What would you like to drink? I've got a really nice mint liquor. If you prefer, I can give you some cherry liquor."

"The mint liquor will be fine."

"Welcome, my dear Kemal!"

"Thank you! I'm so happy to see you!"

"Me too!" Meline said, raising her glass. "To Turks and Armenians!"

"As for me, I'm just toasting Meline! I drink to your love!"

I was eager to explain to her the places I'd traveled to and seen this summer, and the people I had found and spoken with. After we imbibed our liquor I began to speak:

"My dear Meline, it's so wonderful that you told me to go and see for myself. I did what you said. Only Van and Aghtamar I wasn't able to visit. I was going to fly from Ankara to Van, but I couldn't find any airplane seats because of all the troop dispatching. I couldn't see going all that way by bus. Please forgive this one shortcoming. I will definitely go and see it in the coming years."

"That's fine. You went to Amasya, to Aşkale, to Kars and to Ani, right?" That's enough already… But tell me all about it at the restaurant. Let's go before we're late."

As we were leaving, I didn't have the heart to step on the Armenian carpet that was laid out in the little hall in the entrance. Before I could tell her once again about my reluctance to step on this carpet, she spoke, as if she had been reading my thoughts:

"Kemal, my dear, the carpet is supposed to get old and worn out. Let it live along with me! Walk on it with a clear conscience, without fear or hesitation!"

Every time I came to visit, this carpet had sung a new song, had told a different tale. It reminded me of all manner of totally different events.

Just like in her own life, in Meline's house everything was in its proper place, everything made sense. Everything was measured…. In Meline's house there was a lamp, large or small, in every corner. They were all continually on. Each lamp had its own function. Some were to illuminate a painting or photograph, others for plates or carpets… but all of the lamps lit up Meline's life. In Meline's world there were no dark corners. If they appeared, she would try and illuminate them the moment that she noticed their presence.

We had reservations at the Chinese restaurant in the Ratingen Market. We sat at a table before the aquarium in which red fish swam. They welcomed us as we sat down. They swam happily in their miniature sea, every other one pressing its lips against the glass of the aquarium and wishing us a good evening.

As always, Meline was dressed simply, tastefully and elegantly. That evening she had selected the color brown. The brown of her blouse complemented her brown eyes.

I ordered the roast Chinese duck with vegetables, Meline ordered vegetarian Chinese food.

"Let's take from one another's plates. Let our food be different, our tastes the same!"

Meanwhile, the fish danced with the bubbles in the aquarium….

The red wine that we ordered arrived before our meals. Meline raised her glass again to Turks and Armenians; I again limited my toast to Meline.

"Now then. Let's hear what you saw and experienced last summer," she said, opening the conversation.

And so I began to recount the evening meal in our garden in Honaz, my siblings' concerns, my elder brother's statement that "This Armenian thing isn't like the Greek issue!" and my mother's judgment "Aren't Armenians also human beings? Don't they have a God? You go, son. And go to Tokat, too! Send my greetings to the old Armenian woman who cured my headaches. May she be blessed!" I told her, in order, of how I found Zaruhi in Amasya, of going to Aşkale, to Kars, to Ani, and about my doubts and fears when traveling from Taşova to Erzurum.

"Meline, my dear, if I hadn't felt you beside me in Erbaa I would have given up on the idea and turned around. You gave me strength and courage. The little Kemal inside me said, 'How will you ever be able to look in Meline's face again?' I saw your face in the darkness. You were smiling, but you didn't say a word. Your silence gave me courage. If not for you, I wouldn't have seen Ani or gone to Aşkale. I couldn't have understood you, I couldn't have knocked on the door of your world. May you be well! It's good that you told me to go and see for myself before speaking. But now, please: you tell a bit…"

We held up our glasses of red wine and toasted Armenians and Turks.

Meline fell silent. I could see that in her mind she had drifted back to some distant place in her memory. Wherever they were, the fish in the aquarium stopped moving and were all swimming in place, as if they too were waiting for Meline to speak….

She finally spoke, saying, "Where should I start?" and with that she opened the door to the world that made Meline who she was….

> My mother was from Sivas. My father was from Kangal. He was a wagon driver…. During the time of that great disaster, an Alevî family protected my father.
>
> My mother was married in Sivas when she was fourteen years old. She had a daughter and a son. The evening my brother was born they took away her first husband. That's the way it went! At eighteen years old, my mother became a widow with two children!

Silently, two teardrops formed in Meline's chestnut-colored eyes, one the color of Sivas, the other the color of Kangal… one, a brother, the other, a sister.... She was silent. She averted her gaze from me and turned her head toward the aquarium. Gazing at the fish, she wiped Sivas and Kangal from her eyes... After a bit, a smile appeared on her face like dry leaves blown about in an autumn storm.... This was another Meline...

That's how it is, Kemal! Our world has been formed with sorrow and bitterness.... much bitterness. The light of our sun burns with bitterness. I'm speaking with you about this for the first time. I've even forgotten some of these fires, but even their mention brings feelings of bitterness!

After that, the family immigrated to Istanbul.

During the time of the Byzantine Empire, there were a great number of Armenians living within the empire and even in the capital Constantinople. After conquering the city, Mehmet the Conqueror turned it into the capital of the Ottoman Empire, and brought in a great number of Armenians, large groups from Anatolia and the regions of Armenia, for the purpose of rebuilding it and making it more beautiful than before, as well as for replenishing its depleted ranks of artisans and master builders. By imperial decree, the Greek Orthodox Church established its patriarchate in Fener, while the Armenians established theirs in Kumkapı. In the course of his relations with the Armenians, with this decree Mehmet officially recognized the Armenian Patriarchate as a separate religious sect. Along with a photograph of Mustafa Kemal, the Sultan's edict is hung on the wall of the reception room of the Patriarchate. Over time, the Armenians who had been brought in the early days of the empire became an inseparable part of Istanbul, an essential color within the city's ethnic and religious tapestry. The Armenians of Istanbul suffered great hardships in 1915, but they weren't subject to the Deportation. Ever since the beginning of the Republican Period, the Armenians who survived the calamities of 1915 migrated from Anatolia to Istanbul.... My mother and father came to Istanbul then, as well. My mother from Sivas, my father from Kangal....

During those days, all of the immigrants came to Tophane. The Anatolian Armenians first set foot in Istanbul at Tophane. From there, they began to spread out to other parts of the city....

Those were very difficult years...

My mother remained a widow for twelve years, remaining under the roof of her father-in-law until she was thirty years old.

After that, she remarried by means of a matchmaker. I was from that marriage.

> My father worked as a concierge at apartment buildings around Şişli. I first came into the world in the concierge's apartment of one of these buildings.... It was an enormous structure, and its inhabitants were cultured, tolerant people.

Slowly, slowly, Meline recounted the traces of her life, the small milestones of her odyssey, and the sharp turns and steep climbs in the road of her life.

"Afterward, I'll tell you all about this at great length!" she said, once again closing the books of her life.

"My dear Meline, before I met you, I once read in the newspapers when I was young about 'the Tin King' Mıgırdiç Şellefyan... I was so mad, thinking that all of the Armenians were just like Şellefyan. I supposed that the reason for our poverty was the Armenians and the Jews... We were leftists, revolutionaries... but we didn't have the slightest idea about even one part of the world in which we lived... To say it directly, not only didn't I know about you—I didn't even know about myself!"

"That's how we were always explained! That's how we were always described to the Turks, to the people of Turkey."

"As a person, I certainly have many faults... But if I hadn't met you, my humanity would have remained lacking. It's thanks to you that I began to get to know Armenians. In loving you, I began to love Armenians. With this love for you, I began to notice all the prohibitions, prejudices and taboos that had been stuffed into my head. Because of your very existence, I began to understand myself."

"Stop, Kemal! You're going to make me cry!" Meline said, "Those things are nothing! I'm going to tell you everything.... Afterward, we'll decide where and when to meet again—but don't let too much time pass before we meet again.... let's do it as soon as possible.... And next time, let's not do it like this, in a restaurant.... We'll find somewhere where we can sit alone and speak as long as we want.

The past that made Meline who she is

The best place to talk was my house. For the date, we decided by telephone for Monday, January 11, 1999.

On that afternoon it began to snow. She was so upset, she didn't know what to do. There were snow flurries, blown about by an icy wind. The heavens were shrouded by snow-laden clouds. Evening fell early on the city. I closed the shutters early in order not to have to see the cold, darkened skies.

I waited for Meline with some concern. The roads might be iced over. Traffic might have become clogged. As the appointed time approached, I put water on for tea. As the time arrived, I was already steeping the tea. "She must be freezing out there on the roads," I thought....

At four o'clock on the dot, there was a knock on the door. It was Meline. I quickly ushered her in. Her hands and face were frozen, but even in this snowing weather, she hadn't neglected to bring spring flowers. As always, there was a smile on her face and she was dressed to the nines. She brought a light and warmth to my home!

"Meline, my dear, your hands are like ice. It's snowing and windy outside. Let's have some tea first of all. You've come some way, so come sit down and recuperate from your journey. After that we'll talk."

"I'm not tired. Thank God, I'm strong and healthy. And there's a lot to talk about. This evening I want to fully explain to you all the events, the suffering and memories of those days that I only briefly mentioned at the restaurant. But I don't know where to begin.... Maybe you should ask questions...."

"What I'd like to know first of all is what your experience was in that great massacre and conflagration. You said that your mother was from Sivas and your father, from Kangal. But how did they escape from that ring of death?"

My mother was born in Sivas in 1902. Her name was Vartanush. 'Vart' means rose in Armenian. 'Vartanush' is a very common name. It means 'sweet rose.' But my mother's life was anything but sweet. Instead of sweet roses, the only thing that grew in her spring and summer years were sorrow, fear and sadness.

When the disaster of 1915 came, she was just a young girl on the verge of womanhood. Like all of the Armenians, she and her family came face to face with death. I don't fully know how they were rescued, why they weren't sent away in the Deportation. She never told me the details. The only things that stick in my memory are some images, like cut up film stills, jumbled and disconnected....

There were four girls and one boy in her family. Her mother wanted to marry off her daughters as soon as possible and thereby reduce her own obligations and responsibility. At that time, there was no room for sentimentality. In those days, it was a question of life and death. The conditions demanded it. She married my mother off when she was fourteen years old. She gave my mother's older sister to a man who was a widower. I don't even know if this man had any family or anything... I only heard from my mother that he wasn't killed because he was a miller; they didn't deport him because they didn't want to be without a miller in the area.

My maternal grandmother's name was Beğik. Her husband's name was İnok. Those aren't names that are used any more in our day. Where they came from, how they got them—I don't know that, either.

After marrying off two of her daughters, my grandmother took her two younger children, a daughter and a son, and brought them all under the protection of an American woman named Miss Kraft, who worked during those years to gather up all the orphaned children and surviving Armenians who had lost all their family.

Who was this Miss Kraft? What did she do? What aid did they receive from her institution? Was she a missionary? A member of the Red Cross? I don't know any of this. I'm very curious about this as well. But until now I haven't been able to find even a crumb of information, not the slightest trace. From what I heard from my mother, Miss Kraft rescued hundreds of those who survived the massacres, children and adults, young and old. And she rescued my grandmother and her three young children from starvation.... then she sent them to Istanbul. She also arranged that many of them would go to Thessaloniki.... I'm so curious: who was this rescuing angel? Who? I still want to know....

I told you earlier that my father was from Kangal. They called him 'The mad monk's grandson,' which means that there was probably a monastic connection somewhere in his family. Perhaps his grandfather was the monk of the village.... The fact is, I don't have a very clear idea what my father did for a living. On my father's side, our name was 'Tarpinyan,' which means 'blacksmith.' After the Surname Law was passed in Turkey, my father began to use the Turkish equivalent of Tarpinyan, 'Demirji.' His first name was 'Ohan,' which is a holy name in the Gospels. Ohan, Ohannes, Yohannes, they're all religious names that come from the same source.

How did my father survive the calamity of 1915? I only vaguely remember the things they told me. My father died young. I was still small. What I still remember was that my father hid among the dead bodies. After things calmed down a bit, he went to the house of an Alevî family he knew in the village.

This family took my father into their home. They protected him; they looked after him and put up with him. They raised him. My father got married in Kangal. But whom he married, or how they got married I don't know. From my father's first marriage he had a son named Sarkis Mkhitar and a daughter named Meline. But this girl died from meningitis. After that, his wife died, too. That's how my father was left a widower.

My older brother Sarkis is fifteen or sixteen years older than I am. He was a really good tailor. He immigrated to Canada. He's retired now, but he still lives there.

The Turkish family that protected my father later immigrated to Istanbul, and they brought my father along with them. The family had a son by the name of Nuri. He was older than my father. He was a police officer. I met this Nuri when I was a little girl. We'd visit each other all the time, like family.

I told you that my mother was married when she was fourteen. They had a son right away. Four years later, they had a daughter. The night that her daughter was born, they came and took her husband away. But it didn't have any connection to the Deportation or the massacres. In fact, by the time her daughter was born, the Deportation storm had already passed. But they sent him off anyway! That was the last they saw of him. He died afterward. My mother was widowed at age eighteen. She gave her daughter, who was born half-orphaned, the name 'Hayganush.'

The name Hayganush comes from the root 'hayg.' The Armenians call themselves 'Hay.' Only non-Armenians call them 'Armenian.' So Hayganush means 'Armenian girl.' It's a very common name.

My older sister Hayganush is now seventy-five years old. She lives with her daughter in New York. Her entire life passed without ever seeing her father!

After the death of her first husband, my mother couldn't live with her family any longer in Sivas. She found a way to immigrate to Istanbul. That was in 1921 or 1922... the years of the War of Independence.... those were difficult days. My mother, her two children, her in-laws: all five of them rented a little cubbyhole of an apartment on a narrow street behind Galatasaray Lycée called Kumbaraci Yokuşu. At that time it was a Greek neighborhood. There were Greeks living in the basement floor of the building in which my mother's family stayed.

They were like five dry leaves that the storm had torn from their branch and blown all the way to Istanbul. They began to rebuild their lives in this one-room little world in the middle of gigantic Istanbul... That was the beginning, that was how they started out! You could say it was a battle just to survive, a life-and-death struggle. Try to imagine my mother's situation: an eighteen-year-old Armenian woman, widowed with two children.... Their traditions and views were totally eastern: rigid and from the village: you didn't speak in front of her father-in-law; you showed respect to your elders; you'd do all the work in the house; you'd only leave your one-room world when absolutely necessary; you wouldn't speak with any males... not with anyone; you didn't have a private life whatsoever; and much more along those lines. Try to imagine that, if you can!

This whole experience profoundly affected my mother's spiritual world, her habits, her behavior and her ideas.

I laugh when I think about it... there's this little sewing box that my mother preserved from that one-person world. Inside it were her needles, thread, and various odds and ends... This little sewing box was like my mother's treasure chest... She never let anyone touch it... Nobody was allowed to open it. Later on, after I'd grown up, I used to think a lot about that sewing box. Why was it so special for her? I should have asked why....

During those long years that she spent in that lonely, isolated world, the sewing box was her only private possession, all there was of her private world.

Those five persons began their lives again in a single-room apartment.

They didn't have any money accumulated at all. And even if they had, you couldn't live off it forever. The difficulties of making a living then began. They had come from Anatolia. On the one hand, they were accustomed to a more conservative lifestyle. There she was, a young widow. At first, her father-in-law didn't want her to work outside for fear that something would happen to her. But the hardship of making ends meet pressed heavily upon him.

She started to work at a tobacco factory run by the *Regie du Tabac* in Tophane, near their house. She'd walk to and from work every day. On the one hand, she was raising her children, on the other, they were slowly getting used to life in Istanbul. They got to know the other Armenians who had survived the disaster and came there from all parts of Anatolia, as well as the local Armenians, Greeks and Turks. The traces of their great calamities began to fade a bit. They began to forget some of their sorrow and heal their wounds. That's how people are... You put down your roots and grow where you are, no matter where it is... Some died, and others lived. My elder brother grew up and began school. He became a tailor's assistant. He became enamored with the Greek girls in the neighborhood.

My mother slowly began to emerge from her one-room world and to work cleaning the house of a German family that had fled from the Nazi genocide; they lived on Aci Çeşme Street, behind Galatasaray, not too far from her house. She became very friendly with this family. They understood each other very well. Their similar experiences drew them together. I remember very clearly, that later, when I was a child, we would go with my mother and visit that family. My mother would bring some of the sweets, pastries and food that she made, and they'd eat together and drink coffee in the afternoon. We'd then return home before the man of the house came home.... They had a daughter named Sylvia. We used to play together. Later on she married a Turk...

During that time my father, who had meanwhile come to Istanbul from Kangal, found work as a concierge at a big apartment building in Küçükbahçe Street, in Şişli, just one street away from what is now the Atatürk Museum. He lived there, too.... but, as they say, 'Being alone is only suitable for God'... He felt the obligation to build a new nest.

An Armenian woman came along then, who knew my mother Vartanush and my father Ohan. She introduced them to each other.

My mother had been a widow for twelve years—my father, too. Both of them were children of Anatolia who had been uprooted by the storm and deposited in Istanbul. Both of their lives were steeped in sorrow and bitterness, each one was an Armenian who had suffered the vicissitudes of fate... but it was necessary to remarry, they thought. One had lost her husband, the other, his wife. So they married.

A few years of their marriage passed before my mother became pregnant. But she didn't want to bring another child into the world. My mother already had two children from her previous marriage and my father had one from his. It was very difficult just getting by at that time. A fourth child would just bring more hardship for the family. My mother wanted to abort me. 'Hope or no hope, I don't want another child!' she said. It was at that time that her father-in-law from her previous marriage passed away. When she went to the funeral, she revealed her position to her mother-in-law. 'I'm definitely going to abort it!' she told her. She was going to do whatever she was going to do! But her mother-in-law took her over to a corner and gave her a good dressing down.

'Girl, I will break every bone in your body! Under no circumstances will you have an abortion! They tried to completely blot us out, roots and all. But a handful of us have survived. I tell you, we should reproduce, our line must continue; the branches and shoots that weren't burned in the fire should blossom again! If I could give birth to more children, I would—and not just one! If I could I'd bring another ten into the world! I'm going to see that you have that child. Listen well to what I'm saying, girl! Do not murder the child that is in your belly! You've remarried, and this child will bring a blessing to your table, and love to your house! I will break every bone in your body, if it comes to that!'

My mother spent many dark days and sleepless nights wondering: was she right? Or was her mother-in-law right? Was she fooling herself? Or was she seeing clearly? What would the child do? Would it accept her decision, or her indecision? Would the child ask whether or not it should be born? But while she still was in the throes of indecision, time was passing. Then, in 1938, I arrived in the world early one morning with the sun....

My father was beside himself with joy at the fact that I turned out to be a girl. 'I will name her!' he said. 'May it be auspicious and a good omen! I grieved much for my daughter Meline who died. God has given me my heart's desire. In Meline's place, we have a new daughter who is like a ball of light! Her name shall be Meline!'

And that's how I received the name Meline.

Long afterward I spent a lot of time looking into the meaning of the name 'Meline.' There's 'Melina' in Greek, 'Meline' in Armenian. It's connected with ancient Anatolian civilization, and ancient Armenian mythology. According to some sources, the old name for Malatya was 'Melitine.' As for the mythological connection, 'Meline' was the name of the goddess of multitude and blessing.

I was born with the sun.... I was given the name of the goddess of blessing. With the sun in one hand and blessing in the other, I began my life in the bosom of the enormous city of Istanbul, in a concierge's apartment into which the sun didn't shine....

Meline, the concierge's daughter

I first opened my eyes in a concierge's apartment, as the daughter of a concierge. My father worked in a grocery shop close to our home. We only had the chance to see my father in the evenings. My mother and we children ran the affairs at the apartment building.

As the youngest of four siblings, the only child of my parents' second marriage and the only small child in a huge apartment building, I was like the building's mascot. I came and went freely in all the apartments. Each one of the apartments was a completely different world. With my child's mind I took things from each one of those worlds. I learned things from each of them, too. Gifts were always bought for me at holidays and when we had an outing; I grew up as the apple of everyone's eye.

No one denigrated us or looked down on us simply as 'a concierge's family.' I felt myself fully as one of them.

The building had seven floors. One family lived on each floor. Among ourselves, we called the families according to the number of the floor on which they lived. For instance:

The family of Melike lived on the first floor, directly above us. They owned estates in Adana. They were a wealthy Turkish family. We called them 'the number ones.' 'Melike Abla' was a gem of a human being.

The 'number twos' were a Jewish family from Salonica. The others called them 'dönmes.' They were greatly disliked.

On the floor above them lived the widow of a pasha, 'Haminneciğim.' I spent more time at Haminneciğim's apartment than at anyone else's. She had a girl who took care of her. She was like a house cleaner. Haminneciğim never lifted a finger to do anything. From morning until evening, she sat in her special armchair before the window. Everything came to her. I made Haminneciğim laugh. I represented a distraction, a way to pass the time pleasantly.

On the fourth floor was a real Jewish family. They owned a large wholesale warehouse. They were very kind to me. They had twin boys. We would play together.

On the fifth floor lived 'Aunt Ebru' and her family. She herself was an Armenian. Her husband was Turkish. He died from some disease. Aunt Ebru's daughter's name was Nigâr. She was half-Turkish, half-Armenian. Later on, when I was going to primary school, she married a Turkish ship captain.

On floor six lived a wealthy Armenian family from Kayseri. They owned some furrier shops the Tünel District. Their daughter Rona studied at the Sorbonne University in Paris. She was a world-class beauty; she knew everything, was informed on every subject, and a sweet, good-hearted girl. She also helped me out a great deal, as I'll explain later.

The seventh floor was occupied by the heirs of the Nişastaciyan family. They didn't communicate very much with us or any of the building's other occupants.

As you've heard, in our building, Turkish, Armenian and Jewish families all lived without strife or coming to blows, with mutual love and respect. There was peace of mind in our building. All of these families were very worldly, established people. And I grew up as if I, too, were a child of the wealthiest, most cultured families; it was a happy childhood.

In her own mind, my mother never thought of herself as just 'the concierge's wife.' We weren't your average concierge's family. No one ever called down to us, saying, 'Vartanush Hanım! Go buy this, go fetch that! Ohan Efendi, take out the trash!' My mother would have never stood for this, nor would the culture and sensibilities of the other occupants have allowed them to do so....

We were the poorest and most crowded family in the building. Even I myself knew that my mother and father couldn't get along. There weren't any beatings, but my father didn't like what my mother did, my mother couldn't stand my father's behavior. But even if there was a fight in the evening, by the next morning everything was forgotten.

When I became a young woman, I tried to understand why my mother and father couldn't get along. Basically, both my mother and my father were still aching from the emotional and psychological wounds that had yet to heal. I never saw either my mother or my father laugh with all their hearts, never saw them completely happy. But I did see those happy laughs and the hearts which bloom from happiness in Niğâr, Rona, Melike and others.

My father never said a thing. He was silent. He had been rescued from the dead and had grown up all alone in an Alevî family. Afterward, I began to understand my father very well.

Our apartment building had a lush, green backyard garden. Right outside our window there was a mulberry tree, a beautiful magnolia tree and even roses! I awoke in the morning to the sound of birds. There were nightingales singing in the magnolia. In one corner of the courtyard there was a horse stable and a lean-to shed for housing a feuilleton. But I never saw either a carriage or horses. They had been there in the old days, and the place for them remained standing.

The owners of the apartment building had been palace jewelers. Their name was Nişastaciyan. They owned another apartment building directly across from the Atatürk Museum. I used to go there, as well. Most of the Nişastaciyan family had died off. The only one left was an old woman. This apartment building was like a palace. All of the things in it were antiques. When this last surviving woman finally died, their heirs went on a feeding frenzy, sifting through the goods. They went through her entire estate, selling off everything.

Our apartment building was on Küçükbahçe Street, number nine: the 'Abrak Apartments.'

There were groves of mulberry, linden, and fruit trees at the bottom of the street. If you walked through the mulberries and lindens you'd come to Yildiz Palace. The city limits at that time ended at the upper side of the Şişli Mosque. The Karagözyan Orphanage was outside the city limits at that time. The upper end of the Şişli Mosque was covered with bright green mulberry groves. We would go there frequently during the summers. Every family rented its own mulberry tree. Everyone knew which tree was whose. Everyone ate from their own mulberry and picnicked at the foot of their own tree.

Istanbul was a different city back then.... It hadn't filled up with peasants from the villages, like it is now. The people of Istanbul were different, so was the air and the water....

At Melike's apartment I learned about the Turkish tangos and other fashionable songs of the time, as well as about the famous artists, Yaşar İnce, Münir Nurettin Selçuk and the rest.

Nigâr used to sing classic Turkish music. She taught it to me, as well. I caught on quickly. 'Meline,' they used to say, 'come, sing us a song!' I'd come running for the chance. I sang very well, too.

Rona, who had studied at the Sorbonne, taught me French when I was just a little girl, even before I began elementary school. Whenever I'd go see her, she'd ask me a few sentences in French; I would be so happy if I knew them....

From some people I learned to sing, from others, good manners, and from still others, how to set a table....

But my mother never spoke to me about the past, about what had happened to her. We spoke Armenian within the family. My parents spoke to each other in Armenian, argued in Armenian. They spoke Turkish as well, but my mother often warned me: 'Be careful that you don't speak Armenian outside the house! You be very careful! Even be careful among the other families in the building who you go visit!' For my little girl's mind, the reasons for her fear and caution were unfathomable. Nevertheless, within the family there was something of a secret compact. You had to always be on your guard and circumspect. You could do everything, and know everything, but you only go so far...

I think I said that I'd go visit every family in the building. But the apartment I'd visit the most was Haminneciğim's. I could probably even say that when I was a child, I spent more of my days with Haminneciğim than at home with my own mother. It was as if I was her granddaughter.... One time, they forgot to bring me a present for Bayram. Oh, how I cried, how I wept! At that, Haminneciğim quickly sent her son, 'Uncle Sedat,' who had come from Ankara to celebrate the holiday, down to the market to get me something. He bought me some little leather shoes covered with red velvet and silver embroidery and I shut up. I kissed Haminneciğim's hand.

One day, a few words of Armenian slipped out of my mouth when I was talking with Haminneciğim. I just sort of spoke them without thinking. Haminneciğim heard this and sat there stunned. She got a strange look on her face and then I was stunned, too! Then, Haminneciğim, who never got out of that chair, who never set foot outside her door, now stood up and grabbed my hand, heading for the door. We quickly went down three flights of stairs to where my mother was.

'Girl, you whore!' she said, 'When did you find the time to teach this girl Armenian?'

But you have to understand, there was no insult contained in this question. At that time, such curse words had a very different meaning, a whole different sense. It was actually a sign of intimacy when you could say such words or use such expressions....

Anyway, I was very, very sorry that I had let slip those words in Armenian. I tried to understand with my little girl's brain why Haminneciğim had dragged me down three flights of stairs and called my mother a whore.... After that, I was very careful never to accidentally speak Armenian again.

The Capital Tax

I still hadn't begun grade school when at one point a dreadful, silent panic took over our building. Conversations began to be whispered, and secrets kept from me. No one called my mother or father over to their apartment any more in the night or evenings. All concierge's duties were done in the daytime, at clearly prescribed times. Then, one night, the 'Number Threes' called my parents up. I was going to go too, but they ordered me to stay at home. That just increased my curiosity and concern. Afterward, very late at night, my mother and father came back to our apartment carrying things, some wrapped in papers or material, others not. They then placed them very carefully in the room at the very back of our apartment.

'Don't tell a soul!' they said. 'The Capital Tax has come out... They're going to search the Number Threes' apartment. These antique things are going to remain with us for a while.'

I was four or five years old at that time. I didn't have any idea what had just happened. Still, I could comprehend that it was something secret, something dangerous....

During those days, it seemed like the Capital Tax was the only topic of conversation. I did my best to eavesdrop when the adults were speaking: 'This Armenian was exiled to Aşkale... that Jew was going to be sent to Aşkale.... the goods and property of such-and-such a Greek was being sold to pay for his tax debt... What shall we do? Is this going to come upon us too?'

And while all this was going on, one day a bunch of people I didn't recognize came to apartment number three. Silence fell upon the entire building.... But I quickly snuck out and went to the 'Number Threes' apartment. The strangers were turning it upside down. They picked up some things and carted them off. I remember this as if it were yesterday. I can still see it clearly....

But they didn't come to our apartment. The things that the 'Number Threes' had hidden at our place remained there for a long time. Now and then, I would open the door to that room and look inside... Afterward, they came and took them back to their own apartment....

For some time, this event put a cold shadow over the happy, sunny atmosphere that had reigned in the building until then. For the longest time, I couldn't even sing songs or anything to Nigâr....

This little incident left indelible marks on my childhood... All my life, I was deathly afraid of raids and searches, of bureaucrats coming to confiscate our goods....

"Don't let the Girl end up a blind chicken!"

My father was a typical 'man of the field.' His deeply ingrained Anatolian peasant habits, such as his cynical view of life, his defensiveness and his everpresent concern about tomorrow—none of these ever changed.

I was seven years old at the time. The other kids my age were all beginning school. My mother wanted to enroll me, and I wanted to go, as well. But my father came out against my mother:

'Don't start her too early! Don't let the girl end up a blind chicken! Don't make her start school too early or she'll be crushed! Let her start one year later!'

On this matter my father had his way. I began school one year later, so as not to end up 'a blind chicken.'

I remember that day so well. I went with my mother to the Armenian primary school in Feriköy. I was so happy.... so happy! I felt like I was walking on air.

But I came in for a shock as soon as I entered the school: the school building was old and battered. It was run-down and neglected, the desks were all old. I went to the bathroom—Good Lord, what a stench! It was practically impossible to even enter it! I'd never seen such things in our building.

'I'm not going to this dirty school!' I told my mother, but my mother, my father and my siblings all told me stories to convince me to go: 'You'll get used to it after a while!' 'You can't change schools in the middle of the year!' 'We'll definitely send you to a different school next year!'

At that point, the neighbor girls Nigâr and Rona entered into the picture. I cried to Haminneciğim a great deal. I pouted and played hard-to-please. But she also repeated what my mother had said. So, swinging back and forth between wanting to and not wanting to go, I made it through the first grade and into second grade.

At the beginning of the second grade, even before school began, my mother rolled up her sleeves and went to work: she was going to find me a clean school. She asked around and made inquiries. She found a Catholic school in Harbiye. It was called the *Ecole du Soeurs*. It's still there.

My mother took my hand and brought me straight to the school. They didn't want to register me. They sent me back to my school in Feriköy. But the Armenian school didn't want to give me permission to leave and go to another school, because they didn't want to lose students, or some other reason. Finally, and as a result of my mother's insistence, they did provide us with a letter of release.

On the way, my mother opened the letter and read it: 'this student has not advanced to the second grade.' She was furious! She tore up the letter and threw it away.

I finally was enrolled in the second grade at the nuns' school, but through a somewhat adventurous manner.

There were Catholic, Protestant, Armenian and Greek Orthodox churches in Istanbul. There were even some Armenian Catholics, as well. In other words, they were tied to Rome. But they were actually a pretty small group. But no matter how small they were, everyone accepted the existence of Catholic Armenians. According to the Treaty of Lausanne, they had the right to open up their own schools in full security. In recent years, the number of students decreased as more and more of them emigrated abroad. But they continued their own existence. Basically, this Catholic primary school was the nuns' school, meaning that they only accepted girls. The nuns ran the school, cleaned the school, and helped in the instruction.

So I began second grade. This school was as well-kept as the Armenian Primary School in Feriköy was neglected. It was spotless. It was perfect for me. I was so happy to go to this school. They had a lot of money. They even gave us a special discount on the tuition because we were the family of a doorkeeper.

I completed the school with great success. It sparked within me the desire for education. I should explain to you later the ideas that this desire put into my head. But that's enough for today, my dear Kemal.

"O.K., we'll leave it there for today, Meline my dear" I said. "You're tired, and it's already late."

I looked outside. There was a fine snow falling. Everything was covered with white.

"The roads are slippery. You should go before it gets too late, Meline, my dear. Only, the thing that's stuck in my mind is that Miss Kraft, the one who saved your mother, her sisters, and hundreds of Armenian children. Who was this person? How did she save them? I'm very curious. We should look into this. Next time we get together, let's let each other know what we have found out about Miss Kraft."

"Let's indeed look into it, Kemal! Who was Miss Kraft? Who was she?"

Kirkor Ceyhan

"I'm from Zara, I've always looked for Zara…"

Who was Miss Kraft? What sort of person was she?

Meline hadn't heard anything from her mother about this woman who had rescued her. I was very curious. Meline was, too. Together we began to look for little bits of information about this Miss Kraft. First, I checked encyclopedias. Nothing. Who should I ask? Who might know? After consulting with Meline about it, I began to assemble sources and books concerning the Armenians and to read them.

I came across the book *I Grew Up with Songs of the General Mobilization*, by Kirkor Ceyhan. I read the entire thing in one sitting. Kirkor Ceyhan makes brief mention of Miss Kraft in his book. When I came across her name I became excited. I'd found what I'd been looking for. I immediately found Kirkor Ceyhan's number and phoned him. I introduced myself and told him about my interest in Miss Kraft. Could he speak to me about her?

"By all means!" he said, "Come on over!"

On the afternoon of March 19, 1999 I stood in front of the door of a house close to the Rhine river, in the midst of greenery and flowers. I knocked. The air had been washed clean by the day's rain.

The person who opened the door was a man who looked to be in his seventies, but with sparkling eyes, a glowing countenance and an honest smile. He introduced me to his German wife, Ilse. We sat across from each other at a round table. He examined me: who exactly was this person who'd come to speak with him? For some time, I felt that he was looking me over, proofing me. After that, we warmed up to one another.

It was as if we were both yearning to speak about our past and present, safely, openly, without prohibitions.

"So, who is Kirkor Ceyhan? Can you tell me?"

"Kirkor Ceyhan is as I explained in my book. They call us '*külek suyu.*'"

"What does that mean, '*külek suyu*'?"

It's a type of water vessel like a bucket. It's open on top. And you can see the bottom of it. The mouth of a ewer is narrow. You can't always tell what's in it: water, wine or poison. We, on the other hand, are like a '*külek suyu*,' wide open... there's nothing hidden about us! I'm from Zara!"

And that's how our conversation began. I told him about Meline. I explained that I was looking for information about Miss Kraft, who had rescued Meline's mother from death. Who was this Miss Kraft? I wanted to know.

> What I know about Miss Kraft, I learned from Şehrazat Hanım and her husband, Garabed Ağa, when I went to middle school in Sivas. That was in 1941.
>
> The American College in Sivas was on a hill in the northernmost part of the city. They had at least 2,000 donums of land. Surrounding the entire thing was a wall some two meters high. On its western side, the college bordered the Surp Nishan mulberry orchard, on its eastern side, the place where the Bayrampaşa river flowed along the Pirkinik Road, and in the north, the outskirts of the village of Pirkinik. Before the general mobilization in the First World War, the village of Pirkinik had been a Catholic Armenian village. This village had provided transport services for Sivas. The famous Armenian poet Taniel Varujan was from

this village. Before the Armenian 'mobilization,' Armenians lived in the Höllüklük district, where the American College was located.

Miss Kraft was an American missionary. When the Armenians were 'mobilized' during the years 1915-1916, she worked at the American College in Sivas. During the calamities that befell the Armenians, when they were forcibly marched into Deyr-i-Zor and the deserts of Syria, there were hundreds of children left abandoned in the mountains and on the roads. They were utterly destitute. They were hungry, impoverished... when the dreadful events of the Deportation had finally passed somewhat, the American Red Cross organization sent aid committees to Anatolia. These aid committees gathered up all the children that they found on the roads and in the mountain passes. They also collected those who had found refuge within Kurdish and Turkish families—from whom some were given back willingly, others sold for gold coins. The committees took them all to the American College in Sivas. The children, widows, young girls and surviving males were cared for, and then sent off to various places in the world, some to Istanbul, others to the rest of the world, via Salonica. The number who were sent all over the world via Salonica was very large. Miss Kraft was the one who directed this aid at the American College.

At the college, they didn't just give them food and drink; they also taught those who were of school age. Miss Kraft was a very humane, brave, tall and beautiful missionary. She also had enormous breasts. Like jugs.... Those surviving Armenian villagers who saw her would say 'she ties sacks to her breasts.' I also heard this from these villagers.

My father's eldest sister Şehrazat and her husband Garabed Ağa both found refuge with Miss Kraft, along with his younger sister Güvher Hatun and her husband Hovsep. They worked the land at the American College as well as various other tasks. Garabed Ağa plowed, sowed and harvested the land with a pair of oxen. He and Şehrazat had four children from their marriage.

They received reports that my father, my mother and the entire family had been deported. Hovsep quickly told Miss Kraft and said that he wanted to help. Miss Kraft quickly sent Hovsep with blankets, some coins and some food to our family, which was wandering on the roads. Although he wanted to spare the children from the Deportation, the colonel who was responsible for the convoy of deportees did not leave them be. They deported my father and all of the individuals of his family at the end of 1916.

Afterward, Miss Kraft wished to make her breasts smaller. She forced the chief physician at the American Hospital, Hovsep Efendi, who was

Kirkor Ceyhan, Zara

a very famous surgeon, to perform the operation. Hovsep Efendi said, 'Impossible, it's very dangerous!' but she wouldn't relent. And unfortunately, Miss Kraft didn't survive this operation. At her funeral, there were thousands of persons who she had helped. They came to bid her a tearful farewell into the next world.

The assistance activities at the American College in Sivas continued after Miss Kraft's death, even until the signing of the Lausanne Treaty in 1924. After the treaty was signed, the Americans had to pack up and leave, and the supervision and administration of the college was left for the time being to the attorney Tevfik Bey. Because he was so old, Tevfik Bey wasn't able to deal with all of these matters as fully as necessary; many of the college's functions were transferred to my aunt's husband, Garabed Ağa.

Those women and girls who had survived the calamity of the Deportation, some by hiding in the mountains or hills, others by finding refuge with some or other person—some by becoming servant girls, others by becoming the concubines or third or fourth wives— slowly began coming to Sivas where they would stick their heads in at the American College and get a bowl of soup and support. Garabed Ağa devoted his life to helping these people. He became a branch for these people who had escaped death to hold onto, a father who helped to find spouses for these poor women who were left with no one else in the world. They would come and pass through there. But they all remembered Miss Kraft, that good woman who gave them the hope and courage to live during the blackest, darkest days of their lives.

"And that's as much as I know! That's everything I heard!" he said in conclusion.

"Kirkor Bey," I asked, "the Deportation began in April, 1915. But they sent your father and his family away at the end of 1916. How is that? How were they able to remain in Zara all that time? And why did they then deport them so late?"

"Please, don't address me as 'Bey' (Sir, Mr.)! I'd be happier if you called me Ağabey (brother)' he said, and then began to explain:

My father, Simon Cihanyan had been a teacher at the Zara Armenian School before the Deportation. I never saw him teach. During my childhood, he was a well-known and well-respected master builder.

During the summers he worked in far off places; he'd come back to Zara when the winters would begin. He loved me very much. He was a very happy, bold and talkative person. I used to listen to him tell stories of the things that happened to him. My father used to talk about my mother a whole lot. I should now tell you about the things I heard from my father.

The only way to escape death

They sent my father to the Balkan War in 1912. But in those years, there was a custom in the Ottoman Empire. From among every two men going to war, they would draw lots to select one person to be 'without a helper,' meaning those who had no one else who could support their families while they were away at war. Then, those who were selected by lots to be with the 'helper-less' wouldn't be sent to the army. In those days, they would separate those going to war into two groups: 'those with helpers/protectors' and 'those without helpers/protectors.' It came from the old phrase, "*Allah muininiz olsun!*" (May God be your helper!), and meant something like 'May God protect you!'

Look how lucky my father has been! He was saved from going to the Balkan War because he drew the 'helper-less' lot at the local army office.

But the Ottomans themselves weren't saved from the disaster! This mobilization was just a precursor of the World War to come. Ten or twelve months before the general mobilization they took my father and his relatives into active military duty. The age of those first conscripted into the military was a little advanced. The youngest among them was twenty-five. And when the war finally began, they began conscripting men who were already thirty-five and forty years old.

In earlier times, there had been no military unit stationed in Zara. But as soon as the war began, Enver Pasha's Military Staff decided to station the Tenth Regiment in Zara and built a large barracks in which this regiment would be housed. The military barracks and other lodgings were to be built on the western edge of Zara.

But who would build them? Who would do the work? There was no need to look far! Zaza at that time was famous for its artisans. Almost all of the artisans came from the Armenian community. Stoneworkers, iron workers, master builders, carpenters, building frame makers, tinsmiths, locksmiths, blacksmiths… they were too numerous to count…. All of them good craftsmen. The Ottomans took the lot into the army. But unlike in other places, these Armenians and other non-Muslims weren't automatically sent to the labor battalions. The need was so great that they were instead entrusted with the task of building the Zara barracks. They quickly set themselves to the task…. At that time the Ottomans actively entered the war. The entire world was aflame… The different countries began to devour one another.... On the Eastern Front, the Ottomans and Russians fell upon one another.... At Sarıkamış, in the Allahüekber Mountains, thousands of soldiers froze to death.... Things began to take a turn for the worse. The Ottoman government, under the direction of Talat Pasha and the Union and Progress Party, issued the 'Law of Deportation' so as to deport all the Armenians in the East to the deserts of Syria. It said something like 'All Armenian master craftsmen shall be taken from their homes and systematically and in full security resettled in the south, in al-Jezirah (N. Iraq) and Syria.' That was in the spring of 1915.

I don't know whether he did it for virtuous reasons or not, but the person who was responsible for constructing the barracks, a tall, swarthy-faced Damascene corporal by the name of Yahya Bey didn't want to leave the construction half done, and more importantly, he thought for a long time, trying to find a way not to send to their deaths the Armenians who worked so hard and so intelligently... He called for a work break early one day and gathered up all the Armenians.

'Friends!' he began, 'My friends, listen to me now with all your hearts and all your attention! I have been with you for months, now. I know how hard and how well you've all worked.... We are all extremely pleased. I see just how much of a service you've provided to our state, to the Ottoman Empire.... But according to the order that I've received today, the entire Armenian nation, without exception, is to be subject to deportation.... Now, listen to me well. You've understood what I've said....'

'After this introduction, let me now say what it is I wanted to tell you: This is perhaps the most difficult thing I've ever had to express in my life. I did not sleep the entire night. I've been trying to devise ways to save you from this deportation, to protect you from this great calamity that you are to face. The only way I could think of is this: I will take a written petition from each and every one of you, and it will be dated much earlier. I will put it into effect immediately. In this way I will be able to protect you from the disaster of deportation. In your petitions, you will say, 'I plead before our great Sultan that, from this day henceforth, I be allowed to abandon Christianity and accepted into Islam!' Do not worry about what comes after. This evening, everyone go home and speak with your fathers and mothers, think about it and discuss it and decide. You should choose a name for yourselves, and tomorrow morning, come and sign your petitions of conversion.

'This decision is a very difficult one for all of you. If it were up to me, I would not have an easy time making such a decision. But the times are such that you must act according to your minds, not your hearts. I am speaking to you openly: You are all facing death! The decision you make will determine whether you live or die. Continue to be Christians on the inside. There is no other way! Your children's lives are also dependent upon your decision... The current conditions dictate that this is so. Look to the future: you will be able to continue in your own faiths as if nothing happened.

'Tomorrow morning I will expect you to have taken on Muslim names, and to have made your decision. Hurry! To your houses!'

My father, my mother, my father's mother all stayed up and spoke and thought about it until midnight.... It was very difficult for my seventy-five-year-old grandmother to change her religion.... But in the end she, too, submitted...

'Come,' she said, 'let us take out our crosses one last time, turn away from the sun and pray for Jesus Christ our Lord to forgive us!'

Together they all took out the crosses to which they were deeply attached and prayed.

'You see, Jesus our Christ, that we are facing death... What will happen to us and our children? Please forgive us God, and his son, Jesus. We promise that you will still occupy the most exalted place in our hearts!'

After that they sat down and chose names for themselves. My father became Ibrahim, my mother, Naciye, and my grandmother, Şahiban Hatun...

The next morning, on the way to the barracks, no one could look anyone else in the face. Everyone was caught up in their own, strange embarrassment and shame—everyone felt that they'd committed a grave sin.... Afterward, they all convened before Corporal Yahya Bey.

He was an intelligent soldier and an understanding man, this Yahya Bey, and he knew how to lead and direct matters. He made a brief speech:

'I don't know what all of your decisions are. But I see that you are filled with sorrow and fear. Your God and Prophet see all things; they understand the difficult situation you are in, and they know the thoughts of your heart.... May you all be well! Come now one after the other and sign your petitions. Let everyone speak the name that they have chosen for themselves.'

All the paperwork was completed that day. Then everyone began to joke with one another:

'Simon, may your conversion be auspicious!'
'And yours!'

'And what name did you choose?'
'Ibrahim, Simon Ibrahim!'
'It suits you. Most appropriate. I chose Muhammed!'
'Oh ho! May it be auspicious! It's perfect for you!'

A few weeks later Yahya Bey again gathered everyone together. 'What now?' they asked themselves.

'Be well, my friends! Your conversions are going fine, but you know, there are obligations to being a Muslim. If our Padishah were to check one day, what would you say? From today you will have to also fulfill the obligations of being Muslims.... You will be circumcised first. Afterward, a hoja will come and teach you the prayers, supplications, Suras from the Qur'an, and the proper way to pray. But first, circumcision!'

In the tent the regiment's standard bearer, who had become a master by gelding the officers' horses, shortened every man's prized possession amid shouts and screams! Their wounds were small, although some of them bled profusely.... Amid their shouts and howls of pain the circumcisions were completed... After that the hoja came for a bit and left... He chanted some prayers.... Some Arabic Suras began to be read in an Armenian accent.... The church was turned into a mosque... And in that way, the barracks was slowly but surely built....

Afterward, the Ottomans lost the World War.... Trying this, then the other, until they had pushed this mighty empire into the war, they wrenched people from the land, from their homelands by the hundreds of thousands; they slaughtered people by the hundreds of thousands; the Talâts, the Envers, the Nâzims, the Şakirs, the Bedris—they all fled by German ship to Odessa, and then on to Germany, where they sought refuge...

England, France and Italy occupied Istanbul and the lands of the Ottomans as conquerors in war.... A court was established in Istanbul to bring to account those who had the blood of Armenians on their hands... Not having the nerve to face it, death sentences were handed down to the escapees in absentia....

The real persons responsible for carrying out the Deportation and its horrors, the members of the Special Organization (*Teşkilat-i Mahsusa*), fell to fighting for their lives.

The responsible member of the Special Organization in Zara and the town's prominent members, all those who had the blood of the Armenians on their hand now assembled the Armenians before the municipality building. The mayor, Recep Efendi, explained the situation:

'Whether or not the things done to you by the government which has now fled, by the Committee of Union and Progress, were right, what's done is done. From this day onward you are no longer Muslims. You can revert back to your own religions. The mosque will again revert to being a church, and we will reinstall the bell! Go now, and may your religion be blessed!'

It was as the Damascene corporal Yahya Bey had said. Three years after having become Muslims, they again reverted to Christianity. The men had been circumcised, it was true... nevertheless, everyone recited prayers on end for Yahya Bey for having saved their lives.

But as soon as this matter was concluded, a new and greater disaster befell my father. Two Armenians who had escaped the Deportation by fleeing to the mountains came to visit my father's house one night. They asked for assistance. My father would never turn away old friends. He hid them in the house. But three months later they were informed on and captured. My father and all eight persons in his house were immediately forced to go into exile. Five adults and three children then marched all the way to the deserts of Syria. My grandmother was the first to perish, from hunger and deprivation. After that the children died, one after the other....

Kirkor then began to cry. There, in the garden of his wife Ilse's house in Bonn, seventy-three-year-old Kirkor Ceyhan broke into loud sobs and weeping.... Even the spring breeze that had been blowing softly from the banks of the Rhine now ceased. Not a single leaf rustled. I sat their with Ilse, grieving. We didn't move or make a sound.

Finally, Kirkor Ceyhan himself broke the silence. He began to sing a song:

Ayrıldım kavuşamam	I was separated, and could not be reunited
Küstürdüm barışamam	I gave offense, and could not be reconciled
Göz açtım seni gördüm	I opened my eyes, and I saw you
Yad ile konuşamam	But I could not speak with a stranger

"My mother used to sing these songs from the time of the general mobilization when she was weaving rugs" he said, continuing the conversation, "I was raised on these songs!"

Afterward, they went as far as Urfa. By then, the British had taken over the Deyr-i-Zor region and their deportation ended there. What was left of my father's family was sent back to whence they had come. For a while they stayed in Besni. But later on they came back to Zara....

The past years in Zara

I was born in Zara in 1926. I spent by childhood and youth in Zara. I lived on the air and water of Zara. That's where my roots are.

My father was a master builder. My mother used to weave very beautiful rugs. She used to sing these heartfelt songs while she would weave them. I grew up within these dreadful nightmares and fears. Those were years of scarcity. I experienced some very grim deprivations. They committed great cruelties and injustices against me. The other children would beat me. I didn't even know that I was an Armenian, whatever that was! My father's name was Simon, mine was Kirkor... I received a lot of blows because of my name. Even my teacher behaved harshly toward me. They were ignorant people. My schoolwork was very good, though. I got the best grades. But my teacher crossed out my name. He didn't send my school records to Ankara. In those days, the school records of the students who did the best work were sent to the Education Ministry in Ankara. The teacher didn't send mine because my name was Kirkor. With my child's mind I revolted against this. The first rebellion in my life was because of this.

'Why aren't you sending my records?' I asked.

'Oh ho! Are you openly defying me, then?! You're a Turk, aren't you?'

'I am, but my name is Kirkor!'

I couldn't call myself Armenian. We never said a thing to anyone. Who could you complain to? Who would make any effort to defend your rights? They'd have you crushed if you complained! There was great fear. But as a child, with a child's sense of the world, I couldn't stand for these injustices. My father and mother were unable to defend me. But I was very good at math and at singing. My father used to have me solve math problems.

I finished elementary school in Zara. That was in 1938. The year that Atatürk died. I can still see those days clearly before my eyes...

I wanted to study. I didn't even have shoes that fit my feet. I ranted and raved, threw temper tantrums in order to study... My father finally sent me to his sister in Sivas. I began school again at Sivas Middle School, but the torments that I suffered in Sivas over the next five or six years broke my spirit.

I was so afraid. What would they say in Sivas? Would they cross out the name Kirkor again? Would they expel me because my name was Kirkor? I would have terrible nightmares. I was terrified. There wasn't any other Armenian child in that middle school or high school than myself. I was all alone. I felt unsafe. There was no one to stand up for me or with me. I would jump out of my bed at nights, in great pain from this feeling of my spirit being crushed. I worked very hard. I was the best, most industrious student in my class. I helped my friends with their lessons. I would even give them my notebooks.

Finally, I finished middle school.

I wanted to go on, to high school, to university, to study in the best schools. My one and only wish was to learn. I would be a man of learning, and nobody would be able to humiliate me or crush me by calling me an Armenian. I would defend the rights of those oppressed Armenians, I would teach those Armenian children who were unable to learn because of poverty or fear. But it was not to be! It just wasn't possible. We were very poor. We were practically destitute!

I returned to Zara. I was planning to be a man of science. But instead, I ended up as a tailor's apprentice.

The year was 1941. It was during the war years. The fact that I couldn't go to high school made me ill. I felt cursed. At night I dreamt about going to high school and university. But in those days it was back to the tailor's shop....

I began to quiet my yearning for school somewhat through reading. I read everything I found in the library in Zara. I started with Refik Halid, Sabahattin Ali, Sabri Ertem and such. Then, I became familiar with Panait Istrati, Gorky, Tolstoy and Dostoyevsky...

But the more I read, the greater my anger. The more I read, the more I began to understand what the world was like. Slowly but surely, my fears disappeared. What I mean is that I could see that there were others in the world who suffered anguish. I wasn't the only one being mistreated, suffering from want.

Every book I read, every writer with whose work I became familiar, showed me new things. I began to take an interest in politics.

I began to read American literature... I discovered the works of Steinbeck, Jack London and Faulkner. I found so much in these works. They all told stories of people who were anguished and suffering.... I was very inspired by Stefan Zweig's book *Decisive Moments in Human History*.

But the yearning within me to study never abated. I wrote a letter to the Getronagan Armenian Lycée in Istanbul. I explained my situation to them. No answer came.

But apparently, they'd accepted me as a student. They even invited me to the school, but when the letter came, my mother tore it up and threw it out without showing it to me, thinking that it was something bad for her son. I only learned these things much later in conversation. By then, my chance had passed.

During those days, when I was burning with desire to continue school and taking and reading every thing I could find in the library, a soldier by the name of Hüseyin Avni arrived in our town. He had been stationed there as punishment. We met while reading at the library. He had gone to prison because of the 'Naval Academy Incident.' When he was done serving his sentence he was punished by being 'exiled' to the thirty-sixth regiment in Zara....

We began to give each other newspapers and books to read. He knew Nâzim Hikmet and Kemal Tahir, and corresponded with both of them.

He gave me John Steinbeck's *The Endless Struggle*. He gave me *The Grapes of Wrath*. I read them and was dumbstruck! What awesome novels these were! The things that happened on the other side of the world!

I began to understand, by hard experience, how the world really worked. I began to witness and understand injustices. But I couldn't say a word. The Armenians simply lowered their heads and did their best not to be seen or noticed. They were a humiliated and beaten down people with wounded personalities. But when I saw these things the rebellion rose within me. But how? With whom? Against whom?

I began to feel suffocated in Zara. In Zara nobody could open their mouths about anything. If I were to speak out, I would stand out and simply end up being caught in the middle.

The injustices I saw were being done in plain sight. In 1934, it became forbidden for Armenians to have Armenian surnames. I didn't know how it was in Istanbul. But the Armenians who lived in Zara, in Sivas and other cities in Anatolia had their last names Turkified. Our name was 'Cihanyan.' It was changed into 'Cihan.' I was eight years old when my name was changed.

They destroyed the famous Armenian church in Zara in broad daylight. Those beams, pillars and walls that couldn't be destroyed with sledgehammers and axes they completely demolished with dynamite.

The famous Armenian church in Sivas was used as a military depot. One night in the 1940s, during the mayorship of Rahmi Günay, they tore it down completely. Some other churches that remained standing in other cities in Anatolia were simply abandoned to the elements. They made it illegal to repair them.... I don't know how many churches remain today in Anatolia. If you were willing to kill the Armenians and deport the Greeks, what's to prevent you from destroying churches? But what was the crime of churches which didn't even have any congregations left? Weren't they a part of the cultural wealth of Anatolia?

What was the state so afraid of? Did they want to be able to say, 'Look, not only aren't there any Armenians left in Anatolia, there weren't any here in the first place!' What, can you plaster over the sun? By simply saying that there are no Armenians, can you erase Armenian history and cover up the crime that has been committed?

The destruction of all these churches, the mandatory changing of surnames—all these things brought fear upon people... made them feel totally alone, as if their lives had been spared only by the help of some chance act or another.

Just as people were beginning to get over their fears and trust in the state again, the disaster of the Second World War came upon them. A good many of those in Ankara began to act according to their assumption that Germany was going to win the war. Nationalism and chauvinism reigned supreme. From among those non-Muslims who had nursed the wounds of oppression and cruelty that they had suffered between 1914-1934 and had returned to their normal routines, who were willing to forget the past in order to look more hopefully on the future, they took those age twenty and up into military service. But they didn't give them the normal gear of the Turkish soldier. Instead, they gave them brown uniforms, of the same color that garbage collectors wore. They were called the *Gâvur askeri* ('infidel troops'). They didn't issue weapons to the non-Muslims. Instead, they set them to tasks like road building, guarding the rail lines and such. They stationed them in valleys and dry river beds.

This situation produced fear—even panic—among the non-Muslims. The rumors that spread from mouth to mouth were unnerving. There were claims that they were to be killed, but that Field Marshall Fevzi Çakmak, the Commander-in-Chief, had stepped in, saying, 'They are my servants, they have become soldiers. No one shall lay a hand on them, no one shall annihilate them!' So, according to the story, he had thereby saved their lives!

These rumors caused great fright among the Armenians, Jews and Greeks who lived in Turkey. But even as the non-Muslims began to restore their confidence somewhat, saying to each other, 'There's no reason to fear, our fears are ungrounded!' the disaster of the Capital Tax Law then came upon them.

The Capital Tax utterly wiped out the property and possessions of many of the non-Muslims. In the winter of 1942 they were deported to labor camps in Aşkale, near Erzurum.

These developments, coming one right after the other, shook the non-Muslim population to its core. The 1915 massacre, the Deportation and brutality were all carried out by the Union and Progress Party, during the Ottoman period. But then the Sultanate was destroyed and the Republic established in its place. So why were these things happening to us now? Weren't we now all citizens of the Republic of Turkey? Why did the state want to do these things to us? We, who had fulfilled the obligations of citizenship to the letter, Armenians, Greeks, Jews: why were we being treated like criminals? Were we responsible for the mistakes of history?

Some of those who had fled and been saved from the calamity of 1915 and now lived in Russian Armenia had joined the army of Czarist Russia. Some of them had killed many Turks and Kurds in revenge when the Russian forces entered Erzurum and Erzincan in 1916. How true this stuff was I didn't know, but I had also heard that they crowded Turks and Kurds into mosques in Sarıkamış and Hasankale and set them ablaze.

But were we responsible for these events?

Anyway, in 1946, while I was wearying my head with these things, I got married. In that same year, I was conscripted. I did my military service in Erzurum. I was in the service when my first child was born.

While I was serving in the army, I made the acquaintance of a painter named Feridun Ertaç. He was a very cultured man. One day he gave me Franz Liszt's Rhapsody Number 2. 'Here, take this and give it a listen!' he said. I did so, but didn't like it at all.

'What's all that noise he's making?' I said.

'Go, listen to it again!' he said, urging me.

And this time, the more I listened, the more I liked it. I began to feel a strange and different pleasure than I had known before. And that's how I began to listen to classical music... And ever since then I've never stopped listening to it.

I finished my mandatory service in 1949. At that time, there were more than one hundred members of Armenian families left in Zara. But then a way out appeared for us. I came to Istanbul in that year. There I apprenticed with a tailor for a full year. I got myself a place in Gedikpaşa. I then went back to Zara and brought my entire family to Istanbul. We were eight persons in a little one-room apartment in Gedikpaşa. At first, we began to do piecework, sewing clothing for department stores. Everyone in the family worked. Two years later I opened my own tailor's shop with the money that we had accumulated. We sewed things for the department stores. It was intensive, feverishly paced work that we were doing. Where one person would sew five articles of clothing, we sewed fifteen. And we always did good, honest work. We made a place for ourselves. We purchased a house in Gedikpaşa. Work was going well. We were happy, and thought to ourselves 'Finally: we've made it!'

"I lived through the calamity of September 6-7, 1955"

But as soon as we began thinking we'd made it, yet another calamity befell us. This time, in 1955, we were struck by the disaster of September 6-7. The Cyprus question came up again and tempers were inflamed. The newspaper pages were full of it, the radio was screaming about it constantly. 'Partition or Death!' they proclaimed. Rallies in support of the Cypriot Turks were being held on a daily basis. The crowds were incited with such claims as 'They've bombed Atatürk's house!' For the first time in the history of the Republic the government gave permission for a rally to be held in Taksim Square, at eight in the evening. Were they going to allow a rally to be held in the evening in the middle of Beyoğlu, where the majority of the population was non-Muslim? Would you give permission for an evening rally, under the cover of darkness?

They took care of Istanbul and Izmir on the same day—at the same hour, even! When it was over, there wasn't a single Greek house or shop that hadn't been torched, smashed or sacked. And along with the Greek property, Armenian and Jewish property was also burned and destroyed. But Turkish homes and shops that were on the same street, right next to Greek shops, would be left untouched. Everything had been planned in advance, the houses and businesses of non-Muslims had been marked. The people who had been entrusted with the task showed that they themselves hadn't been marked. The main target was the Greeks. But the Armenians also got their share of it, as well.

Beside our home in Gedikpaşa was the home of Vasil. I can still see him before my eyes, as if it were only yesterday.

The looters came, like in a procession. In their hands they had axes and sticks.

'Is there a Greek house here?' they demanded.

'No, this is an Armenian home!' I answered.

'Well, that's even worse! Attack it, boys! Smash it!'

Then they proceeded to break and turn over every place. They defiled Greek women and children. They set churches aflame. They beat all of the priests who they found and cut off their beards.

There was a church across from our house. My father had served as a sexton there. The looters came at night and pounded on the door.

'Hey! Don't you have a Turkish flag? Why don't you display it?'

My father said: 'This is an Armenian church. Please, don't destroy it! Please!'

Then they began to crowd around my father and rough him up. The primary school director, Sitki Bey from Kırşehir, heard the shouts and came down the stairs and intervened. 'Do not do this!' he said, pleading with them. It's eleven o'clock at night. Who hangs out their flag at such an hour?'

'Are you an infidel?' they demanded, grabbing the director by the collar.

'No, I'm the school director! I'm a Turk!'

'Show us your identity card!'

'It's in my house!'

'Go and get it!'

Sitki Bey went and brought his identity papers and showed them, proving he was indeed a Turk…. He was very afraid, but through his intervention, Sitki Bey had rescued the Armenian church from the flames.

The looting finally ended. So did the pillaging and burning. They did what they had set out to do. There was even a whistle, a cue! The looting, the burnings, the beatings, the attacks… it all remains in my memory!

Afterward, they arrested a lot of innocent people and punished them, claiming that it had been the communists who had been responsible for the events. A handful of intellectuals who had had no connection to the events were even sent into exile! One of these was my close friend Dr. Hulusi Dosdoğru. There wasn't a thing that they didn't do to him!

I spoke frequently with Kemal Tahir and his circle. After reading his books I wouldn't be able to sleep at night. After reading his books, I began to understand, not to see the Turks as the enemy, but to perceive the Turkish reality. The more I read, the more I understood the Turkish reality, the nationalist feelings inside me began to give way to a love for humanity. I loved both Armenians and Turks. There was no more enmity left inside me!

And the more I read, the more my desire grew to develop my aesthetic sensibilities. I still found pleasure working as a tailor. But I had become a well-known tailor in Istanbul by sewing clothing for famous and wealthy people. The books that I read changed my view of the world. I could now see my surroundings, the things that I had experienced, more clearly than before. I took great pleasure from culture and art. The more my cultural world grew and developed, the better my tailoring became.

The Armenians had been artisans and master craftsmen in the days when non-Muslims used to intermingle with Turks and Kurds. They used to be specialists in their occupations. It's still the same way. But the Armenian wasn't trying to be superior to the Turks or the Kurds. He was just trying to overcome the conditions in which he lived. Naturally, along with this, the tradition of master craftsmanship and the transmission of masterly abilities from father to son also played a role in preserving this continuity.

But living as a minority in Turkey today forces a person to be more cautious.... You must be careful and mindful from every direction, and to be aware that you are always under scrutiny. You must always be industrious. There is bitterness and suffering in every Armenian's past, and in every Armenian living in Turkey today. Their spirits are wounded, damaged. Their personalities bear the traces of the unforgettable disasters of the past. If you're an Armenian in Turkey, that means you've escaped death. Ultimately, you're a humiliated Armenian!

Under these conditions, laziness and failure are unacceptable. Everything to which you set your hand you must do as well as you possibly can. In your life's struggle you simply have to be smart, long-suffering, tolerant and industrious, so that you can win the race where the odds are stacked against you. The state closes off many avenues to you. If you're an Armenian, you cannot be either a governor or a military commander. If you're Armenian, you cannot find work in government service. If you're Armenian, you'll end up in one of the good, free professions. If you're a doctor, you're a specialist; if you're a tinsmith, you're the best tinsmith in town; if you're a tailor, you're the best tailor. Only in that way can you succeed in the uneven life struggle in which you find yourself....

These were the conditions that caused me to become a master tailor. I was one of Istanbul's most famous tailors. I earned a lot of money. But I never had peace of mind.

'I should pack up and go to a more peaceful country!'

The events of September 6-7 had a great impact upon me, upon all of us. What sort of thing was this, anyway? They didn't give us a moment's peace. We pass our entire lives in a cloud of fear. It's one thing for us to deal with it, but what is these children's crime? There's no end to it. I should pack up and go to one of those countries where I can live without fear....

I set my mind to it: I'll go to Russia, to Armenia! During those years I was a big supporter of the Soviets. The Russian consul came to my tailor shop. I sewed clothes for him. We got to be good friends. We spoke frequently.

I began to work toward going to Russia.

The Russian consul warned me:

'Leave this business (of moving to Russia). Look, you've got a shop here. You earn well. You're in a good position. You won't find these standards of living in Russia, in Armenia. Give it up and come, if you wish. But don't be sorry afterward!'

'No,' I told him, 'I'll go to a country where I can live in peace, without fear, and earn my living!'

In 1965 I went to Armenia over Kars. All eight of my family members went.

We had only begun to open our things at the border when I noticed the difference. I had presumed that they would be helpful. But it appeared as if it was the Soviet secret police that screened us! They opened up the trunks of books. They looked through the books one at a time. I loved Boris Pasternak's *Dr. Zhivago*. I had brought it along.... But they found it among my books! 'Ha!' one of them said, 'How can you read this?' Then they began to search more thoroughly.... And when they turned up a book by Trotsky, how furious they were at me! One day after entering Armenia, they took me to the KGB headquarters in Leninakan where they interrogated me.

'What are these books?'

'Why did you come here?'

They intimidated me from the moment I arrived! They did their best to make me nervous and uncomfortable!

But I had gone to Armenia and the Soviet Union with great love and hope in my heart. And it was because of this love that I had thrown the Russian consul's warnings to the wind....

And already there, at the border, as they began searching us, I realized that I had made a mistake. But I said to myself, 'Let's wait and see. Don't get discouraged already on the first day...'

With each passing day, I began to understand the reality of Armenia and life in the Soviet Union more closely, by seeing it and living it first hand. It wasn't like anything that I had read in books.

My children continued their school in Leninakan. My eldest son finished high school there at the Gogol Lycée. He then entered the State Chemistry Faculty. I would go to parents' meetings at my children's schools. I would speak about the shortcomings that I saw.

My aunt, who had come to Armenia in 1946 with her husband, a Greek partisan, warned me, my spouse and our children:

'What are you saying?!?' she said, upbraiding us, 'You can't just criticize things freely like that! Everything you say, every criticism you make, every behavior of yours is written down! Hold your tongue and keep your mouth shut! Otherwise, you'll end up in Siberia! It's not like Turkey here!'

One of my paternal aunt's daughters had been one of the orphans whom Miss Kraft had rescued.

She had only been able to reach Armenia in 1920 after a thousand and one difficulties. Her husband had been Minister of Provisioning in the Armenian government. But that was all we heard of the matter. He had occupied a high position, but they were afraid to tell me or my family any more about it.

Everything was very open: the fear in Armenia was worse than that in Turkey! In Turkey we were afraid to speak, but we spoke anyway. But in Armenia, they'd pull your tongue out by the roots!

In Armenia, I spoke with Armenians in Leninakan who had been sent to the labor camps in the Gulag Archipelago and forced to work for twenty-five or thirty years before being released and able to return home. These people didn't have any teeth left, and their health was completely broken. They had been destroyed.... All those things that they claimed were lies were actually true.

It seemed as if the people who, relatively speaking, lost the greatest part of its population to the Gulag Archipelago were the Armenians. And I'm not saying these things to talk badly about Armenia—that's actually how it was! There wasn't any freedom in Armenia in 1965. When would it come? Nobody knew...

Needless to say, we were greatly disillusioned. We couldn't live in Armenia! We had to return to Turkey immediately!

I set myself to moving us back to Turkey, but it was a lot harder to leave than to return. They wouldn't let us go. It was only with great difficulty that we were finally able to win the right to exit the Soviet Union and Armenia.

We had entered Armenia on January 29, 1965. Eight months later, in October, 1965, we were able to return to Istanbul. Thank God we were able to return from our Russian odyssey with the same number of persons with whom we had begun it, with no loss of life, ha, ha!

I now think that I must have been out of my mind! How could I do such a thing? Why would I drag a family of eight persons into such a disaster without thinking about the end results?

I had burned my bridges when I went to Armenia. 'I'm never coming back!' I had said. I sold my house, I left my shop where everything was prepared, and gave it all away to my assistant, who I had brought up and taught, for whom I had arranged a marriage, and whom I had now made owner.

We returned to Istanbul, and despite everything, my country and Istanbul were both beautiful! But I had to begin again with nothing.

My Turkish assistant, who I had married off and to whom I had left my shop without taking anything in exchange, was now the shop owner. I went to him and explained the situation. I wanted my shop back. But he wouldn't give me a thing—not even an iron! When I went back a second time, he said 'Don't let this communist back in my shop ever again!' and they didn't....

I wrote it off as a lost cause! I opened a new shop in Beyoğlu. I took out an advertisement in *Cumhuriyet* newspaper: 'Kirkor Ceyhan has returned from his European travels. He has a tailor's shop in Beyoğlu!'

My customers began to come back. I was able to rebuild my business. I purchased another house. I had no lack of money. I earned a great deal.

My eldest son began university. Those were the years when the generation of 1968 were most active. My son was friends with Deniz Gezmiş. He began to skip school. I grew afraid. I'd look down the road, waiting for him every day. When he was late, I'd worry that something had happened to him. Would he return home safe and sound in the evening? Even very young persons and professors were shot down in the middle of the street... Once again, the fear of death enveloped me....

I sent my eldest son Shahnur to study in France in 1970. My relatives in Marseilles were going to help out. My son found work for a short time, and then registered for school. He continued to both work and study.

My daughter Vartuhi finished lycée in Istanbul. Shahnur called her to come to where he was. He finished university in Marseilles. I also sent my younger son Arsen to Marseilles when he finished Galatasaray Lycée. I sent my children living expenses from Istanbul.

It was during these auspicious days that my wife Vartanush died of cancer. She was forty-six years old. I remained completely alone. I had lost my taste for living. I could only find happiness beside my children.

'I've always looked for Zara...'

At the beginning of 1980 I left my tailor shop again and went to Marseilles. It wasn't possible to work, and you can't live off savings forever. I left tailoring to be a fruit seller. Together with my children, I opened a fruit stand. I learned as much French as was necessary to run the business. I earned good money, too. In 1982 I met my German wife Ilse, in France.

My son married a French girl, my daughter married a French man. At that point, the road called me again. I returned to Istanbul.

Ilse and I married in 1985. We went to Germany and settled in Bonn.

In my entire life, I've never become attached to any single place! I've never been able to settle in! I've always gotten fed up with every place I've gone, every country in which I've lived. The restless yearnings inside me have never abated. I'm from Zara. That's where I sent out my roots. Every other place to which I've gone has made me unhappy because it lacked something. I can't get Zara out of my head.... I was with my people when I lived in Zara! Zara formed me.

The world has become my homeland, but inside me, the only homeland is Zara! I remain an inhabitant of Zara....

Here, listen while I sing you a song from Zara! Whether I was in Russia, France, Germany or Istanbul, I've always loved songs from Zara.

Dağlar sen ne dağlarsın	Mountains, Oh, what mountains you are!
Kardan kemer bağlarsın	You fasten your belt of snow
Gül sende bulbul sende	There are roses found on you, nightingales...
Neden durmaz ağlarsın	So why do you continue to weep?

After reciting it, Kirkor began to weep again... How beautiful he recounted it, laughingly. From whence had these tears come? He was unable to continue the song. Then he continued, but the last lines were almost swallowed up in sobbing... I remained sitting, silently. I felt strange... Again, he attempted to recite the song, but it was impossible... He tried a different song:

Kevengin yollarında	On the roads of.....
Çimeydim göllerinde	I was the grass, amid the flowers
Hey anam hey...	Hey, my darling, hey!

İlik düğme olaydım	I was the button in its hole
O yarin kollarında.	In my beloved's arms
Hey anam hey…	Hey, my darling, hey!
Yandan çiçeğim yandan	At my side, [you are] my flower,
Seni severim candan	I love you with all my heart
Keşke sevmez olaydım	If I didn't love you
Ne tez usandın benden	How quickly you would have tired of me
Hey anam hey…	Hey, my darling, hey!

After finishing the song, he began to smile. The clouds of sorrow began to clear from his face, and in their place, flowers bloomed…

"I'm a passionate person!" he began to explain. "In my life there are three things that I have been passionate about: books, classical music and women…

In these three things I have found a salve for my pains and sorrows.

After middle school, the ache and oppression that I felt at being unable to continue to study, at having to give up a life of learning, I tried to rid myself of this abiding bitterness by reading every book I could find, and first and foremost, the classics of world literature.

There was one place inside me reserved for folk songs, another for classical music. Before I got to know and love classical music, I would sing the songs from the general mobilization that I had learned from my mother and father. I still love these songs. This period is best explained through folk songs. These songs never lie! When I began to listen to classical music, I found the perfect solution. I chased away my weariness with classical music. In classical music I found a voice for the storms blowing inside me. From morning to night in my tailor shop I listened to Mozart, Schumann, Chopin, Beethoven, Tchaikovsky, Schubert, and everything else. When I took on an apprentice I told him 'Classical music is going to be played in this shop, if you can stand it, come!' My love of music gave me hope and filled my life with joy… I found my greatest wealth in books and music.

All my life, I have adored beautiful women. I earned a lot of money, and I spent a lot on women…. Ha, ha! I had many girlfriends. And all of my girlfriends were Turks… I didn't have any relationships with Armenian women… I took my revenge by falling in love with them, ha, ha! My wife would catch me. Sometime I would put my socks on inside-out, sometimes I'd re-tie my tie wrongly. Other times she would find strands of hair on my clothing... She tolerated me... After she'd catch me I'd show more interest in my wife.... I never neglected my wife and children.... I never put my children's future at risk.... I received more energy for work by courting beautiful women... And through this love I conquered my fears.... Through this love, I stopped being angry at life.

I've arrived at the age at which I can see the good in any situation. I'm seventy-three years old now. I'm ill... The doctors say I've got chronic leukemia. I've been receiving treatment in Germany for ten years now. The medications I use are very expensive, but my wife's insurance covers all of the expenses for the medicines. I've seen the value that is placed on human life in Germany.... It doesn't make any difference if I was an Armenian or a Turk. I can say here 'I'm an Armenian!' without fear.

I don't know how much longer I've got to live. In Zara I was able to live because of some good, heartfelt people. I'm writing these things down, these days...

My father was an optimistic person. He tended to think good thoughts. 'Whatever happens, at least we're healthy!' he'd say. Sometimes he would tell us stories. My father never held a grudge against anyone, he loved everyone.

My mother used to sing folksongs about the period of general mobilization and about migration.

Göç göç oldu	Wandererers, wanderers there were
Göçler yola düzüldü	The migrants lined the roadside
Ela gözler uyku geldi süzüldü	Their chestnut eyes, drowsy with sleep

She'd sing songs like that and cry. She'd cry, but in such a way that it seemed to me that she was just mumbling! My mother was full of pain. But this pain didn't kill her. She lived to be ninety-eight years old. Because of that she'd often say, 'If I die from anguish, then so be it! What's that to you? Every sort of calamity can befall you. Everyone can die! The last one left will arise again. You don't have time to stand there confused! Don't lose your sense of who you are!'

My mother never learned to read or write. But she was such a strong, hopeful and optimistic woman. My mother and father raised us in an atmosphere of love, hope and optimism. I didn't infect my children with anger. I raised them and nurtured them with love...

I don't have anger against Turks or Kurds! We can't turn back the clock. What happened then is now just water under the bridge. Now, also you can have the same evil appear. Societies discuss the situations in which they find themselves. They argue about them. They kill one another, and they love one another.

What Turks do today to their own brethren, would they do to me? Do you think that the one who would kill me will refrain from doing the same thing to his own cousin? Of course not, because in life, the one who doesn't love himself cannot love another.

I know those who brought this disaster upon us, those who plotted against the Armenians. I still see them. I can still understand why some people would pollute the seas around Turkey. One drop of water doesn't make an ocean, but that one drop carries the same basic characteristics as the ocean. In the same way, one Armenian exhibits the same traits as the entire Armenian nation. But today, only sixty thousand Armenians remain in Istanbul from a population that was once over a million. Every single Armenian is a descendant of those who survived the calamities. There is some measure of the great sorrows of the past embedded in his flesh and bones. Yet, despite this, I wasn't a nationalist. I didn't raise my children to be Armenian nationalists.

'If I've been able to make it this far....'

If I have been able to make it this far, if we have made it this far, it's because my neighbors, my fellow villagers kept us. If it hadn't been so, we would not have been able to survive. In other words, we all made it as a result of a loyalty to every covenant... of a centuries-long friendship. Without this, neither the laws of the Ottoman state nor of the Republic would have protected us.

In Zara, when they were going to pummel me on the street or in school, it was sensible Turks who defended me: 'What do you think you're doing, you cowards!' they would say, 'You're acting as though he were a chicken! Everyone beats the defenseless. If you want to beat something, go hit something bigger than you and see what happens!'

They would extricate us from their grasp and protect us. There were such brave and noble persons in Zara.... It's because of them that Zara remains in my mind.

During those times when the Deportation Law came out, when it was declared that the Armenians had no right to live here and all had to leave, no brave and courageous soul failed to take in his Armenian neighbor, friend or acquaintance. And anyone who helped an Armenian was liable to deportation himself! But there really were such courageous people who took this danger into account and could still come out and say 'Do you know better than we do whether a given Armenian is good or bad? Can we really know the good or bad character of these persons by our own lights, yours and ours?' They may have been few in number, but such people actually existed. There are such courageous Muslims. But how many actually come forth in any society? It gives me hope to know that there are people—Muslims and Turks among them—who keep in mind what's important and hide their neighbors, thereby saving them from death. I am curious about such people...

I am of Armenian origin. I don't love a person simply because he or she is Armenian, but because he is good and intelligent. I love authentic people.

If such persons didn't exist, humanity would perish. The world exists on account of their preservation of the essence and dignity of humanity. It's because of them that everything doesn't collapse. There are both tame and wild dogs in the world. There are Kurds, Turks, Armenians and Greeks....

Let me give you an example: during the general mobilization, the mayor of Zara was a fellow by the name of Ahmet Ağaoğlu Ali Efendi. Ali Efendi had a bosom buddy by the name of Mihran Vartanian. Before the deportations even began, they came to Mihran's shop, pulled him out while he was working and beat him to death. It wasn't known who it was that came to beat him. The assailant was unknown!

As soon as he heard of the murder, Ali Efendi went straight to Mihran Efendi's house. Without delay, he brought his friend's wife and children to his own house. He quickly married his wife and made her a Muslim. By that he prevented his friend's wife and children from being deported and killed. But Ali Efendi never went unto the room of this woman he married. He took care of her and her children for months, for years! He looked out for them, he protected them. When the situation finally calmed down, he took the first opportunity to find a way to send them to America. For years afterward, these people whom he had rescued sent Ali Efendi letters and gifts. They never forgot this good deed. I saw such things myself; I experienced them.

There aren't a lot of this type of person, but they exist!

Those who survived did so on account of these persons. The Union and Progress Party and the Ottoman state at that time had no tolerance, no mercy. The interior minister at that time, Talât Paşa gave very clear instructions: 'Do not let sentiment affect your behavior! Do not give special regard to women and children! Deport all of them!' By 'deport' he meant 'eliminate them and don't leave a trace!' The penalty for not carrying out such a clear order was death.

There were other brave souls like Ali Efendi, who, in the face of death, protected their Armenian friends and acquaintances. And such people weren't just found among the Turks, there were Kurds, too! But after Sultan Abdulhamid II created the irregular Kurdish 'Hamidiye' Regiments in 1891, the Kurds began to harass the Armenians. During the Ottoman era, the largest massacres of Armenians were entrusted to the Kurds. Even so, there were some good persons among the Kurds who rescued and protected Armenians, who hid Armenian children and raised them.

You can't hate the rose simply because of the thorns. In every life there are evil days. But despite it all, you still have to love life itself. And in fact, every day life gets a little better, a little more just. What happened to us was truly an enormous calamity. But despite the enormity of the tragedy, we can't just get embittered about life. Naturally, I will come to the end of my road like all of God's creations. But I will have no regrets. This life will continue through our children. I've never given up hope. I never liked people who had given up hope. Ever since I was very young, I haven't believed in fate. I never acknowledged God. Who are we, and who are others that he would decree that one should be destitute, another rich? It was my character that molded my destiny. That's me! That's how Kirkor is! And I couldn't have done it any other way. It wasn't in my character to oppress others, to exploit other people or use them.

My end isn't far off! I feel like I'm living the last days of my seventy-three-year life. We come and we depart! When they ask me: 'What's do you have to say? What's your testament to this life?' I tell them this: I have loved people. I have sought out people! People are what is most important, neither buildings, nor wealth... People... only people...

For my entire life, I have always desired that the Turks would know themselves; that they would understand where they are in this darkness. I wanted our Turkey to understand this, and to return from this dark place. I've always desired that we should come from a place of beauty, of goodness of positive things.

But it never seems to have gone that way. Maybe after going bad it will one day turn around and move toward the good. I still have hope that Turkey will be a good place one day...

So, my last will and testament is this: Love people. Don't trample on people's rights. Avoid nationalist, religious and chauvinistic sentiments. When people abandon these things they become human beings. Nationalism, and religious and chauvinistic ideas have long brought calamities upon humanity. And nationalism is the most dangerous of all.

I believe that humanity will advance most clearly through love, friendship and knowledge. People must save themselves from these mental plagues. The only way to do this is to read, read and read some more....

I returned home from school on Monday, September 29, 1999. There was a message on my answering machine: "My name is Arsen Ceyhan. I'm Kirkor Ceyhan's son. My father was very fond of you. He passed away at nine o'clock this morning. His funeral will be in Bonn on Wednesday."

Oh, my Armenian brother from Zara! How you loved your home town!

It had been exactly six months before that he had said "The world is my homeland. But within me, my only homeland is Zara!" Afterward, tears began to flow from his eyes like rain.... Ilse and I sat there, grieving together with him. When he had composed himself again, he sang a folk song:

Ayrıldım kavuşamam	I was separated, and could not be reunited
Küstürdüm barışamam	I gave offense, and could not be reconciled
Göz açtım seni gördüm	I opened my eyes, and I saw you
Yad ile konuşamam	But I could not speak with a stranger

I drove my car from Bochum to Bonn. I was going to Arsen to express my condolences. I recalled the things he had told me: I could still see him weeping as he said "I'm from Zara!" I sang the folksong he had recited. The road to Bonn stretched out into the distance.

When I arrived, I was met by Arsen. It was the first time we had spoken. At first, we spoke for a little about the business of publishing the book that he had written about Fikret Mualla.

Kirkor Ceyhan's bed remained empty... I gazed upon the unoccupied mattress...

"They took him to the morgue two hours ago," he was able to say. Phone calls came from Istanbul, from Marseilles... Condolences were spoken in Turkish, in French, in Armenian, in English and in German. Arsen remained all alone there.... The air hung heavy, like lead.

"Come, let's walk a little" Arsen suggested. Outside, there was a cool autumn wind blowing.

We walked along the bank of the Rhine river. Across the Rhine, on the opposite bank sat the German Parliament and the various ministry buildings. It was entirely empty. The capital had been moved to Berlin.

Arsen recounted some of his memories of his father. As for me, I told him my impressions of our encounter six months before. As we walked, the conversation passed from one subject to another, finally coming to the subject of the remaining traces of Armenian culture in Anatolia and Armenian mythology. Arsen had done some research on these topics. His knowledge was broad. He spoke of love, of peace and of preserving cultural values.

"I'm my father's son" he said. "My father was always hopeful. My father raised us without rancor, with love."

The waters of the Rhine rolled by. We sat on the fallen trunk of an enormous pine tree which the raging spring waters had plucked out from some unknown mountain, some unknown mountain pass, and deposited here. The Rhine flowed unceasingly toward the sea.

Arsen said "My father used to say..." and immediately, he was transported to somewhere else.

"The Kızılırmak river flows right before Zara. It's very broad there. In the spring it's very turbulent and overflows its banks. It really upsets people. One time during that season, a fox fell into the Kızılırmak. It got caught up in the current. It struggled to survive and to reach the bank, but no matter what it did, it couldn't reach the shore. The river was great, the fox, small. Even as it looked hopeless, and the fox was being swept to its death, it said to itself, 'Well, I was heading toward the Black Sea anyway!'"

Alas, Zara: Do you feel the longing of your Armenian children who were raised within your bosom? Alas, Kızılırmak: Do you remember the cursed sorrow of that hapless fox that was swept to its death in your raging torrent? Even if you've forgotten, your son, Kirkor from Zara, who lived for twenty years in Marseilles, still hasn't forgotten you...

Meline's hunger strike

Meline and I got together again in the middle of April. It was a brilliant spring day and before we spoke we decided to go out and experience the beauty of the season in the Wattenscheid Municipal Park.

Afterward, we went to my place to speak. I recounted the things that Kirkor Ceyhan had told me about Miss Kraft, and about his life. Meline was distressed at her death and the manner in which she died. From within the depths of her being and thought-world she spoke the wish "May God rest her soul."

After that, it was time to talk.

"So, where did we leave off, Kemal, my dear?"

"You had just successfully completed primary school, Meline."

Whenever Meline began to speak on an important subject, whenever she wanted to draw attention to a specific detail or aspect connected to the events she recounted, she would either laugh and say "Anacığım!" ("Dear mother!") or, smiling, she would use the term "Efendim!" ("Sir!"), making sure to stress every syllable. This time it was "Anacığım!", said laughingly as sparks of love glittered in her eyes:

Dear mother, no one in our family had gone to school past the third grade. I was the only one to receive a diploma for completing fifth grade. Among us, finishing the fifth grade was like being a professor!

But then my father cut it off: 'Enough already with your learning! Now you'll learn to be a seamstress!'

My mother supported my father this time.

'If you study too much, what will you do?' she said, 'First learn seamstressing! Earn your keep!'

'No!' I insisted, 'I don't want to be a seamstress! I won't do it! I'm going to study! I'll even make it to the highest level of school!'

Then the school year came around again. I was at home... All of the other people in the building asked: 'What happened to Meline? Isn't she going to school?'

I couldn't find a reply to give them. My flowing stream had turned stagnant. My blooming flowers had wilted. My feet and hands wouldn't even work... Food and drink had lost their flavor for me!

It was autumn, the month was September. But the air had not yet grown cold. Istanbul was in an Indian summer.

I would sit in the building's garden from morning till night. I didn't go into our own apartment. I didn't even enter the neighbors' apartments that I so frequently went in and out of.

I'd sit at the end of a table that sat beneath the mulberry tree for hours, just thinking. I would speak to myself. The thought of food or drink wouldn't even cross my mind.

'I have to learn,' I'd say to myself, 'I have to learn until I reach the very highest level of school. I have to go to Paris, to Europe, like Rona! There was no endeavor other than learning that could save me!'

My mother and father had no idea of what I meant when I told them 'Sign me up for school!' I knew my father's character. He was stubborn. If I attempted to prevail upon him, he would clam up… and then blow up!

'I have to learn!' I told them.

'But how?' they'd ask.

One day I got the idea of going on a hunger strike. I wouldn't eat a thing; or maybe I would eat, but only in secret. I didn't know. All I knew was that I had cut myself off from eating and drinking, saying, 'Come what may, I *will* go to school!'…

I thought a lot, and in my world—a child's world—I had made my decision. I felt myself totally alone and without any options. But while saying that to myself, one day I suddenly felt like a stranger. And I started to cry, from deep inside. I cried—and how! I cried my whole heart out…. The people in the other apartment heard my voice. Those who didn't hear were told about it by those that did….

'Meline's crying in the garden!'

'Meline has stopped eating and drinking!'

'Poor little Meline, her eyes are all out of tears!'

'Little Meline is crying over school!'

The entire apartment building was shaken up. Even Haminneciğim heard my weeping. She came down the stairs holding onto the banister the whole way. She went to my mother and vented her anger:

'You whore's daughter! Why won't you let my little girl go to school? I'll break your bones! This isn't like the old days anymore! Go! Send her to school!'

After Haminneciğim, Rona the Sorbonne graduate then raised the flag of rebellion. I was still crying in the garden when Rona approached my mother.

'If you don't send little Meline to school, if you don't have the strength to do it, we'll send her. The child has suffered enough. She's cried her eyes out. Not eating like that, she'll waste away!'

After that, she came to my side.

'This can't go on!' she said. 'I'm going to take you this very day and register you for school!'

There was nothing that my mother could say. Rona said 'Come, Meline! Hurry, my child, get dressed! I'm going to take you down to the school and register you!'

She took me by the hand and we traveled by streetcar to the Yessayan Armenian Girls' Lycée in Taksim… She knew the woman who was the school's principal. When we arrived, she explained the situation to her.

'This child has been crying non-stop for two whole weeks because she wants to go to school,' she explained. 'Her father is a doorman. Do whatever you have to, but please: register her for school! Let's together save her life!'

Yessayan was an expensive school. But the principal found a way. She enrolled me immediately.

'Come, my daughter!' she said. 'Congratulations! You will start school right away!'

She then took me by the hand and brought me, without a school uniform, straightaway to the classroom, introducing me in the middle of the lesson and placing me in the teacher's hands.

At the end of class Rona took me back home. Immediately, a school uniform was purchased for me: a navy blue skirt, a white blouse, black socks and a hair net for my hair. And that's how I, by my own initiative and two weeks late, began to study at Yessayan. I entered the school as I wished, through my own child's stubbornness and resolve.

I can still recall how I felt the moment I entered the classroom for the first time. I was very happy, and very excited. Meri, who would over time become my friend and would later go on to become a professor, later recounted to me her recollections of when they brought me into the class for the first time: 'They brought you in as if you'd just been hatched out of an egg!'

"Come, Meline: you'll go on with your life even without your father!"

The Yessayan Girls' Lycée was in Taksim, on Meşelik Street. Across from it was the private Zapyon Greek Girls' Lycée. I would go to school by taking the streetcar from Şişli to Taksim, where I'd get off and then walk the rest of the way down İstiklal Avenue. One end of Meşelik Street ran into Siraselviler Avenue, the other end ran into İstiklal Avenue.

How many times I walked down that short, narrow street! The front door of Yessayan School was exactly one hundred and forty-nine steps from İstiklal Avenue, one hundred and twenty from Siraselviler. This front door gave me life. It made me a whole human being.

Yessayan was a school that provided a thorough education; its teachers were of the highest quality. At noon they provided lunch. We had a sweet little church in our tiny garden there. I spoke the most sincere prayers of my life in that little church.

When I was in the eighth grade, my father fell ill and died. About five or six months after that, the apartment building in which we lived was sold, and we were not only removed from the job of being doorman, but from the apartment itself. We moved into a small house on the outskirts of Kurtuluş.

The entire task of supporting the family fell on my mother's shoulders. My brothers had grown up. I got along best with my older brother. He would take me out for walks and on Saturdays or Sundays he would bring me to a dance hall called Tedansan where they served tea and snacks. I learned to dance from my brother.

After my father died, he acted as both a big brother and a father to me. Over time I learned what it meant to be without a father. I immersed myself in my studies. I always received grades of 'Very Good' for my work. If I ever received 'Average' I would be very upset.

After my father passed away the school's administration stopped asking me for tuition.

The teachers at Yessayan were there out of a love for teaching. Each one was a specialist in his or her own field.

I'll never forget one of my Turkish teachers, Miss Perihan. She began teaching Turkish literature and composition. In my entire life I never saw another teacher who gave lessons as beautifully as she did. As long as I was a Turkish instructor I always tried to make my lessons like hers.

Our mathematics teacher, our philosophy and sociology teacher and our Armenian teachers were all wonderful people, each more precious than the next. At the Armenian schools, they begin French language instruction in the third grade. At Yessayan, we learned Armenian, Turkish, English and French.

Along with Armenian language and literature, all of our science courses—physics, chemistry, mathematics and astronomy were all taught in Armenian. We had Armenian teachers of the highest quality.

Among all of our teachers, the one who had the greatest impact on me was our principal, Madam Kalustyan. She also taught at Galatasaray. She taught us mathematics, geometry and astronomy.

Along with our school lessons, there were also many cultural events. I took part in these with great gusto and enthusiasm. I had roles in the theater productions and operettas. I also participated in poetry reading competitions.

Our lessons were over at four o'clock every day. After school, the cultural activities began, and continued until six in the evening.

I had roles in three different operettas. The last one we did was Lehar's The Gypsy's Passion. There was also an opera in Armenian called Anush. The subject of the opera was a love tragedy. I sang in Anush when I was in the eleventh grade. I had a very good voice. Our music teacher even told me 'You simply must go to the conservatory!' He even gave me singing lessons. A little later, I understood just how much these singing lessons had opened my mind. But I didn't want to be a singer. I didn't like to be a singer and to appear on stage.

Yessayan opened me up to the joy of life. I had always learned from my mother and father to be quiet. But my years at the lycée had opened my eyes. It provided me with the leaven to mature into who I am. I graduated from Yessayan Girls' Lycée in 1957.

"I saw a pair of eyes! It's all over!"

During those years, our teachers didn't only teach at one school. They'd teach five hours a week at Yessayan, ten hours at the Armenian school in Kurtuluş, and another six at some other school. They had to be constantly running from school to school.

Our music teacher gave private singing lessons to me and my friend Meri. We both had very good voices. We used to sing really well. For the singing lessons we had to have a piano, but the only place where there was a piano was the Armenian middle school in Kurtuluş where she taught. Because of that, she'd call Meri and me to the school in Kurtuluş. Anyway, it was close to our home.

I remember when we were students in the last year at the lycée. We were in our glory. I wanted to learn everything. Whenever I learned something new, you couldn't stop me from talking all about it! I was caught up in my love for learning. I was positively brimming over! And I wasn't doing it for the grades, or to pass a class; I was simply giving myself over to this desire to learn that had taken me over. But at that point the only love that I had experienced was for learning, other types of love I had not yet experienced...

One day, we entered the teachers' room at the Kurtuluş Armenian Middle School in order to receive our singing lessons. Some ten teachers were sitting around the table. All eyes turned to us the moment we entered the room. It was then that I saw one pair of eyes for the first time! Oh my God! At that moment, it was finished! I was dumbstruck and remained frozen where I stood! Meri said 'Have a seat,' but I didn't even hear her. It was the strangest thing! I was unable to speak—or to do anything else for that matter! Those eyes had enchanted me.... I couldn't for the life of me tell you what we learned that day or what songs we sang. The sparks that that pair of eyes had given off had lodged in my mind, in my heart, in my entire world!

Was this love? Was there such a thing as love? If there was, for me it was that pair of eyes! If I wasn't inflamed by the passion of love at that moment, I don't know if I've ever been!

"There's one more chance"

During those years, when I was bewitched by those pair of eyes, when I was suffering from the sorrow of not having a father as I was coming of age, my friend Meri's father took my hand and helped me out. He behaved like a father for me. God have mercy on his soul! Nowadays, when I look back at this part of my life, I still remember very well just how precious the kindness and understanding that he showed me were.

My father had died, and we had been forced to leave the apartment building. I felt so alone during those years. There are moments in one's life, there are passages, transitions when a person just wants someone to guide them and take care of them. When they are on the verge of falling, they look for some warmth, someone to reach out to them…

Meri's father did that for me during those days after my father died, when my heart was weighted down with loneliness. He gave me support. He helped to quench the flames of sadness in my heart. I felt as if he was always around, always by my side, just like my own father. He gave me confidence. He was the branch to hold on to, the stretched out hand.

He was a very understanding, very open-minded person. He would take us to the famous nightclub Maksim in Taksim Square.

'Go and see it! Get to know what it's about!' he would tell us. 'Don't go there with others just because you're curious! I'm going to take you so that you get to know all the different sides to life!'

And indeed, that was the first time that I had ever seen the inside of a night club. Meri and I danced all night.

My elder sister's family lived on one of the back streets behind Maksim. Often, when I was leaving or coming to their home I would hear the music emanating from the club, sometimes raucous, other times heartfelt and profound. I grew curious about what went on in that world called Maksim.

Later on, he also took us to famous restaurants and to the beach at Fenerbahçe. When I think back to the Fenerbahçe shore, I can still see that day clearly; I laugh when I think about it. I felt like a little girl at the hamam who was being inspected by a matchmaker. Afterward, there was a man who began to follow me around. More correctly, he had fallen head over heels for me… He followed me everywhere. He even sent his aunt to our little, shared-kitchen, one-room basement apartment in the Kurtuluş neighborhood….

My suitor turned out to be a grain merchant! He was very rich! Meri and I used to laugh long and hard recalling it: 'We went to the beach, and we found a grain merchant!' Years later, a family from Konya also came to ask for my hand. It was clear from their manner what it was that they were expecting.

I put on a short skirt and went next to them. I sat down before them and crossed one leg over the other. Then I took out my lighter and lit myself a cigarette!

They sat there frozen in amazement! They couldn't utter a word—not even to say what they'd come there to ask. They quickly gulped down their coffee and left, practically fleeing.

My mother understood the game I was playing. She was furious at me. But in that manner we maneuvered our way through the treacherous straits....

Every period has its own songs and music, right? During those days, the most popular singers were Hamiyet Yüceses, Perihan Sözeri, Müzeyyen Senar and Münir Nurettin Selçuk. In Taksim there was a very high quality music hall called Kristal. My elder sister lived nearby. I used to hear the songs that were sung there as I'd make my way to her house.

After my sister got married she bought a gramophone that would hold ten records. You could stack them up on the central post, one on top of the other; then you'd just press the button and sit back and listen to the ten songs, one after the other... The song I loved the most was 'Bir ihtimal daha var' ('There's one more chance'). Every time I'd go to my sister's place, I couldn't keep myself from playing that song and listening.

Bir ihtimal daha var There's one more chance
O da ölmek mi dersin 'And is that to die?' you say

It was as if this song was the soundtrack to my life. I had always chosen the possibility of living over dying. During those days, I had taken the path of never thinking about death...

Madam Kalustyan's crime

After I graduated from Yessayan, I continued my relationship with the school. I met with my teachers, and closely followed the developments at the school.

Anyway, time went by, and then there was the military coup of May 27, 1960. They set to work rewriting the constitution. They summoned to Ankara representatives of each religious community and of all sectors of society. Madam Kalustyan went to Ankara in order to participate in the work of preparing the new constitution. She remained there for some time.

The winds of democracy were blowing through society. We felt a great joy and enthusiasm during those days. Everything would be fixed and put in place!

The new constitution was written and put into effect. Madam Kalustyan again returned to her duties at Yessayan.

One day we heard that Madam Kalustyan had been fired by the Ministry of Education! Do you know why? Because she had corresponded with the principal of another Armenian school in Armenian! Can you imagine that? We were already in the year 1965, and corresponding in Armenian in an Armenian school had become a great crime!

It wasn't long before the atmosphere of freedom that had followed the 1960 coup changed for the worse. Director's assistants called 'vice-directors' were appointed to all of the Armenian schools. Much more than any teaching they might do, these persons occupied themselves with gathering information and monitoring the political mood within schools. One day, Madam Kalustyan was fired from the school because of a report from the 'vice-director' who was her assistant!

She was shocked at what had befallen her. But no matter where she turned, she was unable to explain her distress. She tried her best to continue to lead her life in Istanbul, but no matter what she tried, nothing succeeded. In the end, she said 'To hell with it!' She left Turkey amid deep disappointment. She went to Paris in the 1970s. But she couldn't make a go of it there, either. She died of cancer in 1980. Her body was brought to Istanbul for the funeral, and she was buried in the Armenian cemetery in Şişli....

Crossroads

I graduated from the Yessayan Armenian Lycée with the highest grades. My mother hadn't wanted me to study. My family was having a hard time getting by. After my father died, my mother began working as a cleaning lady at the Shell company building in Taksim. She worked hard, and long hours, but she earned very little. My siblings grew up. Some got married. In time it was my turn. My mother wanted to marry me off as soon as possible and thereby conveniently free herself from me and the obligation I represented. I had come to a crossroads. There were two ways before me: I could either listen to what my mother said, find a job and work so that I would not be a burden to her, or I could continue with my school despite everything.

I had experienced this dilemma once before, when I had finished primary school. At that time, they had wanted me to be a seamstress and earn money.... I had rebelled with my child's understanding; through my hunger strike I had secured the right to continue with school. But the current dilemma was more difficult; life had become more complicated. My mind, my heart, and all my senses said 'Continue your studies!' I was either going to break the narrow and confining bonds that surrounded me, or I would surrender to the hard conditions of reality.

In the end, I didn't listen to my mother! I listened to my head, my heart and my feelings. I enrolled in university. I launched out in the direction of knowledge.

Our school principal had told me 'You should go to the Department of Literature.' But my grades in science had also been very good. Why then should I study in the Literature Department of all places? So I entered the Chemistry Department of Istanbul University.

One year later, I left school. I understood that I wouldn't be able to study the sciences. The fact that I was a burden to my mother was pressing heavily upon me. There was no other way but to go to work.

I found a job as a secretary at the Armenian Middle School in Kumkapı. I get goose bumps every time I remember the excitement of that first day that I began as secretary....

I took the streetcar from Kurtuluş to Şişli, then from Şişli to Beyazit. From Beyazit I walked down Gedikpaşa Street and opened the front gate of the Kumkapı Armenian Middle School.

The teachers came. I looked up and there, right before me—that pair of eyes again! The eyes belonged to someone named Kegham İşkol.... Again, I was as bewitched as the first time I saw them. We introduced ourselves. And what an introduction! Within a short time our feelings for one another blossomed. Our friendship slowly transformed into an emotional tie.

At that time Kegham İşkol taught at the Tıbrevank Armenian Lycée in Üsküdar and at the Armenian middle schools in Kurtuluş and Kumkapı.

He was a very influential and persuasive individual. He influenced me greatly. He was then thirty-five years old, a full fifteen years older than I was. He had experienced so much already. He was talkative, happy and full of hope. And a communist. I learned something new from him every day. For a young girl who had only recently graduated from the lycée and only studied at university for one year, and who still didn't possess much life experience, he was everything. He knew everything. He analyzed everything. No matter what he said, he certainly had already thought about it, debated it and spoken about it. It never even crossed my mind to ask 'Really? I wonder....' It continued like this for years and years. I let him into my own world. Already in one of our first conversations he said to me 'You have to continue with your university studies.'

He was one of those types who loved to share. It made him happy to share everything he owned. And to see him happy made me very happy, too.

One year into our friendship, he said to me 'You're going to reenrol in university.' He left the choice of selecting which field to study up to me. I liked the English Philology Department of Istanbul University. But in order to be accepted into this department I had to do well enough on an exam that measured one's knowledge of English, and to write an essay answering the question 'Why do you want to study in the Department of English Philology?'

In the essay, I focused on the theme of 'reading Shakespeare in the original language.' I passed the entrance exam.

I began my studies again in the autumn of 1960. That was a time of enlightenment and freedom that had followed the May 27 coup. We were all so full of grand hopes and plans.

That year, they accepted four hundred new students. The students were divided into three groups, A, B and C, according to their level of English proficiency. The most proficient were placed in group A, the somewhat less proficient in group B, etc. I wound up in group C. But I attended the classes of all three groups. I was placed first in the annual exam, and one day I found myself in group A.

After the fifth semester, I chose 'General Sociology' as my secondary field of study. I took a course from Professor Cahit Tanyol. Professor Tanyol and I got along very well. I translated a great number of socialist writings for him. A very close teacher-student bond developed between us. More than a student, I became like his work colleague.

Five years after I began university again, out of the four hundred students who had begun the program, there were only eight graduates. I was one of them. After graduation, Cahit Tanyol called me to his office:

'You've done really well, both in your English and your Sociology courses' he said. 'I see your success. Would you like to work as my assistant?'

'It would be a great honor for me to work with you as your assistant' I answered.

So, I made a request to be an assistant. I was full of expectation. I assumed that there would be a quick reply to my request, but months passed and I didn't hear a thing.

I sent a request to the Ministry of Education to teach English and Sociology. I wasn't accepted because I was Armenian. In that way, the door to high school teaching was slammed in my face.

After a lengthy search, I found work as a teacher at the ABC Private School in Üsküdar. I was still hoping to receive an answer to my request for a university assistantship. But I was too embarrassed to ask Cahit Tanyol directly.

An entire year passed. Finally I went to him one day and asked:

'Professor, what was the outcome of my request for the assistantship?'

'Unfortunately, my child, it's not to be!'

'Why not?'

'I took your request to the [Academic] Senate. The professors rejected it, saying, 'You can't place an Armenian to teach a course in sociology!''

I was shocked and confused in the face of this reality! I had always thought that acting in a neutral, scientific manner had been essential at the university, but I had been mistaken! The reality was quite different! The truth was, in my own country, in the homeland in which I had been born and raised, it was a crime to be an Armenian!

I thanked my professor for speaking so frankly and not beating around the bush, but inside me, it was as if the flowers of optimism and hope had wilted and died. I began to feel myself a stranger in my own country. This produced a terrible bitterness and sorrow inside me. Yet, no matter how much I tried to break the suffocating brace of this truth, my whole world seemed to be narrowing and closing in on me!

Now that my hopes of being a professorial assistant were dashed, I began to look for a good teaching job. Two of my friends who had graduated from university with me got jobs at the Technical College as English instructors. The school was looking for one more teacher. Without even asking me, they had put my name forward. They didn't mention that I was Armenian.

'Look,' they told me, 'we suggested you as a teacher. But don't tell them that you're Armenian!' The painful experience of the assistantship was still fresh in my mind. This time, I applied, but didn't mention my Armenian identity. They accepted me; I had 'passed through inspection.' But all this secrecy, all of this 'passing inspection' bothered me profoundly: I was very upset that in my own country, even in a city like Istanbul, I had to keep my identity a secret!

During my childhood and when I was a young girl, I never heard a word from either my mother or my father about the great disaster that the Armenians had experienced. Every now and then, my mother would mention Sivas, or my father, Kangal. But they never tried to instill me with the poison of enmity or rancor. In our apartment building on Küçükbahçe Street I had grown up within an atmosphere of complete tolerance and respect for those who were different from you.

I never read about Armenian history, neither in elementary school nor at the Armenian Girls' Lycée. I didn't know anything about the events of 1915, nor what preceded it or what followed it. Nobody had ever mentioned these events to me. For me, Turkey meant Istanbul....

While I was never forward about my own identity in Istanbul, others had picked me out and excluded me, saying, 'You're an Armenian!'

In fact, it was this exclusion and these obstacles that first caused me to look into and think about who I was. Each time my Armenian identity was laid before me as a crime, it increased my curiosity about Armenian history, and about my own family's and my own race's past. The question 'Who am I' became an existential inquiry for me.

It was a great opportunity for me to get to know Kegham and to live with him. His profound knowledge and his broad understanding of the world opened the path before me. Through Kegham's love and through his help, I began to see the events, which, up until then, I had seen but could not understand. Under the warmth of his love, my passion for literature and art, my aesthetic sensibilities and value judgments all grew and blossomed.

My knowledge of both Turkey and of Armenian history expanded greatly on account of Kegham. I became sharper and more alert. When I had questions in my mind that I could not answer, he was both my teacher and my guide. He listened to everything I said with patience, he thought about it, studied it and then gave me an answer. I never tired of speaking with him, discussing things with him. My love for him grew deeper for as long as we lived together.

On a specific day every week, Istanbul's well-known Armenian intellectuals would gather at a certain house in Şişli. During those days, the relations between the Armenian intelligentsia were very close, very lively and very productive. Kegham had a respected place within their circle. These meetings were very beneficial for me. I became acquainted with ideas, opinions and questions that I had previously never heard or taken an interest in. I began to understand the past, the future, and what was transpiring at present. In every one of these relationships and developments, I was at Kegham's side. He gave me strength. I blossomed through my love for Kegham, through living with Kegham; flowers bloomed in my hand, in my heart and in my mind. Loving and wondering at him was a passionate road that led straight toward the good, the beautiful and happiness. Through this passion, the flowers that had opened in my world began to bear fruit.

"Who really was the person behind that bewitching pair of eyes?"

Some people's fate is written in the dewdrop on the leaf of a pink rose. Sometimes, a person gets to know him or herself when they childishly smile at the clouds gathering on a cool autumn day.

I had been smitten by Meline on just such a day, in the teacher training course in Dortmund. The spring flowers in Meline's eyes had bewitched me. As for Meline, she had been smitten and enchanted in a music lesson by a pair of eyes whose owner she didn't know. I was curious. Who was this person who had put Meline under his spell?

In order to understand Meline's world, I would have to get to know the world reflected in that pair of eyes. For many long years, the owner of those eyes, Kegham İşkol, had left his imprint on the life of Meline, which sparkled on the leaf of that pink rose.

And Meline obliged me. Without holding anything back, without keeping a single episode from me, she told me all about Kegham İşkol. She took a deep breath and began to explain:

> I was so smitten by those bewitching eyes, without even knowing who Kegham was or what he did! And at that moment that I was first smitten, I didn't even see who he was, how he looked... I hadn't had the time to even ask what he did.... After our second encounter, at the Armenian Middle School in Kumkapı, I began to see Kegham in his totality, to see a whole person, made of flesh and bones, and to understand him.
>
> Kegham was a native of Istanbul. He was Greek on his mother's side of the family. In other words, an old, venerable Byzantine family. His mother spoke Greek. Kegham also spoke Greek very fluently. He spoke Greek with all his cousins and other Greek relatives. On his father's side, he came from an established Armenian family. Both his father and his uncle had been involved in politics.
>
> Before the First World War, at the beginning of the century, when the Armenians were organizing themselves into political parties, both

his father and uncle had had important political positions. They had even participated in the raid and occupation of the Ottoman Bank in Istanbul, an event that holds an important place in Armenian history.

After this operation, both his father and uncle fled to Egypt. After the establishment of the Republic they were able to return to Istanbul. Because for us, Turkey *was* Istanbul....

Kegham had studied at the Getronagan Armenian Lycée in Karaköy. He had met and married his first wife during his years there. During those years that I had met and lived with him he was still married! His wife was an attorney.

Unlike myself, there were no traces in Kegham's world of the disaster of 1915. No one from his family had perished in this calamity. Because his mother's family was Greek and his father's family were Istanbul Armenians, none of them were deported. Nevertheless, like every Armenian, Kegham felt the sorrow and bitterness of the events of 1915. But during those years we never spoke about the matter. Unlike the Armenians who lived in Anatolia, the bitter memories of the Deportation and its aftermath—an event with which they were forced to contend every day of their lives—were simply not an issue for Istanbul Armenians at the time.

Because of his knowledge of languages, Kegham's father had worked in the Istanbul Customs Administration.

After the Surname Law came out, he was forced, upon the request of his workplace, to change his family name of 'Kerovpyan' to 'İşkol.' Nevertheless, his uncles continued to used the name Kerovpyan.

As long as I lived with Kegham, I was able to see that the fundamental events that had shaped his world had occurred during the Second World War and afterward. The events that had made Kegham who he was had happened to him as a leftist, as a communist.

In 1946, while he was studying in the Philosophy Department of Istanbul University, Kegham had been one of the founding members of the Istanbul University Students Association. During his student years he had been very active in the activities of this organization. It was because of this that he had been 'marked' by the political department of the security services. This 'marking' would appear as an obstacle to him at every juncture of his life.

After the election of the Menderes government in 1950, they initiated a broad campaign of arresting and interrogating those known to be communists. Kegham was caught up in the political turbulence of the time. Things happened to him that he didn't deserve. During his interrogation, he was put in a cell at the political department headquarters that was so narrow he couldn't even sit down. They'd dunk his head in cesspools.... During his questioning, they'd burn his eyes by using very high-wattage lamps. Viewed from outside, you couldn't detect it, but his retinal nerves were destroyed. Only much later did I learn that those eyes that had bewitched me had actually been seared during police interrogations.

His wife, who was an attorney, was a great help to him during his police interrogations and confinement. She never left Kegham alone. It's because of this that Kegham always felt great respect for his wife. But it was this excessive respect which, over time, caused the love and sentiment between them to wither and die.

The tortures that he had experienced had caused more damage to his spirit than to his body. His spirit had been severely wounded. He experienced various psychoses. In thirty-five years he had already amassed a century's worth of life experience. That was why he appeared as such a saint to me. Those who knew Kegham either loved him or hated him. There was no middle ground in the matter. In short, he wasn't just your average, every-day person. For me, it was his extraordinariness that made him so interesting....

Despite all of the bitterness and ruin that he had experienced, he was a hopeful person. He loved life, and he loved living it. He adored women. He had had many amorous adventures. He was a regular Ottoman gentleman, an 'Efendi'.... I was astonished by his enthusiasm for life, and by the hope that sprang eternal in his breast... It was the source of my hope, too!

He held a place of great respect within the Armenian community of Istanbul. He was one of those select people who was fluent in both ancient and modern Armenian, as well as the language of Byzantium. He had written a dictionary of Armenian. During that time, his was a prominent name among Armenian intellectuals. I always felt astonishment at his status in the cultural world of Istanbul.

After four years of confinement, he was acquitted at the end of his trial. He was still in possession of the judgment acquitting him of all crimes. With this behind him, he applied for the position of principal of the Surp Khach Tıbrevank Armenian Lycée in Üsküdar, where he had taught. Those responsible parties at Tıbrevank favored his appointment. They trusted him. Those who had initiated this appeal for his appointment had viewed it as a sure thing. But such an appointment would have to get approval from Ankara, from the Education Ministry, and—even more importantly—his security check would have to be positive.

After his file was sent to Ankara, he began to wait, and hope. 'Times have changed,' he said. He believed that in the trials that were held against him, he had been acquitted of all of those past things. But months passed and still he received no answer. Influential persons intervened on his behalf, but still no reply. He himself began to travel to Ankara. Once he had a very open and frank talk with one of the ministerial advisors.

'I'm sorry,' this advisor had told him, 'but it says in your file that you were a communist! Your security check has come back negative. You could be a thief. Even a rapist. But this, this being a communist... that's something else entirely! No! There's no way you can be a school prinicipal. What's more, you openly state that you're Armenian!'

Kegham was stunned by this outcome. It came as an enormous disappointment to him. I had been denied my right to be a professorial assistant because I was Armenian. As for Kegham, his request to become the principal of an Armenian lycée—something that was his right—had been denied because he was a leftist and an Armenian....

What kind of thing was this?! Hadn't democracy come to Turkey? Weren't we able to live more freely now, more humanely, as members of one of the religious minorities? As Armenians?

We had traveled far, over hill and dale, but when we looked back, it appeared that we had hardly made any progress at all!

One day I sat with Kegham and discussed this:

What had we accomplished?

What happened?

What now?

What could we do about it?

The two of us were steadfast, like the patient rock. But to whom should we tell our hardship? Who would understand us?

If we recounted our pains to the patient rock, would it be able to stand it?

Speak, patient rock! If you were in our place, could you take it? Whose country was it, anyway?

To treat us like strangers in our own country on account of our identity: even 'patient rocks' like us had a hard time accepting this!

'There's no place for us here!' we said. 'If they are going to treat us like strangers in our own homeland, then let's go to another country and be strangers there!'

In our place, what would you do, patient rock?

Part Four

Kegham İşkol's students and friends

"Is that how May is in Istanbul these days?"

How would I be able to find students who knew Kegham İşkol? Whom could I ask? In a matter like this, you couldn't just go around asking anyone! Such a subject couldn't be discussed with just anyone. "Well," I thought, "go find yourself an Armenian!" No Armenian would speak with a person whom he didn't fully trust or know well. And if he did speak, he still wouldn't open up to me fully.

What could I do?

Then I remembered Doğan Görsev. He had been press director during the time that Ahmet İsvan had been mayor of Istanbul. Although he had been arrested and convicted after the September 1980 military coup in the "Peace Association" trial and had, as a result, sat for years in various military prisons in Istanbul, this dear man and able translator had eventually been acquitted. "Brother Doğan," as he was called, referred to himself as an "active partisan of humanism" and was very familiar with the cultural circles of Istanbul....

"How would I go about finding someone who could render me assistance in finding Kegham İşkol's friends and former students?" I asked Doğan.

"That doesn't appear too hard," he replied, smiling. "I've got a dear friend who is Armenian. His name is Zakarya. We were in Metris Military Prison together. He's a good man, this Zakarya, and he's trusted within his circle. He's a very knowledgeable person, an architect, and a very understanding friend.... I don't know which lycée he graduated from, but I'm sure he'll be of some help to you."

On April 30, 1999 I was to fly to Istanbul in order to receive the 1998 Abdi İpekçi Peace and Friendship Prize. The award ceremony was going to be held on May 3rd, at the Doğan Media Center inside the *Milliyet* newspaper building.

I figured that I would remain in Istanbul for four days. I decided that I would devote the time not spent in the award ceremony looking for Kegham İşkol's friends and students. I had no other business to take care of in Istanbul.

Brother Doğan had said in a completely serious and responsible manner, and with a voice that radiated the warmth of love and friendship, that

Zakarya would help me out. Throughout our long friendship I had rarely seen Doğan give a person such a high recommendation.

"Let me call him first," he had said, "then we'll talk!"

By the time I arrived in Istanbul, all that remained for me to do was to call Zakarya.

The newspaper *Milliyet* and the prize committee had reserved rooms in the Dilson Hotel in Taksim Square for the year's recipients. It was already the evening of Friday, April 30, when I settled into the hotel. I called Zakarya and informed him that I was staying at the hotel. Then, at about 9:00 p.m., though still weary from my journey, I left the hotel and immersed myself in the human river of Beyoğlu.

It had been years since I had seen Taksim Square, İstiklal Avenue and the Beyoğlu district at night. How it had changed! How crowded it was everywhere!

The side facing Taksim Square of the magnificent Aya Triyada Church at one end of the Greek lycée was now plastered with huge and hideous cigarette advertisements. These ugly billboards looked as if they had been placed there with the intent of making the church invisible from the square.

The first place I went was the Yessayan Armenian Girls' Lycée, where Meline had gone to school. I walked down the dark and narrow Meşelik Street, which formed a triangle where Siraselviler Avenue ran into İstiklal Avenue.

I thought of Meline. She hadn't been down this street in years. How many times she must have walked these streets and entered this door. I wonder what she said the first time she passed through this door... what prayer did she say?

Still thinking of Meline going over in my mind and the things that she had told me, I walked straight down İstiklal Avenue toward Galatasaray Lycée.

At that time of the evening the human torrent was still too great for İstiklal Avenue. Were most of the buildings really old, or had they simply aged since I had seen them last? Now, they had become so beautiful, these historic buildings. These unique examples of the colorful cultural world which had made Istanbul the city it was.... how filthy they'd become through neglect! The department stores, the shops all attracted one's attention with their colorful lights. But a glance at the upper floors of these

"Who really was the person behind that bewitching pair of eyes?" 205

Zakarya of Ekrek (Kayseri)

buildings housing such colorful and attractive shop windows was enough to shatter any illusions one might have.

Were these the streets of Istanbul, the city in which I had spent my youth and to which I had tied my hopes? Were these the sellers of music cassettes, so selfish in their shouting and blaring music?

And how about the street children, huddled on these street corners, huffing glue! Had Istanbul been so full of conflict and tumult since Byzantine times? If not, had I simply built a picture in my mind of an Istanbul for something that it wasn't?

I turned down some of the side streets: nothing but darkness and filth! I was actually afraid, upset.... I turned as soon as I could back toward İstiklal Avenue, to throw myself back into the human river.

I was in Taksim.... Tomorrow, it would be May 1st.... How many years had passed since my last May 1st in Taksim? The year was 1977. We had dispersed and fled like the remnants of a defeated force, a routed army! The losers had then taken position on the street corners! The street sweepers had gathered up all of the posters, banners and wooden sticks to which they had been attached and taken them to the middle of Taksim Square, where they were burned like the chaff from the harvest. The hopeful songs and slogans of that day now burned in huge flames, throwing off sparks to the heavens. The shimmering redness of the flames played on the faces of the people, the trees and the buildings lining the square. But apart from the roar of the flames, Taksim was silent! Istanbul had covered its face in mourning for its dead children....

I now walked down the same route I had walked back then, looking for traces of my former life... It was not to be found there, but it was indelibly etched in my mind, that Taksim evening of twenty-two years ago..... At that time people had died, crushed by the throng in that narrow opening of Kazanci Street.... In the color of the carnations they donned, in the lines of the songs they had sung, there had been a drop of hope, a whiff of freedom....

And afterward.... yes, now I could see it.... it was right at that moment, right here.... A tank ran over and crushed a young woman, her blood smeared by the tank's thick treads across the asphalt.... and the picture they had printed the next day in the newspaper!

Was this that same Istanbul, whose streets had rung with songs of hope? Was this the same Taksim?

I was unable to fall asleep that night. I lay there for a long time, listening to Istanbul.

I walked down Barbaros Boulevard in Beşiktaş.... Thousands—no, tens of thousands of people, workers, students, men and women, young and old, all swirling around in the festive holiday atmosphere.... I had never seen Istanbul so young, so full of hope... Later on, we marched to Taksim singing marching songs and others.... I had never seen such a crowd, such a spring... And then we were being fired upon from all four directions... then, the crush, being dragged in place... I'm shouting!

I'm shouting and jumping in place. I'm soaked with perspiration.... Where am I?

Morning arrived and found me still awake. The racket of motorcycles shook off what was left of the night from sleep-filled eyes.

It was May 1, 1999. Around 9:00 a.m. I departed the hotel and returned to Taksim. This time, my only role would be that of a spectator. I was angry, unhappy at merely being a bystander.... Before the monument to Atatürk and the Republic on Taksim Square, some fifty or sixty persons were holding a silent demonstration. There were more police than protestors! I was standing at the end of Kazanci Street. The leaders and other members of the Republican People's Party's provincial administration laid red carnations in honor of the thirty-five souls lost on that day.... and I was watching from a distance! Those bearing the carnations were lost in the multitude of television cameramen and police officers, both uniformed and plain-clothed.

Still sour over my new, passive role, I made my way to the Atatürk Cultural Center. The people breakfasting in the café and bakery of the large luxury hotel on the right watched those bearing the red carnations...

So, was this how May mornings went in my city, whose squares once rang with songs of freedom and hope?

Strolling around the Square, I came upon some flower-sellers, who were camped against the base of the high wall of the Water Administration building. I bought a carnation and stuck it in my lapel. I had escaped from the irritation I had felt all morning at being a bystander. Now there was more bounce in my steps. Within my mind, I sang the "May 1st March": "A new sun is born, within ourselves and among the nations!" The Kemal inside began to laugh. A little later, the young woman with the black apron came to my side... She stroked the head of the child within me... Together, and without saying a word to each other, we began chanting the same lines. Suddenly, Taksim was full with people! Istanbul had become beautiful again! Row upon row of pigeons took flight.... coming to rest again on the branches of the surrounding trees, there watching with their henna-colored eyes.... I embraced Istanbul and kissed its eyes in love and blessing!

With the woman in the black apron I walked toward Meline's school. Soon, we were joined by Meline as well... the black-aproned worker on my left, Meline the beauty queen on my right.... Her eyes were like sunshine... her voice, like spring...

I introduced Meline to the black-aproned woman... they embraced... afterward, we knocked on the front door of Meline's school. By then, it was approaching 10:00 a.m. The air had not yet lost its morning coolness....

The school watchman opened the front door... I asked for permission to enter... I wanted to see Meline's school, the benches where Meline had sat for all those years, the schoolyard where Meline had played, the church where Meline had prayed, to touch them, to smell them, to sense them....

"Please, enter..." he replied.

The watchman saw me—but he didn't see my female escorts... I entered. I read the inscription on the left-hand wall: "Built in 1895." It had been built more than a century ago!

I suddenly looked around.... I was alone... All alone I ascended the marble stairs on my right, making my way up to the second floor. The school was spotless.... the classrooms and the corridors smelled of a musk-scented soap.... I entered a classroom. I sat down on one of the benches... perhaps Meline had sat here.... I touched the blackboard, I held the doorknob of the classroom door... everywhere, I sought traces of Meline. Every place, every object in the school smiled back at me like Meline's eyes...

I went out to the garden. I entered the small, delightful Taksim Surp Harutyun Armenian Church situated there in the school's garden. How many times had Meline prayed here during her student years?.... I lit a candle inside the church for Meline; I wished her health, happiness and contentment!.... At that moment, my heart laughed with Meline's. At that moment, religion meant merely a drop of love! The different gods of men came together and merged, with the warmth of love, into one! The language of love, there, in Surp Harutyun Church, was a symphony of silence.

I saw Meline—there! In the eyes of Mary! Their visages both spoke with flowers. Meline merged the past and the future, the oldest Armenian deity with the bright sun of tomorrow, all within the love, the passion of the present.

Zakarya from Kayseri

Zakarya came to the hotel on Sunday, May 2nd. We met for the first time. We had spoken twice on the telephone already, and I had told him, "I'll be sitting in front of the revolving door at the hotel's entrance. I'll be wearing a dark, night blue, checked shirt. I'm short."

The moment of our encounter had arrived. He entered the revolving door and I saw him scanning the faces of those sitting in the lobby. Our eyes met, and I felt a "click" in my heart. He smiled, and his smile, like his face and his stance, radiated sincerity and goodness.

The whole thing hardly lasted a minute. I said to myself "That's the one!" just as he turned to face me. As our eyes met, so did our hearts! It was true…. we had both said "That's him!" at the same moment. Then we introduced ourselves.

We went up to my room on the fourth floor. It was quieter and more peaceful in my room. I gave to Zakarya the gift that Brother Doğan had sent along with me and conveyed his greetings.

I briefly mentioned Meline and Kegham İşkol.

"I'm looking for the former students of Kegham İşkol and others who might know him. Can we locate such persons?"

"Certainly!" he replied without hesitation, "I'm one of Kegham İşkol's students. But we can also find other persons who know him."

"You don't know how happy that makes me!" I said. "What a good fortune for me to stumble upon you! I would like to hear about Kegham İşkol from you. Who was this Kegham İşkol, who bewitched Meline? What sort of teacher was he?" Could he tell me?

And so he began:

> It's been a long time since then. Almost thirty-two years! Let's see what I remember… Kegham Bey, or 'Baron Kegham' as he was called in Armenian, taught me Armenian at the Üsküdar Surp Khach Tıbrevank Lycée for three years. Just like other schools, we mischievous children

came up with nicknames for each of our teachers, according to how they looked and acted. Baron Kegham was one of those teachers for whom we couldn't find an appropriate nickname. Nothing we came up with seemed to stick. He knew Armenian really well. He was a master of the subject. Our teachers were well-trained, knowledgeable persons who loved both their jobs and their students. Baron Kegham was even more fatherly than the others.

The students were a little taken aback by Baron Kegham's class. Most of them had just newly arrived from Anatolia, and they knew Kurdish better than Armenian; even their Turkish was choppy and punctuated. How could he make them less hesitant? Kegham İşkol's task with these students was a hard one.

Each one of us who had come from Karagözyan was assigned a student who had recently come from Anatolia. We were forced to devote certain hours every evening at the boarding school to teaching these fellow students Armenian...

Baron Kegham would make everyone speak Armenian every minute of the day and continually try to teach a couple of new words of Armenian related to the subject we were learning at the time. During his courses, he would work hard to teach the material. Every now and then he became angry; but I never saw him act even slightly on this anger. I never even sensed it. Who knows? Maybe Baron Kegham suffered great distress when we failed our lessons... I still have that impression within me...

Kegham Bey was a swarthy individual. He looked as if he put pomade in his hair every morning before school. He combed his hair straight back, from forehead to neck, and on both sides, too. Even now, I can still see those comb streaks in his hair....

Whenever he would be explaining a lesson, whenever he would give a long discourse on some subject, a little white ball of spittle would form between his lips. I could never understand this.

Sometimes, during his Armenian language class, he would digress into another subject, and would speak to us as if he were our father and we were his children. He was well-aware of our hardships, of our loneliness and of the hard time we had living in a boarding school. He would speak about everything with us when the subject arose, from clothing and finery to table manners, from the relations between friends to sexual topics.

He really was a father to us. He was compassionate. During his class one winter day, he took off his own sweater and gave it to one of my friends who was cold and didn't have a sweater of his own. I'll never forget that moment!

Kegham Bey drank wine. I somehow thought that this wine, the cheapest drink when I was young, had become a steady table companion to Kegham Bey.... As if he received no satisfaction from life other than drinking... as if he had no joy in life other than teaching.... When he arrived in class in the morning, I thought that he'd again lived through sorrowful days. But we never could ask, 'Teacher, what's wrong?' There was never enough of a warmth or rapport between us that would allow us to ask such a question.

We were more or less aware of his private life and his disagreements with the school's administration. These internal disputes within the school's administration and the relations between the teachers all had an effect on us students. We would take sides in the various developments and disputes within the school. We felt ourselves closer to Kegham's side, and we tried to guess what he felt, if not on subjects related to the school, then at least on social subjects.

After graduation I didn't have any more contact with him. Later on I heard that he had gone abroad and was working at a university, and that he had died in Bochum...

Baron Kegham left a deep, positive impression upon us, through his ideals, his fatherly character and his mastery of Armenian. I can see that more and more with each passing year.

"How did this happen?"

The Surp Khach Tıbrevank Lycée, which means 'Holy Cross Seminary' in Armenian, was founded in 1953 by the Armenian Patriarch Hiktanudur Haçaturyan, with the aim of educating and preparing future clergy. In the first years after its founding, and at the time I was there, it was a boarding school where Armenian children from Anatolia came to study.

During those years, the patriarchate had a policy directed toward the Armenians who lived in Anatolia. In the years of its founding, 1953, some fifteen hundred churches and monasteries and hundreds of Armenian schools and colleges throughout Anatolia had simply vanished. The only trace left of them was in photographs and peoples' memories.

Although their numbers were few, there were still Armenians living in many provinces, throughout Anatolia. They had not been totally wiped out. The Armenians in Istanbul were well aware of this situation in Anatolia: how many families were living in which corner of what province, how many school-aged children these families had, etc. Through some or other method, and with greater or lesser accuracy, such information was gathered and kept in Istanbul. Armed with this information, they would go every year to Anatolia and collect the school-aged children to Istanbul, in order to provide them with an education, with the younger ones being sent to the Şişli Karagözyan Armenian Orphanage, and the middle and high-school students living at Tıbrevank. With the intention of 'saving the remnant,' great efforts were made under the trying conditions of the period. And the only way to 'save' this remnant was education. Education and more education...

Those Armenian families that couldn't find an Armenian school for their children in Anatolia sent their progeny to the Karagözyan Orphanage. It was considered a stroke of fortune to be able to go to school. The school administration could therefore choose to take only the most able children from every family. That was the only possibility they had. Those who graduated from Karagözyan and who wanted to continue their education went straight to Tıbrevank, without having to bother looking for another school. During those days, if you were a student at Tıbrevank, it meant you had studied at Karagözyan. If not for Karagözyan, Tıbrevank could never have survived. And it was totally free. Neither those students who did their elementary, middle or high school education at Karagözyan and Tıbrevank were asked to pay a thing. The community's mutual support system took care of all problems, met all needs.

So, as the Armenian population of Anatolia was gradually dying out, the Armenians gathered in Istanbul, and these schools then began to take in students from Istanbul as well. At first, only male students were allowed in, but in my time they were accepting female students, too.

The education and teaching staff of both schools was composed of very select teachers, full of lofty ideals, capable and familiar with pedagogic methods. Like Kegham İşkol, each one was greatly knowledgeable in his or her field of instruction. Most of them had devoted themselves fully to education. At Karagözyan, there was Digin Siranuş, Sarkisyan, Oriyort Mariyam; at Tıbrevank, there was Baron Acemyan, Baron Aratan, and many others....

Our principal was from the clergy. Ever since the school's establishment, its principals had been persons possessing an honored and respected place on the Religious Council. Later on, the position of school principal was turned over to lay persons.

The administrators and the teachers were like our parents while we were at the school. That's how much they loved us, and how much we respected them...

Despite the fact that it was essentially a religious school, the education that was provided was democratic and scientific.

Baron Acemyan's love for physics and chemistry made all of the students love this person very deeply and more than anything else. We worked hard to finish all our physics assignments on our own volition, and without compulsion, just so Baron Acemyan wouldn't be upset. This greatly respected teacher would later immigrate to France. He's there now.

Our teacher for mathematics and geometry was one of the most esteemed architects in Turkey, Istepan Aratan. It was impossible not to love his classes.... After the famous architect Mimar Sinan, it would fall to an Armenian, Mimar Istepan Aratan, to build mosques for the Muslims. I can now tell you that I was an architect. Istepan Bey was the architect who, after Mimar Sinan, built the most high quality mosques in the classic Ottoman style in Turkey.

And he taught at the school not because he needed money, but simply out of love for the subject, and high ideals.

And we worked hard at math and geometry, not out of concern for getting a good grade, but because of our love and respect for Istepan Bey. It was because of our love for our teachers that we loved our classes and succeeded at them.

At Tıbrevank I got to know literature and the social sciences....

Both our teachers and the school administrators placed special importance on the students' cultural development. We read piles of books. During our classes, we could say what we thought without fear. At Tıbrevank we acquired the habit of reading, researching, debating, listening, thinking and following our thoughts through to their conclusion. For this reason, for years after we had left school, these well-trained students grew up to be progressives, leftists. The foundations for my progressive world views were lain at this school. I consider myself extremely fortunate for having gone to this school.

At Tıbrevank, I read Tolstoy, Dostoyevski, Pasternak—all of the classics that the Education Ministry translated into Turkish. I became familiar with the books published by Varlik Publications, one of which Baron Acemyan gave at the beginning of every year to the students, after having selected one especially for each and every one of them.

Tıbrevank had a 'special' place among the Armenian schools. After a certain date, Tıbrevank Armenian Lycée became known as the school of 'hillbillies and leftists'; they were viewed quite inhospitably by certain circles. Our elders became given over to suspicions that the school had veered from the intentions of its founders. It couldn't be said just how much service Tıbrevank graduates afforded the priestly class, but some of these students would eventually fall victim to some of the first 'anonymous assailants' during the turbulent years. No light could be shed on these murders. They were hushed up…. People declined to talk about them. The deaths of these persons were quickly forgotten….

The Education Ministry's curriculum was imposed at our school. Apart from history, geography, and Turkish literature, we also had classes in philosophy, psychology, logic and even Armenian.

But despite the fact that Tıbrevank was an Armenian seminary school, we never got to learn Armenian literature or history. It was forbidden to teach Armenian history at an Armenian school. It was officially forbidden for Armenian children to learn their own history! Forbidden!

Regarding Armenian history, we didn't even have a book or anything. The teachers gave us oral history lessons, all on the basis of their own knowledge of the subject. In our Armenian literature classes, we were allowed to take notes on the condition that we quickly 'lost' them when the Education Ministry inspectors came to the school.

Today, the educational and instructional conditions have declined from where they were in our day. We are now confronted with official demands that even in the Armenian schools, most of the courses be taught in Turkish.

In our identity cards it's written that we are Christians. Our national identity remains unstated. So, in order for an Armenian family to be able to register its child at an Armenian school, it has to prove that the members are Armenian. Think about it! Even without such a proof, is there a single Turkish family in Turkey who wants to send their child to Armenian school? Of course not! If the parents wish, they can enroll their child in the American college if he or she passes the necessary exams. Nobody asks their national identity there. But everything comes to a screeching halt when they just want to go to an Armenian school. A thousand and one obstacles are placed in the way of Armenian families.

Both of my sons went to the Armenian school. I also became closely involved with the school's affairs, serving as a trustee. We had to meet frequently with the relevant government ministries, with the administrators of the educational foundation, with the directors from the Education Ministry.

Just think about it! Before they get permission from the foundation's administrators, the school's trustees aren't even allowed to hammer a nail at the school, even if they use their own money! For example, up until two years ago, we had to receive permission from the General Directorate of Religious Foundations in Ankara if we wished to spend more than five hundred million Turkish Lira (around $300). Now this amount has been raised. The school is old and in need of repair. We wish to collect money as trustees and have the school whitewashed. But we have to go to the ministry in Ankara in order to get permission! The school's administration doesn't have the authority to make the necessary repairs to the school, not even if the trustees volunteer their own time and money! You can't do anything on your own! But these things can be done at other regular schools. The school's administration can resort to help from the trustees in order to carry out the basic needs of the school—but such things are impossible at Armenian schools!

If you'd like, we can go now to the Karagözyan Orphanage in Şişli. You can see an Armenian school with your own eyes! There, you can ask all the questions you wish....

In the schoolyard of the Şişli Karagözyan Orphanage

We left the Dilson Hotel. The air was warm as we strolled together to the Karagözyan Orphanage. We received permission from the watchman and entered the schoolyard. The yard was surrounded by walls and trees. The flower beds were well-maintained. The surroundings were spotlessly clean. We sat down on a bench in front of the main entrance gate of the three-story school building. Above the entrance there was a plaque saying, "Karagözyan State Orphanage. Established: 1912." We sat there and spoke in the cool of the garden.

Zakarya began to drift back to the world of his youth and began reminiscing:

My childhood years were spent here, at this school! Now and then I come here and sit on this bench. I sit and think about my childhood, about my village, and about my past and future. This bench is one of my places for thinking and talking to myself. During my years here, the school yard and garden used to stretch all the way to the cemetery. It was vast. Every year they'd hold athletic contests on this field. One part of it was covered with mulberry trees. We used to eat our fill of mulberries. I'd miss my village and my family. During the first days after I arrived I would go and find myself a quiet corner at the foot of a mulberry tree and cry to myself... Afterward I got used to the separation, the homesickness... There! Do you see it? There's not even a single tree left. When Bedrettin Dalan was mayor of Istanbul, he cut down my beloved trees and put a market place and a parking lot there. All that was left to the school was this little patch here. Where are the kids supposed to play? Where are they supposed to run? In recent years, some people who don't think about anything but money, such circles cast their gaze on the school's garden. If they could, they'd tear down the school itself and erect a big skyscraper in its place..."

Zakarya told all about the schools where he studied, about his teachers, but he didn't say a word about himself, about why he had arrived at the orphanage.

"Where are you originally from Zakarya?" I finally asked. "Who are you? What is the yeast that leavened you? What is the land, the past that made you who you are?"

He fell silent. His gaze dropped to the toes of his shoes, to the concrete. I couldn't tell where he was gazing. After a while he lifted his head again. He raised his eyes to the school nameplate and stared at it long... Was he reading it or evaluating it? Was he searching for someone? Something? I couldn't tell.

His eyes still fixed on the plate, he said "I'm from Kayseri. I was born in the village of Ekrek in 1950. I went to the primary school in Ekrek for the first grade."

Then he turned his head in my direction. Facing me, he smiled bitterly.... He took a deep breath. He looked troubled as if he was about to tell a secret. Would he tell me it? Or wouldn't he?

"The other children of the village beat me every day when I went to school!" he said with a shudder. "They would beat me!"

> It was about one and a half kilometers between the school and our house. The way was a rock-strewn dirt path. We would leave our earth-roof house at the base of a big rock, and then there was a big bend in the road before we got to the school. After turning the bend you couldn't see our house anymore.... The people in our house couldn't see me even if they wanted to.
>
> After that bend, every day for a whole year, I received blows from every child, large and small, in the village! Out of some two hundred houses, there were only two Armenian families left. Us, and my mother's mother. One Armenian had married Said Ağa and after that, I had a Muslim uncle. In the old days, Ekrek had been an Armenian

village with seven hundred and fifty households. They were killed even before they could be sent off on the Deportation. No one survived except for a few babies. Everyone was gone! There were two churches in the village. My mother told me that on the order of the District Governor of Bünyan, one of them had been dynamited and fire bombed; its ancient doors were sent to Istanbul. Not a stone was left standing of the two churches.

In 1924, the town of Ekrek, which had been almost entirely emptied of Armenians, was now settled with those Greek Muslims from the population exchange. We called them the *muhacirs* (migrants). It was the children of these emigrants who would block my way every day at the bend in the road. 'You Armenian bastard!' they'd say, 'C'mon, let's see you take out your cross!' Then they'd hold three of my fingers together and try to make me make the sign of the cross. Striking me on the head, they would chant, 'Hey, you dog! You infidel, son of an infidel! Let's spit on the cross! Let's hear you say the Shehada! Isn't that how it is?'

At that time, I didn't know what it meant to make the sign of the cross; I'd receive a few slaps and run straight to school to escape the curses and insults.

I'd arrive at school crying every single day. My teacher never said a thing to the children who beat me. He told my mother and father instead. My mother was angry and grieved. As for my father, he was a poor, miserable horse shepherd. Those who would have been arrayed against him in this matter were the village's toughest families. He got angry at me. If he hadn't, he would have cursed and boiled over with helplessness.

I still carry within me the fear from the beatings that I received on the way to school and the cursed sadness of the humiliation that I experienced as an Armenian child. No matter what I do, I can't rid myself of them!

On the one hand, my father wanted to send his children to school, but on the other, he felt helpless that his child was being beaten on the way to school every day. He felt all alone.... In Ekrek village, my whole family felt all alone! To whom could he complain? Who would listen to the sorrows of a miserable horse shepherd? Was such a person even considered a human being? Was any honor accorded him? If the children who beat me, who spat on the cross that they made me make with my fingers and tried to make me say the 'Shehada' were like that, would even bigger persons treat me any more like a human being?

Some nights they would even stone our house. They would rain down rocks upon our house! It felt like the earthen roof of our house was going to collapse. But my parents, neither my father nor my mother, dared to even go outside and say 'Who's doing that?!' or look for the people who did it. The only person in the village who would protect us was my school teacher, Mustafa Alimci. Many nights he and his wife would sleep at our house. Before it would get dark, they would walk in plain sight of all the other villagers to our place. Those nights we slept more soundly.

During the Christmas and Easter holidays some of the village children would come and visit us; they'd come and receive their treats and go. At that young age, I couldn't fathom how they could do that, and I'd stand there, shocked and amazed. My mother and father had some other friends in the village, but not one of them would speak out under any circumstances against the people who intimidated and humiliated us.

It was during these fearful, bitter days that my father did what he did. He took me and brought me to the orphanage in Istanbul and enrolled me in school there. It was this school that saved me from becoming a frightened rabbit, and made me into a person! This orphanage was what restored the joy in living to all of the destitute, miserable Armenian children from the East, the Southeast and Central Anatolia!

Every time I pass this orphanage I feel happy. But it gives me a little 'twinge' of sorrow inside as well. Sometimes I will hurry past the front gate without stopping, but others, I'll come in and sit here....

Later on, I graduated from the university and became an architect; I'm approaching fifty now... I always wanted very much to examine those feelings deep inside me... to take a close look at the circumstances and conditions that made me who I am.... but it never happened; I couldn't do it! I consciously avoided dealing with myself...

My father never told me about his own past. Even after I began thinking more or less about these matters, I still wasn't able to ask him... It was as if there was an unspoken agreement between us: I didn't ask, and he didn't volunteer any information!

All that I know about their past I learned from my mother and from her mother. From time to time they would recount some events—albeit they were usually just snippets. What I can still remember from those stories is the personal history that made me who I am:

The things my father told me...

My father's name was Hovsep. He was from the village of Karahallı, near Yozgat. My father was the son of Zakarya, who was one of five brothers: Yakup, Agop, Boğos, Zakarya and Gülbo. I was named in remembrance of my grandfather... I remember that my father used to list the names of thirty-two close relatives in one breath: Ardaş, Tercan, Zartar, Bedros, Kadem, Haci Emmi, Artin, Ohannes, Mıgırdiç, Lusin.... the list went on and on, of these ancestors, these relatives of mine who arise and awaken on the Day of Resurrection... but not one of these members of our line remained alive! I told you, didn't I, that not a soul was deported from the village of Ekrek. Everyone was finished off right there, through what they called 'easier methods,' or a 'short cut.' When my grandmother used to get angry, she'd get beside herself and say things like 'Did *you* ever see a baby trying to nurse from the breast of a dismembered woman? I have!'....

The children and infants remained up for grabs. Although the Americans were in many places in Anatolia, they first gathered the children remaining in the Kayseri region and put them in the American colleges and Red Cross centers. Afterward they brought them to America by ship.

My father came from a group of seven brothers. But from these seven brothers, his parents, uncles and others, he was the only one who survived. Later on the Americans found him. They brought my father to the Talas American College in Kayseri. He stayed there for one year. He learned a little English. During the second year he was there, he ran off with one of his friends in order to go and look for his family. But he didn't find a single relative. While he was there, without another relative in the world, a Circassian family took him in. But my father wasn't able to save himself from becoming the family's servant.... They raised him within their family; they also used all manner of threats and intimidation in order not to set him free. My father acted as this family's servant until he was thirty-five years old! His main job was to look after the horses and act as a stable boy!

From Kayseri there was pasture that stretched as far as the eye could see, all the way to Sivas. It was called Uzunyayla (Long Meadow). The best horses are raised in that meadow. My father was the horse tender of Uzunyayla.... He understood the language of horses and their pain very well. He knew and understood the horses' wounds, their bruises, their bone fractures and dislocations, their aches and pains... One thing that caused my father pain was that they called him 'Kurt Duran' ('Duran the Wolf) in Uzunyayla. Afterward, when he settled in Ekrek village, this was somehow changed into Duran Ağa.

After my father was released from service by the Circassian family, he left Yozgat and began to look for his relatives. Wandering here, there and everywhere the road eventually led him to Ekrek village, near Kayseri. There, he met an Armenian family. According to what my mother later told me, he was a miserable wretch of a person, with a quilt draped around his shoulders and nothing but twenty sheep to his name. He didn't even have any identity papers... He was only able to register himself on the population rolls with great difficulty. Over a period of three years, in certain months he did road work under the auspices of the army. Time passed.... Meanwhile, he met my mother. She was a resident of Ekrek village. Why had my father come to Ekrek? How? She never told me a thing. When she'd come to these matters, she fell silent, as if it were a great secret.

Their marriage was somewhat difficult. At first, my grandmother didn't want to give my mother to my father. 'I raised her,' she would say, 'and is he going to enjoy the spoils?' But in the end, they did marry....

My grandmother's nickname was 'Deli Dilber' (Mad Beauty). She didn't have a single living relative or acquaintance: not her husband, nor her brother, nor any other relative. She lost them all on that dreadful day of life or death. After that she eventually went mad from having to live among those monsters who had done this terrible deed and having to protect her sons and daughters. In a way there was some measure of rebellion in my grandmother's madness!

I always heard from my grandmother that my grandfather's side had been very rich.... My grandfather had been the head of an armed gang. He and his band of five hundred mounted horsemen had roamed through the mountains protecting Armenians. It was an enormous family. His name was well-known in the entire region. But from that five hundred-strong mounted family only my mother survived!

All of the property belonging to both my mother and father's side of the family was confiscated by the state, claiming that the owners had been 'subject to deportation.' Later on, it was given to the rural chieftains and wealthy members of the village. What was left was given to the immigrants who arrived after the population exchange.

Left without even a handful of dirt from their families' possessions, my parents were able only with the greatest difficulty to purchase three plots totaling twenty donums. These lands were also parched and barren. Barely enough to live on, not enough to get rich!

The lands around Ekrek village were not very fertile. The villagers would clear the rocks from a patch of earth and work it. The lands most conducive to cultivation belonged to the immigrants. In fact, right next to the few portions of land of the two Armenian families was a small but well-watered *bostan* (orchard-garden). My mother made immense efforts to obtain this garden. We raised all manner of fruit and vegetables in this orchard-garden. The other villagers were jealous of our garden.

First, my elder brother came to study in Istanbul, then, I followed. My other brothers never did study; for both Armenian families it came to a point when they were no longer able to live in Ekrek. One night in 1960, without any announcement and without a sound, they loaded up all of their belongings in a truck and left for Istanbul. The village had almost no knowledge of this departure, this flight from the village. The orchard-garden, which had been grown amid great hardship and with a thousand and one hopes, was now left to the same fate as the rest of the rocky fields around it. After coming to Istanbul, we never again returned to the village or asked about our fields or property. The land registration is still in our hands, but the villagers have since taken it over, planted and harvested it....

My mother told me about our history, but even more so, my grandmother. My grandmother was like an ocean of knowledge. She'd often say, 'Cursed is he who denies his origins!' She'd stand me in front of her and say 'My son, if you have a blemish on your soul, there should be a blemish in your eye as well!' What she meant was 'If you think bad thoughts, you'll go blind! Don't do evil!'

We were six children: four boys and two girls. My father would discuss everything with us, joke with us; he also treated us very warmly, he loved us and was affectionate toward us. I have very fond memories of him. We used to sit, knee-to-knee. He was very talkative.... Some things he would go on about, telling them for hours on end.... but others, like our family or origins, or what had happened to him personally, he never discussed...

For years, my father worked as a porter in Istanbul. For a while, he was the watchman at the Armenian cemetery in Şişli. For a period he worked with my mother, carding wool in Zeytinburnu, and sorting hazelnuts in workshops. Later on, he worked as a janitor at the Sahakyan school. Throughout his life, he earned his daily bread from the sweat of his brow. But despite all odds, he denied himself of everything so that he could send six children to school. He even managed to send four of us through higher education. I always remember my father with great gratitude...

I never saw in my father even the slightest visceral reaction against Turks or nationalist rancor.... I could never understand how, even though he suffered great and bitter sorrows and lost everything, he remained so tolerant. But that's how it was. I can say that I never discussed 'our history' with my father. Among us, within my family, it was as if there was an unspoken understanding that we didn't discuss our past. Our past was never brought up. When my father would get together with his friend, Master Sarkis, they would talk long about the past and future. Sometimes, they would even laugh uproariously. This piqued my curiousity. I would eavesdrop on their conversations.

There weren't any feelings of rancor or enmity in my family. I had a lot of Turkish friends, not because I was a leftist, but because my father had raised me and formed my personality with love and tolerance. What I got from my father was not rancor, but love for humanity.

A man seeking his village...

The world is small, the storm great.... The storm of the Deportation killed the children of human beings, but others found refuge here and there, and the surviving orphans were cared for by people from four corners of the world...

Uncle Drtad from our village was seven years old in 1915. He saw everything. He lost all of his relatives. He was left without anyone in the world. Later on, he was found by the American Red Cross, and brought to Boston with other orphaned children.

He grew up in America, owned a business, married, grew rich and lived to a ripe old age... But the older he got, the more his interest and longing grew! He made a vow, 'Before I die, I will go back to Ekrek again, if nothing else, I will see the Barren Plain in my village.'

His nephew is a journalist in Beirut.

Together with his wife, he went to Egypt with a tour group in 1978. The land has a pull on people. Upon going to Egypt the yearning within him increased once more. Out of this yearning for the land, they separated from the tour group. 'No matter what, I will find another Armenian from Kayseri, from Ekrek, and I will go to my village!' he said.

They arrived in Istanbul. But how would he go about it, how would he find such a person? He went straight to the Armenian Patriarchate in Kumkapı. He asked those persons from the village of Ekrek in Kayseri who were known as 'Çökelekeci' ('Curd eaters'). From the Patriarch's records, he found no information, but an Armenian who happened by the Patriarchate pointed out the way. There was a woman living in Samatya known as 'Deli Meryem' ('Mad Meryem') he told Uncle Drtad. She was sort of the unofficial head of her neighborhood. If anyone knew anything, it would be her. At one time, Deli Meryem had come from Kayseri. She knew all of the Armenians from Kayseri. She also loved helping people out. She was crazy, but she wasn't stupid.

Uncle Drtad followed the man's instructions. He located Deli Meryem. When he told her what he was seeking, she took him by the hand and led him straight to our family. She knocked on our door: 'Nurse Gülbeyaz! Nurse Gülbeyaz! There are people here looking for you.'

We ushered her and her guests in and she asked, 'Are you from the Çökelekeci family?'

When my mother answered 'yes!', seventy-year-old Drtad threw his arms around her... They both began to cry, my mother and Uncle Drtad! For the first time in sixty-three years, he saw someone from the village of Ekrek...

In this way, he had completed his odyssey of being able to experience this moment, of being able to see the 'Barren Plain' before he died....

My grandmother told me the story of how we came by the name Çökelekeci:

One of our family members was desirous that our lands be returned to us. He ate the cheese curds left over from their provisions. They stuck in his throat. But what water was there on the Barren Plain? He died because of this piece of dried cheese curd.... After this happened, the name 'Curd eaters' stuck.

Uncle Drtad and his family were staying in a luxury hotel in Istanbul. The day they found us they quickly moved in with us. We were fifteen people in this impoverished little, two-room apartment that usually housed eight. They spoke very good Turkish. All of the Armenians spoke Turkish. Drtad went on for hours recounting his childhood up to age seven, his remaining without any relatives or acquaintances, his going to America and his life there.

On the second day of his stay with us, he proclaimed, 'If only you'd take me to my village, to Ekrek!'

At first, we couldn't imagine this old man traveling from Istanbul to Kayseri and from there to Ekrek. But he insisted.

'I came all the way from America. I'm not going back without seeing Ekrek and the Barren Plain! If I die, at least I would die on the earth where I was born!'

After that, he took all the responsibility upon himself. We set out. When we finally arrived in Ekrek, seventy-year-old Uncle Drtad became youthful, even childlike!

He told me all about the village and drew me a sketch map of it while we were in Istanbul. 'This is the road to Kayseri. This is the Barren Plain, and before it is the Girls' School, on the right side of the road. Here's the church. Over there is the cemetery. Right here is where our house is!'

When we arrived in the village he located each one of these places, one after the other, as if it had only been yesterday that he had left. Even at his age, he wanted to see the old areas where the Armenians had lived, the church and the houses. The heat of the summer day weighed heavily upon us, but he kept a brisk pace, all the while saying, 'This one's yours,' 'That one's mine!' He wore me out, and his wife also lagged behind.... He took pictures of everything he saw—he even took pictures of golden thistles, blackthorns, denuded pears and olive seedlings, or had me take pictures for him.

Of the church, all that remained were the foundations. He found the Armenian cemetery next to the newer, Turkish one. He looked for the graves of his family members and other relations. He found some of them amid the bushes and groves of trees. There were very beautiful headstones, or more correctly, crosses (*khachkars*). Each one was a story, a human epic. Each one a monument carved by a master's hand. The stones were embellished with a delicate, intricate carving. The crosses had flowers carved into them. The names of those who had come and gone were written upon the crosses. At one point, Drtad found the grave of one of his relatives. He began to read the inscription. He became distressed and fell silent.... he withdrew, deep within himself....

What a shame that so many of the graves and crosses had been smashed and piled up by grave robbers. They'd even dug up and taken parts of the church foundation.

The town's villagers, who had heard and seen us now gathered around us.... Drtad became ever more animated! He talked and explained, and the more he did so, the looser his tongue became. He told of his life in Ekrek until age seven, of the calamity he suffered, of being rescued from death, and on and on.... But what he spoke of the most—just as my mother had done—was his lineage, what had come upon them, and without omitting a single thing he recalled all of those things that they had forgotten, explaining everything from the very beginning.... He acted as if here, in Ekrek, he was somewhere in America... He said everything that came into his mind, lambasting and abusing everyone present... I began to grow afraid. But it would have been shameful to caution him.... In any case, my elder brother was a government doctor in Pınarbaşı. The inhabitants of Ekrek knew him well. On account of this we were able to act more calmly.

My elder brother was a great idealist. He went to primary school in Ekrek, and to Tıbrevank for middle and high school. When he was still a student, he used to say, 'I'm going to become a doctor and work in Ekrek!' And in fact, that's just what he did! When he became a doctor, he was appointed to Pınarbaşı, which was the closest provincial district to our village.

We wandered everywhere, saw everything. Eventually, evening came. 'Let's go to Pınarbaşı and stay at my brother's house' I said. 'We can come back tomorrow, if you wish.'

'Impossible!' he said. 'I came all the way from America. I'm not going back without spending the night on the earth where I was born! If you want, you can go! I will remain here alone, as a guest in someone's house!'

The villagers—God bless them!—were very hospitable. 'Leave him. He can stay here!' they said. 'If the rest of you wish, you can stay here as well. We have enough beds for everyone, thank God, and enough food for all!'

That night, we all slept in Ekrek. We ate various courses that had been arranged on a large, round tray; we slept under the same earthen roofs that we had slept under as little children, but there was no one to throw stones or force us to make the sign of the cross!

We stayed in Ekrek for two nights. The second day, we continued to walk around the village, up and down all the streets, seeing everything. Again, evening came on the second day.

Uncle Drtad had me draw a tiny outline of the village in a delicate and detailed map. He drew everything that there was, and in its proper place. He drew in Bozkaya, which was near the village, and the remains of the Girls' School that resembled a rock graveyard. 'I will look at this again when I get back to America!' he said.

I was shocked. Looking at the map that I had now drawn by examining the village, I saw that it was identical with the map that he had drawn for me in Istanbul from memory! He hadn't left out a thing! Maybe he had me draw it just so he could check whether he had forgotten something... To think that all of that had entered and remained in his memory since he was seven years old!

Two days later we bid a fond goodbye to the village. When we reached Kayseri, Uncle Drtad had aged, becoming seventy years old again.

We returned to Istanbul, and from there we saw Drtad and his family off on their trip back to America. A while later we heard that some persons from the village of Ekrek had given a bad interpretation to Uncle Drtad's having come all the way from America. 'Maybe they were looking to dig up buried treasure?' they asked themselves.

Those who have experienced these things know what it means to long for the earth where one was born, to yearn for some remembrance of their past; they who have experienced these things know such longings, which can't be valued with money, whose burning desire can't be extinguished with gold....

"Why didn't I look into my own past?"

I thought about myself: why have I never looked deeply into my own past, even until now? Why, although I have spent countless hours examining the history of many other countries, have I never bothered to examine the history of my own country? When Uncle Drtad, who came all the way from America in order to see his own village, to look for his own roots, why hadn't I traveled from Istanbul to Ekrek?

During my years at Tıbrevank, during my years at lycée, the longing began to develop in me for a world, for a country in which I could live freely and as a human being... These ideas of freedom, brotherhood and equality all began to take root in my mind, in my personality. These longings, these ideas, these values were no passing fancy; they were the characteristics that made their mark on my life, and that made me who I was. But I never regretted the path I took, the road I traveled. I wasn't ashamed of my past, or of my own history. I never hid who I was.... But today, when I look back now to the past, I see that there are some things lacking, some things that I missed....

Near the end of my university years I began working to establish the Association of Progressive Youth. Later on, I was politically active in the Association of Technical Employees, the Council of Architects and many other institutions. I became a member of the Communist Party of Turkey.

I was arrested during the military coup of September 12, 1980 and tried in court. I was kept in the Metris Military Prison with Brother Doğan for three years. In the end, I was acquitted. I had been arrested six months before Doğan.

I asked myself, why hadn't I thoroughly looked into and investigated my own origins, my history and my culture? I've thought a whole lot about this subject in recent years. The conclusion I've come to is that we fled from many of these things entirely! It's painfully clear that I didn't do the right thing. This is a criticism I have of myself, of my generation. I'm an Armenian. But like the other leftists in this country, on the outside I was a 'Turkish leftist.'

Fear had prevented me from thinking otherwise, from understanding otherwise, from seeing otherwise. During all my years: in the village, in school, at home and in the workplace, fear was everpresent. The subject was taboo. There were prohibitions. It was forbidden for me to learn my own history. It was forbidden for me to ask about my own origins. Only very late did I perceive the error in this. But now, years later, I still don't know real Armenian history very well.

My own condition, and that of many Armenians like me, is somewhat special. We were people who employed our preferences differently after a certain date. I can honestly say that through these intellectual and political preferences we forgot that we were Armenians. We were persons who defended internationalism, universalism, whose concerns, ideals and struggles were different. With this mentality, we struck out on a different path.

Many of my friends made special effort to learn both Armenian history and literature. They looked into and researched their past and what had happened to them. These friends felt confident enough to discuss these things publicly. Their labors on the subjects of Armenian history and literature are now branching out in totally new directions.

The special situation of myself and all Armenians, and our present thoughts and feelings do not allow us to forget the great sorrows and bitterness we experienced during the 1915 Deportation, the 1942 Capital Tax, the attacks of September 6-7, 1955 and the 'Compatriot! Speak Turkish!' campaigns of the 1960s.[*]

Every part of the past now interests me.

Those who are Armenian in Turkey today can understand what it means to live during times when a minister of the interior calls 'Armenian spawn!' when speaking to the press in regard to Abdullah Öcalan,[†] and what it means to live daily with such humiliations.

Violence and fear prevent a person from thinking sound thoughts. Prohibitions and taboos distort a person's vision to the point of

---

[*] Such a campaign was first introduced in the 1930s.
[†] The Kurdish leader of the PKK.

blindness, they infect his thoughts to the point of mental illness. As a result, they completely pass over painfully evident truths, concrete events from the past, as if they simply don't and never did exist. They try to avoid them. Their human and social consciousness becomes blinded by prohibitions, fears and suspicions. They attempt to avoid shedding light on these conscious truths to which they have been blinded by fear. They close their eyes, their ears and their voices to them, and they even avoid others who do see them, hear them or speak about them.

As an Armenian who doesn't attempt to hide his identity, I run into such cases and such persons all the time. My two sons are continuing their education at Armenian schools. When a stranger or one of their new acquaintances asks them the name of the school they attend, my children look into my eyes… they are hesitant to answer… and I speak on my children's behalf. After I say the name of the school, I add that it is an Armenian school. No one has ever specifically intimidated my children. Nevertheless, my children, who were born and raised in Istanbul, feel themselves as 'foreigners.' What a shame that we haven't yet succeeded in erasing this 'foreignness' or 'alienation'!

During my years at high school, I never experienced any particular attack, reaction, injustice or insult on account of being Armenian. Many of my Turkish friends want to know whether or not anyone ever bothers me or disturbs me, particularly on this topic. They continually protect me.

When I was taken into custody—the very next day after the September 12, 1980 Coup—they reminded me that I was an Armenian! Only in custody did I experience the bitterness of being Armenian! The forty-five days I passed in custody were what I paid for my entire life until then. I was arrested and taken into custody on the charge that I was a member of the Communist Party of Turkey. Those were the days when torture in this country was as merciless, violent and brutal as it's ever been. But above all, I was an Armenian! My Turkish friends who were there were also tortured and beaten. But I was singled out and suffered the special punishment of having been an Armenian. For forty-five days, in the corridor where I would be made to wait before entering into the interrogation room, I would have to come and be the whipping boy for the guards!

'Hey, you Armenian bastard!' they would say, and they would give me either a punch or a kick from behind.

'So, is it up to you to save Turkey?' they would ask and give me a resounding slap on the head from behind.

Other times, it would be, 'Hey, you infidel, son of an infidel! Was it your job to become a Communist?'

I'd receive blows on the way in and the way out... As for me, I would keep an account of the things I experienced in the interrogation room. The pains during interrogation were different! For my inquisitorial executors, what was important was not that I was an Armenian, but that I was a member of the Turkish Communist Party.

Those children and adults back in Ekrek village, the ones who had tried to get me to spit on the cross and say the Shehada, what sweet and pleasant creatures they were in comparison!

Just like hundreds, thousands of others then in custody, I was subjected to all manner of torture, humiliation and barbarism for forty-five days. The traces of this period remain with me until today. Some nights I still can't sleep; I have nightmares. I wake up screaming sometimes.

These traces, the tortures I suffered... I don't even discuss them much with my wife. I haven't told her anything—I can't!

Zakarya again fell silent! I listened to the things he had said still as a stone. I didn't want to disturb the world into which he had drifted off. He looked to the side. He got up and went over to the red roses that were three paces in front of me. He bent over and took one of them in his hand. I thought he was going to pluck it... but he just stood there, bent over, breathing it in... He was too gentle and merciful to even pluck a rose. The scent of the rose remained on his fingers, and he smiled as he smelled the fingers of his right hand. His face changed as he did so. The tension that had been there now dissipated as his contours softened. His voice became happy....

Did you know, my wife is Turkish. She's from Şebinkarahisar.... She's the best woman in the world! There are those moments in life that you never forget. But life is like this red rose. The flower comes with the thorn. During the forty-five days I was in jail and my almost three years in prison, my wife didn't leave me there alone for even one day... During those times that I was tortured, when I was between life and death and my hope was flagging, my wife gave me the strength to go on. The flame of love between us warmed my otherwise darkening world!

Zakarya again stopped talking and drifted off into his inner world. His eyes remained fixed on the roses there before him. It was as if his mind, his thoughts and his feelings had all been locked up in one moment of life.

During the first year of our marriage, when I was in custody, Jale brought a bouquet of red roses to be given to me...

I was a reserve officer in Diyarbakir...

I had come to Istanbul for a one month change of atmosphere.... When the month was over, I purchased my return ticket from the Kâmil Koç bus company... Just as the evening that I was to get on the bus approached, I was arrested and taken into custody...

How could I explain?

Where should I begin?

I never told these things to anyone... I didn't even want to remember them myself...

I had delayed my military service for a long time. I had long since passed the age of military conscription. During the general tumult following the 1980 Coup, I wanted to resolve this problem. My odyssey first brought me to Izmir, then to Diyarbakir. I did almost five months of service at the Headquarters of the 7th Army Corps in Diyarbakir. I had a desk job. My job was to process a number of strategic changes directed at defense and to put them on the map.

The 7th Army Corps had, in the wake of the 1980 Coup, become the main detention center for the region. Every day, people were brought in by bus and deposited there. The arrested and those who had gone through interrogation and were awaiting trial were housed inside three old stone buildings that had originally been horse stables. They were in an awful shape. The stables had been surrounded by wire mesh. It was prohibited to even approach this wire mesh, which was surrounded by soldiers at every step, facing outward and away from the stables. Not even the officers were allowed to enter the stables. Special functionaries who came from outside the unit brought in persons according to their lists, and others were taken away, according to different lists.

Everything that happened did so in our plain sight. I could sense in my heart what these people experienced! It became unbearable for me! I had a nervous collapse. The things that I myself had experienced, the beatings I had received as a child in the village of Ekrek, the things that I had experienced in the Davutpaşa and Metris prisons had all left deep scars on my body and my soul...

Sometimes, I compared the things I saw and experienced in Diyarbakir with those things that I had experienced during the three years that I was in prison. I thought that Metris and Davutpaşa Prisons were a lot more 'comfortable'!

While I was doing my military service in the 7th Army Corps, I fell ill. I had to stay in hospital for fifteen days. They gave me a month of leave for a change of atmosphere. I came to Istanbul. I strolled and did some sightseeing as my friends had suggested. Slowly, my health returned. The evening that I was to return to Diyarbakir, I was arrested at my own home. An officer came by to take me. They brought me in a jeep, escorted by two military police officers to the Central Command in Beşiktaş. Because I was a soldier, the law demanded that my interrogation had to be done by soldiers. At the Command Center, they gave some rest time before my interrogation, which would continue for several days. I remained there for a week, altogether.

After they took me into custody, my wife Jale, my older brother and my stepfather all asked around until they found out what had happened to me. Jale asked a captain at the Beşiktaş Command Center about me. At first, he said, 'He's not here!', but when she persisted, he finally relented. She gave him money and clean clothing to be given to me. He refused to accept them.

From there they sent me to the First Department.* For me, the days I passed at the First Department were like a lifetime! There were seven of us, crowded in a one by two-and-a-half meter cell. It was impossible to lie down or to stretch out. We were subjected to severe violence, too.

As for Jale, every single day she posted herself in front of the door of the First Department awaiting news of me. Here she also came across the captain with whom she had spoken at Beşiktaş. She asked about me. She wanted him to pass on the money and clothes that she had brought. The captain scolded her: 'What? You're here again, girl?' But in the end, she prevailed in having the money delivered to me. When I received the money, the world was suddenly mine again. I wasn't alone!

The fifteenth day since I had been brought to the First Department coincided with our first anniversary. That day I was beaten very badly during the interrogation with my eyes blindfolded. When they brought me back to the cell, I couldn't even stand up. Amid the aches and pains, traces of my life one year earlier blew through my mind.

I was blindfolded throughout the entire 45 days of my interrogation. There was a lot of typing at one point. Finally, they said 'Sign!'

'I won't sign anything without reading it!'

---

* The "First Department" was the department of Turkey's National Security Directorate that dealt with those persons suspected of "political crimes," and was notorious for its brutality.

Then came another round of beatings, as they said, 'Who do you think you are that you would read your own confession?' I resisted. In the end, they lifted my blindfold a little and I read it.

'I never said this! I refuse!'

That led to another series of blows. They beat me silly! Then they took me and threw me back in the cell. A few days later they brought me back to the interrogation room. If only briefly, they gave me the chance to read my confession again. They had made several corrections and amendments. Thinking that it was the lesser of evils, I signed...

After this adventurous 'signing ceremony,' they brought me back to the Command Center in Beşiktaş. There, I was again taken to interrogation.

'They weren't able to break you at the First Department,' they said. 'But we will! You're even going to have to pay for those flowers that that stupid wife of yours brought on your anniversary!'

When I heard that, I felt the warmth of the sun rise within my mind, my heart and my soul! To think that my beloved wife, the most beautiful woman in the world, my Jale had brought flowers to the First Department to be given to me! Even if I died now I wouldn't care! My Jale had brought me flowers! Who cares if they didn't give them to me! I didn't care what happened after that!

With the strength that I received from this love, this joy, I passed, with a clean conscience and head unbowed, the arduous, week-long interrogation, after which I was brought before the judge at the Selimiye Barracks. Afterward, my three years of confinement at the Metris Military Prison began. But Jale never left me, not during my interrogation nor during my time in prison.

Zakarya was silent again, lost in his thoughts. After a bit, some tears began to form in his eyes and run down his cheeks. They were as bright as Jale's roses, as pure as her love! He didn't wipe them away... Perhaps!....

As soon as he felt them, he said "Come, let's go home!"

"Let's go, my sensitive Armenian brother!"

Jale of Şebinkarahisar

"Zakarya, my brother," I asked, "Is there a florist on the way to your place? Take me to a flower seller before we get home!"

'What for?' he asked.

"First, take me to a flower seller, please, then ask why."

Zakarya's eyes began to smile. He didn't ask any more questions. He seemed to understand what I was thinking.

He pointed out the florist's shop when we got there, but he didn't go in himself, preferring instead to wait at the entrance to the shop. He didn't even glance inside. What sort of understanding and maturity was this?

"Some of these red ones" I told the florist, "and these pink ones, too, please… and the lilies…. from the white ones… and these purple flowers, too…. Could you put in some green, please? Actually, not like that, maybe just the lilies. No, no… don't let the green leaves cover the pink roses…"

Finally, I was able to have the florist give me the bouquet I wanted. A handful of Istanbul flowers… As soon as we left the florist's, Zakarya called his wife and told her that we were on the way. Earlier, he had told her that he would be bringing a guest to dinner.

As we came to his apartment building he rang the buzzer. He didn't just open it and enter, even though he had the key on him.

When we arrived on the third floor, the door of his apartment opened. A smiling woman appeared who greeted her guest with a smile, saying, "Welcome. Please come in!"

This must have been Madam Jale, the very same Jale, or "dew," of which two drops had flowed from Zakarya's eyes a little earlier.* I waited for Zakarya to introduce us. There was no need…. We knew each other from first glance!

"With my gratitude to Jale, who one day, the hardest day of her husband's life, brought a bouquet of roses to the First Department for their anniversary."

"Very pleased to meet you! Welcome!"

I presented the bouquet to her myself. We introduced ourselves. She greeted me warmly, like an old acquaintance or dear friend. An old woman lay down on one side of the salon. Zakarya introduced us: "This is my mother, Jale's mother." After that, their two sons, Arda and Aras shook my hand respectfully.

Zakarya recounted to his wife all that he had done since morning, and what we had done together. He informed her of our lengthy conversation, simply saying, "We spoke a little."

I confirmed this, saying, "We finished off two fifths!"

---

* The meaning of "Jale" in Turkish is "dew."

Jale then explained, "My mother is somewhat unwell. She broke her arm about six months ago.... She's got Parkinson's Disease... She can walk if you hold her arms firmly. Her arm has only now begun to heal."

Zakarya then turned to his mother-in-law, "Mother, dear. How are you doing? Are you having pains again today?"

"Be well, my child!" she replied. "May God bless you! I'm well, thank God!"

I introduced myself. I relayed the warmest regards from Brother Doğan and his wife, Neşrin. Madam Jale had prepared the table and was awaiting us.

"Come, everyone. To the table! I haven't been able to prepare too much. Please forgive me!"

"Please," I replied. "What more could you have made? There's nothing missing from the feast you've prepared!"

Zakarya, Jale and myself sat at the table. Their boys, Ardas and Aras, had already eaten.

"I made both Turkish and Armenian dishes" Jale said. "Eat whatever you'd like."

"I heard your story from Zakarya" I volunteered. "But how did you have the strength to bring a bouquet of red roses to the Political Department of the Istanbul Security Directorate, to have them given to Zakarya? I am amazed both by the greatness of your courage and your love. What's more, what does it mean to be married to an Armenian? What is the secret of this thing? What's the trick? Could you tell me something about Zakarya?"

Zakarya raised his raki glass and toasted me. I toasted both Jale and Zakarya, and how happy I was to have made their acquaintance.

Due to his modesty and maturity, Zakarya appeared a little embarrassed about being the subject of conversation. "You speak. I want to listen. Jale should tell a little about what she saw and experienced!"

When she spoke, Jale impressed me as plainspoken, loquacious, noble and experienced; a person whom God had created with great care.

"O.K., let me first answer your question about who Zakarya is" she began. "In a word, Zakarya is a 'human being' in the full sense of the word. I'm not just saying this to praise him, or because I'm his wife. Anyway, he hates praise and being lauded. I'm just saying it because it's the truth. After I give you some examples, you'll see that I'm right."

"Madam Jale," I said, "I'm of the same mind as you. Even before coming here tonight, I thought to myself, 'Zakarya is a good person!' But I'd still like to hear everything from you. Where did you find the courage to bring him flowers?"

The marriage of a Turk and an Armenian

"Let's go back a bit, before 1980," Jale began. "Those years when everything was so difficult, when social and political activity was so alive.... Those days, different views clashed with one another, and there wasn't any sense of safety or security.... We struggled with all our hearts, all our souls and all our strength.... We wanted the dawn of a whole new age! We were so full of hope, it imbued our work, our thoughts, our dreams... During those hopeful days, I found myself in the same struggle with Zakarya... I worked as secretary at the Headquarters of the Association of All Technical Workers. Zakarya was president. When Zakarya came to the position, he was a decisive person, deliberate in the steps he took, thoughtful and well-respected. He was industrious and creative, and he brought people together. He would always find the points we had in common during debates. He was conciliatory. There was nothing of the dictator about him. Sometimes he would get frightfully angry, albeit rarely. He was not afraid to explain his ideas. Let me say it openly, I was smitten as soon as I saw him. I was enchanted, head over heels for him. I began trembling, and was all upset. If they would have killed me at that moment, not a drop of my blood would have spilled, I wouldn't have felt any pain."

Zakarya then added, "It was the same for me. My heart jumped. All of my senses were attuned to Jale, my antennae were locked on her. Whenever I think of that moment, my heart jumps again. The morning star rose in my heart, and I felt alive from head to toe. Jale was the star that led me at night, she was the sun that lit up my days. The fire of that moment has never died down. Even till now, our love is still blooming. It's never faded."

Jale: "I was hesitant to give voice to the feelings inside me. That's how I had been raised! It was also somewhat difficult to experience sensitivity and emotion amid the social and political conditions of those days, but I couldn't keep it within me. I would go to the Association every day, but I wasn't all there. Finally, I summoned up all of my courage and declared my love for Zakarya! As for Zakarya, he answered 'I love you, too! But have you thought it over well? Are you aware that this love is an all-consuming thing?'

'Yes,' I replied, 'I've thought about it a lot. I want to be consumed in this love!'

And from that moment my world was brighter than before. For a while, we could only share our love by meeting secretly. But all these trysts and this secrecy weren't enough to satisfy our love.

One day, we organized a panel discussion. I was one of the panel's organizers. It turned out much better than I could have imagined. I was very happy. Zakarya was there, too. When we left the hall, we came to a concrete decision. We went straight to a jeweler on İstiklal Avenue and bought each other rings! After that, Zakarya went to a florist and had them make up a bouquet of red roses for me. When he gave them to me, he said 'I love you so much. Let these roses be witnesses to our love!'

I replied 'I love you so much, too! May the stars in the heavens and the flowers of the earth be our witnesses!'

People become more human through those very special sentiments that are bestowed upon objects, through the specific meanings given to them. It's true, a rose is just a flower, but for us, the red rose is a symbol of our unfading love!

We put rings on our fingers, but things got complicated after that. At first, I didn't tell my family. 'I'll tell them eventually' I told myself. My relationship to the party and the organization were those of an average partisan. I worked now as a technical illustrator. Apart from that, I had my duties within the association. I was a member of the association myself. I had never slept at anyone else's house, not even a single night. But the other colleagues at the association sensed the emotional tie between us. And we didn't try to hide it.

One day, one of the women with a position of responsibility within the association came up to me and said 'I want to speak with you.'

'Fine, let's talk' I said.

'You should give up this emotional relationship!' she said.

'Why? It's my own problem!' I told her.

'You work at the association!' she insisted. 'Your problem is everybody's problem! How is it that you think you can just go and marry an Armenian?'

'Aren't Armenians people too? And that's my problem as well! We love one another. It's nobody's business who I love or don't love!'

After that, I had a lot of similar discussions and arguments with other colleagues and friends. Some told me it was wrong, others told Zakarya.

Some of them even went so far as to blame themselves for not having found me a Turkish husband!

This actually caused me to reevaluate my position. What sort of leftist movement was this, anyway? On the one hand, they were always singing and shouting about all persons being equal, 'Workers of all the nations unite!' and all that. But on the other, they were warning me that 'Zakarya's an Armenian. You can't marry him!'

Zakarya: "I also experienced similar hardships. But nobody spoke to me openly about my marriage to Jale… Some of them went absolutely over the top! In their minds, they were protecting the party by reducing the secret life of the party to the point of personal relations. At one of our meetings, one of my comrades, seeing the ring on my finger, even said 'Ooooh! You get married and we're not informed about it?' They neither congratulated me, nor wished me happiness! When I think about it now, it makes me laugh. I'm glad that I followed my heart and married; it's good that we got married! Those who had 'political marriages,' as it was called in those days, broke up at the first sign of difficulty."

Jale then spoke up again: "We overcame all of the obstacles that our comrades attempted to place in our paths. The next hurdle were our families. I first told my mother and bared my heart to her. But she cut me off, saying: 'Girl, it's forbidden to marry outside your religion! Couldn't you find someone other than an Armenian to marry? We are from Şebinkarahisar. No one in our family has ever married an Armenian! I don't want to hear any more about this from you!'

My mother then told my father. He blew his top. They made me go through some really difficult days.

Zakarya's family was also opposed at first. 'It's difficult to make a marriage with a Turk work,' they told him. 'What's wrong, are all the Armenian girls contagious? Is there not a single girl left in this enormous city of Istanbul that you could marry other than a Turk?'

We put our heads together and thought about what to do. What was love? Love was equality: After all that our feelings and our bodies said, there was the mind. Our feelings said 'yes.' Our bodies said 'yes.' Our minds said 'yes.' So let our families and friends say 'no!'

In the end, it was our decision: We would marry!

Zakarya's family respected their son's decision, and wanted to come and ask my family for my hand. But my mother and father said 'They shouldn't come. We won't let them through the door!' No matter what I said, it was not to be.

'Go ahead, don't give me away!' I threatened, 'I'm going to leave and go there myself!' My decision was final. I would go. But Zakarya's parents said 'We're not going to kidnap brides! Everything should be done properly and in seemly fashion!'

We were five siblings: three boys and two girls. Every day there'd be a big blowup in the house over me! One of my older brothers took my side, saying, 'What is that supposed to mean, 'inside' or 'outside' the faith? What century are we living in? Are we supposed to conform to the times? Or are the times supposed to conform to us? Jale is twenty-four years old. She's in charge of her life. Do you support her any more?'

Then he turned to me 'Marry who you want, girl! Let them come to me and ask for your hand. If father doesn't want to give you away, that's fine!' And then, back to my parents, he said, 'The mosque is the mosque.... Don't tell me about your mosque, your ceremonies or your traditions!'

In the end, my elder brother gave me away. Neither my mother, nor my father, nor any of my other relatives came to the wedding. They didn't even give me a dowry....

It was December 14, we were in the fourth month of marriage when Zakarya entered his military service. I was taken into custody on January 5. They released me three months later.

As for Zakarya, he was arrested during the eleventh month of our marriage. It was on June 3: I'll never forget that day. We only found out where he was after twenty-seven days of looking for him.

July 14 was the first anniversary of our marriage. I knew that Zakarya was being tortured, and that he was being subjected to all manner of debasement and humiliation. During the time that I was in custody I had learned very well what 'custody,' 'questioning' and the 'Political Department' were all about. I learned through experience how necessary it was for a person to maintain a sliver of hope, a sincere 'hello,' and a sincere love. And most importantly, I acquired the notion that love was another name for resistance. I had rebelled through Zakarya's love, I had warmed myself on those cold nights with the fire of Zakarya's love. And now, Zakarya was being tortured....

The power of love

You can't buy madness, you know! After considering what the possible consequences were, and knowing full well that they would refuse them,

I went out and bought a bouquet of flowers to give to Zakarya for our wedding anniversary.

I purchased a big beautiful bouquet of red roses and wrote a short note. I went down and knocked on the door of the First Department in the morning. Even if they killed me, I wasn't going home until I had given them the roses for him! When my turn came, I entered the building.

The officer on duty looked at the roses and said 'What's all this?'

'A bouquet of roses,' I replied.

'What's it supposed to be for?'

'My husband is here in custody. I would like you to pass these on to him!'

'Can't be done!'

'You have to do it. Today is the first anniversary of our marriage!'

'What's his name? What organization does he belong to?'

'His name is Zakarya. I don't know what organization!'

'Wait over there!'

Then he picked up the phone and called someone. After a bit a captain came out from inside the building and approached me. I had seen him before, at the Beşiktaş Command Center. He called me inside.

'What do you want?' he asked.

'Today is our wedding anniversary. My husband is under interrogation. Could you please make sure he gets these roses?'

He took the bouquet from my hand with an evil look that seemed to say 'I'll smack him in the head with your flowers!' Then he dismissed me, saying, 'Beat it. Get out of here!'

I left amid insults and hateful glares! I began to wait in front of the guard's kiosk on the way leading to the First Department, wondering if I would be able to see Zakarya if they brought him out. The voices inside me went back and forth:

'This person isn't going to give him the flowers!'

'Maybe he will...'

'Come on, this isn't like before! Get smart! They're not going to give them to him!'

'And what if they do?'

I stood there for two or three hours. At one point, a military jeep appeared. My heart jumped into my mouth. It slowed down as it approached me. A door opened and the captain who had taken the flowers from me got out:

'What are you waiting around here for? Get lost! Don't let me see you around here again, or I'll take you inside!'

I was frozen with terror! The hope that I had been nurturing within me since the morning was now dashed! I returned home downhearted, sure that they hadn't given the flowers to Zakarya.

"What did you write in the note to him?" I asked at that point. "Do you remember?"

"Sure. To this day I can still remember it word for word. I wrote:

> *My soul, my life,*
> *Today is the first anniversary of our marriage....*
> *I'm with you: every moment, every minute....*
> *It gives me strength to love you!*
> *I am the happiest person in the world because I love you, because I married you.*
> *Take care of yourself!*
> *Don't worry about us...*
> *I love you so very very much.*
> *Your wife, Jale....*"

We then raised our glasses in honor of Jale, who had wanted to send flowers to Zakarya when he was under interrogation.

Zakarya then took his wife's hand: "This love, this passion, this support—they all remain until today," he said. "We love one another so much! It was Jale who shored up my confidence.... Up to the very end, she not only supported me, she supported my whole family. During those dark days, those hopeless days after September 12 [1980], she behaved so warmly and closely toward my family—even closer than my own brothers... If my aunt or mother had a problem, they'd run straight to Jale. They didn't speak with me, with my sisters-in-law, only with Jale. If anyone in the family had a pain, she took it on as her own. She knew how to get what she wanted. She was fearless and enterprising. She'd finish what she started. She was warm... She'd bring springtime during the darkest part of winter. Her love was abundant.... It made the deserts bloom. I'm so lucky to have married Jale. She's the best thing that ever happened to me, the foundation of all my happiness.

"It's the same for me," Jale added. "I'm so lucky to have married Zakarya. It's because of him that I love the world, that I love myself. I said earlier that Zakarya is a good person. Look, I'll give you another example. He'd never tell you such things himself.

Do you see my mother over there lying down? She doesn't hear very well, and she can't even stand up or lie down by herself. Six months ago she fell on the stairs and broke her arm. The bone deteriorated. She's old. It took a long time for it to heal. She still can't walk. She has to have special care. My brothers are all sitting well. Their businesses are going fine. It's been a long time since my father died and my mother has been all alone. After she broke her arm, the question arose in our family as to who would look after her. Who would do it? We thought of putting her in a nursing home, but none of us said openly what we were thinking, or really wanted to take upon ourselves the task of caring for her. I raised the idea with Zakarya of sending her to a nursing home. 'Under no circumstances!' he said. 'You don't send an old woman with a broken arm to the nursing home! Bring her here! *I'll* take care of her!' May he be well!

So we brought my mother here to our house. Zakarya displayed the concern, the patience and the understanding that we ourselves hadn't even been able to muster. He spends a whole lot of time with my mother. I work. Our two sons go to school. Zakarya hired a private caretaker for TL 100 million per month. She's a very clean, trustworthy girl. She sleeps here at our house, too. It's a full time job looking after my mother.

We've been married now for nineteen years. I've got two sons. But not once has my mother said to Zakarya 'Well, my son, I gave you my daughter Jale. May you be fortunate and blessed! May you be happy!' When she gets mad at my children she curses them, saying, 'You sons of an Armenian infidel!'—even in front of Zakarya!

Finally, and four full months after she came here, she took the trouble to say 'Zakarya, my son: I've given you my daught Jale. May you be blessed!' But after that she didn't fail to add, 'If only you were a Turk!'

As for my father, he later made his peace with me. When Zakarya was thrown into Metris prison, he came and visited him every week. He tried to encourage him. He tried to get him released. He went everywhere, knocked on every door that he thought might help, in order to convince them of Zakarya's innocence. But no matter where he went, they threw back in his face the accusation that Zakarya was 'an Armenian and a Communist.' These words, the injustice of them made a deep impression on my father. Over time, my father conceded that I had been right: 'My daughter, I don't think we've ever encountered such a child! Before, we were always concerned about how we could ever face our neighbors!'

When my father got to know Zakarya, he came to love him. He told him all about Şebinkarahisar. He spoke about the Armenian neighbors they had there. He recounted how and why Tamzara and the Tamzara river once flowed red! Although it took a while, my father finally reconciled with his son-in-law, they even became good friends....

So, there's your marriage of a Turk with an Armenian. It took love.... it took patience... Would that were all it took!

My own aunt hasn't spoken with Zakarya for twenty years. Because she doesn't respect Zakarya, she has never even come to my house for tea or invited me to hers!

My mother-in-law is a sensible, precious woman.... When I go to her house she never treats me poorly. I've never once seen her behave poorly toward me. She always defends me and embraces me. For my mother-in-law, relations between family members, and between in-laws are very important. She values her in-laws greatly.

"What does it mean to be an Armenian in Istanbul? What are the difficulties of having a life with Zakarya, with an Armenian?"

Istanbul isn't like it appears from the outside. You have to see the hidden aspects of people. Here's another example: My older sister lost her husband at an early age.... According to Armenian custom, my mother-in-law came dressed in black that very night to express her condolences. She wanted to pay her respects and show her sympathy for my sister's and her in-laws' loss. She sat in a corner all night and into the morning, just listening to the prayers that were spoken.

Wouldn't you know it? The next morning my aunt said in front of everyone 'Why is that black-clad woman still sitting here?' My father dressed down my aunt in the most severe fashion, saying, 'All your prayers and religiosity aren't worth a damn thing!'

And he didn't stop there! He didn't care who heard him.

That same day, Zakarya's older sister, according to Turkish custom, left her house in Kocamustafapaşa and came all the way to my older brother's house in Acıbadem to express her condolences. She brought along with her soup, pilaf, chicken and a large tray of manti and yoghurt. My aunt arose and left, saying, 'We don't eat food cooked on the same tray that they cook pig meat!'

You don't know whether to laugh or cry. What's at the base of this intolerance?

Among the Armenians there is a tradition. Food is brought to the house of the deceased for forty days after their passing. After I married Zakarya, I tried to follow Armenian traditions, Armenian holy days, and to cook the foods characteristic of the Armenians—in short, to learn a bit about Armenian life. Everyone was very pleased. We'd sit together and eat together.

We've been married for nineteen years. We don't live in a squatter neighborhood. We live in one of Istanbul's more exclusive neighborhoods, full of educated, middle class people. We wish all our Turkish neighbors happy holidays on all their religious holidays, on Ramadan, during the Sacrifice Holiday. But they have never once done the same to Zakarya on his religious holidays. In nineteen years, not a single Turkish neighbor has ever brought over some of the meat from their sacrifice, because they think it's unclean here.

Over there, not too far from us, there's an Armenian grocer. We got to know each other and speak often. Somehow, I've become like a daughter-in-law to them. Sometimes he explains things to me. The other day he spoke to me. He said that during the religious holidays, the Turks don't come to shop at his place. Their children come secretly and shop.

Zakarya then spoke:

Jale, don't just criticize the Turks. Aren't there reactionary, irrational attitudes among the Armenians, as well? Here, let me give an example: We have two sons. We wanted them to be baptized. But the Patriarchate refused to baptize them, saying, 'We don't baptize the children of Armenians married to Turks.' The things my mother had to go through in order to get them baptized! She went and spoke with the Patriarch. He told her 'They should decide themselves when they reach eighteen years of age!' My mother answered him, saying, 'If these are the children of my son, they won't enter a church after they turn eighteen!' and then turned and left in a huff.

In Istanbul, it's difficult to live as an Armenian, and also to be married to one. But let me tell you, the most difficult part of all is to live as a *dönme* (religious convert). For a person to live as a convert, or a 'secret Armenian,' someone who, although they were originally Armenian, converted to Islam in order to save their lives, forced to live as a Muslim: that's the hardest and bitterest road of all! There are such people in Istanbul and in Anatolia. But it's impossible to find them and talk to them about it.

The reasons for hatred of the Armenians

"O.K.," I said to Zakarya and Jale, "tell me what are the reasons for this hostility toward the Armenians, for this automatic suspicion and prejudice to which they are always subjected?"

And one at a time, they spoke beautifully about the other, whether Armenian or Turkish. Those who got to know Armenians, those who lived next to Armenians, either in Istanbul or in other places, those who lived with them, all spoke well of them. But despite this, there was still this decades-long antipathy, this Armenian "taboo," this suspicion of Armenians. Sometimes these suspicions and mistrust were mutual. What was the reason for this? How must we approach the Armenian question? How must we deal with it? How must we illuminate the relations between Turks, Armenians and Kurds, both from the past and for the future? Jale spoke first:

> Sometimes, I ask myself these same questions. But I haven't looked into them deeply. Over my life I have reached some conclusions. One of these is that there isn't really a true, heartfelt and sincere dialogue or connection between Turks and Armenians. A Turk who has a relationship with an Armenian doesn't really want to understand the sorrow and hardship that the person before him has suffered for having been Armenian. He doesn't even want to think about the immense sorrow in every Armenian's past. In short, he assumes that the Armenian is like himself. Even so, he could work to develop an understanding of the differences between people by acknowledging and giving a sincere respect to these differences.... I've seen such people! They treat me very well, very warmly. But the minute that they learn that I'm married to an Armenian, they change and begin to distance themselves from me. In fact, all I have to do is mention Armenian history and they start to look at me differently! In these last years, Zakarya has been digging around quite a bit in this subject. He's always reading about it and researching it. He knows about it quite well.

Zakarya then chimed in. "I wouldn't say that I know it better," he said, and began to tell me his thoughts and views on the subject.

> It's true that in recent years I have been devoting a fair amount of time to studying Armenian and Turkish history. I have begun to form some clear ideas. But I'm just an architect. I'm not a historian, of Armenian or any other history. It's a difficult question. But I could recount some of the points that have come to me tonight over dinner. Relations

between Turks, Kurds and Armenians are not only a subject of history. There are also social, economic, cultural and spiritual aspects.... There is a whole bundle of multi-faceted relations that are not that well known. What's more, this is a subject that also has a number of international dimensions....

What are the reasons for hostility toward the Armenians? How can this hatred be erased? What must be done? How must we look at this subject? These are all such difficult questions! You can approach them from such different angles. It's crucial that you approach them with the right intentions! The questions you ask and the answers you come up with will depend on your objectives and your intentions. It doesn't seem possible to explain this immense, historical event with just one approach.

Before we start, we should establish some facts:

First, even before the anti-Armenian actions of 1915, things were different in Western Anatolia than they were in Eastern Anatolia. The great hardships, and the vicious bloody conflicts that were experienced in the Eastern Provinces were not experienced in Istanbul, in Kütahya or Izmir.

Second, regarding the aforementioned subject, the people speak one way, the leaders another way. The things that happened are spoken about freely within families, at coffee houses, in conversations, anywhere where people sit together and speak in small groups. Grandfathers, grandmonthers, fathers and mothers will speak freely about what they think, or what they saw and felt.

I've frequently heard from people 'There were some Armenians in our village. They killed them!' or 'They killed the Armenians of the village in that valley. I saw it!' or 'My grandfather was an Armenian,' 'Our family is of Armenian origin, afterward we converted!', 'My grandmother was Armenian. They sent her away on the Deportation!'

And so much more than that! Today, if you just ask them, sometimes the old folks will tell you the most amazing things.

Naturally, there are also those from among the Turks who have a different account of events. Even if few in number, there are Turks here and there who give similar accounts of the events, and in a similar fashion.

In my personal opinion, you have to look at the subject from many different angles in order to properly understand it. If we want to really look at this enormous, complicated historical event, we have to avoid those approaches that mask its more emotional dimensions, and its tragic aspects, that lead us into a dead end, or that prevent us from fully confronting our history.

To fully understand the Armenian question, you need to study, inch by inch, the last three centuries of the Ottoman Empire—particularly the last century. You have to look at the relations and disagreements between the Ottoman State and all of the other countries, England, Germany, France, Italy, Austria and Czarist Russia, among others. The Armenians played an important role in these relations for several centuries.

The European states' demands for reforms should in no way mask the fact that the Ottomans themselves were working to create a modern, centralized state. On the one hand, you have to conduct a meticulous examination of the Ottomans' relations with the states of Europe, while on the other you have to study, in parallel with these relations, the Ottomans' approach toward the various nations within Anatolia and the Ottomans' relations and problems with these component nations and communities.

It's impossible to explain and understand the hostility between the Armenians, the Turks and the Kurds without the objectives and goals of the Kurdish irregular mounted 'Hamidiye' Regiments that Abdulhamid II created, without objectively and scientifically studying the Kurdish question that has existed from Ottoman times until today.

In the same way, you can't explain this enmity without studying and researching the reasons that the various nations, who for centuries had lived under Ottoman sovereignty in the Balkans, on the Arabian Peninsula and in North Africa, embarked on wars of independence, one after the other, against the Ottoman state, without understanding the nationalist current of the period and its results.

The constant concern within the Ottoman Empire as they watched their borders shrink, their empire be partitioned and eaten away at the edges, all this ultimately produced very ghastly results.

It's very important to study the intellectual currents at the beginning of the Twentieth Century, the views of the Young Turks, and the political views, objectives and directions of struggle of the Committee of Union and Progress. We also have to look at the relations between the Union and Progress and the Armenians, and the elections of those Armenians who were on the party's list of candidates, and the Hunchag and Tashnag Armenian revolutionary organizations.

The seeds of anti-Armenian enmity must be sought in the Union and Progress Party's attempts to create a 'national economy,' to form a Turkish national identity, and their foreign political and military 'adventures,' which aimed at extending Turkish sovereignty throughout Central Asia. The clash between the goal of creating a 'national economy' on the one hand, and the dominant role played by the Armenians, Greeks and Jews in Ottoman economic life on the other were one of the main reasons for the hostility toward the Armenians and Greeks. Along these same lines, Armenian and Greek capital, which prevailed in Ottoman commercial and economic life at the turn of the century, had been reduced to almost nothing by the 1920s. This enormous transformation, which occurred within a very short period, has a great deal of meaning for a person who wishes to understand history.

The Armenians really wanted to find a niche for themselves within the Ottoman Empire. Of all the different minority communities, the Armenians were the most devoted to the state. They didn't want to break away from the empire, they just wanted equal rights within the Ottoman State. The Armenians were the leaders in Ottomanism in the empire; but they wanted to live as Armenians, with an Armenian identity.

This demand for equal rights didn't coincide with the Young Turks' conception of 'Turkishness'; it ran contrary to the aims of the Union and Progress Party. The Unionists didn't accept any of the Armenians' demands, no matter how justified or well-intentioned.

The Armenians were the first community to embark on the process of nationalism and enlightenment, and they made great progress in this direction. But, unfortunately, at a crucial historical juncture, they disappeared, along with their economic and cultural presence.... A handful of self-seeking adventurers turned the Armenians, the Turks and the Kurds against one another; these peoples who had lived side by side, and even among one another for centuries. They accused the Armenians of collaboration; 'Uproot them entirely!' they said. They created imaginary enemies. Their real objective was to create an economic and social life devoid of Armenians and Greeks. In exchange for this annihilation, economic and cultural life passed into the hands of others. During the last century of the empire's existence the Armenians had assumed a very important place in the cultural and economic life of Eastern, Southeastern and Central Anatolia. During those days, every corner of Anatolia was filled with educational and cultural centers. But as we came to 1918, there weren't any Armenians left to give life either to educational or cultural life, or to their accumulated cultural wealth. In a period of history when the Armenians were all alone, all of these historical, social and economic developments had paved the way for their deportation.

Throughout history, those who don't wish to share with others their power, or the economic, social or cultural wealth have always resorted to force. In my opinion, the bloody and brutal events of the Republican period were simply a reenactment of similar events from the period of the Ottoman Empire. The imposition of the Capital Tax and the events of September 6-7, 1955 were not coincidental. They were simply a continuation of the bitter events of the Ottoman period under different circumstances.

Only one week ago, I spoke with a Turkish friend of mine. He told me that the first person to found a theater in the Ottoman empire was an Armenian; the first person to write an opera was Armenian; the first architectural school was founded by an Armenian; the first person to compose songs and write the musical notation was an Armenian. No matter what important field of expertise you're talking about, no matter what profession, the leading members were all Armenian. What was it about them?

"The Armenians," I added, "who in these lands had fulfilled such important duties and played such decisive roles in every field of expertise, from the Ottoman Treasury to its economic life, from art to education, they were declared as enemies and traitors and annihilated." Our conversation continued long into the night....

Imagine an entire state that avoids looking into its own past in a scientific, historical manner. Imagine a state that intentionally teaches its own history to its citizens, to its people in an incomplete and flawed manner....

Nations that refuse to look objectively at their past are condemning themselves to a dark present and future. By completely denying or ignoring the enormous calamities and bloody events of their past, they are destroying the mental health of their society and the individuals who comprise it. What is right and true is to be able to come face to face with one's own past, with an open mind, without bias or any hidden agenda, and armed with knowledge and a clean conscience, and to be able to then make an honest accounting of it.

Germany has today been able to establish a freer and more liberal social order only because it illuminated the black pages of its recent history and made a moral accounting of the bloody events of that period. We, too, can turn to the darker pages of our own history and shed light on them. The illuminating of our past will assist us in passing through the present evils in our society and establishing a more conciliatory and peaceful life for ourselves, amid social and personal freedom.

But let's be realistic! Just as enmities aren't created overnight, they won't disappear overnight, either. What's important is that we are able to advance in that direction, with good intentions, in confidence and without fear, in order to be able to shed light on these realities and to change the present conditions. The sooner we begin this long-delayed task, the sooner we'll be able to bring about social peace, friendship and brotherhood… This task isn't just of interest to the Armenians, but to everyone who lives in Turkey. The Armenians were some of the most deeply-rooted flowers ever to bloom in Anatolia, one of the most brilliant pieces of the cultural mosaic of Anatolia…. Those who wish to make Anatolia a garden that only grows one type of fruit have thereby decreased its blessing and its cultural richness.

In my opinion, we still need to be reconciled with our own history; we must not flinch from facing our past, because everybody wins from such an encounter. We will only bring honor to ourselves by developing a culture of peace, and we'll be able to face the rest of humanity with a clear conscience and with our heads held high.

Compared to forty or fifty years ago, Armenian history and Turkish-Armenian relations can be discussed far more openly than before, it can be written about and sketched. These are encouraging developments… My hope is that these positive developments spread, and find some resonance within Turkish society; that mutual friendship, love and trust take the place of enmity, rancor and suspicion.

We raised our glasses to these positive, encouraging developments.

Jale then brought a tray of fruit to the table; apples, oranges, loquats, bananas, green almonds…

"Please" she said, proffering two apples, "we didn't eat a thing because of all this talking and note-taking." Someone once said that "we are like half an apple," but I think they we're somewhat mistaken. Each one of us is a whole apple, complete. I'm a Turk, Zakarya, an Armenian… but through love and respect we can bring these two elements together, unite two different worlds. Both of us are the flowering branches of a young sapling!

I loved Jale and Zakarya more with each hour that passed. These two flowering sapling branches had illuminated Istanbul and Turkey for me....

Master Sarkis of Karaman: "We shouldn't have let him beat the priest..."

I was planning to return to Germany one day later, but the things I heard from Jale and Zakarya had piqued my curiosity. I asked Zakarya whether or not he knew such old persons in Istanbul who were intimately familiar with the deportations and its aftermath, and especially whether he might be able to locate some Armenians who had survived by converting to Islam, and whether or not he knew some other persons who knew Kegham.

"I know one such old man," he said. "Master Sarkis. He is a piece of living history. He still has all his faculties, too. He is very familiar with the events in question. He was even born during the deportations... but I'm not sure if I can track him down right away. Let me look into it, let me ask around. This may take a little time."

I delayed my return to Germany. Two days later we managed to communicate with Master Sarkis. He came with Zakarya to the hotel where I was staying. The persons who appeared before me had a face shaped by laughter, snow-white hair and was immaculately dressed.... The day had turned very hot.

"Let's go somewhere cool and quiet" I suggested.

"Let's go to my place!" Zakarya said.

"Thank you for your kind invitation," I said, "but today is a work day.... your wife is at work. Your mother-in-law is ill. I don't want create any inconvenience."

"But at a tea house or café our attention will be disturbed by all the noise and hustle and bustle. And anyway, we won't be disturbing anyone at my place."

Master Sarkis then interjected:

"Come, I'll take you to a place. That way, we can both stroll and see something on the way."

We walked along Istiklal Avenue toward the Galatasaray Lycée. When we came to Çiçek Pasaji (Flower Arcade) we turned right. We entered the Fish Market. We followed Master Sarkis down through the market, amid the calls of the produce sellers, the merchants and the customers with whom they were haggling.

"Where are you leading us, Master Sarkis?" I asked.

"To Heaven! To the Seventh Heaven! Come, follow me. Zakarya's maybe seen it already, but you've never seen such a place!"

"And where might this Seventh Heaven be?"

"You'll see it presently!"

We walked a little further. We passed the various restaurants lining the pedestrian promenade. Master Sarkis stopped between a grocer's stand and the shop of a house-slipper seller.

"We've arrived!" he announced, and motioned to an iron door. If he hadn't said something, I would never have noticed the black iron door squeezed between the grocer and the slipper salesman.

Beyond the door was an entrance hall of five or six meters in length. On the right side of the hall was the administration center for the Three Khoran Church Foundation, on the left were stacks of candles and the room of the church watchman… The entrance hall opened onto an extremely bright and well-lit garden, framed in marble. In the middle of this bright garden was a beauty that dazzled the eye! For a moment, I stood there, frozen.

"Here's the Seventh Heaven. Come, take a look!"

Master Sarkis then began to speak, explaining and expounding like an art historian or master architect:

> Here, for you, is a cool and quiet Seventh Heaven, in the middle of Istanbul! Here, in the middle of the Beyoğlu District, is the Three Khoran Church, which is one of the unparalleled examples of beauty created by Armenian architects. It is the second most important Armenian church after the Patriarchate building in Kumkapı. Do you know what 'Three Khoran' symbolises? The Three Khoran are God, the Father; God, the Son; and the Holy Spirit. The Three Khoran represent the unity in this trinity.
>
> There are thirty-three Armenian churches worth seeing in the different districts of Istanbul; in Kumkapı, in Fener, in Balat, in Ortaköy and in Üsküdar. According to some research, there used to be over 1,500 Armenian churches and monasteries in Anatolia. Today, the majority have either fallen to rack and ruin, or even disappeared completely. In fact, the fables, epics, songs, churches and other historical works belong to all of us. This is part of our wealth. It has to be preserved… Those things that are still standing have to be protected with the utmost care; not one stone or brick should be disturbed.

The site for this church was purchased in 1805. A wooden church was built here in 1807. Over time, the wooden church grew old and rickety, and a stone church was built in its place in 1907. It is said that the white marble stones which surround the church garden were brought over from the Armenian cemetery and church which once stood on the place where the Divan Hotel now stands.

Master Sarkis led us around the garden, always explaining.... A section of the garden on the left side of the church was covered in hanging arbor. Underneath the arbor, it was very cool. It led from the garden on the right side of the church out onto a back street.

"If you want," Master Sarkis offered, "We can view the inside of the church."

"Let's see it!" I exclaimed. "If we've come this far, I'd like to light candles for both Meline and Kegham."

I took two candles from the pile. From the inside, the Three Khoran Church was a completely different place! It was a quiet, sedate, soothing world unto itself, in the midst of unimaginable beauty, nestled there amid the bustle and roar of Beyoğlu and its Fish Market.

I lit the candles and made a wish for Meline's health, well-being and happiness, and the illumination of Kegham's eternal abode. In the silent light of the candles' flame, I felt as if I could see Meline's face. Two drops of flame, flickering with the beat of my heart!

We went outside. We sat down on the bench, upon which was written "Princess Islands Municipality," in the dark, cool shadow of the overhanging arbor covering the side garden. Like the shade under which we sat, our conversation soon turned to darker things....

"Master Sarkis," I asked, "where does your title come from? In what field are you a master?" As I awaited his answer, his face turned thoughtful, but he remained silent.

In order to spur him to conversation, I spoke about my own encounters with Meline, Kegham İşkol, my travels to Ani and my conversations with Zakarya.

"I know" he finally answered, "Zakarya told me. I was curious about you. Until now there are a good number of people who have wanted to speak with me, but I've always refused. But you caught my attention. I liked the idea of someone coming here all the way from Germany and seeking me out, seeking us out. As for my "mastery," it's a long story. I did carpentry for fifty years.

You asked about Kegham.... He and I were very close. He lived in the area around Şişli. I'd go to his house now and then and drink strong black coffee. I knew his first wife well. She was an attorney. She helped Kegham out a great deal. Kegham was a very cultured, very knowledgeable, very decisive and very brave man. He was very swarthy and tall. He made some very important contributions to Armenian culture. He put together an Armenian dictionary.

We taught together. He was one of the few people who knew the old classical Armenian language.

But what made Kegham who he was were his ideas. He was one of the honest and decent leftists. He was a man of his word. He loved his country. But they forced him out of Istanbul. He left his country and went away... He went to Germany and never returned again. Even in death he remained there... Is that how you treat such a man, such a scholar? Tell me, are such things done to a person who can author a dictionary? To a researcher?

They intimidated him, they threw him in prison, they ruined his peace of mind, they chased him out of the country... Did this save the state? Did this end poverty? Bring down inflation?

I never met his second wife. Ah! Now I remember.... I'll never forget. When I mention Kegham—God rest his soul!—it all comes back to me. I am a 'master of good deeds'! There was a time when they used to hunt for all manner of books; those who produced 'dangerous' books were punished. I made a beautiful book cache for Kegham.... Ho, ho! I'll tell you these things, but don't write them down! Look, even in the grave he's mixed up in matters! Ha, ha! There were two chests, one which fit inside the other. That was my idea! Go ahead and look, you won't find such a thing anywhere! He was very pleased. Kegham: now he was a great person! He came from an old Istanbul family. You understand what that means, one of those very unique Istanbul gentlemen... There aren't many of those types left...

Kegham used to say, 'Master Sarkis, I want to be a teacher, in order to save a child, to save an Armenian child!' You understand: one of those people who labored and toiled out of love, out of passion.

His work at Tıbrevank was to raise honest, hard-working, gentlemen. He could have done it even better if they would have allowed him to do so. But they didn't give that poor boy a moment's peace....

"Master Sarkis," I said, "you are a carpenter, but you intimately involve yourself with culture, books, architecture and intellectual pursuits in general.... What I'm saying is that you're not like other carpenters I've known. Can you solve the mystery for me?"

"The answer to this mystery, the source and reason for being the way I am, is my mother. My mother knew French, she played piano. She was a teacher who was very devoted to reading and teaching others to read. My life's greatest passion, my most indispensable habit is reading. I even used to write poetry when I was young. My mother was the one who instilled in me this habit of reading. But then came the Deportation, and she regretted ever having come into the world.

My mother graduated from the Armenian College in Tokat. She became a teacher. My mother's family is from Tokat. My father's side is from Kayseri... From Talas, in the province of Kayseri.... She met my father in Karaman, in the province of Konya, and married him, thinking she would put an end to her poverty... But even after marrying just for the sake of being married, she wasn't able to prevent a single thing from happening to her.

One from Tokat, the other from Talas; you might ask 'What strange twist of fate brought them to marry in Karaman?' It's a long story, but I should tell it to you. This is what I learned from my mother:

There was a massacre in Tokat in 1895. It lasted for four hours.... After four hours the order came from the Sultan saying, 'Stop!' My mother would cry when she'd tell me, saying, 'With my own eyes I saw the dismembered bodies of Armenians being carted off in horse-drawn carts!'

Her father and uncle were tailors. They brought the first sewing machine to Tokat. Because her uncle was lame, he used to arrive at their shop and leave again by mule. When the massacre began, my mother's father fled, but her uncle wasn't able to escape. They caught him and killed him in the doorway of his shop.

Together with her mother, her father and her three sisters and one brother placed a ladder against the garden walls and climbed over, going from house to house until they made it to the French school, where they were given refuge.

After this massacre, her father contracted meningitis somewhere and died. Her siblings all got some paralytic disorder.

The doctors told them to go to a warmer clime, but at that time, after my father's death, my mother wanted to leave the school. But despite the difficult transition, her mother made sure she finished college, saying, 'No ifs ands or buts. You will study!'

After my mother finished school, the family traveled to Istanbul with the intention of going on to Egypt. But when they arrived in Istanbul, their relatives took them in, and they eventually forwent the idea of going to Egypt. They settled in Istanbul. My mother was hired as a teacher at the Armenian School in Gedikpaşa. She worked there for a while. During that time, my eldest aunt and next oldest aunt got married.

"We married in order to put an end to this poverty!"

During that time, there was a need for a teacher at the Armenian School in Karaman. They sent my mother off to Karaman.

Taking her mother with her, my mother went to Karaman and began her work... Time passed, and my mother, long having passed marrying age, remained unmarried.

She became acquainted with my father. At that time, my father had come from Talas to Karaman and settled there, where he worked as a banker; in particular, he bought and sold cattle and horses.... I heard a little about this from my father. When he was in the mood, now and then he'd say things like 'I lost fifty-seven thousand in gold lira during the deportation calamity!'

This is the way that my mother married my father, who was very rich, in 1911. When my mother would later mention her marriage, she let out a sigh of pain, saying, 'I married, hoping that it would put an end to this miserable poverty! But we couldn't imagine what great calamities fate would bring upon us.'

In the first years of their marriage, they built a nice little home for themselves. My father was a banker, my mother, a teacher. She knew French... she played piano. Imagine for yourself: they had hardly begun to taste happiness when the deportation order came in the summer of 1915. They only had a few days to prepare for the deportation. My father was very attached to his carpets. He had many very valuable carpets in his house. He quickly gathered them and rolled them up. They entrusted them to the District Official for Karaman, Müftüzade Ahmet Efendi for safe keeping. Before they actually set out on the deportation, most people believed that they would eventually return. My mother was pregnant at the time, and very far along, too. They took along the things that they were allowed to take... Then, without even understanding what had happened, they found themselves in a convoy procession of deportees.

The calamity they call "the deportation"

Thousands of persons were deported, sent away in convoys.... Where to? Nobody knew and none came back alive.... Some say to the deserts of Syria, others say to Deyr-i-Zor, to Halep, to Resülayn, to Meskene, to Rakka...

They walked the whole way, with gendarmes at their head... nights they would be made to sleep wherever they were, no matter how infested by snakes, centipedes or scorpions. Every day, a new place to bivouac.... there was no halting, no resting... then came the hunger, the want, the disease, the attacks, the looting, the kidnapping of women, the rapes.... each day worse than the last... On one day, the eldest of two daughters died on the way. They buried her and continued onward... My mother was pregnant... But the child inside her wasn't going to wait for better times to emerge.... At an overnight stop, early one morning, long before dawn, she went into labor, and as a result brought them a son into the world....

As soon as it was daybreak the gendarmes arrived: 'Get up!' they said, 'Take down your tents!'

My father pleaded with them: 'Please don't, Mr. Gendarme! Please don't, Mr. Soldier! My wife gave birth only hours ago! With your permission....'

But they weren't having any of it. 'You ass, son of an ass!' they said cursing him. 'You infidel, son of an infidel! We wish to wipe your race off the face of the earth, and you bring another child into the world?! We want to annihilate you and you dare produce more?!'

Then they struck my father in the face....

He went back into the tent and said to my mother: 'Arusyag, please forgive me: we have to get up. We're going!'

The child that was born was my elder brother.... He died a few days later... He hadn't even opened his eyes....

With each passing day the conditions on the deportation and migration worsened. People foraged like animals for any bit of food they could find.... They were beset by hunger, by weariness, by the filth and by outbreaks of typhus.

My father's mother died of typhus just before they reached Kilis. They buried her in a ditch! There was no orderly stopping place... Where were they being taken? To Aleppo! Where? To Iraq! Where in Iraq? Where in Deyr-i-Zor? No one ever returned to say!

The long column of deportees was driven from place to place, from camp to camp amid a thousand and one hardships.

There was a dreadful fright and commotion! Death and fear were everywhere! It was prohibited for a Turk to give even a piece of bread, even a cup of water to his Armenian neighbor of forty years! It was prohibited for a Kurd to show even the slightest human compassion to an Armenian! It was forbidden for a Turk to marry an Armenian woman to save her! Armenians couldn't even spare themselves from being deported by converting to Islam like in the old days! That was the law! And the order came from the very highest places.... from Talât. It was even forbidden for an Armenian to help another Armenian! It didn't matter who it was, or for whatever humane reasons it was being done: giving aid to an Armenian deportee—even a drop of water to one dying of thirst or rags to clothe his naked back—was a crime punishable by death! But they were free to attack the deportee columns, to kidnap their women and children, to kill them or sell them in the slave markets! So that you understand: it was forbidden to help them live and permissible to kill them!

My mother told me:

'One day in the Syrian desert we arrived at the banks of the Euphrates river and halted. Hundreds of persons, women, children, entire families, young and old, were all suffering from dehydration. But the army posted sentries between the deportees and the water, forbidding them from approaching the Euphrates to drink! The people began to die from lack of water....'

My mother was a courageous, knowledgeable woman who knew how to get what she wanted! If not she wouldn't have been able to survive!

She looked and saw that there was a military barracks up ahead. She went there and said to the soldier who was guarding the door:

'Mr. Soldier, Sir, are there any persons inside the barracks from Konya?'

'I've got one friend from there!' he answered and shouted 'Rıza!'

After a short while Rıza emerged from inside the barracks.

'My son,' my mother asked, 'are you from Konya?'

'Yes, I'm from Konya!'

'Where in Konya?'

'From the Karaman district....'

'Which village?'

'The village of Binek! And where are you from, sister?'

'I'm also from Karaman!'

'Who are you?'

'I'm the wife of Çerkezoğlu Gazaros!'

When he heard this, the soldier turned white. He was on the verge of tears. He then asked my mother:

'Is my uncle here?'

'What will you do?'

'Before I entered the army, Uncle Gazaros treated me very well' he began to explain....

It turned out that Rıza's father had been a dear friend of my father. At the time, Rıza was just a small child.... He had delighted Rıza every time he came to the village by bringing him food and clothing.... In that way, my father eventually became something of a spiritual uncle to Rıza....

My mother said to Rıza:

'Rıza, my son, we're dying of thirst. They've posted soldiers on the banks of the Euphrates and won't give us water. Whatever else, give us a sip of water!'

Rıza immediately turned around and ran back into the barracks. He came back bringing two large copper pitchers. My mother brought them and gave them to the deportees who were dying of thirst. Bringing it to one person at a time, she distributed the water. 'Through Rıza we were able to distribute the water to the deportees. We saved some five or ten people from death in this way,' she told me.

They remained there, near the Euphrates, for a few days. Rıza was a great help to my mother. The children couldn't even speak because their blood sugar was so low. Children whose blood sugar gets too low can't speak or laugh. It makes normally happy active children into silent, listless things. They get this lifeless, stupid look in their eyes.

Karaman was famous for its sesame *halvah*. But my father never liked it. One day, Rıza gave my mother some three or four kilos of sesame halvah that he had brought from his village. 'Sister, take this halvah and distribute it among the children,' he told her. 'Let them eat it, so that they might be able to talk!'

My mother took it and came with it. At that point my father wasn't aware of what was going on. He was hungry... For days he had been destitute and out of sorts. My father asked my mother if there was any food left.

'Yes, there's Gazaros' halvah. Have some if you want!'

'Ha! Are you teasing me in my time of hunger?' my father said in irritation.

'Not at all! I'm telling you the honest truth! The sesame halvah is from Gazaros, and it came all the way from Karaman!'

'Where did you find it?'

'Rıza from the barracks gave it to me' she said, and as she said so, my father began to cry...

She then divided up a portion of it among the children... another portion she gave to my father, and what remained she ate herself.

Once the children had eaten the halvah, they began to speak again, even to the point of chatter.

So there you have it! On the one hand there were orders commanding that 'no assistance be given to the Armenians or to the deportees!' But some civilians and soldiers, thinking of old friendships and intimacy—even with full knowledge of the punishment that awaited if they were reported—gave a few sips of water, a few pieces of bread, or even some halvah that they had brought from their village as Rıza did. They brought smiles to the children's faces.

This is what makes people into human beings. These are the friendships to which I give importance.

Some people get angry when they hear these things. 'You're lying!' they say. But folk songs don't lie! They express the song of the hearts and of the minds of the people. Allow me to sing to you a little bit. I learned these songs from my mother:

Suvarın dağında bir selemmiş	There was a basket on the mound
Ermeni muhaciri tifoya düşmüş,	The Armenian deportees fell sick with typhus
Kuvveti olanlar sincara kaçmış	Those with the strength fled to the Sinjar [mountains]
Kuvveti olmayanlar çöllerde kalmış.	Those without, remained in the wastes
Yol verin candarmalar biz gideceğiz	Let us pass, gendarmes, and we will go
Annemi babamı biz bulacağız!	We will find our mothers and fathers!

There are a lot more songs like this. My mother used to sing them... Oh, oh! Now I'm starting to get depressed... Whenever I sing these songs I begin to feel down. I'll light a cigarette; that always helps dissipate the bad thoughts. Then, I'll start singing again as soon as I remember the songs....

Yürüye yürüye geldik Arap çölüne	Marching, ever marching we reached the deserts of Arabia
Aç kala kala düştük biz derelere	Hungry, ever hungry, we descended into the valleys
Mevlam Ermeni'ye sabırlar vere	Lord, may You grant the Armenian perserverence
Dini bir uğruna giden Ermeni	The Armenian, the one who goes to a Divine fate,
Dini bir uğruna giden yiğitler.	Brave are those who go to a Divine fate.
Tuzsuz olur Arabistan fıstığı	The pistachio of Arabia has no savor
Taştanmış Ermeni'nin yastığı	The Armenian's pillow is a stone
Böyle miydi Osmanlı'nın dostluğu	So, is that what the Ottomans call 'friendship'?
Dini bir uğruna giden Ermeni	The Armenian, the one who goes to a Divine fate,
Dini bir uğruna giden yiğitler.	Brave are those who go to a Divine fate.
Ermeni Ermeni çirkin Ermeni	The Armenian, the Armenian; the ugly Armenian
Ermeni'nin yoktur asla dermanı	The Armenian who never has succor
Padişahtan gelmiş kırım fermanı	The Decree of Slaughter has come from the Sultan
Dini bir uğruna giden Ermeni	The Armenian, the one who goes to a Divine fate,
Dini bir uğruna giden yiğitler.	Brave are those who go to a Divine fate.
Der Zor çöllerinde naneler biter,	Sprigs of mint grow in the wastes of Deyr-i-Zor
Nanenin kokusu cihana yeter,	The smell of mint is enough for this world
Bu ayrılık bize ölümden beter	For us, this separation is better than death…

Dini bir uğruna giden Ermeni	The Armenian, the one who goes to a Divine fate,
Dini bir uğruna giden yiğitler.	Brave are those who go to a Divine fate.

My mother would sing these songs when she was sad. Shall I recite a little more, but this time singing them?

Master Sarkis began to sing, but with the wounded voice of an eighty-three year old's heart...

There was no one else there in the church courtyard. The songs that Master Sarkis sang from his heart, which had originally been sung with the parched throat of the deportees of 1915-1916, now echoed off the marble church walls, then bouncing upward and outward, toward the Golden Horn, and into infinity.... The sun had risen high enough to peer down upon us in the church garden. The bench upon which we sat cast a shadow, as Master Sarkis began again where he'd left off.

They sent my uncle to Deyr-i-Zor. The wagon drivers he met on the way told him 'The massacre has begun!', so he left his wagon and fled.

My father always said that it was the Circassians who carried out the massacre at Deyr-i-Zor. From Deyr-i-Zor it was a six-day journey to Aleppo by wagon. Many folk songs were sung about Deyr-i-Zor. I've forgotten most of them, but I remember a couple of lines that might give you an idea:

Sabahtan kalktım güneş parlıyor	I arose one morning, the sun was shining
Çeçenler oturmuş mavzer yağlıyor	The Circassians sat there, oiling their Mausers

After I grew up and attained the mind of an adult, I spoke a great deal with my father and my mother, and with other people who saw and experienced the Deportation, the marches into exile, and—call it what you will—that great calamity, that great slaughter, the operations intended to obliterate the Armenian nation. I've tried to read everything that's been written and published on this subject. I've thought long about the things that happened to me personally. I've tried to consider the events' effects and injury on all the people who lived within Anatolia and within the Ottoman State as a whole at this time: on the Kurds, the Turks, the Armenians, the Greeks, on Muslims and Christians...

But I haven't been able to get my mind around it, to understand it fully. I still can't.... How can they have acted in such a carefully planned and brutal manner as this? I'm eighty-three years old, and through the course of my life I've seen a great deal of bitterness and suffering, a great deal of oppression. I've experienced a bit myself... But I still can't grasp the mindset, the thought processes and the cruelty of those who planned and carried out this enormous, disastrous action...

Let me first say that, just as has been frequently said, there were among the Armenians some who committed crimes, who betrayed the Ottomans and collaborated with the British, the French or the Russians; there were even some who attacked and killed Turks or Kurds... Let's begin by admitting that these things that are said are true. But did all of these things justify the extermination of the entire Armenian nation, a nation that had lived throughout Anatolia, from Edirne to Kars, from Trabzon to Iskenderun, and which was long known as 'the loyal community'?

There are all manner of creatures, all types of fish living within the ocean. The shark lives there and so does the dolphin... Do you have to drain the entire ocean in order to catch a few sharks?

Within one year, the Unionist Ottoman government of Talat, Enver, Cemal and Bahaettin Şakir wiped out all trace of the Armenian population in Anatolia—by this did they save the six-hundred year old Ottoman Empire from collapse?

Interior Minister Talat Paşa, who was one of the Unionist leaders who planned and implemented this 'draining of the ocean' bragged at that time: 'In three months, I did more to solve the Armenian problem than Abdulhamid had done in thirty years...'

And did all this prevent the Ottoman collapse in 1918 and the subsequent occupation of Anatolia? In terms of oppression, he did much more than Abdulhamid, but in the end, didn't he have to flee his own country on board a German warship?

Before 1915, Anatolia was an ocean containing many different creatures, fish of all shapes and sizes. It was replete with all manner of peoples that you can imagine: Turks, Greeks, Kurds, Armenians, Jews, Assyrian Christians, Arabs, Circassians, Laz.... Before 1915, some one third of those living within the borders of present-day Turkey were Christians, non-Muslims.

Today, no more than 60,000 Armenians and 3,000 Greeks live in all of Turkey. Where did all these people go? By drying out this ocean, did the Unionist regime succeed in bringing peace, happiness and wealth to the peoples of Anatolia?

It's a shame for these people, it's a shame for those cultures which had originally appeared and flourished in Anatolia for thousands of years, which gave Anatolia its color and its power. It's a shame for those minds that think, for those stars that light up the dark night of the country, for those suns which shower their blessings down upon the country!

According to the central plan that they designed, everything was done quickly and systematically. First, all of the leading members of the cities, towns and villages were to be rounded up for deportation: all the spokespersons, respected members of the community, all the thinkers, writers and artists. They were then taken off and liquidated.

The Armenians within Istanbul itself were largely left untouched. Some two hundred and seventy Armenian intellectuals from Istanbul were also gathered up and deported. Everything was planned down to the last detail!

And everything was done so as not to leave a trace of their deeds! No witnesses would be left to their crimes. And certainly, nothing was photographed. A tight censorship was imposed on the press....

This is information that anyone who is interested can easily find and read about. If Master Sarkis the carpenter can find about and learn about it, then you certainly can...

My father told me about these things... And my mother would correct my father and fill in the holes he'd left. I've got these images still in my head, they're indelible, like the film stills of a tragedy.

One of these images is interesting in that it shows to what lengths some people would go during the deportations. It's the story of a 'madman':

I told you that the convoys of deportees were driven from one place to the next during the operation; that's true, but life still went on in some ways. Even amid all this, people would still find for themselves reasons to laugh and enjoy themselves.... One time, very close to Aleppo, the convoy from Karaman and the one from Kayseri merged. It was one enormous procession of deportees.... In this procession, there was one madman... nobody even knew his name. He had become separated from his own convoy and lost all trace of them, so he attached himself to the one from Kayseri.... and he really acted crazy! They'd cry out, 'The madman's coming, the madman's coming!' and others would shout: 'Catch him! Catch the madman!' or 'Look out! He's getting away!' Those trying to catch him would grab him anyway and anywhere they could! The madman would just laugh and bleat like a goat; they'd grab him from the front and the back.... Those in the deportee convoy would grab him here and there and then laugh as he ran away....

'Come, madman, help us fix this horse cart!' they'd say, 'Come, have a ladle full of water!'

The madman would comb his hair with a backscratcher and say, 'I'm going to fix the wagon!'....

My grandmother from Kayseri knew this madman, however... She told my mother and father 'That man's not mad. I know him well from Kayseri. He's Aram Andonian, the writer and historian. He's one of our intellectuals. He wrote a book called *The Balkan War*. Look out for him. Don't hurt him!'

So at the first chance she had, my grandmother took the opportunity to approach him at a time and place that others wouldn't notice. 'Come here, Aram Andonian Efendi! Come with me!' she said. The madman was stunned, but keeping up his act, he followed my grandmother to the place she led him.

'Aram Andonian Efendi,' she said, 'I know you. Stop with that madman routine. Don't be afraid. Give me your hand! There's no need for all this... It's much worse for us to see you in such a state!' So he sat within the tent and spoke with my grandmother, my mother and my father...

'In the convoy in which I came here,' he said, 'everyone knew me. It was very dangerous for me to be recognized. I feigned illness so that I could separate myself from the convoy. After that, I started to act like I was crazy and joined the convoy from Kayseri. Don't tell anyone about me! I want to separate from the convoy and make it to Aleppo. But only wagon drivers can enter and leave Aleppo right now. If I knew a wagon driver, I'd have him take me... The end of the war is near... It's already clear that Germany is going to lose. Let's make frequent stops, let's not lose hope. We need to live and behave like tortoises, we need to protect ourselves like tortoises. Like tortoises, we need to shore up our wills against these disasters that come from outside.... But again, please be your kind selves and don't tell a soul!'

At that time those among the Armenians who had horse-drawn carts or wagons could come and go to Aleppo in order to carry things and see to the needs of the soldiers guarding the convoys.

My father said to a driver that he knew: 'Look, this poor madman doesn't stop his wailing. I don't know if he's twisted his ankle, his tooth hurts, or what the problem is... but for God's sake, could you please find it in the goodness of your heart to squeeze this madman into the back of your wagon and to take him to Aleppo?'

The wagon driver was a sympathetic man, so, two or three days later, he put the madman on the wagon pole at the back of his 'Tatar wagon'—there was no room within the wagon itself.

When he arrived in Aleppo he looked back, but saw that there was no one there! Had he fallen off? Had he run away? Had he died? It wasn't clear, but there was no sign of him....

That's how life is... a little gap between hope and fear... Life is a little beam of light, sparkling between fear and death!

Do you know what 'couch grass' is? What 'everlasting' plants are? Have you ever seen the flower called 'bloody tears'? You uproot it from the ground and pile it up at the edges of fields and gardens. It'll pass the whole summer like that, but if it just gets a drop of water and a bit of earth, it grows again. Do you know what 'erisylpas' or 'snake vetch' is? In Anatolia, it grows at the base of plants and inside piles of threshed grain. From within its bright red flowers, it puts forth seeds that resemble little cobs of corn. It's poisonous. Otherwise, all the animals, the wolves, the birds, everything else would eat it. It eats its own progeny. The life of the snake vetch is dependant upon its seed being poisonous. That's what life is like. Every form of life has to defend itself in some manner. Within each form there's some defense mechanism, some characteristic with which they keep themselves alive. That's how humans are too. But they preserve themselves through their intellects, through their will to live, through their hope...

After my mother lost the boy child that was born at the beginning of the deportations, she buried him under the foot of a rock and went on and became pregnant again. Just look at how life works: just look at this hope!

One section of the convoy from Karaman remained on the outskirts of Aleppo. Aleppo was partially better than Deyr-i-Zor or Resülayn in the Meskene District.

I came into the world in a camp called Jabul in the area around Aleppo. It was a place that had a salt lake nearby.... That was in 1916. Neither my mother nor my father could remember the exact day. So when was I born? In 1916... and that's as far as it goes...

How is it that I lived and didn't perish like my predecessor? I still have no answer to this mystery, this riddle. But it may not just be me; could it be that there are hundreds of other Armenian children born during the deportations surviving until today? And maybe, even under these harsh conditions, there were hundreds or even thousands of persons who evaded the grip of death and went on to live long lives. Look at me: I'm eighty-three years old. And I'm still healthy, thank God. I don't know a single doctor! I've had some close encounters with the Angel of Death in the past... I was sure he would take me several times, but he didn't! I didn't let him! Ha, ha, ha!

What I'm trying to say is that when a person comes face to face with death his attachment to life multiplies tenfold in order to enable him to make his line continue. Maybe a person's cells and genes actually change....

Maybe it was our good fortune to live in Central Anatolia instead of the western part, because the deportations were not the same everywhere and at every period. People are different, conditions are different in different places... There were plenty of Turkish provincial governors, district governors, soldiers and officers, German generals like Liman von Sanders, German officers and missionaries, nuns, nurses and orderlies, who put themselves in harm's way, risking not only their lives, but their work and their positions as well, working with whatever means they had at their disposal to prevent the Armenians from being sent to their deaths. There were those sons of men who were faithful and righteous, who listened to the voice of their conscience, despite all of the official commands and orders.

My mother used to tell this story with the sense of having a great emotional dept:

My great uncle was serving in the Ottoman army with Cemal Paşa in 1916. He received news of the whereabouts of his sister's husband, of which camp he was in. He approached his commander and pleaded with him: 'Commander, Sir; my elder sister and her husband are in a camp not far from here. With your permission, I would like to see them. And with your permission, I would like to have them sent to Istanbul.'

'You can have your sister and her children sent, but not your brother-in-law,' the commander said. 'Go, see them. Here's a letter giving you permission. Take them to Istanbul!'

So my uncle hopped on a horse, and arrived at the camp accompanied by two other soldiers. The Armenians all gathered around him, saying, 'An Armenian officer has come. He'll save everyone!'

My uncle sent the soldiers back to whence they had come. 'I'm going to spend the night here,' he told them, 'You go on back!'

Night came, and my uncle said to his elder sister, who was my mother: 'Elder sister, do you know why I've come here? I prayed to God that he let me see my sibling's face one more time!' God has heard my prayer. Thank God I have been able to see you once more. I've got permission from the general, I'm going to take you and the children to Istanbul!'

'And what about your brother-in-law?' my mother asked. But my uncle couldn't say a word.

'Tell me,' my mother insisted, 'What about your brother-in-law?'

'I was only able to get permission from the general to release you and the children!'

'Look, my brother! This man has lost everything. All that he has left in the entire world are his wife and two children. I can't just go and leave him. I couldn't do such a thing. Go now, may you have a safe journey. What else can I do? Stay alive if you can... We are living in such a time that a person must save his own life if he can, but must not poison the lives of others in order to save his own soul. When we married we promised each other to remain together, both through the good days and the bad. I cannot leave this person now!'

These were the sort of conditions people experienced during the deportations. Despite everything, their humanity didn't perish. It won't ever perish.

It's said, for instance, that during the deportation of the Armenians from Izmir, the majority were saved from deportation by the decisive stance of Liman von Sanders. It's also known that the deportation of the Armenians of Kütahya was prevented and then delayed by the provincial governor there.

During those days, helping Armenians was seen by some as a capital crime, by others as treason. But if we look back now, after so much time has passed, we rejoice at the self-sacrificing, moral behavior of some persons, and remember them with compassion and reverence.

Beginning in April 1915 and continuing for three months, the Armenians of the East, of the nine eastern provinces in which most of them were concentrated, were entirely uprooted and driven off into the deserts of Syria. The most deaths occurred among the Armenians of this region.

Beginning in July 1915, the Armenians who lived in Central and Western Anatolia—outside of Istanbul and Izmir—were deported; their fate, too, was to be marched off to some unknown calamity. By December of that year, the operation of uprooting all of the Armenians within the Ottoman borders, tearing them away from their homes and their regions had been completed. The following year, 1916, was as harsh period as fate could have decreed for the hundreds of thousands of persons who crowded the camps on the sides of the roads in the Syrian wastes, or on the roads leading to Syria.

As of 1917, conditions improved somewhat. In 1918, the Ottoman Empire was defeated and surrendered unconditionally, and the leaders of the Union and Progress Party were arrested and tried in Istanbul for the 'Armenian massacres.'

When the British occupied Arabia and the French took Adana, Iskenderun, the Alexandretta Province, Urfa and Maraş, it was announced that the those who had been deported would be allowed to return to their own country of origin. But in order to return, it would be necessary to first acquire written permission.

My father went to Aleppo and asked an acquaintance of his from Kayseri: 'Look, we are going to return to Karaman, but the government there has since changed. To whom do we make our request? From whom will we receive permission? The French are in Adana... How are we to return, which road should we take?'

The acquaintance replied: 'Do you know who will take care of matters for you? That so-called 'madman' of yours at Meskene. He'll do it!'

'How?'

'There's no 'how' to it! You just go to army headquarters on the second floor of the Baron Hotel in Aleppo. You'll find our madman there. He'll take care of the whole thing. He provides return permits for Armenians!'

At that point, my father was utterly baffled. But he went to Aleppo and to the Baron Hotel as instructed. He knocked on the second floor room. And sure enough, the person who opened the door was the very same 'madman,' Aram Andonian Efendi, who was now staring him in the face! But he was dressed very snappily, and looked very well groomed....

They embraced, and Andonian Efendi quickly ushered him inside and offered him food and drink. My father's host said: 'Hey now, let's have a look at you, Çerkezoğlu Gazaros! You were a great help to me. How is your mother? Is she well? Where is she now? And your wife, your children?'

'All are safe and sound, thank God!' my father replied, and explained his problem: 'We want to return to Karaman. But how do we do so? Can you tell me?'

'I swear, Çerkez Efendi, if it were up to me, I'd tell you not to go. It's still unclear what the future holds. Nevertheless, if you wish to return, I will organize the necessary documentation for your return.'

So, after four years of deportation, wandering and exile, our family was finally able to return to Karaman. I was three years old when we returned. I still have a few weak traces in my mind about the conditions during the Deportation. But they are too faint to allow me to explain it.

As for my life after our arrival in Karaman, I've got a very clear memories.

Those members of our family who remained alive faced the greatest difficulties upon returning to Karaman. Their houses and properties had been totally demolished. They no longer had as many houses as when they had left. They repaired what they could… and began their lives again with what they found. But the government again began to act in intimidating ways toward them. There were good people who afforded them support. My uncles' families and a great many other Armenian families from Kayseri opted not to return. We went back together with a few other families.

In 1919, war broke out again, this time with the Greeks… They wanted to recruit more men into the army. My father didn't go. Instead he ran away and hid. There were some *yörük* nomads whom he knew in the Taurus Mountains who gave him much assistance. He knew them from the time before the Deportation, when he had bought and sold livestock and worked as a banker.

I earlier told you that my father worked both as a banker and a livestock dealer before the Deportation. One day in 1909, my father went to Adana and purchased a young bull. It was on that very day that the attacks against the Armenians in Adana began. They killed all the Armenians that they saw in the market and looted their property. My father fled and went to these nomads in the Taurus Mountains who he had gotten to know, where he sought refuge. That's how he saved his own life.

You must endure what fate brings to you

When he fled from the army, he went to these same nomads. The nomads weren't the ones to inform on a friend who sought their assistance, or to hand him over to the gendarmes.

My father spent a full six months hiding out with these nomads in the Taurus Mountains. They made a *cura* for him, one of their traditional stringed instruments, and he purchased a salt container to take with him. He would wander from rock to rock, from mountain spring to mountain spring, and sometimes he would help the nomads out as well.

One day, as he was laying down next to a spring and thinking to himself, a young nomad woman came to the spring. She took down the child she was carrying on her back, washed its face and hands and gave it to drink from the waters. She then pulled out her breast to suckle the child.

Upon seeing the woman suckle the child at her breast, my father suddenly thought of me. He began to miss me badly.... Soon thereafter, he said to his nomad friends, 'Thank you so much, May God grant your every wish! I am going now. I'll hide out a bit longer in Karaman. That which is fated to happen to me shall happen, God be praised! I will never forget the kindness that you've shown me!'

And one night he secretly made his way back to his home where he hid....

Every day, they called my mother to the provincial police station.

'Where's your husband?' they would ask her.

'I don't know,' she'd reply. 'I swear, I haven't seen him! He went to Gülnar and to Anamur. I don't even know if he's still alive!'

I'll never forget the way our house was built.... It had a courtyard and a huge door. On the right side of the house was a wooden staircase. There was a balcony at the top of the stairs. My mother used to take me and let me play there.

It was like my little window onto life. Sometimes, when I would be playing there, I would see something from the window like a phantom shape. I'd get scared and run to my mother's side.

'Don't be afraid, my son,' she'd say, reassuring me, 'there's nothing there. You just saw a ghost. I'm here, see? Go, go on back and play!'

Actually, it had been my father, who would come out of his hiding place in order to be able to secretly watch me. 'Take my son out to the balcony and let him play' he'd tell my mother, 'Let me watch him a little.'

I was four years old at the time. My mother and father were both people who had survived the deportations. They had passed through the gauntlet, so to speak. They had taken moisture from the blowing wind. They were alert every single moment. For whatever reason, they wouldn't let me see my father, thinking that a child might innocently let something slip.

Even so, one night I fell ill. I had a high fever. I lapsed in and out of consciousness. My mother was very afraid and she went and told my father. My father came in quietly and held my head. He placed a cool, damp cloth on my forehead. At one point I opened my eyes and saw my father. I still remember calling out 'Father! Father!' Then, a little while later I fell unconscious again. Morning came and my fever went down. I got better, but then I began crying and asking 'Where's my father?'

My mother said 'Shush! There's no father here or anyone else. He never came. You were dreaming!'

I didn't believe my mother. I was sure I'd seen my father in the house! After that, my mother didn't let me go outside of the courtyard anymore.

We had a next-door neighbor named Fatma Hanım. Across from us was a Greek family of a mother and a daughter. At that time, the population transfer of the Karaman Greeks had not yet taken place. But everyone in the neighborhood were spies. They didn't like us.

Anyway, one time I found the door to the courtyard open. I can still remember it as if it were yesterday....

Fatma Hanım took my hand and pulled me after her. It was the time when the apricots were just ripening. The walls of our respective gardens abutted one another. There were many apricot trees in our neighbor's garden. I saw them and Fatma Hanım said to me, 'Sarkis, is it true that your father is in the house? If you tell me the truth I'll give you an apricot.'

'He's in the house,' I replied, 'My father is in the house.'

'God bless you,' she said. 'Come, take three apricots for yourself.'

As soon as my mother saw the apricots, she pressed me for information. 'Who gave you these?' she demanded.

'Aunt Fatma Hanım' I said.

'What did she ask you?'

She asked 'Is your father in the house?' and I said 'Yes, he's in the house.'

'You did something very wrong!' she said, scolding me.

I understood the error I'd committed; but I said what I'd said. I really wanted those apricots. But afterward, I was very sorry...

My father and mother immediately took preventive measures. Fatma Hanım reported us immediately. The gendarmes came to our house and searched everywhere, but they weren't able to find my father. Even so, they ordered us to clear out of the house, saying that they were going to turn it into a hospital. The next day we moved out.

There was a fellow in our neighborhood by the name of Mehmet from Kayseri. Before the deportations my father had taken him in and treated him as his own son. He raised him, married him off. Mehmet loved my father greatly. When my father came down from the mountains, he was able to come back to our house through Mehmet's help. He would always watch our house and be aware of what was going on there. When he learned that we had been cleared out of our house, he came over at midnight, in the darkness. He brought with him a turban and the clothes of a religious teacher. He had my father dress in these and in that way he was able to secretly ferret him out to his own house.

In the morning we went to Kayserili Mehmet's house. As soon as we arrived the gendarmes came and raided the house. They caught my father, threw handcuffs on his wrists and took him away, pummeling him all the while.... I still remember that moment: my own crying, my mother's hysteria and my father being taken away....

My father remained in jail for a period.

It appears that our Greek neighbor had seen my father and Kayserili Mehmet as they left our house and went and reported it.

When my mother learned this to be the case, she said to the neighbor, 'I hope to God that you are struck down, that he sticks a knife into your neck!'

Two days later, it was heard that the mother and daughter at our neighbors had been murdered at the foot of their stairs. 'The soldiers who came to ask for *rakı* murdered them' they said. I don't know if it's true or not.

My mother was later sorry, saying, 'Oh Lord! I know I asked for this, but did I say you should do it so quickly?'

My mother didn't long hold a grudge against anybody. She supposed that the deaths of the Greek women had come about because of her own curse and she was very sorry. When she would recall this event from time to time she would blame herself, saying, 'Oh Lord, when I told you....'

Ah, wait! Now I remember it well: when my father was in jail a horse-drawn carriage came one night and stopped before our door. There were gendarmes inside. Both my mother and my father were inside it in chains. I didn't know why and I began to cry. They took me into the carriage as well. We all went down to the Karaman train station. They sent my father off to Ereğli.

While we were waiting at the station, my father gave my mother a piece of paper. It read: 'Alusha, there are honorable people in this country, too. I wrote down the names of those persons who owe me money. Go collect my debts and don't let the children go hungry!'

The gendarmes quickly came and snatched the paper from my mother's hand. 'What's that?' they asked my father, upbraiding him, 'What did you write?'

I can now feel the darkness of that night before me!

My father had friends in Ereğli; the Deli Mustafa family took him in and helped him out a great deal.

My father later sent us a telegram: 'Go get a travel document from the District Governor and come to Ereğli!'

During that time, any Armenian who wished to travel from one place to another had to first get a travel document. The Armenians had no freedom of movement.

My mother managed to get the travel document she needed. Everything that was in our house was deposited with the local head of Karaman, Müftüzade Ahmet Efendi for safe keeping.

We took the train to Ereğli. A woman met us at the station. I was standing in front of my mother. We stepped down from the train. She took us to the house of an Armenian. It belonged to a friend of my mother and father during the deportations.... We remained as guests in the house of Aunt Sultan. We waited for my father... one day, two days... still no father!

'Where is he?'

'Kirkor's family called yesterday evening. He's coming in the morning!'

But morning came, and father still didn't come!

Uncle Kirkor, who had called my father to his house, now arrived.

'Where's Gazaros?' we asked.

'Gazaros was going to come to my place; we waited, but he never arrived. We started to worry, so we came to ask you!'

At that point we all began to cry! My mother, my elder sister and I.

One, two, now three days, and my father was nowhere to be seen!

Days became weeks, and still, no father!

We were still staying at my Aunt Sultan's house. It was a pitch black night, the heavens were thundering, lightning was flashing, and rain was coming down in buckets. My mother would pray constantly at times like these: 'My God, protect those who are stuck on the roads or in the saddle! Protect those who are hungry and thirsty and in strange and foreign places! God, do not let people be swept away in the deluge or the torrent!'

Shortly after her prayers, the rain began to lighten up. There was a knock on the door. My mother took the gas lantern in her hand and shone it out the window, calling to us 'Get up, children! Get up!' Then she opened the window and peered out into the darkness. Again, there was a knock at the door. My mother opened the door and let out a surprised 'Oh! Father!' Father had arrived! He was sopping wet! Over his shoulder was slung a saddlebag...

Then, all of a sudden, I was holding onto my sopping wet father! We all hugged father with all our might, and he embraced us all as well.... There, within Aunt Sultan's house, we were walking on air. Our spirits were hovering above as if we had died and been resurrected.

Then Aunt Sultan and her husband and children came out... The room was bursting with people.... happy, elated people!

Like the day on which my father was to have gone over to Uncle Kirkor's house, the gendarmerie commander summoned my father.

'Çerkezoğlu Gazaros,' he said, I heard that you had a purebred horse like an Arabian. Give me this horse! I am in need of a swift steed.'

'I shall give it to you, commander sir' my father replied.

'Where is it?'

'In the village of Krallar, in the district of Mut. It's with Abdullah Bey.'

'Send two children there to retrieve it and bring it to me!'

'I swear, commander sir, even if you were to go there yourself, Abdullah Bey would not give it to you! They are thrifty and frugal people. Without my going there personally, they won't give a soul the horse I've entrusted to them. If you are afraid that I will flee, send two gendarmes to accompany me, so that I may go and retrieve the horse and bring it to you.'

For some reason, the gendarmerie commander grew angry at this... He bundled my father off to exile in Kayseri. My father remained there for fifteen days. He went to the Armenican College there. Afterward, he found a way to return home.

When the guests had left, my father took out the gifts that were in one of the compartments of the saddlebag. From Talas he had brought a pair of American ankle boots for me; a haircutting machine for himself; for my mother and my sister he had brought some dresses with ornamental ribbons sewn into their borders.

The next morning I put on my boots and strode out into the street. I wanted to show them off to everyone. In those days, only the children of rich families wore ankle boots. We wore rawhide sandals known as *çarik*. And if we couldn't find those we would go around barefoot.

Çerkezoğlu Gazaros, who only five years earlier had been a well-respected banker and livestock merchant in the village and who had sat on a capital of 57,000 gold pieces, had now become a penniless, unemployed and powerless individual. Before the deportations he had wanted to call in all his debts, but apart from a few honest individuals, nobody wanted to pay their debts to him. Each time he wanted to collect on his debts, he had to go and ask for a document allowing him to travel. Even though he had survived the deportations and returned alive, his debtors still didn't want to repay what they owed. Just look how low some people will sink! There are many folk songs about this!

They would make up some excuse to delay paying my father what they owed him, always promising to pay at a later date.

Ver Ömer'e	Give to Ömer [what you owe him]
Yaz duvara,	Write [the amount you owe him] on the wall
Duvar yıkıldı,	The wall collapses
Hesap silindi!	The debt is erased!

Some of those who owed him money even made threats! 'Forget about these debts! Forget them!' they'd shout after him. One person who owed my father a great deal of money sent three thugs to threaten to kill my father. Because of this, my father was afraid to go to Adana.

He appealed to the courts. He engaged the services of an attorney. The judge admitted that the property belonged to my father, but rejected his petition anyway, claiming that there was an order from the Interior Ministry strictly forbidding the surrender of such properties to their owners!

The gist of the matter was clear. The Deportation had overthrown the old order entirely. My father's commercial holdings had been reduced to nothing. All of his property and possessions had been confiscated under the pretext that it had belonged to one 'subject to deportation' and was thus 'abandoned' or 'ownerless property.' It was impossible to get it back. But even so, my father remained happy and hopeful.

My father was interested in horses. He was very knowledgeable in the art of taking care of horses. Before the Deportation he had entrusted his horses to a groom. After his return, he was forced to become a groom for other horse owners.

My mother was a teacher, but the Armenian school had been closed and she was unable to work. But even this destitute, debased life was a thousand times better than what they had experienced during the Deportation.

My mother, my father—all of us were so thankful to have escaped the clutches of death. But even though some persons survived the deportations, the mental and emotional scars, and the fear all remained within them. The survivors never managed to shake off the 'mortal fear' that they had experienced.

"I am going to send my children to school, no matter what!"

And it was under these very conditions that my mother began making every effort she could, saying, 'No matter what else, I am sending my two children to school.' But there wasn't any Armenian school in Ereğli. The education that was provided in Turkish schools at the time was so far behind that of the Armenian schools as to be beyond comparison.

At that time, French language instruction was mandatory at the Armenian schools. For us the only possibility of getting a good Armenian school education was to be found in Istanbul. My mother did everything she could, wouldn't let the subject go, and in the end managed to bring my father around to her position. My father would remain in Ereğli, and we would go with my mother to Istanbul.

When we arrived in Izmit by train, I saw the sea for the first time in my life. I was dumbstruck with awe! Water everywhere and without end! The entire way to Istanbul I stared out the train window at the sea....

We got on the ferry at Haydarpaşa, across the Bosphorus from Istanbul. Istanbul was a completely different world than the one I had known.

We stayed with our relatives until we found a place of our own. We rented a place in the area around Gedikpaşa. My older sister went to one primary school, I went to another. My mother spared no effort to ensure that we would be able to go to school. She worked as a cleaning lady, she did seamstress work, she cleaned stairwells... she even swept up hair clippings at barbershops! She didn't rest, night or day!

In 1932 my mother had to take my sister out from the fourth grade. She was going to go to Syria to get married. After that my mother's whole plan began to unravel. I was forced to leave school too. We returned to Ereğli after that.

Summer vacation was over. My father told me, 'Get ready, it's about time for school to open again,' but my mother told him the truth:

'Sarkis left school.'

'Why?'

'What do you mean, 'Why?' We've found notebooks, but we can't find shoes. We give the money for school fees, and there's not enough left over for bread! How is this child going to study on a woman's wages?'

My father felt strange. He stood there, thinking. What's the world coming to? Çerkezoğlu the Banker can't find enough money to send his son to school?!?

'I will send my son to school' he said. 'And I will send him to the French school!' I supposed that my father had a secret stash of money somewhere. But my mother asked:

'How are you going to do that?' she asked.

I'll sell my horse and use that money for school!' he replied.

'O.K., so let's say you sell your horse this year and send your child to school with the money. What are you going to sell next year in order to pay for his tuition?' And after saying this, my mother began to cry. She didn't cry often, and by bursting into tears, she was signaling that she had lost hope. In other words, the dream of my going to school was becoming more distant.

Then, I got to be seventeen or eighteen years old. I would write poetry. I read books. I did a lot of traveling and wandering. After not speaking it for years, I began to forget the French I had learned at school. When my older sister went to Syria to get married, my mother went to the district official of Karaman, Müftüzade Ahmet Bey, to whom we had entrusted our bales of expensive carpets before the Deportation.

'I've come to take back three or four of our carpets for my daughter's dowry' she said. Müftüzade Ahmet Bey made all sorts of excuses, though. He spoke of obligations and outstanding debts. My mother returned home empty-handed and crestfallen.

In this way, my father wrote off the things that we had deposited as a trust. My sister got married and left. I remained alone with my mother and father.

But what was I to do in Ereğli? I grew older, life was passing by. In the end I began to learn carpentry alongside a carpenter that I knew.

You have to start somewhere! I started to learn carpentry. I moved up from apprentice to journeyman, and eventually became a master carpenter myself. I made my living through carpentry. I even taught it to my sons.

We were called 'infidel soldiers'

It was on the tenth of June, in the year 1941 that I was conscripted into the military. During those years they took non-Muslim men between the ages of 12 and 32 into the army. Camps were set up in Afyon, Yozgat and Sivas. We were kept separate from the regular troops.

They only gave us brown uniforms, and no weapons were issued to us. We were called *gavur askerleri* – 'infidel soldiers' – and we weren't given the training or duties of regular soldiers. Instead, they made us do forced labor. There wasn't a single place that we weren't sent. From Afyon to Erzurum, I worked every place, every kilometer of the rail lines. My stomach still turns at the very mention of the word 'train'!

I worked in Balıkesir and in Aydın. I spent a winter under a bridge in Gebze. What we did was corvée work: breaking up the earth with pickaxes, filling up handcarts and dumping the dirt somewhere else.

When the outcome of the war became clear our military service was also ended.

I'm afraid that if there's ever another war, we're going to get the worst of it again, like the other times, because any time there's a war, we are the first to face trouble and have our lives turned upside down.

During the First World War, the country's Armenians and Greeks, all of its minorities were subjected to a great calamity. During the Second World War we didn't face a new deportation of the same scale—there weren't enough Armenians or Greeks left to deport! But all of the non-Muslims were affected by the Capital Tax....

The first stop during this second deportation was Aşkale. While we were working on the railroad tracks we saw the non-Muslims who were being sent to Aşkale by train. Those who were sent were our co-religionists, our fathers, our brothers and other relatives and acquaintances. We were also members of the same community. They recognized us and we recognized them. We could identify them by their sad hand waving, and they could identify us by our brown, 'infidel soldier' uniforms....

In the winter of 1942 I was one of the brown-uniformed soldiers working at cleaning the tracks at Ankara Train Station. The 'travellers to Aşkale' passed by in their trains. The inhabitants of Ankara came out to watch as if they were watching circus animals, with their constant curiosity, their helplessness, their silence, their anger, their good intentions.... Most of the Ankarans just stood there silently, but there were some who shouted out in angry voices 'May you go and never return!,' 'Good riddance!,' 'Be thankful that you've lived this long!,' 'May you bleed back the blood you've sucked from the nation!,' 'Someone will keep your wives company while you're gone!'

As if the deportees to Aşkale were responsible for all the poverty, black marketeering, profiteering and wartime conditions....

The people had been conditioned in this way: the newspapers, the cartoonists had put the blame on a handful of persons being sent off to Aşkale.

They sent them from Ankara to the Malatya region. We had a camp on the banks of the Euphrates at the time. There we worked breaking rocks, digging and removing dirt, and performing maintenance on the rail lines. The letters that my father sent me regularly were intercepted. Only those of my mother arrived.

I began to have the most evil thoughts. One night, I saw my father in a dream: I was in the tent when he came to me. He was dressed entirely in black. 'Come, father!' I said, but he remained silent. Then he turned around and left. I ran and ran, trying to catch him, but my foot got caught on a tree root and I fell into the mud. I struggled and struggled but was unable to extract myself. I was bathed in sweat.

I awoke, feeling like I was suffocating. I went outside and washed my face and hands. The night was pitch black. I found myself unable to get back to sleep and lay there awake until the morning. 'Sarkis, you've lost your father!' I said to myself.

The thought stuck in my head. I began to plan my escape from the army. I spoke with a trusted friend and told him my thoughts and pains. I was going to take the first opportunity that came my way. I wasn't thinking clearly.

One day, while I was plodding my way deep into the foliage on the banks of the Euphrates, the unit commander suddenly appeared before me. I had been imagining that I had already fled and was strolling around in Ereğli. I came to my senses. I greeted the commander and he acknowledged my greeting.

'Come over here, next to me, Sarkis' he said to me. 'Relax, but listen well to what I say. In every life there are good days and there are bad days. A person also has to endure and get through the bad days. I like you, Sarkis, but I like my task even more. You say you're going to flee, but I'll catch you the moment you try, and I'll send you up to the court martial! Your military service will be voided! Pull yourself together! All people get crazy thoughts. Soon we'll be going to Balıkesir. I'll give you leave when we pass through Kayseri… You can go to Ereğli and see your mother and father. That's a promise! Just don't run away!'

It was almost another full month before the 'brown-uniformed military division' traveled by train to Balıkesir. The commander stood by his word. He gave me a week's leave when we got to Kayseri.

I arrived in Ereğli shortly before dusk. I went to my house and Uncle Kirkor came out to meet me.

'Welcome, Sarkis!' he said.

'Thank you, Uncle Kirkor!' I replied, but didn't dare to ask 'How is my father?'

Kirkor went away and as he was leaving I thought to myself, 'Sarkis, if he turns around and looks it means that my father has died!' and just like that, he turned around and looked!

Just as the sun was setting I entered the door to our house. My mother was startled and dumbstruck. Then she hung her head and began to cry.

I went up the stairs and entered the house.

'Mother, where is father?' I asked.

'He got sick, so we sent him to a hospital in Istanbul!'

'You sent him to Istanbul barefoot?' I asked, not believing it for an instant. 'Why are his shoes here at the base of the stairs?'

Then she began to sob, weeping loudly.

My father had apparently died on the night that I saw him in my dream.

And that's how my father passed from this beautiful world!

One week later I returned to the Balıkesir district. I explained the situation to my commander and thanked him for the help he had given me.

Eventually my military service came to an end, and I returned home to Ereğli. I returned to carpentry. I enjoyed the work I did because I knew how to read and write, and how to manage my books. I did good work, too. My reputation spread.

During those years they established a 'Village Institute' in İvriz. New buildings began to spring up all over the sparse plain around there. Both the male and female children of the village began to work there and they began to give lessons within the classrooms that they themselves had built.

I made all the benches, the chairs and desks at the İvriz Village Institute. I came and went to İvriz very often during that time.... Although I myself wasn't able to study, the desire to learn and go to school continued to burn within me. I used to invent excuses or pretexts to go over to the institute....

They used to always sing together, play together. Enlightenment was going to begin with the villages. The dusty plains of Anatolia were going to bloom.

Those young boys and girls, how they played violin, how they used to build walls and work in the fields. I saw with my own eyes the world that was being created through faith, through hope, through music and folksongs...

These rosy-faced village girls, with their military ankle boots on their feet and their school bags on their back used to go shopping arm in arm with the boys. I spoke to those to whom I had taught carpentry.... Each one was full of hope from head to foot.... each one, a fresh sprout, bursting forth on the dry plain.... I used to join them for dinner. I ate from their soup kettle.

They used to sing a march together; I still remember a couple of lines from it:

Sürer eker biçeriz güvenip ötesine	Trusting in the future, we march, we plant, we sow
Herkesin kazancı kendi kesesine!	Everyone's profit to his own pocket!

A lot of people didn't like these things at all! Among the animals, it's only the cat who eats its own young. It mistakes its own offspring for a mouse and eats it. As for us, they mistook us for a lot of things, and ate us; they wanted to devour us.

Our only crime during the Deportation was being Armenian; during the Capital Tax, it was being non-Muslims.

The Village Institutes were a great hope for greening the sparsely vegetated plains of Anatolia. But they immediately mistook it, too, for a mouse! 'Let's close it!' they said. 'It's a nest of communists!,' they claimed, 'The toilets at the institutes are all full of the aborted fetuses of the girls who go there!' The things they said about the institutes! But the real intentions of those who slandered the institutes and wanted to close them down, their real fears were very clearly expressed by a rural notable from Eskişehir, who said, 'I don't want the ass that I will ride to be smarter than me!' This phrase was well publicized during that time. In the end, they caused great damage and finally destroyed the Village Institutes.

Moving to Istanbul

After my father's death I remained for a while longer in Ereğli to look after my mother. But it had already become increasingly difficult to live in Ereğli. About half of the Armenians had moved to Istanbul or abroad. I began myself to feel alone and insecure.

I spoke with my mother about it. Together, we decided to pack up and move to Istanbul. We rented a place in Yedikule, and I set up shop for myself in Kumkapı. I struggled to get my business established and to earn enough money for us....

At that time I was in my early thirties. The years passed by like water. I had hardly blinked my eyes and it was already 1949.

I was still unmarried. All of my contemporaries were already married, with homes and children. I didn't have a thing. A real pessimism began to descend upon me.

One day there was a wedding celebration in front of our house. Everyone was happy and having a wonderful time. I went to the tavern instead. I drank and drank, drank and felt sorry for myself! I got really drunk... On the way home I stopped and rested my head against the iron gate before an elementary school and cried my eyes out. No one stopped to ask me, 'Why are you crying?' I thought about my own childhood, about my father's death, about having to leave school because of our poverty, about my friends.... It's very difficult to have all these bad thoughts, to feel so alone... You wander the streets like a drunk, even when you're not, up one street and down the other, speaking to yourself.

That wedding, the wretched state I was in that night, they all made me a little smarter, a little wiser. I pulled myself together and got my head on straight. I spoke with my mother and I resolved to marry. I ended up marrying a young woman seventeen years younger than myself. We are still together. If only she had been twenty years younger! Ha, ha, ha!

It was 1950 when we had our first child.... After that, two sons more.... One of them became a dentist, the others are in commerce.

I also managed to put my business on a firmer footing and become established in Istanbul. My mother stayed with us.

I worked from morning till night and was very tired, but I never completely exhausted myself. My house was full of peace and tranquility. There was always food on our table. We were at peace with ourselves. We were happy. Our children were a joy and a blessing. My mother's passion was to send her grandchildren to school.... when she was able to read to them, her joy was without bounds.

I used to chase away my weariness by reading. I wouldn't be able to fall asleep without reading. The more I read, the more I developed my passion for art, the better I worked the boards or lumber. I took great pleasure from the mastery reflected in the pieces I created.

While I was still in Ereğli I didn't get very involved in politics, but since coming to Istanbul I began to read more systematically. And the more I read, the more I saw, the more I understood.

The more I understood about how things were, the more I understood the past and the present, the more they came alive for me. The fears of Sarkis, who was born in Jabul during the Deportation in 1916, gradually began to recede. I began to engage in politics, to follow developments via the newspapers, the radio and books, and to subject them to my own analysis.

I'm an Armenian. And what's more, I'm one of those who survived death! Fear worked its way into my bones. If others have five senses, I've had to have ten! In any case, I'm a member of a minority community. I'm also a citizen of the Turkish Republic; I pay taxes, I fulfill my obligations to the state to the letter, and I love my country lately...

After the Aşkale affair, a good many of my friends and acquaintances got up and left the country for America, France or somewhere else in Europe, Canada, Australia—anywhere in the world, saying to themselves that no matter how well they did here, every time there's another mobilization, they were going to get it in the neck. They're always telling me, 'Come, it may be good there in Turkey today, but tomorrow, who knows? You'll catch it again!'

But I didn't go. I always say to myself, 'Sarkis, you were born in Anatolia, and in Anatolia you'll stay!' Because I love my country. Because I went to Istanbul and fell in love with it. If I'm in pain, if I grow weary sometimes, the blue waters of the Bosphorus take away my pains and weariness. I'm staying in Turkey; I won't leave! I'll never entirely give up hope!

The night of September 6-7, 1955

As I said, the situation gets turbulent sometimes, different powers contend with each other! You can be sure that it's going to mean trouble for us before it's all said and done.

It was five years since the Menderes government had come to power. Nothing at all had changed.... just a lot more American cars on the streets. The call to prayer had been in Turkish, then they changed it back to Arabic. The Village Institutes were closed. Soldiers were sent to Korea.... Anyone who spoke out was squashed by the government. My senses were alert! I could smell an evil wind starting to blow... The smell of blood was wafting from the dailies, from the news agencies!

Every day we were inundated with reports out of Cyprus.... 'The possibility of war' they kept repeating. God help us!

When there's a war, or the possibility of one, you can be sure to expect something from the government. Throughout our lives, we had learned that the hard way. During the First World War the calamity of the Deportation almost wiped us out entirely. During the Second World War, we became the brown-uniformed infidel soldiers or were sent to Aşkale! In the papers and on the airwaves they shouted like the harbingers of disaster: 'Palikarya! Get ready. We're coming!,' 'Partition or death!'

Woe unto us! If only there would be no war on Cyprus! If we could only escape the disaster of war!... This time, we were certain to bear the brunt of it again! We would be the whipping boy! The weakest of us would have to be beaten so that the Sultan's anger would be appeased....

I was on edge, expecting some sort of disaster...

At the time I was building the interior furnishings for a shop in Karaköy. I was working late, but I still hadn't been able to complete the job. Finally, I called it quits for the night, resigning myself to having to come back the next day and finishing up the last remaining tasks.

I left for home, walking to the bus stop. A boy selling newspapers was shouting 'Read all about it! The Greeks have bombed Atatürk's house!'

'Hurry, Sarkis!' I said to myself. 'This is going to end badly! Be quick, Sarkis! Don't wait for the bus! Hail a taxi and make it home!'

The newspapers were selling like hotcakes. They were being snatched up as soon as they appeared. You heard newsboys shouting everywhere. I bought a paper and took a quick look at the headline! This was definitely going to end badly! And we were going to get it the worst!

'Keep moving, Sarkis! Don't dawdle! Get in a taxi!'

I hailed a taxi and got in. I went straight to the shop in Kumkapı. When I got there I quickly locked up my shop and bolted it tightly. I lowered the rolling shutter and locked it. Then, I quickly caught another taxi straight to Yedikule.

I had only recently moved to a new place in Yedikule. I had renovated and rented the home of a Greek family on Gençağa Street in a Greek neighborhood in Yedikule. My mother had no idea of recent developments.

No sooner had I gotten to the corner of our street when they began breaking things and shouting!

'Oh no, Sarkis!' I said to myself, 'That which you feared has come upon us. Pull yourself together! Be careful: Don't fall into the hands of these monsters! They'll eat you alive!'

My mother hadn't yet noticed what was going on.

'What's that, Sarkis?' she asked me when I got home, 'What are they howling about?'

'For God's sake, keep your voice down!' I said. 'This isn't what you think! Hurry! Get the children and go up to the top floor! And don't make a sound. There's real trouble brewing. Don't ask what!'

I was prepared. I had hung large Turkish flags, both at home and at the shop. Even when my Turkish neighbors didn't hang theirs, I made sure to hang mine at every holiday. Even if they didn't appear to have hung theirs, we would be blamed for not having hung ours...

I quickly displayed the flag from the window. On our street there were only two flags flying, one at our house, and one at the house on the corner.

I was in a Greek neighborhood but had only just moved there. They didn't know me, hadn't met me. Nevertheless, I was always alert and cautious. I'm not one to go out and introduce myself easily. My only chance was not to be recognized.

I went up to the top floor.

'Mother,' I said, 'Go, quickly and dress yourself differently. Go and dress like a Muslim woman, cover your head! If they come here, you shouldn't be wearing anything colorful! If they ask, you say 'God be praised, I'm a Muslim!'

My mother had had experience with this in the past! Ha, ha! She'd seen better days! Ha, ha! She'd survived deportation to Deyr-i-Zor... She immediately grasped the seriousness of the situation. She dressed herself in Muslim dress... She looked like a Muslim, born and raised! I hardly recognized my own mother!

She then began to order me around:

'Do this! Do that!' Then she told me, 'Go, sit outside! Sit in front of the house! Don't be afraid my son! I'll take care of things inside the house. You deal with what's going on outside. Do what you have to do. The Lord Jesus will protect you! God will protect you! Don't be afraid, my son!'

There was a little disturbance. I came out of the place I was hiding. I plucked up my courage and sat in front of the house, alert to the developments transpiring on our street. Whatever was going to happen would happen. If they attacked our house, then they'd have to go through me first! The only way that they could touch my mother and my family would be by killing me first! I was going to be steadfast, not budging.... I wasn't going to give an inch!

You should have seen how they came. Soon the street was full of them!

The one in front had hung a Turkish flag around his neck, like a bib. That was his protection! After him came the looters. They smashed some things, threw over others... beating, striking... My God, my God.... Gençağa Street in Yedikule was caught in the vice of death!

May God strike them down! May he strike them down in their tracks!

I glance enough to see the church engulfed in flames. The historical church in Yedikule was burning. The sparks even began to reach where I was. There was a young bride living in the basement floor of the apartment building across the way. She was Greek. She came out of the building, crying. She fled down a side street. The poor thing! She was waiting for someone to come to her aid. But I wasn't able!

My nerves were being stretched to breaking point! But I had to appear calm!

Three persons then approached. They stopped in the middle of the street. One of them was blonde with a drooping mustache. With his eyes and brows he motioned to our house. I understood: he was from the neighborhood; he knew who was Turkish, who was Greek. He was showing the looters the different houses, one by one.

I quickly approached him and placed my hand on his shoulder. He looked at me.

'Young man,' I said, 'I live in the house you just motioned to. Look at the flag flying from it. It's in the summer house on the top floor. There's no one there. But I live on the lower floor. Don't make any mistakes!'

He couldn't even bring himself to ask 'Who are you?' Then he withdrew and left without another word.

Later on, a young man appeared. He was a puny, weak thing. He stood there, looking at my house.

'What are you looking at?!' I demanded. 'Who are you looking for?! Can't you see that this is a Turkish house? And if there used to be an infidel living here, what does that matter to me? I'm here now. Go on, take your cart and get out of here!'

And that way I managed to fool him.

But across the street, they smashed up and destroyed the houses of the Greeks.

I saw one leave clutching a sewing machine, another a carpet, a third holding a pair of shoes.... Anything they could find... anything that could be taken....

In the end, they tired themselves out with all the looting and destruction! I called them to my side: 'Come, sit down! Take a breather!'

So they came over and sat down next to me. They rested a bit but were still too excited to speak.... I gave them water. My mother made some coffee and brought it out. Looters' coffee! It was unbelievable. The looters spared our house from being pillaged!

Afterward, someone blew a whistle. Everything felt a bit odd. They then snatched up the things that they had looted and flitted off like a scared flock of birds!

It was one o'clock in the morning. There I sat, on the bench in front of our house, still clutching my demitasse of coffee. An army corporal came along, accompanied by a number of soldiers. This is exactly what he said to me:

'I commend you, young man! You've picked a wonderful time and place to sit back and savor your cup of coffee! Every Turk should be like you! But finish your coffee and go inside, now. Don't remain outside!'

'Be well, Commander Sir!' I answered. 'Be well. I hear and obey!'

I went back inside, but as soon as I did so, all my strength left me. I locked the door and collapsed, leaning against the door for support. I closed my eyes... and said a prayer of thanks for having been spared from death once again! Thank God we'd been able to think our way out of this disaster! But what of the young bride, fleeing and weeping, weeping and pleading? What of the burning church? What about the looted houses? What about the young Greek women in front of the Gedikpaşa police station, half-naked and with their clothes torn, desperately trying to cover and protect themselves against shameless hands!

How did the world come to this? Once again, we were struggling against death, but in other parts of the world people were able to lie down and go to sleep at night without any such fears. My children were speechless from fear! What sort of world was this?!?

After that, I saw a completely collapsed four-story building on Gençağa Street. The workers who had worked building the crudely constructed building belonging to the Greek Yorgo tore it entirely to the ground. without any thought or regard for their previous labor. It was unbelievable! How can a person destroy the very building that he has built himself? What manner of hatred, what sort of thinking, what sort of belief was this? I couldn't comprehend this.

Afterward, I called for my mother to come back downstairs:

'You can come down now, mother! We escaped this calamity! Thank God, we've evaded death!'

My mother came over to me:

'You were scared, my son! May God bring disaster upon them! But how many times now have we experienced this fear of death? How many times have we endured? Everything has its limit. Even the stone eventually cracks. The iron melts. But we are stronger than a stone or iron.... Get up, my son. Come away from the door. Lock it and come have a drink of water. You were very scared. May God visit a thousand disasters upon those who commit such acts!'

Those who prepare such calamities for others will eventually meet with disaster themselves! They are digging their own graves! That's how the world works. Nobody has a monopoly on curses! In this world, the one who sets the fire will be consumed by it, the one who destroys will be destroyed! The ones who bombed Atatürk's house in Salonica had their necks broken and that was the end of them!

After the night between 6-7 September, 1955 there wasn't a single Greek shop or store left in Karaköy, on İstiklal Avenue, in Galatasaray that didn't have its windows smashed and its goods looted. Along with those belonging to the Greeks, Armenian businesses were also destroyed or burnt down.

The next day we went to my cousin's perfume shop on İstiklal Avenue. They had even smashed the perfume bottles themselves! There wasn't a single thing left unbroken! Beyoğlu and Karaköy looked like war zones.

My mother asked my cousin about what had transpired on İstiklal Avenue, in Karaköy and surrounding areas. I recounted the things that I had seen. He was sorely grieved. 'Thank God, at least we weren't hurt!' he exclaimed, 'May God spare us from future calamities!'

My mother had a habit of singing these beautiful folk songs whenever she was upset. I think I told you, my mother also played piano. But I could neither afford to buy a piano for her, nor a house that was large enough to accommodate one.

The events of the previous night, and the disaster that had passed over us had affected her greatly. She began to softly murmur one of the well-known Armenian folk songs:

Ne zalim bir dünya ki	How cruel the world is
Cana yakın bir arkadaş yok	There is no one I can call 'friend'
Derdim çok, çaresi yok.	My pain is great, but there's no balm
Çare var da, çare olan yok.	There is a cure, but not for me
İyi günlerim geçti gitti	My good days have come and gone
Derin acılarım kaldı geriye	All that remains is a deep sorrow within

The songs my mother used to sing were generally sad ones. But she didn't like it when I'd say that. She had learned these songs when she had stayed in Istanbul, at the Tashnag Party's[*] youth club next to the Armenian School in Gedikpaşa. My mother had been a member of the Tashnag Party ever since she was a young girl. Politically speaking, she didn't care for me one bit. 'Shithead communist!' she used to call me! She herself, her sons-in-law and the husband of her oldest sister were all Tashnags.

As a family, we had been raised on this stuff. My mother's resilience, her will were healthy and hard as stone. She never lost her faith or her

---

[*] "Tashnag," shortened from "Hay Heghapokhagan Tashnagtsoutiun," the Armenian nationalist political party that was formed in 1890.

hope. This optimism, this love of and faith in humanity, this streak of rebellion, they all came from having been a party member ever since her early youth. My mother's influence on the development of my personality—and on my political ideas, in particular—was very great.

My mother had more fight in her than my father; she was more imperturbable.

It doesn't seem to matter what I say, it always digresses into something else!

After the disaster of 6-7 September, 1955, the trend of Greeks and Armenians leaving the country accelerated. People didn't have any more faith in the country. 'To hell with it!' they said, and left the land where they were born and raised, albeit with great sorrow and tears in their eyes....

But this wasn't the end of it.

After 1960, we thought that we might see a little peace and quiet, but then they began with the 'Citizen, Speak Turkish!' campaign. Where ever you were, on the bus, the streetcar, in a taxi, at a coffeehouse... if they heard Armenian, Greek, or some other language that they didn't understand people would give a nudge on the shoulder and warn you: 'Citizen, Speak Turkish!'

This campaign increased during the events on Cyprus in 1964. Throughout the whole crisis, I was terrified, wondering if we were going to experience another disaster. But it wasn't just me personally. All the non-Muslims were afraid: the Armenians, the Greeks and the Jews were all terrified.

The Cyprus Intervention in 1974 once again accelerated the emigration of the country's Greek population. By that time there were hardly any Armenians left to emigrate or flee. But people left their parents, their homes and went... The only ones to remain behind were tombstones and some 'unloved' individuals!

I was going to go to the Soviet Union. In 1973 I received the right to become a citizen there. But I didn't go. I love my country too much! But it still doesn't love us! And we don't seem to be able to make them love us more! We don't know how. Maybe we should find someone to teach us, or maybe a love potion? Ha, ha, ha!

What's the reason for this century-long hostility?

Sometimes I sit and think about all the things that have befallen me over the course of my brief—my interminable—eighty-three year-long life. Why has it been a crime for us to simply be Armenians? What has been the unpardonable crime of Çerkezoğlu Gazaros? Of Arusyak, the teacher from Tokat? Of the master carpenter Sarkis?

I was born during the Deportation, I wasn't able to go to school because of my family's poverty, I was a 'brown-uniformed infidel soldier' during my military service! Even after that, when I thought I'd finally get some peace of mind, I had to go through the events of 6-7 September, 1955, and I was still, for many long years, unable to travel from one city to another in my own country without a travel permit! 'We'll give you liberty!' they'd promise, and then they'd silence me, saying, 'Citizen, Speak Turkish!'… As if that wasn't enough! Every time there's some crisis on Cyprus, every time the winds of war start blowing, they're breathing down our necks again, trying to crush us… I demanded my rights, and they called me: 'Communist! Leftist!'…. What haven't I had to put up with? What is my sin, for which I'm forced to pay into eternity?

I've given a great deal of thought to these things…. a very great deal. I read, I asked questions, I demanded answers, I scoured Armenian books for any information I could find. I studied the Turkish ones line by line. I did carpentry all those years in order to support myself, but I did all these things in order to be able to live, in order to find out who I was….

Now, let me ask you: If an Armenian person whom I didn't know from Adam killed a Turk, what would my mother's, my father's and my own guilt be in this matter? If you caught the culprit you would give him his just rewards, no? But if you failed to apprehend him, would it be right to take out your distress and anger on a child who was born during the Deportation?

Or let me pose another question: You're a great empire. Forty different states are created upon your ruins. When necessary, you take pride in the fact that you once brought your forces as far as the gates of Vienna. So why didn't you treat the different peoples within your empire equally? Europe eventually made great advances and surpassed you. They moved ahead in science and technology. The Enlightenment began in France. The idea of nationalism was born. It spread in waves throughout the entire world. But you prevented it through imperial decree. Can ideas be destroyed with rifles and cannons? Can you kill them? Can you outlaw them? Can you hold a child guilty of a crime when it's still in its mother's womb? And if you can't prevent it from being born, do you take out your anger and irritation at the innocent, defenseless child? Is this justice?

Of all the different peoples within the Ottoman Empire, the Armenian community was the most faithful to the state and the Sultan. For this reason they were even called 'the loyal community.'

But this community was the one that placed the greatest importance on reading, writing, on science, on thinking, and on its own culture. As a state, you brought printing into the country in the eighteenth century, but the Armenian community had already introduced it into the country and was printing books here a hundred years before you did. What's the crime in this?

You're the emperor. You're the sultan. You established schools in order to train slaves, the Armenian community established schools for the sake of knowledge. You taught Arabic for the sake of the Qur'an, but the Armenian community taught its children French for the sake of science and technology. Is this a crime?

Some people call Abdulhamid 'the Great Ruler'; we call him 'the Red Sultan,' because the assaults against Armenians and Greeks began just as soon as he came to the throne.

You forbade the Armenian community from bearing arms. You made it a crime for any of the Armenian villagers to carry weapons to defend themselves against the Kurds who attacked them. But in 1891 you founded the Imperial cavalry regiments called the Hamidiye Regiments—forty-eight units, each with five hundred horses!—for the purpose of attacking the Armenians.

The Kurdish rural notables and lords would kidnap the girls and young brides of Armenian villagers and violate them. During the harvest time, they would come and seize the villagers' crops. The Armenians would appeal to the courts. But you rejected their petitions out of hand, without even examining the merits of their complaints, saying, 'The testimony of Christians is not acceptable!'

If they raised their heads to speak, you'd beat them back down; if they opened their mouths to express their pain, you'd cut out their tongues.... They were left without any choice; they reached out their hand to others, and you tore off their outstretched arm...

Tell me: if you had been in my place, what would you have done?

Place your hand on your heart and tell me honestly: if the times and fortunes change, and time comes for the slaves to demand their freedom, to demand equality, is that a crime?

The Armenian community was one of the first communities within the Ottoman Empire that developed a national consciousness... But the empire considered this idea, this 'nationalization,' this awakening as a capital crime, worthy of death... And this mutual tension, this sniping and picking at one another finally came to a head. And the Ottomans finally attempted to 'put an end to the Armenian saga,' in a period in which the Armenians found themselves trapped, in a time when the Ottomans finally felt themselves at liberty to act, in 1915....

Within a three month stretch, the great Armenian nation was reduced to a handful of survivors. The Ottomans knew full well that these survivors would never again trust them, that they would never again be the loyal friends to them as before. For this reason, they saw all of the few remaining Armenians as guilty from conception.

Tell me. If my grandfather was guilty of some crime, is it just to try and punish me for the crime?

I say this as Master Sarkis the carpenter: the state must not promote hatred... Individuals may feel enmity toward one another, but states must never have such hatred toward their own citizens!

If you do so, you acknowledge the right for others to do the same thing to you. This is a law of nature...

If you are a state, you need to know statecraft! Greatness doesn't mean oppressing the weak; it can defend the rights of the weak, of minorities; it can prevent the oppression of the minority by the majority.

The times have changed. The old world is no more! The old enmities and the tribal mentality and custom of clannishness that go along with it can't continue any longer.

The world is becoming one, Europe is uniting. So why don't you embrace your own citizens, why do you chase your educated and enlightened people out of the country? Why don't you foster love instead of hatred? Why do you nurture and promote this century-old hatred like some sort of blood feud? If Master Sarkis the carpenter can think of these things, why can't you?

Tell me the truth! Put yourself in my shoes and think about it for once!

'I've never been a nationalist'

I was never a Turkish or Armenian nationalist. Whatever I have done in my life, I've done it with love. I loved carpentry; I loved leftist politics. I've never been ashamed of anything I've done. Have I always been right? No. I've made mistakes, too. But I've always proudly borne my deeds, both good and bad. There's a saying in Anatolia: 'Let the mare who gave birth to it be ashamed!' In other words, if someone does something wrong, let them be ashamed of it. But I don't have anything that I need to be ashamed of, or that has offended others. I never worked with ulterior motives or false pretenses. So does that make me crazy or smart? I still don't know myself....

As I said, I'm no nationalist type. I'm a man of the Left. But you might tell me there are nationalists on the left as well. Fair enough! The most famous leftist back then was my friend Zihni Anadol. He passed away. May he rest in peace! Around 1965 he used to publish a newspaper called *Türk Solu* (The Turkish Left).

One day, as we were walking down Yüksekkaldırım Street toward the Galata Bridge, he said to me:

'Hey Sarkis, you should write for our paper!'

'I don't know how to write' I told him. 'I'm a carpenter!'

'So write something having to do with your trade!' he said.

'I'm not going to write about things connected with my trade; it would be boring for your newspaper.'

'Why's that?'

'I'll tell you: the Magirus company came to this country, and it became "Turkish Magirus." Migros came and it was turned into "Turkish Migros." Pirelli came and it became "Turkish Pirelli." Pardon the expression, but no matter what gets stuck up this people's ass, they have to put "Turkish" in front of it! Now you're publishing a paper called "The Turkish Left." If it's really "Turkish" like that, what business do you have with it? Should I go and found a paper called "The Armenian Left"? Should I work for the "Armenian Left"? Is that how it's going to be? I want to be united. I want to work for the development of my country, but you've gone and published "The Turkish Left." Since when does the Left need a national stamp? But let's not beat around the bush. I won't write for a nationalist paper.'

After that, Zihni Anadol didn't say anything. As we walked he thought and thought. By the time we reached the top of the Galata Bridge, he opened his mouth and said 'You're right!'

Since I've grown old, I've started to look for traces of my childhood

After many long years, at age eighty, I finally got up and went to Karaman. I wanted to find and see some things in this place where I had passed my childhood, things that had to do with me, that belonged to me. It's a hard thing to explain.

So I looked high and low. But to no avail. Everything had changed so much. Our house had been right next to a church. When I was there, I asked an old man there about the Karaman Church.

'Don't bother!' he said. 'They tore it down and destroyed it.'

But I insisted, 'Can you show me the place where it stood?'

So he brought me there. 'Here's where it was!'

But in finding the place where the church had stood, I was able to locate our house: they'd turned it into a prison!

The church had been called the Çeşmeli Church (The Church with the Fountain). There had been a beautiful fountain in its courtyard. If nothing else, at least that had been preserved.

When people see such things, they get excited. After all, my mother had been married in the now-destroyed Fountain Church. They say to themselves, 'Here's where I grew up! Here's the street where I used to play!', but when they look now, they see that nothing remains of the church, of your house. And then they get bitter and their heads fill up with bad thoughts.

I guess it was a silly idea. As if it were possible to actually find some traces of my childhood there! I went over to the prison and ran my hand along the wall. I saw my mother, my father, my sister all before my eyes. In the garden next to our house where the apricot trees had been, now stood an apartment building. I had even forgotten the name of Aunt Fatma Hanım, who had coaxed my tongue out of my mouth with apricots, and had been the reason for my father's arrest.

I approached the soldier who was guarding our erstwhile home—now a prison.

'My child,' I said, 'I've got a request for you. This prison used to be our house. I grew up in this house. Would you let me have a stone piece of the wall of my house?'

He was a bit surprised and confused.

'What are you going to do with the stone, uncle?'

'I will put it under my pillow and sleep on it!' I told him.

At that he laughed. Maybe he thought I was crazy. Nevertheless, he went and, taking out his bayonet, pried a piece of stone from the wall where the plaster was peeling, and came back and gave it to me.

'Be well, my son!' I said to him and left.

I traveled from Karaman to Mut, and from there I went to the village of Krallar (Kings), which is located in the meadow called Sarsanlı; Yaylası. I went to Krallar because that was where my father had left his famous horse, and where he had gone and hidden when he was in trouble. And the people there really did greet me like royalty. I went and visited the house of my father's dear friends. Their grandchildren were still living there. They hosted and entertained me in their houses. We spoke to each other and recounted the old days.

My father had written a letter to their grandparents in 1922. This letter had been passed down from the grandparents to their fathers, and from their fathers to them. They brought it out and gave it to me, seventy-six years after it had been written!

'Take it as a remembrance of your father!' they said. 'It's more suitable for you to have the letter than for us to keep it!'

Have you ever heard of such things? Such loyalty, such friendship are practically unheard of!

This is the real Turkish people.

Ha! Then there's the Mufti of Karaman, Müftüzade Ahmet Efendi, the person to whom my father had entrusted so many baled up carpets, who then didn't just sit on our carpets, he sat on those of everyone who trusted him to keep their goods.

One of them was a simple villager: he had kept a letter from my father for seventy-six years and then returned it; the other one was a mufti: he took possession of loads of stuff that had been entrusted to him to keep safe! They're both Turks! There's all kinds within this nation! Which one could you do without?

You can say the same thing about the Armenian nation. You can't dismiss the whole nation as rotten just because you see one bad apple....

It's not important that you make a mistake, what's important is that you are able to perceive your error and you try and ensure that you don't make it again. What's important is that you show love and respect for one another. It's on the foundation of mutual love and respect that you can build trust.

'We shouldn't have let him beat the priest...'

I've talked a lot. But it was good to talk... I don't think about death anymore, but it's not far off... I'm eighty-three years old... If they would come to me now and ask me, after all that has happened to me, 'What do you have to say to all the Turks, the Kurds and the Armenians?' I would tell them a story that my father once told me. Let these be my last words!

My father used to tell this story about the events of those days, but it's as relevant for today as it was back then:

One summer day in the area around Antep, an Armenian priest, a Kurd and Turk decided to go out for a walk. Eventually, they became thirsty, but there was no water to be found. Their tongues became thick and their mouths dry from the heat and from their thirst. It was the time when the grapes in the vineyards were perfectly ripe.

Master Sarkis of Karaman: Ever since I've grown old, I've sought out traces of my childhood...

They said to one another, 'We'll die of thirst if we don't do something! Let's go into one of those vineyards and pick ourselves a couple of bunches of grapes and eat them.' They called out for the owner of the vineyard, but there was nobody around. So together they went into the quiet vineyard. Just then, the owner of the vineyard appeared.

'Peace upon you!' they said to him.

'And upon you be peace!' he replied.

'Please excuse us,' the Turk said, 'We shouted and called out, and nobody answered. We were very thirsty. That's why we entered the vineyard. We'll be happy to pay for what we took.'

The owner of the vineyard was also a Turk. He looked the three men over and understood that they were an Armenian priest, a Kurd and a Turk from their dress and their speech. His anger would not abate. He was going to attack them, but he didn't dare because there were three of them before him. So he turned to the Armenian and said:

'Look here, you: Even though this guy here ate from my grapes, he's a Turk. May he be blessed! We don't withhold anything from our brothers. He can eat his fill! And this other one, he's a Kurd. He speaks a different language, but he's our brother in religion. May he be blessed too! But you, you infidel, son of an infidel! How do you dare to enter a vineyard when the owner's not there? Why did you eat from my grapes?'

Now the owner's words pleased the Turk and the Kurd.

'Well, we sure got out of that fix!' they said to themselves.

Then the vineyard owner laid into the Armenian.... he gave him a good hard slap and pummeled him until he had laid him out flat!

Then he started on the Kurd: 'Hey, you stupid Kurdish beast! Since when has it been your place to go into Turkish vineyards when the owner wasn't there and eat his grapes?!?'

When he heard this, the Turk was pleased!

When he saw that he was in for a beating, the Kurd began pleading, 'No! Stop! Don't hit me! Please! It's a shame!' and he groaned with every blow that the vineyard owner landed. Finally, the owner knocked him out, too, and laid him next to the Armenian.

Now it was the Turk's turn.

'Hey, you!' the vineyard owner said to him, 'we share the same religion, the same language! Why didn't you stop the Armenian and the Kurd from entering into the vineyard of a Turk when he was not there?' and then he really let him have it! He beat him silly, breaking his nose, bloodying his mouth. Then, when he was out cold, the owner laid him out next to the Kurd.

Then, with a blustery voice, he warned them, 'Alright now, let's see if you ever try again to enter the vineyard and eat the grapes when the owner's not there....' And then the Turk turned toward the Kurd and whispered, 'We shouldn't have let him beat the priest...'

Part Five

Crypto-Armenians

Crypto-Armenians

I had spoken with Zakarya, Jale and Master Sarkis about those persons called *dönmeler* (converts) or 'crypto-Armenians,' who had survived the calamity of 1915 by abandoning their old religion and becoming Muslims, but preserving their old beliefs to varying degrees. I was very curious about the situation of such people. I learned that some Armenians who had converted to Islam, especially in the regions of Tunceli, Adıyaman and Diyarbakir, had gradually forgotten their own languages and begun to speak Kurdish, but nevertheless continued to very secretly practice their original religion and maintain their original faith.

They even claimed that there were Armenians like this in Istanbul. We tried to locate some of these people, but all of our efforts proved fruitless. I couldn't find a single crypto-Armenian in Istanbul.

When I returned to Germany, I immediately telephoned Meline. I briefly told her about Zakarya, Kegham's student, and about getting to know Master Sarkis and our conversations. She was thrilled by Jale's delicacy and her resistance.

Meline had also heard about the existence of crypto-Armenians, but she'd never had the opportunity to speak to one. She told me that the crypto-Armenians were like 'closed cabinets' that you couldn't pry open, that they didn't talk about their own secret worlds to anyone, but that she was very curious about their lives, their feelings, their beliefs. "We simply have to try and find them!" we resolved between ourselves, "We'll find them and speak with them!"

"But how would we find them? Whom could we ask?"

I spoke to some Armenian friends that I had met in Germany, but they failed to provide me with any new information.

I then asked my Kurdish friends from Tunceli.

"Sure," they told me, "there are great number of Armenians in the Tunceli area who survived by accepting Islam, and who adopted Alevî beliefs!"

And so I had found some tracks leading to my quarry. I would have to follow them, step by step. It looked like it would be easier and safer to try to contact those crypto-Armenians who lived in Germany than those who remained in Istanbul, Adıyaman or Tunceli.

I next inquired within the Armenian community and Kurdish associations in Cologne. Both places told me that they had heard of such people but didn't know any personally. What should be my next step?

I asked some friends from the Turkish-German Human Rights Association in Cologne.

"Yes, there are Armenians who converted to Islam and have become Kurdish!" they claimed, but they, too, were unable to provide me with the name of anyone who might be able to establish contact with them.

I next thought that I might be able to find such people by means of some other friends who were very familiar with both Kurdish and Turkish circles and well respected by both. I spoke with Kemal Uzun, a fellow-teacher who was among the most well-respected and trusted members of the Turkish-Kurdish Friendship Initiative, an association that had been established in Cologne in 1992. "Let me look into it!" he told me.

One week later I received a call from him:

"I found a Kurdish Armenian from Adıyaman. Let's go and see him together. I'll introduce you. Maybe he'll speak to you."

I was delighted. I arrived at Kemal Uzun's house at the appointed time, brimming over with joy and excitement. Together we went to the house of the Kurdish Armenian from Adıyaman.

The teacher Kemal Uzun said with a laughing face and assuring voice:

"This is the house of 'Kurdish İbrahim,' who comes from Kâhta, near Adıyaman. His real name is 'Haci* İbrahim,' but he never went on the Hajj; he was given that name at birth! You can talk with him about everything openly and honestly, and ask him anything you wish. Kurdish İbrahim is a friend of mine and is trusted by everyone. He is honest, intelligent and sensible."

After Kurdish İbrahim opened the door, Kemal introduced me:

"This is Kemal, my namesake and colleague. He's very interested in the Armenians. I brought him to you. You can speak to him without worry."

Haci İbrahim had an open, honest face, a face without guile that lit up when he smiled. The whiteness of his aged mane augmented the brightness

---

* *Hacı* is the Turkish form of "Hajji," the Arabic title reserved for Muslims who have gone on the "Hajj" or pilgrimage to Mecca.

of his face. He smiled when he spoke, and as he did so, he made those listening to him smile as well:

"On the assurance of Master Kemal the Teacher, I have agreed to talk with you," he began. "I'll tell you everything I know, everything I've seen and experienced."

The Armenian Haci İbrahim from Kâhta

"I didn't really understand who I was! My mother tongue is Kurdish and I feel myself to be Kurdish. But I'm Armenian by blood. My mother and father were both Armenian, through and through. I grew up in a Kurdish village. I didn't know a single word of Armenian. The Germans always ask me 'What's your nationality? What's your identity?' and I answer them 'I came from Turkey. My mother tongue is Kurdish. I'm of Armenian origin. My religion is Islam. In Germany I'm an *Ausländer* ('foreigner'), and in Turkey they call me *Almancı*.'"[*]

At this we laughed, and he laughed along with us. After that, in order to appease his own curiosity, he asked me:

"Turks aren't very fond of Armenians; they don't usually concern themselves with the sorrows of the Armenians. So where did the idea come into your head to seek us out and ask about our lives?"

So I told him all about Meline, about the professional development course in Dortmund, about the fact that it had never occurred to a single one of the one hundred and fifty Turkish teachers she had taught over a six year period to ask their instructor Meline, "Say, you're an Armenian: do you have your own language and culture?", that I, too, had been one of those who didn't ask, and that I had been very disturbed and affected by my own insensitivity.

Kemal Uzun then added, "Is it easy to get people to think enough to ask?"

I continued, telling Haci İbrahim that I had set out on my odyssey in order to be able to understand the reasons for my own insensitivity and to

---

[*] A Turkish neologism that has its origins in the large Turkish "Guest worker" presence in Germany. It refers to Turkish citizens who have either relocated to Germany or been born there to émigré parents. In contrast to the term *Alman*, which is simply the equivalent of the English noun/adjective "German."

be better able to know and understand Meline, a person whom I loved greatly; I recounted how I had gone to Ani, how I had learned from Zakarya, Jale and Master Sarkis in Istanbul of the existence of Armenians who were called "converts" (*dönme*), but that I hadn't been able to find any to speak with myself, and that that was what had lead me to his door.

"Be well!," he responded. "Welcome, then! You've eased my mind! When I get my tongue back, I'll tell you what I know. But first, allow me to make you a little uncomfortable. The Turks and Kurds call us 'converts,' but I don't like this word at all. For those of us who were originally Armenian but converted to Islam, it's more correct to call us 'crypto-Armenians.' We call ourselves 'our kind' (*bizimkiler*)."

They gave me the name 'Haci İbrahim.' No one ever explained to me what I was. Our village was a Kurdish village called Tukaris, it belonged to the town of Kâhta. It was a big village, but there were only two Armenian families in it: ours and a family of shoe makers.

Until the age of nine I never once heard that we were of Armenian origin. My father never said a single word to me about this subject. My father was a blacksmith. We had a very big house. One of the rooms in the house was used as the 'village meeting place,' another one for Qur'an lessons. I learned what I know about my religion during the Qur'an lessons that were given in our house.

Sometimes, on winter days, the youth of the village would gather in the village meeting room and talk among themselves, and at others, the old men would get together and tell 'war stories' or stories about the infidels. I used to really love the war stories. Whenever I'd listen to the tales about the infidels, my anger and hatred for non-Muslims would grow, and I'd be happy that I wasn't one. I'd turn to someone sitting close to me and ask 'Who are these infidels?' In my child's mind, I was sure that I would kill one of these 'infidels' with my bare hands if I ever caught one!

One time, when I was contemplating just how I would perform such a terrible deed, my elder sister came to visit. She had gotten married one year before. We began to talk and I expressed to her my hatred of these infidels.

'Whoa! Slow down, little brother!' she said. 'Don't you know? Our family used to be infidels! Our father and mother are both Armenian! Even though your name is Haci İbrahim, even though everybody knows us as Muslims, that's really what we are!'

I was dumbstruck. Then I began to feel very bad.

'Why didn't you tell me?!?' I demanded.

'You think it's that easy?' she said, explaining to me. 'How could I have explained it? What would have happened if you accidentally let slip to someone else? You don't tell those sort of things to children! This is an important secret that has to remain just among us.'

After I spoke with my sister, I closed up within myself. I didn't want to talk to anyone. Where had this whole Armenian business come from? All that time I had been cursing the infidels, and now, suddenly, I was one myself! Now what was I supposed to do? Even the word 'infidel' bothered me...

And it was during these troubled days that a great disaster befell my family. One night, they broke into my father's blacksmith shop and robbed it. In the middle of that enormous village they knocked down the wall of a shop and made off with everything they found, from the shoulder-scale to the pliers, from the scissors to the yardstick! And that wasn't enough for them, apparently: they even cut up the bellows for the blacksmith's furnace with a smith's knife!

After this robbery, my father was no longer able to do any iron work or horseshoeing.

Who had done it? Why? We didn't have any idea.

My father was very grieved. 'We can't stay in a village in which they knock down walls and rob a blacksmith's shop!' he exclaimed. And because of this, in 1952 we were forced to move from the village to Kâhta.

"My father's prayers"

After learning about my family's Armenian origins, I began to pay very close attention to my father's behavior. During the days, he went to prayers five times a day, and during the night he would go into a room alone and close the door and pray.

'Father,' we asked, querying him, 'you pray during the day and you pray at night. What do you say when you're praying?' He didn't get angry at us, but a peculiar smile appeared on his face. 'You don't know it!' he said. My father's daytime prayers were performed in plain sight of everyone, but his night supplications were performed alone, behind a locked door. He didn't know the Arabic prayer formulas very well.

'Father, what do you recite during prayers?' I persisted.

'My son, I'm calling upon God. I pray from my heart. God accepts my worship of Him,' he answered.

After I turned ten or so, my father began to talk to me. He began to trust me. By constantly asking, I learned all about my parents' past, and what had happened to them. The things I heard were unbelievable.

Over time, I got to know some others of 'our kind' in Kâhta, other crypto-Armenians. We had both close and distant relatives there. I made the old ones tell me all about what had happened to them. I even started paying close attention to the recollections that they mentioned in passing. The stories that the older Kurds told were positively bone-chilling.

My father had owned a lot of land. I still remember the things they told me. It's still there, like it was carved in marble.

My father's name was 'Ali.' Much later I learned that his original Armenian name had been Shimaver. His family had originally come from a village on the plain of Muş. 'The name of our village was Arakli,' he told me. A large river flowed through the village of Arakli. It was a big, verdant, lush, well-watered village, almost like a town. It had a church and a school. Its shops were a center for commerce for the whole area. It had three different mills. One of them had belonged to a relative of my father.

My father was one of six brothers. All six worked in blacksmithing. They were well-off individuals. But the tranquility of their lives was shattered even before the Deportation. There began to be attacks against them here and there from the surrounding areas. After a while, there was no more security for either life or property.

During those years, missionaries used to come to the village and gather the elders together in the church and speak with them. The things they spoke about would quickly be known throughout the village, passing from one mouth to another.

The young men, in particular, wanted to arm themselves and defend against the attacks. But the priests and the old men prevented them from doing so.

'Under no circumstances should you attempt such a thing!' they would warn. 'That will be the end of us! Nobody will be able to do a thing. The English will save us!' they would say.

Some of the old men would fret and complain, saying, 'These young men will bring disaster down upon us!' But over time, rumors began to circulate: 'They're coming today!' 'They're coming tomorrow!' 'They're going to round us up and ship us off!'

'They can't come here!' others would counter. 'And even if they do, they won't be able to do a thing. We've got the English to back us up!'

And such a day did eventually come. Everyone could feel it. Fear and distress hung in the air. The tension was palpable in the village. Everything was silent: people, animals, even the stones and mountains, waiting.... in fearful anticipation of the storm that would break upon us.

This is how my father would recount the events of that day and its aftermath....

'The things that befell my father...'

It was during springtime. Some five or six of us children had gone over the hill that faced the village in order to graze the lambs. We let the lambs graze until the evening, let them fill their bellies while we ran and played. That evening, as we were driving them back to the village, just as we had reached the top of the hill, we looked down at the village. There was something strange going on there. Smoke was rising from the village, and there was a buzzing sound emanating from it. Fear took us and as we came closer we could see that the animals were running madly in all directions. Where were the people? We couldn't see a soul.... We looked again and saw that the village was burning!

We were too afraid to go back into the village. We abandoned the lambs and ran straight toward the mountains to flee. We hid ourselves in a cave we knew. We spent the night there. We could see the village from far off. The morning came, but there was still no sound from the village. We were still too scared to enter it ourselves. The five or six of us hid ourselves in the cave for three days.

On the fourth day rows of people began coming toward the village, in processions or convoys.... We emerged from our hiding place and went up to a person who was marching in one of these processions. They were processions of Kurds. They were coming from the countryside aroung Ağri and Kars. We asked them lots of questions, and plied for information. These long lines of Kurds had fled from the Russians.... So we joined them, and 'fled' along with them. We weren't afraid of Kurds. And they didn't say a thing to us.

After going quite a ways, we arrived at a totally deserted village. Some of the Kurds with whom we were marching decided to remain in the village. We stayed with them. This village had been an Armenian village, like the other empty villages we had seen on the way. The inhabitants had suddenly up and left the village, along with all their goods and property. The Kurds settled in the empty houses. The animals were still in their pens and stables. Even so, there was plenty of bickering among the Kurds, arguing about who deserved what, or who got the bigger share...

A Kurdish family took me in. I was given the task of minding the animals and of shepherding them. Those Kurdish families who needed a shepherd divided up the other Armenian children among themselves. We would go every day with the Kurdish children and graze the animals.

One day, when it was snowing, we were very cold. But we didn't have a fire. 'One of us should go to the village and bring back a fire,' we said. 'We should light a fire. That way we can both warm up and dry out our bodies and clothes'

'Who's going to go and bring it?' we asked.

'You go and bring it!' they told me.

Going over hill and dale, I reached the house in which I was staying. It stopped snowing and the sun came out. Ever since the grab for the abandoned Armenian property, relations between my own master and our next door neighbor had been tense. As I arrived at the house I saw our neighbor sitting at the base of the wall cleaning his weapon. 'Oh, ho, What's this?' I said to myself. I began to have a very bad feeling about it. I was aware of the enmity between our two houses, and I grew a little afraid. Nevertheless, I continued on and entered our house. I quickly took a few large burning embers and placed them between two cow patties, and then set out again for the pasture. Out of the corner of my eye I spied our neighbor: he was holding his gun. I hurried past him, terribly afraid. After I had walked a bit, I heard the sound of gunfire. Still holding the embers, I broke into a run, making my way as best as I could through the snow.

I didn't know how far I would be able to run. My back began to hurt. At one point I turned and looked back. I had left a trail of blood in the snow! I examined myself and tried to explore the place on my back where it hurt so. There was blood all over my arm. My neighbor had been shooting at me! I apparently hadn't notice that I'd been shot because of the fear and the newness of the wound.

Because of his hatred for my master, our neighbor had wanted to cause him damage by killing me and leaving him without a shepherd. Anyway, the death of a 'infidel' shepherd wouldn't be enough to cause division between two Kurdish families; it wouldn't be enough to lead to a blood feud! This was our neighbor's way of settling accounts.

Even wounded, I managed to make it back to where my friends where, but by then the pain of the wound had become unbearable. I was burning up!

The older children were experienced enough to know what to do. The wound would have to be cleaned with snow. First they washed off all the blood with water. Then they rubbed the wound clean with snow. The pain was so great that I passed out. They brought me back to the house where I stayed.

I slept in the stable, together with the animals. They took me there and lay me down, wounded, on my bed there.

Toward evening, two of the other Armenian children who lived with other Kurdish families came to me. One of them was a relative of mine, older than me, who after hearing about what happened, came and covered the gunshot wound with fresh, warm ox manure, as he had once learned from his father. The manure compact remained on me for three days. After that, I regained consciousness. When I opened my eyes, there was my cousin, sitting next to me.

The ox manure really had helped the wound to heal! I had returned from the dead.

We stayed in this Armenian village for three or four years. After that, the enmity and hatred became too great. My master decided to take his family and leave the village. We set off on the road. For a time we migrated from place to place in the areas around Adıyaman and Diyarbakir. Finally, we came to Gerger. At that time, Gerger was connected administratively to Malatya. In Gerger I separated from the Kurdish family. That was in the 1920s. I found shelter with an Armenian family that had survived death and the deportations. They were all alone. They were looking for someone who they could put to work. I was already a teenager by then. I was young and strong. They liked me and treated me as if I was their own child. They protected me and helped me out....

For the whole time that I stayed with this Armenian family I worked as a blacksmith's apprentice. I learned blacksmithing very well. It had been my father's profession as well.

I married a hardy (*canberkli*) Armenian girl from the village in which I lived. She was still very young. But she didn't have any living relatives whatsoever.

A little while after we married, we moved to the village of Heniş, on the banks of the Euphrates, so that I could open up my own blacksmith's shop. In this area, the only Armenians left alive were those who had trades, like blacksmithing, tinsmithing and coppersmithing. There weren't any Kurds who were artisans or tradesmen. Because there were very few Armenians left who did such work, they were at a premium and much valued.

There was a large village near Heniş that was called Tukaris. There was a person living there by the name of Osman Paşa. He had been a commander in one of the irregular Kurdish 'Hamidiye Regiments' that had been formed during the reign of Abdulhamid. His son, Bedri Paşa, was the headman of the village. His reputation had spread throughout the region.

Anyway, this Bedri Paşa had heard that there was a blacksmith in Heniş. Heniş was a small village. Tukaris, on the other hand, was the administrative center of a sub-district, with some two hundred families. But it didn't have a single craftsman or artisan....

For this reason, Bedri Paşa sent a messenger saying, 'You will come to Tukaris. Here, you will undertaken blacksmithing under my protection and patronage!'

During those days, coming under Bedri Paşa's protection and patronage was a fortunate thing indeed! Nobody could give me problems! Overjoyed, I immediately obeyed Bedri Paşa's command. I moved to Tukaris. I was about twenty-five or twenty-six years of age then.

I opened a blacksmithing shop in Tukaris. I was the only blacksmith in the whole Tukaris sub-district. Here's where I really established my business and got my affairs in order.

'We were all alone, living in fear... '

And that's the story of how, after 1915, my father went from the village of Arakli, in Muş, to the sub-district of Tukaris, in the provincial district of Gerger, in the province of Adıyaman.

I was born in Tukaris in 1943. I spent my childhood in this village. We were only two Armenian families out of two hundred households in that Kurdish village. Our family did blacksmithing, the other one was a family of cobblers.

At first, my father was the only blacksmith in the entire region. Later on, a Kurdish blacksmith arrived. A short while after that, they broke into my father's shop, as I explained earlier. In 1952, we were forced to move to Kâhta.

In Tukaris they had given my father the name 'Ali,' but they still knew that he was an Armenian. I myself didn't know.

When the Second World War broke out, they conscripted my father into the military, along with other Armenian and Assyrian Christian men.

In those days, they called it in Kurdish *eskeri beşik*, when they gathered up all of those who were Armenians or Christians and sent them off without doing military duty.

They gathered up all the non-Muslim men in the region, young and old, and carted them off to Diyarbakir. There were even fathers and sons doing military service in the same place. These people were set to work in places that were called *işocağı*, or work camps. Forcing the non-Muslims to perform labor in these work camps was a preventive measure. The regime thought that in any war that might break out the minorities might collaborate with the enemy! My father worked for three years in the work camp in Diyarbakir.

After settling in Tukaris, my father and our whole family had converted to Islam. As I already told you, my father was a person who prayed regularly and frequently. There were two rooms in our house in which Qur'an lessons were given. He gave me the name Haci İbrahim. Despite this, when the Capital Tax Law came out in 1942, one of the Kurds informed on my father during the time when he was laboring at the work camp, saying, 'This one's an Armenian,' and that opened the way for him to be forced to pay the Capital Tax, too.

My brothers were still small when my father was performing his military service at a labor camp. We didn't have much of anything in the way of property. I didn't have anything that was mine except my mother. Nevertheless, they assessed us a TL 500 capital tax obligation.

After my father returned from the work camp, he was able to muster up the five hundred lira only with the greatest of difficulties and paid off his tax bill. That's how he saved himself from being sent off to Aşkale.

During the period of my childhood in Tukaris, I never heard a thing from either my mother or my father about the things that had happened to the Armenians. My father simply didn't talk about it. As for my mother, she had been very small at that time, and didn't remember a thing. Only later were they able to draw on their memories. We didn't have any close relatives left. My father had been one of six brothers, but I didn't have a single surviving uncle, aunt, grandfather, grandchild or cousin left. The disaster had taken them all and wiped them out. My father didn't have a single relative in the world. On my mother's side I only had one uncle. Much later he found my mother when he was looking for lost relatives.

We were all alone! We lived in constant fear, but nobody said a thing.

Under no circumstances did my father want us to get into fights with the Kurdish children. And not just that, he didn't even want us to look at the Kurdish children who were always fighting with one another! During my childhood and youth, I could never understand the reason for this. I'd ask myself 'Why is my father raising us to be so fearful?'

One time, the Kurdish children were getting in a fight with one another and I watched it. My father saw me watching it and he grew angry. He came over to me and gave me a good hard slap. I fainted! I only regained consciousness at home. Only much later did I understand my father's fears. He knew full well just where a fight between two children could ultimately lead.

After moving to Kâhta I learned this myself through experiencing it. If two Kurdish children fought among themselves, those in opposing camps usually parted amicably, and things would resolve themselves. But if one of our children fought with a Kurdish child, the matter would grow into more than just a fight between children: it became a fight between a Kurd and the son of an infidel. Even if the infidel's son was in the right, no one would come to his defense; the infidel was always blamed!

Throughout my youth I suffered the pain of this humiliation a great deal. I would eat myself up inside every time I experienced such injustices or humiliations.

These fears made me close up and turn inward. I developed a fear of conflicts and would run from all fights every time people came to blows.

I'm just about sixty years old, and I can't recall ever having been in a fight with anyone. I even think it over for a couple days before arguing with anyone.

Others of 'our kind' in Kâhta

After coming to Kâhta, I saw many people who resembled us. Most of the guildsmen and artisans in Kâhta were of 'our kind.' I learned both up close and from a distance that some of them were even our relatives.

We developed close relations with those of 'our kind' in Kâhta. I began to feel surer of myself. These people who came to our house to visit told me all about events that I had never heard about in Tukaris.

Slowly, we became aware that we weren't Muslim, but instead were those people known as 'infidels.' We heard and discovered that there were even some people practicing Christianity in the mountain villages and in the area around Gerger.

We were astonished at the things we heard: 'How is that possible here?' we asked ourselves, 'What's all this?', 'How can they do such a sordid deed?', 'What do they hope to gain from remaining infidels?'

Even though my name was Haci İbrahim, sometimes others would insult me, and call me 'infidel.'

Over time, and as I got older, I started to get to know those of 'our kind' up close. Among them secrecy was the rule. By listening, sensing and doing, I learned what to say and what not to say in front of Muslims. I began to understand what people were thinking from their looks.

Most of those of our kind were persons who appeared to be religious, prayerful individuals. Among them were even some who had gone on the Hajj, and who had devoted their goods and property to the mosque or for Qur'an lessons. Nevertheless, I knew that most of 'our kind' secretly performed their own brand of worship. Even my father would perform his rituals at night.

There wasn't a church in Kâhta. Most of 'our kind' still secretly performed Christian worship rituals and celebrated Christian holidays. They gave their sons prophets' names like Aziz, Yakup (Jacob), İbrahim (Abraham), prophets who were accepted and common to all of the religions. As for the girls, they were given names like Hatun, Sultan and Meryem. You'd never hear about a Muhammad.

Some of my friends used to criticize me, saying, 'You've become a Muslim!' I would get mad and respond 'And you're Christian!' The division between us was along the Muslim-'infidel' divide. During those years, we still weren't aware of what it was to be an Armenian, of an Armenian identity.

I learned about the calamities that had befallen the Armenians from the old folks who visited our house. As I grew older, I wanted to learn about every great sorrow and as I learned I also grew afraid that such a thing would come upon us again.

More than anyone else, I heard from our distant relative Veli Dede, who came to our house frequently, about the calamities that the Armenians had gone through. His memory was vast, and he never tired of telling of his recollections of events.

When I finally saw him again in 1990, I made him tell me once more the recollections he had first recounted when I was a child and a teenager. Thinking that this was something that should be remembered, I video-taped him from start to finish. Here's the video cassettes, here. I spoke with him in Kâhta on July 22, 1990. He was ninety years old at the time. Four months after speaking with me, Veli Dede died. His voice and his vision are all that remain for us.

Veli Dede knew Kurdish, Armenian, Syrian (Aramaic) and Turkish. While I was filming him, others who were listening who knew Kurdish would translate for me when he spoke in Kurdish. But sometimes he spoke Turkish, other times, he spoke Syrian.

Despite the fact that he was already ninety years old, Veli Dede's mind and memory were sound. He hadn't forgotten the name of a single place or person. He even had a detailed memory of the various events themselves. If you wish, we can listen to those things that happened to an infidel named Veli Dede.

Those things that Veli Dede experienced

We took up Haci İbrahim on his proposal. Kemal Uzun gave up on the idea of leaving. We followed Veli Dede's words with rapt attention. And Haci İbrahim translated all of the Kurdish portions into Turkish.

In Haci İbrahim's video tapes, Veli Dede appeared from his dress to be a Kurd. He was a swarthy, completely animated, and cheery-faced old man. He sat on a divan and spoke of his memories to Haci İbrahim and those around him… and spoke… and spoke:

> The name of our village was Holbiş. Now it's called Sütlüce. At that time there weren't any of these new names you now hear. The names of the villages were changed after 1960. I never got used to Sütlüce. For me, Holbiş sounds nicer. So I'm from Holbiş!
>
> Our entire village had one hundred and fifty-three households. Of these, twenty-seven belonged to our relatives. We called those who remained behind 'converts' (*dönme*). All of them were Zaza Kurds.*
>
> My uncle Kirkor Ağa was one of the wealthiest and most famous rural notables in the area. People knew of Kirkor Ağa and our family from Gerger to Kâhta, from Holbiş to Kâhta. We got on quite well with the Kurds. There were never any fights or disputes between us.
>
> The *kaymakam*, the local government official, informed my uncle that we were to be deported some ten days before the event:
>
> 'A hard and fast decision has been taken,' he warned him, 'They're going to deport you all!'
>
> 'Kaymakam Bey,' my uncle asked, 'Why didn't you give me news of this earlier? Maybe I would have found some solution. I would have found some way for us.'
>
> 'Kirkor Ağa' the kaymakam said, 'I only heard about it myself today! Do you think I want to send you off into exile? But there's nothing I can do to prevent it. I can only give you ten days' warning!'
>
> My uncle then told the rest of us what had happened. 'Impossible!' we protested, 'It cannot be! What did we do to deserve this? Why would they exile us from Holbiş, from this earth where we were born and raised?' Even when the deportation decree was announced, we still refused to believe it.
>
> But in the end, whether we believed it or not, the fateful day arrived!

---

* Although ethnically the Zazas are thought to be closer to the Kızılbaş than the Kurds, they are generally considered one of the various Kurdish subgroups. They are predominantly Sunni in religious orientation.

At first they took my uncle and father and sent them to Old Kâhta. When we saw the very great Kirkor Ağa being sent away, we were at a loss for what to do.

Several days later they gathered up the rest of us; we were all brought to Narince, which is a sub-district of Kâhta. But it wasn't just the Armenians from Holbiş who were sent to Narince; they sent and concentrated all the Armenians in the region there. There were a great many Armenians. I'm not talking about just a couple of hundred persons… it was far more than that. While we were waiting in Narince, Kirkor Ağa and my father returned to us again.

There was utter pandemonium. We had no idea what we were going to do, where we were going.

When my uncle heard about the deportations, he hid his gold in Holbiş. I guessed the place where he had hid it.

We remained in Narince for three days, in the place where we had been concentrated. Some cried to one another, others lost track of one another….

I was fifteen years old at the time. I followed events with interest and with fear. I looked after my brothers and helped my mother.

In Holbiş there was a Kurdish provincial lord by the name of Sabri Ağa. His one burning obsession was to find the place where my uncle's gold was hidden. He came from Holbiş to Narince. At that time, the administrative head of the sub-district was Ali Tezel… Sabri Ağa mentioned my uncle's gold to Ali Tezel, and they sat down and tried to figure out how to get their hands on it. 'If anyone knows where it is, his nephew Minas knows' they said. 'Minas is a very clever boy. He knows what's under everything. Let's go put him to the task! We'll bring him to the village after the convoy heads out. He'll show us where the gold is!'

My name was Minas back then. Later on it became Veli.

The district head Ali Tezel came unto us with Sabri Ağa. They asked my uncle for me.

'Kirkor Ağa,' they said, 'you're going on with the procession, but at least let Minas remain with us!'

'Why Minas?' my uncle asked. 'Why should I leave my nephew here?'

'Is it so bad if one of you remains behind? Isn't it clear what tomorrow will bring? And Sabri Ağa likes Minas, too!'

My uncle gave me to Ali Tezel. But I didn't like Sabri Ağa. I sensed that his intentions were bad.

The procession of Armenian deportees set out. It was not clear where they went. Within the dust and smoke, the calling and shouting, I found a way and fled. I covered my tracks. I marched secretly, following the convoy, until I finally caught up with my family, which was bivouacking on the banks of a river.

That night we went to Tukaris. It's present name is Akincilar.

In Tukaris, Osman Paşa, whom I have earlier mentioned, had been a commander of the Hamidiye Regiments approached my uncle.

'Kirkor Ağa' he said, 'Should we meet one another in front of fountains? Are we really to experience such days? If nothing else, you should at least come to my home!'

'Be well, Osman Paşa' my uncle replied, 'but please forgive me. I cannot leave the procession!'

Upon hearing this, Osman Paşa ordered that food be prepared at his house. He provided food for the entire procession. He had the food for our family sent separately from that of the others in the convoy, because one notable treated another notable differently than the ordinary persons in the convoy. He showed him more honor.

During the Deportation, at resting places he had our family separated from the rest of the convoy, and honored us as in other places. Osman Paşa's servants brought us our food. They treated us with the utmost respect. We passed the night in Tukaris.

The next day, they woke us early and brought us to the village of Merdi, on the banks of the Euphrates. We remained at Merdi for three days.

In the village of Naserdin, which was on the other side of the river, my uncle had a Kurdish plowman by the name of Hüseyin. When he learned that we were coming to Merdi, he came and located my uncle. He wanted to give us assistance.

My uncle told him:

'Hüseyin, if you wish to do us a favor, go get my nephew Minas and bring him! Some day there may be survivors. We will return, and when we do, Minas will be able to assist the survivors more than we will!'

'Kirkor Ağa,' Hüseyin replied, 'I will bring Minas, but the gendarmes at the head of the column won't let him go. When night falls Minas should come and wait under that enormous tree over there. We'll take him from there and bring him across. Don't worry! We will look after Minas and raise him like one of our own!'

That night, after it grew dark, I was making my way straight for the big tree when my foot caught on something! I looked down: it was a corpse! I was very scared! I went a little further—another corpse! After that, every two or three steps there was a corpse!

For the first time in my life I was really scared. I was never afraid!

I made my way to the tree and waited under it, but Hüseyin, who was supposed to come and take me, didn't arrive. I waited for a while, but I didn't see anybody coming or going. I was all alone! Then, I became afraid again. I went back to the camp in a state of dread. I made my way into the convoy.

My uncle asked 'Minas, my son, why have you come here?'

'Things are bad, uncle!' I replied. 'As I approached the tree, there were corpses at every step. I was scared. And nobody showed up. So I came back!'

'In that case, stay with us. Don't be afraid!'

After staying in Tukaris for three days, we went to the village of Hellis, on the opposite bank of the Euphrates. We crossed the river with a boat from Hellis. After the entire procession had crossed over by boat, my uncle embarked and crossed over as well.

In Hellis, my uncle gathered the entire family together and spoke to us:

'After this, I cannot go come with you any further! I have seen the pain and suffering of my children and grandchildren. I do not want to see anymore suffering and pain of my daughters or daughters-in-law!'

We all came to him and kissed his hand.

After that, my uncle summoned the inhabitants of Hellis. The villagers knew my uncle because he was a rural notable. They gathered around to listen to him. He distributed all the gold he had on him to the miserably poor villagers.

Finally, he called one villagers to his side:

'Take these two gold coins!' he said. 'I have a very important request of you. I do not want to see the suffering of my wife and children, of my daughters-in-law or my daughters. I know how to swim very well. Even with this old body of mine, I can remain on the water for three days and nights without drowning. Take these gold pieces! My death shall be a blessing unto you! I shall throw myself into the Euphrates! It's very fresh water. If I should float to the surface, you will make me sink!'

And so, the very great Kirkor Ağa threw himself into the Euphrates and killed himself. The Euphrates took my uncle up in its current and downstream. We were very sad and afraid. We felt ourselves alone and abandoned.

A short while later we arrived at a place with many trees, on the Gendere Bridge, at the edge of a steep precipice. At that point they separated the men who had come of age from the rest of our family. First, they made them dig graves. Then they killed them and buried them! All that remained in the column were women, children and old people.

'They snatched my mother and took her away'

There were some ten to fifteen gendarmes accompanying the column of deportees. In addition to these, there were some of Sabri Ağa's servants, from the village of Holbiş. Throughout the deportation, Sabri Ağa called the shots. At certain points along the route, the gendarmes would hand over the column to other gendarmes and return whence they had come.

We continued on our journey, eventually coming to the village of Hoşin, near Hilvan. In this village there were a number of Kurdish men who began picking out the beautiful women and girls from the convoy that they wanted for themselves.

My mother was a beautiful woman. They came and turned her around, inspecting her. My mother cried and pleaded with them.

'Please don't! Please don't!' she cried, 'Have mercy on my two children!' Others in the column pleaded as well. The women were all crying to one another. I didn't want to leave my mother's side. With one hand my mother held tightly onto the hand of my little brother, and with the other, to mine. I was crying hysterically, wearing myself out so as not to have to give up my mother!

There was one of the name of Haci Halil, from the village of Honi, who wanted to pull my mother from the column and take her away with him. Those who knew him pleaded with him: 'Don't do it, Haci Halil! This poor woman has two children. They took her husband away from her on the way!'

My mother pleaded herself: 'Please don't! Please! Even if you don't have pity on me, take pity on my children!'

In order to save my mother from Haci Halil's clutches, I bit his hand. He gave me a good slap to the back of the head. I went flying. But I got up again and hugged my mother tightly.

'That little jackass, son of a jackass!' he said cursing me. 'He goes to his death without a sound, but he cries for his mother!' And then he began kicking and slapping me. I didn't have enough strength to rescue my mother. Haci Halil from the village of Honi gave fourteen gold pieces to Sabri Ağa, who was in charge of the column and then took my mother and left.

I sat there crying with my brother for a long while. Along with my mother, the Kurds had snatched up other women and girls and taken them off to their villages. There were others weeping as well. But the convoy didn't stop. We set off again. We walked and walked. The next village we came to was Kızılkaya.

The column then came to a halt at one of the spring heads for Kızılkaya. In the village there was a notable by the name of Osmani Mahmud Ağa. He had long ago come from a village in Adıyaman. Later, he came to Kızılkaya and became the head of the village. In the old days, Kızılkaya had belonged to those from Siverek.

My brother and I were in a miserable state. I had to carry my brother on my back. Should I look out for myself or for my brother? And the others in the convoy: should they look out for their own children or for us? There was hopelessness and misery along the whole length of the column!

My uncle's wife, Meryem, found a way out of our situation and went to the head of Kızılkaya, Osmani Mahmud Ağa, and entreated him:

'If only you would take these two children. Look at them: they don't have a mother or father left. Perhaps by your grace, these children can be rescued! May it be attributed to your mercy and munificence! And Minas is a very good boy! He's a clever child! Whatever you ask him he'll do. He's very skillful. He's well-behaved!'

'But will Sabri Ağa give him to me?' Osmani Mahmud Ağa asked.

There were soldiers accompanying the convoy, but the real authority was Sabri Ağa. Osman Mahmud Ağa went and spoke with Sabri Ağa, and the latter consented.

'Fine. You can take him with you!' he said.

That night, Osmani Mahmud Ağa came and took me and my younger brother. The next day the column set out again, while we remained in Kızılkaya. One after the other, I had lost my father, my mother and all my other relatives and acquaintances. And now, all of a sudden, I and my brother were left all alone. A Kurdish family that was neighbors of Osmani Mahmud Ağa had taken from the convoy an Armenian girl who was from our village.

Once there, I began to work as a shepherd for Osmani Mahmud Ağa's flocks. The Armenian girl was put to work as a servant girl. Now and then, here and there, we would see one another and speak.

My master had told me 'From henceforth, your name will be Veli! And your brother's will be Muhammad. Forget the name Minas!' Up to age fifteen I had been Minas. Can a person forget his name so easily? But when nobody called me Minas for some time, I eventually became Veli, and Veli I remain. The neighbors also changed the name of the girl from my village who was their servant girl. She became Ayşe.

Osmani Mahmud Ağa was a tyrant of a man. His wife, his children—everyone was terrified of him. He beat them frequently.

One winter day, while I was out minding the flocks, I dozed off for a bit out of weariness. I was awakened by the sound of the sheep running around in a panic. I looked up and saw several dogs attacking the sheep. I went running and began to hit them with a stick in an attempt to rescue the sheep. I beat them, but the dogs kept on attacking the sheep without the slightest letup.

During that time a horseman who was passing close by saw my predicament and shouted:

'No, no, no! The wolves will eat you! Get out of there!' and fired both his guns at the wolves. It wasn't dogs attacking the sheep, it was ravenous wolves! I had thrown myself into great danger without even realizing it!

At the sound of the gunshot, the wolves took fright and fled. But before doing so, they had strangled and killed one of the sheep.

When I came home that evening, I carried the dead sheep on my back. When my lord saw the dead animal he became angry. Even without asking what had happened, he gave me two hard slaps.

'You jackass, son of a jackass! Where do you get the idea of sleeping and giving the sheep over to the wolves?'

His wife, Bege Hanım, heard the shouting and cursing and came running: 'Don't hit the child!' she pleaded. 'How should he have known if it was a wolf or a dog?'

'Get lost!' he shouted at her, 'Keep out of my affairs! This son of a cur dog fell asleep! He fell asleep and the wolves attacked the flock!'

That time I managed to avoid getting any more blows! God bless Bege Hanım. She rescued me.

That night, Osmani Mahmud Ağa didn't give me any dinner. It was very cold out, and I sat in front of the door, shivering violently from hunger, fear and cold. He wouldn't even let me come in the house. I could see the fire of the hearth from the other side. Because they were so afraid of Osmani Mahmud Ağa, they didn't dare to say to me, 'You're cold. Come sit by the hearth. Have a bite to eat.'

After a while, Bege Hanım came to me. Very softly, she said: 'Keko! Keko! Go lie down on the straw!'

I didn't have a choice but to do what she said. I went over to the straw and burrowed my way into it.

Several hours later I heard Bege Hanım slowly whispering for me: 'Keko! Keko!'

'What is it, Aunt Bege?' I replied.

'My son, I've brought you a little food!'

God bless Bege Hanım! She was such a good person. She mothered me and treated me like her son. She was the opposite of Osmani Mahmud Ağa, she treated me very well. If I didn't perish during that time from hunger or from the beatings, it was only because of her goodness.

Columns of Armenian deportees continually passed through the village of Kızılkaya. They would bivouac there for one or two days and then load up and go straight to a place called Rakka.

Because I knew Armenian, Osmani Mahmud Ağa would make me sell hard-boiled eggs and bread to the Armenians who camped near our village. And it wasn't just me: many of the residents of Kızılkaya went among the columns selling food. Some of them would try to forcibly collect gold from the Armenians in exchange for measly scraps of food.

One day while I was selling eggs and bread, I asked one of the deportees, 'Where are they taking you?'

'They're taking us to Murat!' they replied.

'What they call Murat is down on the Euphrates a little further,' I explained. 'They're going to take you and kill you all there!'

'No, they're going to take us to Rakka!' they said.

None of them knew what lay in store for them. They hadn't even heard where they were being taken. But even if there were some who sensed this inside, they didn't tell a soul, so as not to dishearten the others.

Those who heard my warning didn't want to believe it. Nevertheless, there was a certain disturbance and uproar among them. The things that I had said were passed quickly from mouth to mouth. The deportees clung to any shred of hope, and would have even embraced a serpent if they thought it might save them.

One day, when I was herding the sheep between the nut and apricot trees, somewhat distant from the banks of the Euphrates river, a woman came carrying a child on her back. She approached me. The top of her head had been shattered. When I saw it, I grew afraid.

With her hand she gestured to her mouth and to the child on her back.

I understood. She was telling me they were hungry.

'Are you *Hay*? Don't be afraid! I'm also *Hay*!' I told her. In Armenian, we call Armenians *Hay*.

'I'm Armenian!' she said.

'Where are you coming from?' I asked.

She gestured to the rock outcroppings of Görni, on the banks of the Euphrates.

'Do you see those rocks?' she said. 'They threw us from the top of those rocks into the Euphrates!'

'How did you survive?' I asked, still amazed.

'They threw so many people that the water near the base of the rock was full of corpses. My child and I fell together on top of some corpses. I didn't die. Crawling over the bodies, I eventually made my way to the bank and survived! We've been starving for days. The area has been very inhospitable, and we have no one who will help us. Where should I go?'

Osmani Mahmud Ağa gave me one and a half loaves of bread every day. I still hadn't eaten my bread that day. I gave it all to the woman.

'I work as a shepherd here for a rural lord. I don't have any family left! How can I help you? Go straight to the village. Maybe someone there will help you!'

'We have no one who will help us! Be well!' And with that, she went off, her child still on her back, and disappeared into the trees and bushes.

The Armenian disease

It was in the spring months. My brother Muhammad became sick. He got bad diarrhoea. His insides turned to water. He couldn't even hold it in. I couldn't find anything to help him. From one day to the next he grew weaker.

One day, he soiled the balcony. When our master saw that, he flew into a rage. He began shouting and cursing:

'What is this supposed to be?! This infidel's child has soiled every corner of the house!'

His wife intervened:

'He's a child! He's sick! He's not doing it on purpose. I'm going to clean it up presently.'

Still angry, Osmani Mahmud Ağa called to me:

'Veli! Come here! Your brother is soiling every place!'

'He's sick, my lord!' I replied.

'I don't want to hear about anyone being sick! This child will make us all sick! Take this son of a cur dog and throw him in the lake! If you don't, then take him and go somewhere else! I don't care, just get lost!'

Muhammad had only now begun to walk again. The diarrhoea was gradually subsiding. He was sick, but he was still my brother. How could I just throw him in the lake?!?

But I had no choice. Bege Hanım couldn't help me this time. She was afraid of Osmani Mahmud Ağa and fled inside.

The lake that he spoke of was actually a deep spot in the Euphrates river.

My brother hugged me tight, as if he understood what was going to happen to him. He held me very tightly and began to cry. I was crying too. We were all alone in this great big world. Who knows where my mother was at that point? I thought that I would throw myself in the lake, too. But in the end, I didn't.

I got to the top of the rock around the base of which the Euphrates flowed. My brother was crying. I was crying, too. What was this calamity that had happened to us? Where was my mother? Where was my father?

It was as if my brother's weak little arms had grown strong. He wouldn't let me go. At one moment I was trying to peel his arms off me, grabbing him by the leg. Two or three times I put it off; I closed my eyes and tossed him from the rock, down into the waters of the Euphrates below....

My brother let out a shriek.... And what a shriek! His cry echoed off the rocks. I began to run from there as fast as I could, without even looking back to see whether or not he'd actually fallen. How far did I run? How long did I cry? I don't know.

I couldn't go back to the house. I didn't want to go back. I didn't want to look anyone in the face. I cried and ached until the evening. My brother had been my one ray of hope. I could speak with him; we played together; we laughed together... After throwing my brother into the river, I now remained totally alone in the world. My heart and spirit were broken. If only I had died along with my brother! But that's how life is. A person says 'Let me die!' but doesn't!

That night, I snuck back to the house and crawled into the straw. The next morning they came looking for me and found me. I had to lead the flocks out to pasture. I couldn't even look at the rocks from which I had thrown my brother. His cry at that moment has never left my ears!

After killing my brother, I almost completely isolated myself. Every now and then I would commiserate in Armenian with Ayşe. She was the only person with whom I could share my pain. One evening I went to Ayşe and inquired about her:

'She was sick,' they told me. 'We sealed her up in the hollow place that was in the rock. Go and see!'

I ran quickly to the rock outcropping. They had bound Ayşe inside the hollow and closed it up after her. Ayşe was lying there in a miserable looking state. She had died!

In those days there was an epidemic that they called 'the Armenian disease' that swept over people and finished them off. They would kill the Armenians who caught this illness out of fear that they would spread it to others. But this epidemic, this 'Armenian disease' quickly spread. Neither my brother's nor Ayşe's deaths could stem its spread.

At first, Bege Hanım took ill. She became bedridden. After that, Osmani Mahmud Ağa himself took ill. Then, their youngest son... Every day more of the inhabitants of Kızılkaya were carried off by the disease. There weren't even enough people left to dig graves.

There was no one left to tend to Osmani Mahmud Ağa's flocks. Men, women, young and old—everyone was bedridden, struggling for their lives.

I remained completely well. My master was now dependent upon me.

'Veli, my son,' he said to me one day, 'go make me some *bulamaç** and bring it here!'

'My lord, I don't know how to make *bulamaç*!' I replied.

'Put the saucepan on the fire; then put in some water, some flour and some *pekmez*.† Then boil it like soup. Bring it to me so that I can drink it when it's still hot. Maybe that will help...'

I prepared it according to his instructions. But it didn't look like what it was supposed to be. Nevertheless, he drank it, one spoonful at a time. That was the first time I had ever heard kind words out of his mouth. He even said a prayer for me!

'God bless you, Veli my son! May you find favor in the eyes of God! If not for you, I wouldn't even have been able to drink this soup. Now, listen to me and listen well: Get on my horse and go to the village of Hoşin. I've got a very good friend there. His name is İmam. He's something like a doctor. Please send him my regards and tell him: 'Osman Ağa is sick. He has called for you!' Then, set him on the horse with you and bring him here.'

I went to Hoşin. When I got there I asked around until I found İmam's house. He had also taken ill. I found him sitting in a corner of his house, shriveled looking and curled up.

---

* A thick soup of flour, butter and sugar.
† A molasses made from reducing fruit, especially grapes. It is used as a sweetener throughout Anatolia.

'May it pass quickly!' I said. 'Osmani Ağa has sent me. He sends his greetings and asks if you might come and examine him if you can manage it. He himself is very ill.'

'In the name of my Lord, I too am sick,' he replied. 'I don't think I'm capable of going all the way to Kızılkaya and coming back. But since you've come this far, I can't say no! Did you bring a horse?'

'I did.'

'Put me on a donkey. I'm not able to get on a horse. Let's try to reach Osman Ağa in time.'

So we returned to Kızılkaya with all haste. As soon as we reached the house we heard the sound of Osman Ağa's daughter-in-law weeping. She was in mourning. Osmani Mahmut Ağa had long since given up the ghost.

How were we to conduct the funeral? There wasn't a healthy man in the entire village who could dig a grave or carry a coffin.

İmam returned to his village. I went to another nearby village. There everyone knew me as Osmani Mahmud Ağa's servant. I had also gotten to know the notables and persons of authority there. I went to the house of Sabri Bey, one of my master's good friends. He greeted me finely.

'Hail, Veli! Welcome!'

'Thank you, may your life be long!' I replied. 'My master has died…. There are no healthy men left in the village to conduct his funeral. I came to request assistance.'

'You have my condolences, Veli. We would like to go to Osmani Mahmud Ağa's funeral. But here, in this village, there are also no healthy persons left. I myself am sick. I'm not even in a condition to stand up! Go to the village of Kaynaklı. There you should relay my greetings to Yusuf Ağa. He should be able to find you some healthy men. May nothing stop the funeral of the great Osmani Mahmud Ağa!'

I went to Kaynaklı as he instructed. There I found Yusuf Ağa and explained the situation to him. I relayed the greetings from Sabri Bey.

'I swear, there is not one healthy man left here! The entire people have been affected. Nevertheless, Osmani Mahmud Ağa's funeral must not be held up! Let me take a stroll through the village. If I find anyone capable of standing on their feet, I'll find them and bring them here.'

Yusuf Ağa returned after a while with two elderly men he had found. Then the four of us, Yusuf Ağa, myself and the two old men set out by horse for Kızılkaya. We reached the village in the afternoon. Toward evening we managed to return Osman Mahmud Ağa to the earth.

I didn't have the right to remain in Osman Ağa's house, but where else could I go? With whom else could I stay?

I said to Yusuf Ağa, 'I've got no one left. What should I do? Please help me.'

'Osmani Mahmud Ağa has no more need for a servant boy. Come with me, be my servant boy!'

We returned to Kaynaklı together. I became Yusuf Ağa's shepherd. Yusuf Ağa was a good person. He never beat me, or cursed me or insulted me. He gave me food. I never went hungry. I worked as his shepherd for an entire year. In the meantime, the situation stabilized a bit. During the previous year, news had reached us at one point that the Assyrians would be pardoned.

One time, when I was bringing the flock to the well to drink, I came across a caravan that was going to Urfa to trade. They were also drawing water for their animals.

One of the members of the caravan pointed me out to his colleague and asked him, 'Do you know who this child is?'

'No!' the other replied.

'Shepherd boy,' he said, addressing me, 'do you know who we are?'

'You look like someone or other that I know, but I can't say who you might be.'

'You're Minas, right? The nephew of Kirkor Ağa from Holbiş?'

'Yes. You're also from Holbiş, no?'

'No. We're from Nefsi Gerger, the village next to Holbiş. We're on our way to trade in Urfa.'

'Take me to your village upon your return!' I said. 'I'm all alone here!'

'Done! We will be back here in three days. Wait for us, and be prepared. We'll take you to Nefsi Gerger!'

And they were true to their word—God bless them! They brought me to Nefsi Gerger. From there I went to my own village of Holbiş. Five years had passed since I had left. Our house, our home, our property and possessions—all had been looted and divided up.

Like an unwanted pest who won't be shooed away, I managed to get my hands on one small edge of our property. There was great fear in the air. I was never able to shake off that fear of death. For years, I couldn't manage to free myself from it. I worked. Man, did I work! I managed to recoup a great deal of our property and possessions. I married, had children.... but the shriek of my little brother whom I threw in the lake continued to ring in my ears. It still rings. To this day, I can't bear to hear the cries and screams of children!

After me, there were a few other hangers on, here and there; altogether, some ten or fifteen more Armenians returned... survivors, people who only with a thousand and one difficulties had managed to escape death, but who were now left with no one else in the world. I eventually found out that my uncle's wife was now living in the village of Istahola.

But I never heard reports of anyone else in the family. What had happened to my mother? Was she still alive? I didn't know. I always believed that one day I would find my mother. Often I would see other women and mistakenly think that they were my mother. I waited for my mother for years. I'm ninety years old and I'm still waiting.

We were all moved by the things that Veli Dede recounted. After having escaped death with great difficulty, and at times through mere luck, he had been forced to adopt Islam. Veli Dede had passed the great majority of his life as a *dönme* (convert), as a crypto-Armenian.

"Attack the infidel quarter!"

The video tape came to an end. Haci İbrahim began to recount those things that had happened to him from the point he had left off.

There were enormous difficulties that the Armenians suffered and endured during the deportations. And here before you is Veli Dede: an example of those who survived—and how they survived. But even though these survivors tried to rebuild their lives and go on afterward, it wasn't easy at all. And I know just how hard it was. I experienced it on my flesh and bones, in my dreams and my waking thoughts, in my fears and humiliation.

I'll never forget: in Istanbul, after the events of 6-7 September, 1955 it was as if the Muslim youths formed a front against us. Those of us who remained in Kâhta had no news of the events in Istanbul. But before we knew it, some Muslim youths began to divide up among themselves the homes, the daughters, and the wives of those persons of Armenian origin, calling them 'infidels'—even the old men! They waited, biding their time, saying, 'Just let one more thing happen, just one more incident, and we'll do as we wish. Just let the mood get a little troubled and tense, and we'll loot all their goods.'

We were all living under a great cloud of fear and tension at that time. Nine more years passed after that; it was 1964 when the events in Cyprus came to a head. The newspapers and the radio all spoke of what the Greeks were doing on Cyprus. The people were whipped into frenzy.

Over the summer, films concerning Cyprus were screened in the movie theaters. Every evening, after the films were over, the crowds would stream out of the cinemas and many would shout 'attack the infidel quarter!' and assault the quarter near the Adıyaman Church, where there were many Christians living. Late into the night they would throw rocks at our houses. There were certain people who organized these agitations. These attacks managed to instill a great fear in the people. The Armenians in Adıyaman, the Assyrian Christians and the crypto-Armenian Muslims were all afraid to venture out of their houses. No one had forgotten the dreadful bitterness and fear of the past. People were afraid that they would simply be assaulted on the streets, that people would break into their houses and loot them.

Finally, the events on Cyprus cooled down, but they had had a devastating effect on the Armenians and Assyrians still in Adıyaman and Kâhta! These people, who no longer felt themselves safe, now fled to Istanbul, to Iskenderun, to Adana or to Mersin.

After 1970, we began to feel a little more secure again. Progressive, democratic societies were established in Adıyaman and in Kâhta. These organizations were established both by our youth and those of the Kurds, and they struggled for shared objectives. The Kurdish youths gave assurance to our youths about not having to hide their origins, and being able to speak openly about their identities or beliefs. Within the framework of such tolerant, sincere relations, where there were no hidden agendas, many young men began to say, 'I'm an Armenian by birth!', 'I'm an Assyrian!', 'We have a different faith!' People were slowly coming to the point where they could relax and breathe freely, where they could smile and go to bed without fear.

But there were certain political movements that didn't like this new, auspicious situation. Soon, the rumors began to spread from mouth to mouth: 'The Armenians are reorganizing!', 'They are going to reopen the churches of the infidels!', 'The Armenians are going to reclaim the property of their fathers!'

With such rumors circulating, the mood of peace and reconciliation began to deteriorate once again. Slowly but surely, covertly and silently, the population of Adıyaman and Kâhta began to have their minds poisoned, and the brief period of tranquility and security that our kind had just tasted for the first time now began to give way to fear again.

After the 12 September, 1980 military coup those of our kind, and the Assyrians, were subjected to great pressures and humiliations. Those who humiliated the Armenians and Assyrians received support from certain 'high up' political movements. Nobody wanted to claim the Armenians, the Assyrians or 'our kind.' At that time, a good many persons who felt themselves without any other options threw up their hands and fled to Germany or other countries in Europe. They sought political asylum in these countries. Many of them were completely devastated, while others managed to rebuild their lives. In order to feel themselves a little more secure, many Armenian, Assyrian and crypto-Armenian families settled together in a few cities in Europe. They established communities where they would be able to practice their beliefs freely. In our day, in one district of Cologne alone, there are some fifty or sixty Armenian and Assyrian families from the area around Adıyaman.

Those of our kind who live in Germany or other countries in Europe still have many relatives in Istanbul, in Adıyaman and Kâhta. These persons tell us, 'Remain in Europe. There you can do what you want in freedom; here, we'll get it in the neck again!'

Our relatives and relations in Adıyaman and Kâhta all have their own trades. They are known as Muslims within their milieus. We don't want to cause them difficulties or trouble. When we get travel permits and come to visit, we—our children, ourselves—all of us conform ourselves to their way of life. Whether we like it or not, the fact is that we speak and act differently among ourselves than we do around Muslims.

Sometimes, when I am just among our kind, I say to them, 'We are Armenians by birth and by nature. Our religion and our worship are different. Why are you hiding it?'

'What does that mean 'We're Armenians,' they reply. 'What do we have? We have a little peace of mind. But in the end, we're bound to lose that, too. For you all [in Europe], the environment is friendly and pleasant. When your visa is up, you'll return to Germany. But what are we going to do? You go be yourselves, but keep quiet over there! Don't bring disaster down upon our heads here!'

This double life is a very difficult human condition to be in... very difficult. Inside you're one thing, outside, you're something else!

You've become a Muslim, but you haven't forgotten your origins. You can go on the pilgrimage, become an Islamic religious teacher. But you can never erase the mark of being an 'infidel' from your forehead. Even if you think you've erased it, others haven't. When things get tight, when push comes to shove, they never hesitate to throw it at your feet, saying, 'infidel, son of an infidel!'

Our kind are very fearful of both normal Muslim converts or born Muslims, because the real Muslim convert behaves like a true Muslim in order to prove to himself that he is a real Muslim, in order to preserve his position in society. Sincere Muslim converts can very easily tell us apart from normal Muslims. They perceive the coded messages that pass between us. It's for that reason that converts are even more dangerous for our kind.

There are converts who study Islam and become prayer leaders. These are the ones who struggle to make us into true Muslims, they feel like it's their mission to do so.

In recent years, there have been some converts who have become ardent members of dervish orders. Among the people, these people are known to have been of Armenian origin. They are given nicknames in Armenian. But they become the most fanatical religious chauvinists. What they do when they can is to humiliate those of our kind that they know. No one is more merciless to a convert than another convert!

"Milla Çelebi roused me from my slumber"

I graduated from the Institute of Art and came to Germany in 1970 as an apprentice worker through the Institution for Locating of Employment and Laborers. I was a supervisor at the Deutz factory in Cologne. I worked at that place for twenty-three years straight. Then I retired.

During my first years I lived in the factory's workers' dormitories. In the workers' dormitories people were more open to others, more sincere. Close friendships were forged there, like those of work colleagues or people you do your military service with. It was healthy. Factory life tended to bring out people's true nature, whether good or bad.

While I was working at the Deutz factory I got to know a Kurd from Batman by the name of Milla Çelebi. We became friends. We worked together in the factory and roomed together in the workers' dormitory. Before coming to Germany, Milla Çelebi had served as an Imam in Batman for seven years. His knowledge of religion was very deep. He had graduated from the *medrese*.* He liked Molla Barzani's political movement in Iraq.

At that time, I didn't have any interest or connection with politics. I was a 'closed box.' I hadn't told anyone that I was of Armenian origin. I may not have been a pure Muslim but liked Islam. I voted for the right-wing parties. I got angry at the leftists.

One day we began talking about one thing and another, and I told him that I was of Armenian origin, but that I felt myself to be a Kurd. There was a great turmoil inside me.

Milla Çelebi listened to me and accepted it with great understanding.

---

* A school for Islamic study. Something like a Muslim seminary.

'Haci İbrahim, why do you hide your origins?' he said. 'Whatever your origins, you should be able to say so without shame or hesitation. If you're Armenian, then say 'I'm an Armenian!' If you're Kurdish, say 'I'm a Kurd!' A person has to accept his own identity. You've become a Kurd, but your origins are Armenian. You can change your religion but you can't change your Armenianness. But you have to express your own identity without fear and without internal distress!'

Milla Çelebi's circle was quite broad. He was a lively and well-liked person. He spoke with Kurds, with Turks, with Armenians and with Assyrians, and had friendships among all of them. When he'd introduce me to his circles, he'd say, 'Haci İbrahim is Kurdish but he's originally an Armenian.'

At first, I didn't want him to introduce me so, but I got used to it. No matter what I did, there remained inside me a fear that I couldn't get rid of. And Milla Çelebi eventually helped me to grow more comfortable with being Armenian. I finally got to the place where I myself could say 'I'm Kurdish but I'm of Armenian origin.'

When people would introduce themselves during a meeting or a conversation, they would openly declare the city and region they were from and their ethnic or religius identities. I would disguise my identity somewhat, saying, 'I'm from Kâhta. I'm a Kurd,' but afterward I would upbraid myself, saying, 'Why did you hide the fact that you're Armenian? Why are you afraid to state your origins?' There were times when I would feel like shouting 'I'm Armenian!' at the top of my lungs—but I didn't! I'd stay silent. Even in a place like Germany, I'd just close up inside myself. God bless Milla Çelebi for saving me from all of this depression and fear.

It was on account of Milla Çelebi that I began to read the daily papers. Slowly, my political views changed. I started to like the 'Deniz Gezmiş's of the world. And as I read, I began to learn how to think, how to speak; I began to understand the way things were. And the more I understood, the calmer I became. The more my world became enlightened, the more my fears receded.

When I received a travel visa to Turkey in 1975, I came and married a girl from among our kind. Among us, marriages were always contracted between ourselves. We neither gave our daughters to marry outside of our group, nor married the daughters of outsiders. That was because a bride who came from outside could learn our secrets. And if one of our girls was given to outsiders, it would be possible in the future that if there was some misunderstanding or difficulty between the couple, they would humiliate her, or call her an 'infidel's daughter!' Such humiliation would be unbearable.

My older sister was a very beautiful girl. There was a Kurdish notable who had grown up with my father and served him for years and who wanted her for his son. Risking everything, he refused to give my sister to him. 'We don't have a bitch for some foreign dog!' he said. Nevertheless, because he was afraid that they would kidnap her, he quickly married her off to a bald, ugly, poor nobody of a shepherd who was one of our kind.

These are difficult things! You know you're doing wrong, but you can't do what's right. Sometimes your head says one thing, your heart another.... The inside of these things angers me, the outside angers you!

We raised our children with a Kurdish identity. We gave them Kurdish names. Our oldest daughter went to middle school in Germany. One day there was a person from our kind visiting us. My daughter came home from school. She was very distressed. She hinted that something had happened.

'What's wrong, girl?' I asked. 'Did something happen at school?'

'Yes,' she replied. 'There's an Armenian kid in our class. He's very bad. Today we got in a fight. He called me 'Dirty Kurd!' I wanted to hit him. How does he think he can call Kurds 'dirty'?!'

One of our guests couldn't contain themselves and said:

'Well, my girl, what's your origin?'

'I'm a Kurd, through and through!' she answered.

'Look, daughter. We are Armenian in origin!' I said. That was the first time that I had said anything about it.

'No!' she cried. 'That's impossible! I can't be Armenian! I'm Kurdish! After this I can't be Armenian! Why didn't you tell me before? Where did all this Armenianness come from?' And then she began to cry. It was only with great difficulty that I got her to stop....

My daughter entered a crisis over this. She neglected her studies and more. She was furious at me and at her mother. We were also very sad. We understood that we'd made a mistake. But that would be for our daughter to deal with. Our daughter was suffering because of our mistake.

Very slowly, we explained that being an Armenian wasn't a bad thing. After that we explained how, even though we were originally Armenian, we had assimilated among the Kurds and become Muslims. But the brain of a child couldn't comprehend all this. How had these evil events happened? Could we explain it in a way that our child could understand? We spoke about the bloody, bitter things that had happened to our forefathers. But the child, who listened to these bitter recollections, began to feel enmity and hatred toward the Turks and Kurds. It was very hard to explain to her why she shouldn't feel hatred toward the Turks and Kurds.

But never underestimate a child's mind! They think of things that never occur to us. They ask questions that we never think to ask. This double life that seems so normal to us—behaving one way inside, another in public—strikes a child as nonsense.

We think we're going to be the ones to teach them something, but in the end, it's they who have something to teach us.

With our younger children, we told them the truth about everything from the outset.

Red mark in their identity cards

It's very hard to be one of the crypto-Armenians, converts, or our kind. Maybe it's not so difficult in Istanbul. There's a throng of people. It's so chaotic that no one bothers with what others are doing! But in places like Adıyaman and Kâhta, the lives of our kind are very, very difficult.

No matter how much you think you're hiding your true identity from outsiders, they still know. At some moment when you least expect it, they pull out the fact that you're Armenian and throw it at you. You can shrug it off to some measure when it's just your neighbor or some ordinary person, but whatever details about your life that the normal people on the street may not know, or may have forgotten, you can be sure that they'll use such details against you in the offices of the state. They do evil to such a person! I personally witnessed such an injustice when I went to visit Turkey three years ago. Let me tell you the story and you can decide whether it's right or wrong:

I've got a friend; he's completely Muslim… He's the son of a father who converted out of belief. He's a graduate of the Trade High School, a democratically minded young man by the name of Yakup.

Anyway, he was looking for work. He'd heard that they were looking for a typist at the Adıyaman Department of Justice. He applied. He sat for the tests, and he passed both the typing and the cultural tests. The examination board informed him of the results.

He came home elated and told his mother and father the good news. They, too, were delighted that their son had passed the exams and found work.

Yakup assumed that there was nothing left but to wait for the notice of official appointment. Three days passed, then five, then a week, then a month.... Good Lord, even after two months had passed, there was still no notice.

It was then the first days of the summer vacation. I ran into Yakup. He was utterly dejected. I asked him what the problem was.

'Don't ask, uncle!' he replied. I took the qualification exams and passed them. But it's been two months and I still haven't received notice of their decision. I don't know what to do, I don't know to whom to turn!'

'Come,' I told him, 'let's go to the Department of Justice. I've got a close acquaintance there. Let's talk with him. Maybe he knows something.'

Yakup cheered up at this proposal. Even his voice took on a cheerier tone. Together we walked to the Department of Justice.

I hadn't seen my friend in a long time, but the moment he saw us he ushered us in. I explained Yakup's situation to him. I asked him the reason that the order for Yakup's appointment hadn't arrived.

'Wait here for five minutes,' he instructed us. 'Let me speak with my colleague who deals with these things.'

A short while later, he returned. He motioned for us to come with him and took us to his colleague.

'Please forgive me!' the colleague said. 'We took out your file and looked through it. Here, have a look yourself....'

The outside of the dossier was stamped 'secret' in red ink. He opened the file and read out what was written inside:

'... After it was determined, during the national security check, that [the applicant] was an Armenian who had converted to Islam, his appointment was halted...

Yakup was completely devastated!

'How can this be!?' he demanded. 'We've been practicing Muslims for years now! We pray and observe all of the religious rites. I don't do it, but my father goes to pray five times a day without fail. How can this be? How!?'

Yakup could in no way accept this injustice against him. We informed his father of what had happened. He, too, was shocked.

'Who is this, anyway, who tries to make us into Armenians?' Yakup's father exclaimed. 'We've been Muslims for years! We have always done more than our share in the service of the nation. We're not Armenians. Who is making such an accusation against us. I'm going to write to the papers about this injustice! And if that doesn't do it, I'm going to go as far up as the President of the Republic himself!'

But no matter to whom Yakup and his father appealed, doors were slammed in their face. When it was a matter of employment in government offices, they were silent; but when it didn't have to do with employment, they'd accuse them openly of having been Armenians some eighty years before.

"Fear, always the fear!"

To be a convert, to hide one's Armenian origins, entails manifold difficulties. As I said, you face injustice in government offices. Even your Muslim Kurdish neighbor looks upon you with contempt. The Turks don't like you either. A person who is of Armenian origin will always be hesitant and fearful, thinking 'If they understand that I'm Armenian they will take all my property and possessions; and if they don't lay their hands on my things, they'll cause me physical harm!' So they hide their true identities. They are plagued by the inner fear that they'll lose everything. And these fears grow to an intolerable state.

Maybe the children of those of our kind who are in Istanbul can establish ties with the Armenian community. But it would be very difficult for those of us in Adıyaman to be in contact with the Armenian community there. They remain silent and closed within themselves, thinking that if somebody ever found out, they would bring themselves needless grief. In Germany and in other countries in Europe, we've got some connection with the Armenian community. Some joint cultural activities have even been organized. We've participated in the Armenian festivals.

During the past year, we went to visit some of our relatives in the Swiss city of Aarau. At the time we were visiting there was an Armenian festival in Aarau. We participated. But the fact is, Armenians who come from the various regions of Anatolia, those Muslims who are of Armenian origin, as well as the Assyrians all possess different cultural values and judgments. Some appear totally western, others, eastern. Those from Diyarbakir, Mardin or Adıyaman want to dance the *halay*;[*] those from Istanbul, on the other hand, or those who have lived for years in Europe want to dance disco.

The Armenians who were born and raised in the West look down on the eastern Armenians in their Kurdish garb. At the Armenian festival in Aarau, first it was the young people who enjoyed themselves. After that, they gave way to those of our kind, and to those from Diyarbakir, from

---

[*] A folk dance from eastern and southeastern Anatolia.

Mardin and from Adıyaman. We danced the *halay* to our heart's content.

What I want is that everyone should be able to express their own identity freely and without fear. Whoever wishes to believe should believe, and those who don't shouldn't have to, and people should be able to talk about who they are, whatever that is. If you're Armenian, you should be able to say 'I'm Armenian!' Let there be no more discrimination in any society, in no place of employment or government office! Let no one have to hide their ethnic, racial or national identity from their children. Is that too much to ask?

Sultan Bakırcıgil: "Infidel ants!"

I told Haci İbrahim that I wanted to speak with a woman from the crypto-Armenian community.

"I'll look into it," he said. "I've got a few acquaintances; but it's not easy getting them to speak. I'll let you know if I manage to convince any of them."

Ten days passed since that conversation. Then, Haci İbrahim called with a happy message:

"I found one of those I was looking for! She'll talk. Come to Cologne tomorrow evening."

I was there at the appointed hour, knocking on the door. Without entering, we set out for the house of the woman he knew. Her husband and their children met us with sincere hospitality.

Haci İbrahim introduced us. And then, before anything else, he explained at length my purposes and why I wanted to speak with them. That gave them confidence. Before we arrived at the house he had also given me the necessary background information on the woman with whom I was to speak and on her family.

We drank our tea and warmed to each other with small talk. Then Sultan Bakırcıgil spoke:

"My name is Sultan. I'm from Adıyaman. I learned that I was Armenian when I was seven years old" she said, starting off her explanation with a smile. Apart from the occasional question, I didn't interrupt her as she spoke. Sometimes she laughed, other times she grew sad and melancholy, and at others she even cried. But she opened wide the gates of her inner world:

Once, when I was seven years old, I was killing ants with my friend Fatma, who was also the daughter of our neighbors. There were both black ants and red ants. Fatma said:

'Come, let's kill these red ants. These are the infidel ants. Leave the black ones alone. Those are the Muslim ants!'

That was the first time I'd ever heard ants separated into 'Muslims' and 'infidels.' I was confused.

'What's an infidel?' I asked her.

'What do you mean? You're an infidel, too. Those red ants are your ants, the black ones are mine!'

I didn't understand, but I was very upset. I didn't want to kill the ants. I left the game and went home.

My child's mind was full of questions: Who are we? Are we infidels? What does that mean? Why did Fatma say such a thing to me? But I couldn't find any answers to my questions. I went to my mother and asked her:

'Mother, are we infidels?'

My mother was surprised and agitated:

'From whom did you hear that?' she demanded.

'Fatma, the neighbors' daughter told me that!'

'Don't you mind. I'll tell you about it someday.'

'Tell me now, mother!' I insisted, and so she did.

'Look, my child. We are Armenians. We are Armenian Christians. They call Christians 'infidels!' That's how it is, my child! We can scrub ourselves seven times over, we can even become Muslims, but they'll still call us 'infidels.' Even if some little hooligan calls us 'infidels,' don't you worry about it! I'll speak with her mother. She won't call you 'infidel' again. Only when you're outside, don't speak a word about what I've told you around others. They shouldn't know what we are! What's spoken about in the house should remain in the house! Don't tell anybody that we're this or that. We're Muslims. That's as much as you need to say!'

From that day forward, I understood that we belonged to a different people. My mother's frequent warnings made me afraid. I felt guilty. I began to pay very close attention to things that were said in our house, to how my father behaved, and to what the old women who came to visit had to say. I listened to the things these old Armenian women said with rapt attention, as if I were listening to a fable, and I grew afraid.

The incident with the ants had disturbed me greatly. And it troubled me greatly to learn that we were a different people. I would ask myself, always looking for an answer to the question: Does that mean we are something bad or evil?

'Look, they're killing the infidel ants. We're also infidels. They're killing us! Just like they did in the old days!'

I couldn't forget about the ants and the effect it had on me.

When my mother's father came to our house in winter, he called me to his side and explained at great length all of the things that had happened to him. I thought he was telling an epic or a fable. But I've never forgotten those things my grandfather told me. I was very scared at those times.

"We don't have anything to laugh about"

My grandfather was a ten year old child at the time. The Kurds came to his village. For three days and three nights they murdered people; then they left. My grandfather was saved by mere coincidence. Those who were killing the Armenians got into an argument. 'Whose gun can kill more people, yours or mine?' Then they lined up ten children in a row and bound them with rope. They were going to have a killing contest! My grandfather wasn't killed because he was the last one in the line. The bullet didn't reach him. Those before him were killed. They all collapsed where they were and remained still. The killers assumed that they had killed them all. My grandfather later untied the rope that bound him and fled. They fired after him. Only by luck or by coincidence did he survive.

He ran and ran until he came to a hidden wellspring. He went inside the well, hoping to hide himself. He glanced over and saw that there were two or three snakes at the edge of the well!

What should he do? If he crawled down in, the snakes would bite him, but if he went back out, they would shoot him! He decided to balance himself on the steps in the middle of the well and stay there. When it again grew dark, he came back out of the well and rested, going back inside when dawn broke again. Repeating this again the next couple of days, he hid out in the well for three whole days.

After that he came to the house of a Kurdish family that he knew. This Kurdish family hid my grandfather for forty days underneath a haystack. They brought him bread and water. They rescued him from certain death. After things had calmed down, he came out of his hiding place. The members of this Kurdish family were shepherds. Even though he had lost his mother, his father and all his family and relations, he didn't flinch from life, he didn't lose his hope; he worked hard and saved his life.

I'd listen to all these things my grandfather told us with great horror.

The old women who came to our house to visit also spoke of the bitter events that they had experienced. During the deportations beautiful women, girls and young brides would be separated from the column of deportees and assaulted. When I heard these things I grew afraid because I was a beautiful girl! It was as if it was a crime to be beautiful. I didn't want to be beautiful.

The things that had happened to my paternal uncle's wife scared me for years. During the time of the deportations a Kurdish man killed her husband before her eyes and made off with her. He forced her to marry him after that. My great-aunt gave birth to two sons by this man who killed her husband. She used to cry, saying:

'I'll never forget what happened. I knew that that man killed my husband. I saw it with my own eyes! He was going to kill me, too. Then, out of fear, I became the wife of the man who killed my husband. I agreed to it in order to save my life. Life is so precious! I'll never forgive that murderer who is the father of my two children!'

Afterward, she'd try to comfort herself, saying: 'God will punish him!'

My aunt was older than my mother. But she would pour out her inner pain and suffering to my mother. I would listen with rapt attention, and then I'd be afraid. I'd have nightmares about it.

During my childhood and when I was a young girl these old Armenian women who came to visit would usually talk about their recollections, pour out their inner grief, and cry. Most of them never smiled.

The internal condition of my uncle's wife was one great sorrow and bitterness. Even when her children were playing happily and carefree, she was always angry at them.

'What are you laughing at?' she would say, accusingly. 'We don't have anything to laugh about! What do we have to be happy about? We need to sit down and worry continually!'

I never saw her laugh herself. I would even ask her:

'Why don't you ever laugh?'

'What should I laugh at?' she would answer. 'How can I laugh? I don't have anything left to laugh about.' And then she would cry, silently to herself. Her weeping would affect me very deeply.

How could a person, a woman, be so grief-stricken, so filled with sorrow? I couldn't understand it. When I'd see how she was, I'd become overcome with grief myself, and for some time afterward I wouldn't be able to laugh myself.

My father had been a child at the time of the deportations. My father's family was very rich. His father was the village notable. In his village there was a Kurd by the name of Şükrü Ağa. Şükrü Ağa had very good relations with my father's family. During the massacres he saved many members of my father's family. He risked his own life and those of his family in hiding my father and his family. He gave them great assistance.

My mother's father was a man who greatly loved Christianity. He used to laugh when he told us how he would appear and behave like a Muslim to the outside world, but inside observe and practice the various Christian rites.

During the month of Ramadan, the drummer would post himself before peoples' doors and bang on them insistently. My grandfather's family would wake up everyone in the house and light all the lights; they would rattle the pots and pans and make noise as if they were preparing food for the pre-dawn meal marking the resumption of the daily dawn-to-dusk fast. To the outside world, they appeared to be keeping the fast. My grandfather would get angry at the drummer and at this or that humiliation

'They've destroyed us down to our roots!' he would grumble. 'There's only a few of us left. All that time has passed and they still won't leave us in peace!'

My grandfather's family didn't keep the fast during my childhood; they would eat secretly during fast times. My grandfather would get very angry and very irritated when he was compelled to keep the fast or made to appear like he was.

My mother was one of seven siblings: three girls, four boys.

My maternal grandfather married off his four sons to girls from our kind. The Sunni Kurds wanted my oldest aunt. My grandfather didn't want to give her to them. They intimidated my grandfather; he finally relented to their demands. Afterward, he would grow sorrowful when he'd think about it. 'I've sacrificed my daughter to the Kurds!' he'd say. Afterward, the Kurds said 'Let's at least give you one of our girls!' But my grandfather wouldn't accept the offer, as he was afraid that they'd learn our secret. 'I've done all sorts of things, but I didn't take in a daughter of the Kurds!' he'd say. My younger aunt was abducted by another Kurdish family. After that, my grandfather grew afraid and gave my mother, who was only twelve years old at the time, to my father, who was already thirty years of age. My grandfather was pleased, saying, 'At least I've saved one of my three daughters!' My mother was glad too, because she'd been rescued from the hands of the Kurds.

My father's moods

My father thought of himself as completely Armenian; he got very angry at any talk of 'conversion.'

During his childhood, he had wanted to be a priest and had even gone to seminary to learn to be one. But his father had said:

'My son, the Armenian population has greatly shrunk. If you become a priest you won't be able to marry. You won't have any children. You won't be able to produce any offspring. Abandon the idea of becoming a priest. Go to a different school. Get married. May you have a whole flock of children! May the Armenian race not die out!'

My father took his father's words to heart and left the priests' school. Instead he went to the government middle school and graduated from there. But in terms of religion he was a Christian, through and through. He would read the Gospels to us every night.

'Listen!' he would tell us. 'The one who listens to another reading earns a good deed!'

My father was always full of hope.

'Things will change one day!' he would say, 'Everything will change! This oppression, this fear, all will disappear. Everybody will be able to say openly 'I'm Armenian'; they'll be able to worship in the church!' He always carried that hope.

He was a government official in Adıyaman. At home we spoke Kurdish. During our time, there were very few people in Adıyaman who spoke Turkish. Almost the only ones who spoke it were the government officials because the great majority of them were Turks who had come from other cities.

My father's Turkish colleagues would come and visit us all the time. We learned to speak Turkish from them. When I began public school I was already able to speak Turkish.

Despite the fact that my father felt himself to be completely Armenian, in order not to draw attention to himself, he forced himself to appear like a Muslim around the other officials, praying and keeping the fasts. But he didn't pray five times a day. He'd go to prayers on the holidays. As for our holidays, for those he'd go to the church in Adıyaman.

Because my father didn't go to work on Sundays, he wouldn't keep the fast. But throughout the month of Ramadan we would get up every day before dawn and light our lights. We would eat the *iftar*, the pre-dawn meal, when everyone else was eating it. We were forced to appear as if we were keeping the fast, too. During my childhood, it seemed like we were playing a game. But when I got older, after I began to understand and I learned that we were Armenian, it got harder and harder to play the game. Sometimes I would be so ashamed of what we were doing, sometimes I would feel so humiliated by it!

It isn't possible to say that we didn't fast or that we openly observed our own faith. There was no tolerance for us among whom we lived. They would only accept us if we behaved like them. You could say we were under constant monitoring. During Ramadan, almost every day at noon, our neighbor's daughter would come to our place to sit and visit. We couldn't tell her 'Don't come!' The girl would listen closely to what we said and how we behaved. And she wouldn't leave… We would secretly slip into the kitchen and eat our lunch. We supposed she didn't know, but one day, as we were going into the kitchen on some or other pretext, she said, 'You don't have to hide it! I know what you do, and whether or not someone keeps the fast!' We were devastated. We were terrified that she would tell others and that everyone would hear about it. We fell into great distress.

In our religion there is a fifty-day period of abstinence. My father wasn't able to observe it, even though he really wanted to. He was a government official. He didn't want the others in his office to find out. He found a solution that suited his situation and personality. Throughout Ramadan he would think of the fast that he kept as being done for the sake of Lent. When he would break the fast, he would pray to God and plead, 'My Lord, please accept the fasts I kept as my abstinence for Lent. Pardon my sins!'

'Father?' I would ask, 'Can you really do that?'

'That's how it is,' he would reply. 'What's important is intent. God and our prophet Jesus see our condition. They understand the hardships we endure!'

My father didn't say his Muslim prayers very often. Every holiday, though, he'd go to the mosque. But he'd say his Christian prayers every day. In our religion, we say our prayers twice a day: once in the morning and once at night. We turn toward the direction in which the sun rises, bend our knees and sit. We make the sign of the cross and pray without any bending or standing.

My father taught us Armenian, and taught us to recite two very short prayers. When we make the sign of the cross, we would say:

Bismillah, velli din, nuru Kudüs, vilakin, amin! (In the name of God, the protector of the faith, the light of Jerusalem, now and forever. Amen.)

After saying this prayer and making the sign of the cross, we say another prayer, either in Turkish or Kurdish. Because I didn't know Armenian, I'd generally say them in Turkish.

My father was a real faithful Christian. He felt himself to be Armenian, through and through. He would always warn us:

'You can go wherever you want to. But no matter what, never be ashamed of the fact that you are Armenian!'

But I was still afraid. No matter how many times my father would say 'Don't hide your Armenian origins,' I would still take the vow every morning at primary school: 'I'm a Turk, I'm honest, I'm hard working!' I saw my being Armenian as a sort of crime, and I was always afraid that my friends would hear about it and do bad things to me.

One day… it would have been in the fourth grade… the children started saying to each other 'Sultan's an Armenian!' One of them came up to me and told me. Since it was recess time, they had all gathered together and were looking at me! I was so afraid! I thought that they would beat me to death or kill me some other way, like my father, my grandfather and my aunt had all told me.

I began to cry. At that moment I felt all alone in the world! I ran to the teacher.

'Teacher,' I told him, 'my friends are all calling me an Armenian and I'm very scared!' He calmed me down, saying:

'Don't be afraid! They're just being rude! I'll go speak with them!'

After that he called all the students together and spoke with them. I don't know what he said to them. Later on, I learned that this teacher was also one of our kind.

During all my primary school years there was always a constant fear within me, a constant feeling of dread that something bad would happen. I was always afraid that something evil might befall me, and this fear gnawed at me day and night.

With my child's perception of the world, I was ashamed at being Armenian, always wishing secretly that we had been born Turks. I really yearned badly to be a Turk, I wanted it more than anything. I was full of sorrow and regret over it.

Thank goodness, I was eventually able to rid myself of the shame I felt inside. As for my desire to be Turkish, during my youth I eventually moved beyond it. I began to accept myself for who I was. And after that, I was able to sleep more soundly.

After primary school, I wasn't able to continue my education, even though I wanted to do so very badly. Because of their fears, those families of our kind didn't send their daughters to schools in other cities.

Their greatest fear of all was that their daughters would be abducted my Muslims and forced to marry them.

Our kind never married out or allowed our children to do so. During my time, girls of Armenian origin were married off very young, before something happened to them.

I also married early. I came to Germany after that. My husband worked in Germany. I used to think that I was freer in Germany, that I didn't have as many fears. In fact, it's true that I feel a lot calmer and safer in Germany than in Adıyaman. But our being Armenian was also seen as a crime in Germany. Even in Germany, for years I was unable to bring myself to say openly that I was an Armenian.

My husband and I speak Kurdish at home. Even though we know Turkish, it's easier for us to speak Kurdish. Kurdish was our mother tongue. We're Armenians, but we don't know Armenian.

In the neighborhood in which we've lived for ten years, they call us 'Kurdish Sultangil' or 'Kurdish Osmangil.' Even this bothers me. Guests come and they say what their identities are. But we can't say that we're Armenians in front of them. The fear has worked its way deep inside us!

I was unemployed for three years. During that period I both raised my child and looked after the infant child of a Tatar family who were our neighbors. They were very good people. We'd always be in and out of each other's houses. One day they'd come to us as guests. During those days, soldiers were being murdered around Hakkâri. The conversation went from one subject to another; ultimately, it moved to the reasons for the conflicts in eastern Anatolia.

Our Tatar friend, this person whose child I had looked after for a whole year, began the discussion by saying:

'It's not the Kurds who are in fact the source of these incidents; it's the Armenians who are behind the Kurds. If you want to stop these incidents, you first have to wipe out the Armenians!'

But both I and my husband remained silent. Neither of us could say, 'But we're also Armenians!'

This incident affected me greatly. So many years had passed, so many Armenians had died, there were only a handful of Armenians left, scattered here and there, but somehow, it was still the Armenians who were responsible and guilty of all manner of evil! What kind of hatred was this?! What sort of notion was this, that even in Germany, it didn't leave us be?! Whenever I'd hear of such things, such unjust accusations, I'd get the uncontrollable urge to shout out 'I'm Armenian!' at the top of my lungs. But I wouldn't and instead I'd turn it all inside and cry loudly and bitterly instead. My hands and feet would shake. I'd collapse emotionally speaking. Because of these incidents I began going to doctors. In the end, we reached the decision to leave the neighborhood, and to find a place in another neighborhood, far away from this one. There we would declare ourselves as Armenians.

In the new neighborhood we told everyone who came to visit us, even volunteering it:

'We're from Adıyaman. We speak Turkish, but we're originally Armenians. We're not Muslims. We're Armenians! That's how you should know us!'

Some would never come back after that. Others would keep coming, saying things like, 'If you're Kurdish or if you're Armenian, it makes no difference to us. What's important is that you are human beings!' All of a sudden I could relax. How much more at ease I felt! It was a whole new world for me!

I'm a little more at ease in Germany now, but whenever we get visas and travel to Adıyaman we still have to hide our true identities and go back to acting outwardly like Muslims so that nothing bad happens to our relatives there. So the difficulties and fears still continue down to our day....

The bitterness of having to hide one's origins

Those who have experienced the bitterness of it know what it means to have to hide one's origins. I work in a hospital as a nurse's aide. Sometimes I speak Turkish, other times Kurdish, according to the situation. At the beginning, they knew me as a Kurd. After a long while, when they'd ask me, 'Are you Kurdish or Turkish?' I began to answer 'I'm Armenian!' I feel more comfortable with myself when I speak openly about my origins, about my identity.

In the department in which I work I gave breakfast and other meals for a sick Turkish woman all day long. I was an assistant. At first I spoke German, after that, I began speaking Turkish to her. We became close after a while. One day we met in the corridor. We greeted each other. Seeing the Turkish motif on the sweater I was wearing, she asked me:

'Are you a Turk?'

'No,' I replied. 'I'm Armenian!'

This smiling woman, who had behaved lovingly to me for a whole week, suddenly changed.

'O.K., O.K.!' she said, and quickly absented herself. As I watched her flee from me, I just laughed. But that's how it is! The Turks still don't accept us as we are. And we're still scared of Turks!

But is it only Turks we're scared of? Not at all! We're also afraid of Kurds. No matter how much we may speak Kurdish, or how much we may love Kurds, when we're among them we still hide our Armenian identity. We're still afraid of the Kurds.

It doesn't matter how much time passes, no matter how old we get, how long we've lived in Germany—we're still unable to speak openly about our own identity, about our present or our past. Before speaking about it, we automatically look around to see who's listening. If the 'coast is clear,' we speak. In the old days, we couldn't even do that much.

The entire environment in Adıyaman is Kurdish. Can we say that we're Armenian in their midst? By no means! There are plenty who have moved away from Adıyaman, others who have fled! Only a few of us remain. It's now been ninety years since the deportation of the Armenians. Most died, and those who survived became Muslims; but we're still called 'converts.' That word 'convert' irritates me to no end! I get very angry when I hear it.

Even if we pray five times a day—and for that matter, even if we were to pray fifteen times a day!—the stigma of being a convert will never be removed from us, the mark of the 'infidel' never erased! Where does this fanaticism come from? What is this selfishness? This hatred? I simply cannot understand it.

You might say that it comes from ignorance, but it really is unconnected to ignorance. It has to do with one's humanity. It may not suit your interests; you may not think like them, but both the ignorant and the learned say 'infidel!' Both the Turk and the Kurd use the term 'convert.' It's the same in Germany as it is in Adıyaman!

There's a Turkish girl who was born and raised in Germany, who finished nursing school in Germany; she's doing her nursing residency in the hospital where I work. She's a happy, sweet thing. She would help me, work with me to make sure the matters in the kitchen ran smoothly. It's like music when she says 'Miss Sultan!'

One day, while we were distributing the lunch meal, a Turkish woman who was a patient at the time asked me:

'Miss Sultan, where are you from?'

'I'm from Adıyaman!' I told her.

'So, are you Kurdish? Or are you Turkish?' she continued.

'I'm Armenian!' I told her.

'I'm from Malatya!' she responded. And that was the end of the conversation. She began to eat her lunch after that. But the young nursing assistant had been listening to us talk. And that was the end of that! From that day forward she distanced herself from me. She broke off relations with me! This same girl with the smiling eyes who had always treated me and addressed me like I was her older sister, now began to give me the evil eye!

Finally, I couldn't take it any more. I asked her:

'Güldane, what happened to you? You used to be different. You didn't used to treat me so coldly. Why did you change all of a sudden?'

'Then I didn't know you were an Armenian!' she answered.

'And if I'm an Armenian, how does that make it different? I'm still the same person; I'm still the same old Sultan! We used to get on so well with each other!'

'I don't want to answer!' she said and cut off our conversation. Nurse Güldane, around whose neck hung a wolf pendant,* never spoke with me again!

I just stood there, wondering to myself what she would do for me if it was I who was ill and she knew that I was Armenian.

Events like these had a profound effect upon me. People always told me, 'Forget about it!', 'Pay it no attention!' But how can you simply ignore such a thing? I was sick for days over what that Nurse Güldane had done.

Sometimes I ask myself: What sort of nation are we that such things would happen to us? If we were really such an evil people, you could say we deserved it. But the Armenians are good people. They're a clean, honest, hard-working nation. So why did these things happen to us? Since we aren't an evil people, it's very hard for a person to be held accountable for all of these evils. The Armenians have never deserved such humiliation.

We ourselves didn't experience that great, horrible disaster, but the great sorrow and bitterness of it remains lodged in our memory… Even the memory of it causes us great sorrow! Although we didn't experience those dreadful days, or the 'deportation to oblivion,' those events have left indelible marks upon us. And if that's us, how did those who actually experienced it deal with it?

In general, the Kurds over there were encouraged to kill the Armenians. Everyone knows that. The Kurds all speak about 'the massacre of the infidels!' They never say 'We did it!' They simply say that 'there was a massacre of the infidels.'

---

* While the lone or grey wolf are traditional symbols of the Turkish nation, during the period of the Turkish Republic it has increasingly been used as an identifying symbol of the ultra-nationalist parties.

When they began to feel what it was like to be on the other side of the fence and to suffer the pain that they had caused others, the older Kurds would say, 'Good! Didn't they kill more than a few Armenians in their time? Now they are paying for what they have done!'

I don't at all blame all Kurds and Turks for what happened. I don't have any problem with you. My grief and pain is with those who planned this disaster down to the last detail and those who carried it out. I would be content if these ones would just come out and admit the truth of what happened.

I don't harbor any enmity, either toward Turks or Kurds! I don't have even the slightest desire to extract some revenge or to settle accounts. There are both the good and the bad amongst Turks and Kurds! I can get on very well with both Turks and Kurds. My problem, my anger and irritation is with those who ordered and carried out this massacre. Those who committed these crimes should be ashamed! May God bring a thousand disasters upon their heads!

I can't even kill a bird. I can't even swat a fly. How am I going to kill a human being? I wouldn't kill another person for all the money in the world!

I just want some peace of mind! I don't want to be humiliated by people calling me 'convert' or 'infidel'; I don't want to have to act like a Muslim when I don't believe in Islam. I don't want to have to hide the fact that I'm Armenian, neither in Germany nor in Adıyaman. I want to be seen as who I am, and I want to be as I am seen.

Part Six

"See what happens to a young man when he goes abroad…"

The years abroad

Meline and I came together again at her house on a Monday afternoon in early June.

Expounding on my earlier mention of these persons over the phone, I now spoke to her at length about Kegham's student Zakarya and about Master Sarkis, who had also known him. Meline was very interested in what Zakarya had had to say. I helped to satisfy her curiosity.

She listened to the odyssey of Master Sarkis' life with tear-filled eyes. We had a good laugh at the story "We shouldn't have let him beat the priest!" But then the merry breeze that blew between us began to subside, disappearing completely. Meline grew serious, and with a voice clouded over by sorrow, she said, "Oh Lord, if only the Turks and the Kurds hadn't beaten the Armenians!" The 'If only's followed each other like links in a chain:

> If only this great calamity had never occurred… If only there were no massacres anywhere in the world… If only the millions of Turks, Armenians and Kurds had lived together in Anatolia like brothers before 1914. If so, Anatolia could have been a true mosaic of religions, languages, cultures and nations.…

> The Greeks and Armenians were a blessing to Anatolia. Can you so easily rebuild and restore so many hearths that were extinguished? Can one so easily preserve a culture that has no owner?

These were the same things that Zakarya had expressed… These were the same things that Kirkor Ceyhan, Vahram Karabent and Master Sarkis had seen and experienced.…

In fact, every Armenian was a single drop in a vast ocean of sorrow. Every Armenian was a flower whose heart had been burnt by fire, a flower struggling to bloom upon scorched earth. This conflagration had not just consumed the Armenians; it had affected the very character of Anatolia and its people.

As Meline, I feel this profound sense of sorrow in this fertile ground which had brought me into existence. But as an Istanbul Armenian, I didn't personally experience nearly as much bitterness as those in Anatolia.

Kegham was the same.… He hadn't lost any of his family in the massacres. But Kegham had suffered very much for the crime of simply having been an Armenian and a Leftist. When we reached our decision to go abroad, we didn't know what hardships and sorrows the coming years and the road ahead would bring.

The injustices that were done to us came very hard for both of us. Who wants to leave their land, the soil upon which they've lived? Who wants to detach themselves from one's own homeland? Do people abandon Istanbul, this jewel of a city, with a light heart and a song in their mouths?

"Give me your hand, Paris"

Being an English teacher at the Istanbul Işık Engineering High School was actually a well-paying job. With the money I was earning I managed to spare myself from having to live in that single-room basement apartment in which I'd lived for so long. I rented a cheery, two-room house that was more to my liking. But my life wasn't just money or a cheery house!

Think for a minute, my dear Kemal: what would you do if you were loathed in Turkey simply for being a Turk, if you lost the position to which you had every right to occupy, simply for being a Turk, if you had to hide the fact that you were a Turk simply in order to be able to get a job as a teacher?

The difficulties of living as a foreigner in Germany, the injustices you often face as a Turk here make you want to revolt. You can't ever feel at peace. But if you can't take it, you can always say to yourself, 'If it gets too bad, I can always pack up and go back to my own country!' But what can I do? What can we do? Where can we go?

Good heavens! I burnt my bridges when I left Istanbul! But I can still see it before my eyes as if I was there yesterday…

At the time as we left Kegham's older sister—Ayda, the one closest to him in age—underwent an operation. 'You go on ahead,' he told me, 'I'll come after my sister has recovered!'

When the plane took off from Yeşilköy Airport[*] bound for Paris on November 1, 1969, my heart remained behind.

Kegham's oldest sister worked as a seamstress in Paris. I went to her place. She was there waiting for me at the airport in Paris.

We reached her house that evening. She lived with her daughter in a single-room attic apartment in a seven-story building. There was neither a bath nor a toilet. The disorder and clutter was knee-deep.

---

[*] Since renamed the "Atatürk International Airport," it is Istanbul's main airport and Turkey's major international hub.

What I saw when I arrived in Paris was a hovel…

We were still living out of our suitcases. We didn't have a place of our own. When Kegham arrived we were then four persons in that one-room attic….

The day after I arrived in Paris we went to a cloth cutting and sewing workshop where my sister-in-law worked. Because it was before the New Year, they were working non-stop. I sat down in front of a sewing machine and began to sew…

When we decided to leave Istanbul I didn't know that I would be sitting in front of a sewing machine in Paris. My hands would be busy sewing clothes, but my mind was thinking about the future. How would this venture end? Where would our decision to leave ultimately leave us? Kegham would come soon. Fine, I'm sewing clothes—but what would Kegham do? How would we get by? My eyes were opened more with each passing day. It wouldn't be possible to work as teachers in Paris.

İşte hendek, işte deve	Here is a ditch, here is a camel
Ya geçersin ya düşersin.	You either pass or fall into it.
Baktın olmaz vazgeçersin	You see it can't be done and give up
Zordur almak bizden kızı.	It's difficult to have a daughter taken from us.

The words to this song were always in my mouth… But our sorrow was not about giving or accepting brides in marriage. We were looking for a branch on which we could come to rest, a bit of earth on which to land. We didn't have either a branch or a spot of earth. But most importantly, we refused to even reconsider our decision to leave…

I informed Kegham of the situation in Paris….

It was a full two months, meaning the very end of 1969, when Kegham arrived in Bonn by train. He had some former students there. He spoke with them about the working conditions in Germany, and about whether it was better to live in Paris or Bonn.

From Bonn, they went to the city of Bochum. A new university was being founded in Bochum, and they would have an Armenian Language Department. He might be able to find a position there…

A short while later Kegham took the train to Paris. We lived together in that little one-room attic apartment. He saw the seamstress workshop. He was shocked! He had never imagined such difficulties!

It never even occurred to us to stroll around Paris and see it…. We sat down and spoke with one another. Kegham told me about his conversations with his students in Germany. The conditions in Paris were glaring. It made more sense to go and settle in Bochum. There was no time to lose. At least in Bochum we had Mihran, Kegham's former student from the Tıbrevank Lycée. Without any hesitation, we decided to go to Bochum.

We arrived in Cologne on January 5, 1970. Mihran met us at the station. I remember that date well, because it's the date of Armenian Christmas.

Mihran was our lifeline at first. We were totally dependent upon him… He concerned himself with everything, from the place where we stayed to the place we worked. He neglected his own affairs and ran around taking care of us. At first, we rented a room in a cheap hotel near the university. There wasn't even a bathroom in which to bathe. In order to wash up we had to either go to the public pools or the dormitory where Mihran lived.

A short while after that, the university went out on its mid-year recess. We waited for the summer courses, which began in April.

Mihran registered us both for the university. There were certain advantages in being a student, the most important of which was that we could attend the university's language courses for free.

When we arrived we didn't know a single word of German. Although I knew four languages, none of them were of any use there. Kegham would perhaps be able to find work because of his thorough knowledge of Armenian, but what would I do?

"Like a fish out of water"

We were both like fish out of water. The world that we had hewed out for ourselves—albeit with a thousand and one difficulties—all remained in Istanbul. We had to start again from nothing…. We felt like two fish in an empty fishbowl. We were desperate to find water in which to swim, air to breathe. We looked at the world around us, we heard the strange voices all around us, but it was all alien to us. When people don't understand, they become nervous and irritable. During those moments of alienation and detachment, there was no purpose, no joy in life. Only those who've experienced it know how difficult it is!

It was very difficult for me to try and begin my life again, but for Kegham it was every harder. There was no hint of the broad social network he had had in Istanbul, none of the esteem that there had been for him within the Armenian community. It was very hard for him to have to request help from his own student for every little thing.

We began to attend a German language course together. We sat together in the same classroom. Kegham, who had known everything in Istanbul, who had always been there to guide Meline in everything, who had always led Meline, now had to sit next to Meline and learn a language with her.

It wasn't long before I began to understand the similarities between German and English. My knowledge of English made it easier for me to learn German. For the first time, my knowledge in something exceeded that of Kegham; I picked up German quicker than he did. This situation gave rise to a number of arguments between Kegham and myself. Maybe it would have been easier if we hadn't gone to the same courses, but there wasn't another course to choose from. He would get upset when he didn't perform correctly, when he spoke incorrect sentences.... I understand it better now. When I think back on some of our arguments, I laugh till it hurts.... Oh Lord, what days those were!

Two months after we began the German course Kegham began to work in the university's Armenian Department. He had to work; we had almost no money for food.

Six months after I began taking the language course, I took the tests and passed them. I was placed first, they told me....

I could already express myself well in the new language. After learning German I gained a good deal of self-confidence.... Inside me, that little doorman's daughter Meline, who had once refused to eat because she was so determined to study, was now smiling.

In her past life in Istanbul, Meline, the doorman's daughter, had built herself an ocean in which to swim, a branch upon which to land. Nothing had been given to her. She had entered the race under unequal conditions, and had reached the finishing line by virtue of her own hard work and brains.

She would rebuild a life for herself in Germany. If she had managed to overcome the obstacles that had emerged in her path after primary school, if she had broken the narrow bonds in which her mother had tried to place her, she would be able to overcome any hardship that Bochum had to offer. Sometimes, my own mind and thoughts caused the 'little Meline' inside me great difficulty, at other times, it was the little Meline who gave me my enthusiasm for life.

But in any case, when I had left Istanbul, I had made a clear decision: Meline was not going back under any condition! So act accordingly! Full speed ahead!

"I have to find a job and start working"

It was in the days immediately following my exam…. One morning after I had fought with Kegham over nothing at all the thought came to my head: I had to find a job and begin working!

I left the house and went straight to the newly built Central Library of Bochum University. While I had attended the German language course I had frequently visited the library. Through talking with people there I had learned where everything was.

The name of the professor who was responsible for the library was Herr Pflug. I received an appointment with him from his secretary and entered the professor's office. If he is alive, his ears should be ringing! I explained my situation to him:

'Herr Pflug,' I said, 'my name is Meline. Only eight months ago I was forced to leave Turkey with my husband. One week ago I finished the university's German language course. Now I have to find work. Might there be any jobs here for me? What jobs might I be able to do here? Can you help me?'

My dear Kemal, you wouldn't believe it: the man took me and brought me straightaway to the center were they kept the original texts and manuscripts. He never asked me another question. All he said was two sentences:

'You'll work here. My secretary will explain the work to you!'

I was beside myself with joy. I had never expected this much. It was such a stroke of good fortune to find work in the university library…

My insides were jumping up and down with joy and excitement! Fortune had come right up to me and looked me in the eye and said: 'Let's go, then. Here's a branch to land on in Germany, a spot of earth on which to come to rest. Full speed ahead!'

"My right to live is finally recognized"

I began to work. For the first time in my life I was around Germans on a daily basis. It was an important opportunity for me for the purposes of bettering my German. I spent much leisure time and ate many meals with the young woman who was my boss and with my other colleagues. My boss's name was Frau Cläre Schuth. My relations with the people around me gradually developed and deepened. I was the only foreigner in our department. We were all practically the same age, and the work environment was very friendly and nurturing. I felt very much at ease there. Because I was the 'new girl,' my friends and my boss wanted to know all about me: Where was I from? Why had I come to Bochum?

Who was I? What was I? What about my past? What about my future? My family, my husband, my children? And so on and so forth… In my halting German I did my best to answer their questions.

They weren't at all shocked or surprised about me being an Armenian. And I was able to introduce myself as an Armenain without any fear or hesitation…. My boss had acquired extensive knowledge about Turkey. To the best extent that I could understand, our political views were pretty close to one another's. It was as if we viewed the world from the same set of spectacles. That was something that brought us even closer together.

One day they asked me why I left Turkey. Without any self-pity or attempt to arouse sympathy for myself, I told them very clearly what had happened. My boss was most affected from the fact that I'd been denied an assistantship because I was Armenian. They also asked me questions about university life in Turkey.

I was the only worker among my work colleagues who had graduated from the university and who knew five languages.

On another day they asked me about Kegham. I told them. During those days Kegham had begun to teach at Bochum University.

One day, my boss approached me.

'Meline,' she said, 'They're looking for an English teacher at the high school in the district where I live. Does the job interest you?'

'Is it possible for me to work here as an English teacher?' I asked.

'Certainly!' she replied, 'Why wouldn't it be?'

So she set up a meeting between myself and the school's principal. Two days later Frau Cläre Schuth and I paid a visit to the house of the school principal in Bochum's Gerthe District. The principal asked me about the work that I did, and whether or not I had worked as a high school teacher in Turkey. I told him about having worked at the Işık Engineering High School. He didn't ask anything else. I was thinking to myself, 'Well, so much for that job!', but the principal said, 'Little miss, come to the school on Monday. I would be very pleased if you would work with us.'

I had never dreamed that he would make such a quick decision. I was delighted beyond belief! My boss was happy too. I thanked her greatly.

I returned home very happy and immediately told Kegham the good news. He was excited as well. But I also sensed a hint of sourness in his smile.

I went to the high school on Monday. The principal introduced me to the other teachers. Then he gave me a tour of the school. We went through my job qualifications and other bureaucratic processes.

The school was a boys' high school. All of the instructors were men, and older. I was the only young woman in that great big high school.

One week later I began my first class. It was middle level English for tenth grade students. That was the first time they had ever seen a female teacher. I was going to teach English for the first time at a boys' high school in Germany! Both the students and I found ourselves sharing a mutual surprise and shock.

'Well, Meline!' I told myself, 'You've really waded into deep water this time. You better start swimming.... you don't have any other choice!'

It wasn't my English that made me nervous—it was my German, which I had only begun learning a year ago. I knew student psychology very well. They weren't going to pull any fast ones on me... even if they knew all the tricks for manipulating teachers....

I worked like mad every evening, preparing lessons. I was always trying to better my German—I didn't have a choice!

I got through the school year without any major crisis or disaster. My students all passed to the eleventh grade.

The director called me in to see him again:

'Miss Meline, you've made a great start, and really progressed. I thank you. You've completed the first step toward being a teacher. Now I would request of you the next and most important step. You must see your students who have passed through the high school unto the very end of their journey, you must prepare them and see them all the way to matriculation! In other words, you must now prepare final examinations for the high school!'

I was going to teach these same students for the next three years, until they passed the matriculation exams at the end of the thirteenth year. I rolled up my sleeves and set to work...

To be honest, during the first matriculation exams I gave, I wasn't sure if it was me or the students being tested. And I still don't know for sure! It was a very difficult matter. The older instructors were skeptical. Anyway, I was the only foreign instructor at the whole school. All the other instructors listened to the questions that were asked and the answers that were given. But I was confident because only English was spoken during the exam. After the first matriculation exam, I said to myself, 'That's the way it's done, Meline! It's over! Your right to live has now been recognized. You can now step confidently on German soil!'

The dictionary of Armenian mythology

After having begun to teach, Kegham received a new job offer. One of the teaching staff of Bochum University's Armenian Department, Professor H. W. Haussig, was overseeing the publication of an immense dictionary of mythology titled *Wörterbuch der Mythologie*. He commissioned Kegham to write the section on Armenian Mythology. It was a very important work.

Kegham devoted all of his energy and time to the preparation of this work. He had already published his own dictionary of mythology when he was still in Istanbul. Professor Haussig had liked this work and proposed that he and Kegham collaborate on the project.

Kegham always worked at home; I had to take public transportation and make three transfers every day to get to my job at the school.

Kegham became totally withdrawn into himself. He hardly left the house. His social relations narrowed significantly. I was forced to deal alone with the outer world.

In all of Bochum, we were just four Armenians: myself, Kegham, Mihran and a female doctor. Now and then, a student from Tıbrevank would come through for a visit. But this narrow little world began to feel constricting to me. As a teacher I had to become more involved in the life of the school. Kegham, on the other hand, wanted with all his might to limit our connection with the outside world. We would get into fights for no reason at all. However, our economic situation had improved greatly. Since coming to Bochum we had moved from a tiny little attic apartment to a roomy and well-lit house.

After entering the working world, I was gradually able to adapt to life in Germany. But Kegham always rightly sought the broad social network and vibrant life of Istanbul. But Istanbul remained far, far away. That had been a different time, a different place. This feeling of being out of place and the accompanying loneliness began to tell on Kegham. He grew depressed. I was desperate to make him happy, and Kegham also worked to make me happy in his own way.

It had been six years since we had come to Germany 'We've managed to keep ourselves afloat—even get established!' we told ourselves.

But at one point they discovered something like a boil growing on Kegham's neck, right over his aorta. At first we were optimistic, but his pains and suffering increased. Mihran's wife, who was a doctor, subjected it to a proper examination. It turned out to be very serious. A cancerous tumor had affixed itself directly onto his aorta!

"There's one other possibility, but it, too, might mean death"

Kegham began to fight against the cancer. He resisted. He wasn't going to surrender to death. It was horrible to see the man I loved waste away a little more from day to day. He underwent a very difficult operation. In order to remove the tumor, it was necessary to cut his aorta. The doctors told us about the very grave complications that might arise after the operation. 'He might wind up paralyzed,' they said. But there was no other way of saving him. He agreed to the operation. He lay there on the operating table, but just as the doctors had warned, while they were cutting his aorta and sewing it back up, his brain hadn't received enough blood, and when he awoke after the operation he found himself to be paralyzed.

In the period before his operation, Kegham hadn't fully understood the situation. But afterward, Kegham became realistic enough to see the bitter end of the affair.

'Let's bring my mother here,' he told me, 'Don't stay here all alone!'

I did what he said. In any case his mother was all alone in Istanbul and had fallen into a state in which she couldn't live by herself.

During the four years in which Kegham was sick, the only German who came to our house to visit was Paul Gerhard, one of my colleagues from the high school. One sunny day he said:

'Kegham, come, I want to take you on a little drive in my car.'

So, the three of us piled into Paul's car. He drove us to a hill from which there was a very beautiful view of the Ruhr river. It was as if we were back in Istanbul, standing on Çamlıca Hill! It was as if the Bosphorus, bright blue, was flowing below our feet and into the endless distance!

Upon seeing this view of the Ruhr river, Kegham was very moved.

'Ah,' he sighed, 'if only we were in Istanbul!' At that I began weeping inside.

Afterward, he pointed to the lush greenery on the side of the hill.

'Look, Paul,' he said, 'aren't those gardens just beautiful?'

'Kegham Bey,' Paul replied, 'those aren't gardens, it's a cemetery!'

'Is that so? Then bury me over there!'

'Whoa! Kegham my dear! Slow down!' I said, 'What are you talking about?'

'Meline, my dear' he said, 'my time's drawing close! When that day comes, do as I have asked, if it's possible! I would definitely like to have my body brought to Istanbul, but even more I want to be close to you.... If I'm in Istanbul, you won't be able to visit me often! And anyway, we've become natives of this place already! Give my watch to my brother in Paris, give my Armenian dictionary to my friend in Osnabrück. Be good, and take good care of yourself! Don't send me back to Istanbul! I want to always be close to you! Look how it resembles the Bosphorus here!'

Black earth under the snow

Less than a month had passed since he had shown me where he wanted to be buried.

Shortly before morning, on January 5, 1980, that pair of magical eyes that had bewitched me closed for the last time, never to reopen. We had arrived in Germany on January 5, 1970. It was as if he had actually been counting the days: exactly ten years since our arrival he left Germany and the world and his soul departed!

After twenty-three years together, Kegham of Istanbul, the man who had smitten me the first time I saw him in the teachers' lounge of the Armenian middle school in Kurtuluş, back in 1957, the man of whom I had said, 'either him or no one!', the man whom I had loved, respected and trusted, the man who had set my life on its journey, this Kegham had now silently disappeared....

The only person I had left on my side was my mother. And she was in Istanbul, three thousand kilometers away.

Winding our way, like a torrent through a valley, being blown like wind over the hills, we had made our way to Bochum! Kegham had been here, and now he was gone! I was all alone at that time! I just let go at that point.... I cried... I cried... but after a while a voice came from somewhere inside me....

'Pull yourself together, Meline! Some die and others live! Look at all that you have... After that you must be stronger!'

All I had left then was my mother, only my mother who held my hand!

'Meline, my child, pull yourself together!' she said. 'You did what you could! He was beset by unendurable pain. You will prosper still! Wipe the tears from your eyes! Come, my child, and let's fulfill our last duty to Kegham as he deserves! Don't go mad with grief! Tomorrow we'll notify his friends!'

My mother's warmth roused me and dispersed the clouds of grief that had surrounded me....

Who did I have to tell?

First of all, I telephoned Paul Gerhard, who lived on the same street. God bless him! He came running even at that early hour. He expressed his condolences.

'May our friends be well, Paul!' I said. 'We knew this day would come, but I didn't know it would be so soon! Do you remember when we went to the hill on the green banks of the Ruhr river, and what Kegham's last wish was?'

'Could I forget?' he said.

'But it's a Protestant graveyard.... what do we do? Do you think they'd agree to bury a Gregorian Armenian from Istanbul?'

'Why not? Even if religions are different, isn't God the same for all? I'll look into it. The fellow who gives religious instruction at our school is also a minister at the Protestant church attached to the cemetery. Let me speak with him.'

So Paul went to take care of the burial permission. After that I notified our little Armenian world, which consisted of only three persons. Mihran and his wife came quickly... In this great, big world we were only four persons: Mihran, his wife, my mother and myself! We hugged one another... We wept to one another! My mother tried to comfort the rest of us.

We wiped away our tears and discussed how we would perform the funeral.

Paul returned, having received the cemetery's permission to have Kegham interred there. 'And while you're there, make sure you get it for three!' Paul had said. 'That's the way the world is... one day you're here, the next you're gone!'

And he was right.... I purchased plots for Kegham, for my mother and for myself.

Some of the church's burial functionaries took Kegham's body and left. The funeral was to be held two days later. Twenty years ago there weren't as many Armenians in Germany as there are now. The only place that there were enough Armenians to come together was in Cologne. We looked for an Armenian priest. We found one only in Aachen, which was two hundred kilometers away.

Kegham was buried on January 8, 1980. Beginning that evening, snow fell until it was knee deep. The air outside was freezing. Everywhere, snow and ice! We gathered in the Protestant church in Stiepel in the afternoon. Kegham was in his coffin. We waited at one end for the priest to come. Because of his distress at the weather outside, he didn't know what to do! Snow gusts and flurries blew and stopped, blew and stopped. The icy wind penetrated everyone's bones. We all froze. My feet were frozen stiff. I couldn't even feel them. I was shivering... We all looked down the road, watching, waiting for the priest to arrive from Aachen. No one could get through. The roads were like ice.

The hour grew late. No one came or went! Soon it would be evening... what should we do?

The Protestant minister from the church approached me:

'I'm a Protestant,' he said, 'but I am familiar with the rules of the Orthodox Church, and with their prayers and rites. If you'll permit me, I will perform the service instead of the Armenian priest!'

I agreed and accompanied by the prayers of the Protestant priest we brought Kegham and laid him to rest in the black earth, under the snow. Then we covered him with the snowy, icy earth.

The Ruhr river flowed silently, endlessly below us. Rivers flow into seas, seas into oceans, and the world keeps on turning.

Kegham of Istanbul had stood and watched the Ruhr flow by from Stiepel Hill, imagining that it was his beloved Bosphorus....

There was not even a word from Istanbul...

Oh, beautiful Istanbul, wasn't Kegham your son, too?

Part Seven

My Heart Laughs with You

Kegham's grave

On the second Sunday of the month I visited Kegham's grave with Meline. The day was sunny and hot, the surroundings were bright and verdant.

The plots of Kegham and Meline's mother lay side-by-side. The tombstones had been specially made according to Armenian custom. The ends of the Armenian crosses were stylized to look like flowers.

"For centuries," Meline said, "Armenian gravestones have all been carved as if they were works of art. The stone carvers worked chunks of volcanic stone from Mounts Ararat and Erciyes, decorating them with sacred motifs from Armenian mythology. The Armenian gravestones are known as *khachkar*, or cross-stone. I couldn't find a master carver who would make his tombstone in this style. This is the best I could have done in Germany. Six years after Kegham's death I lost my mother. We brought her here to be buried. May the two of them rest in perfect peace!"

The top of the grave was decorated with white pansies and Rhododendrons.

Meline spoke a heartfelt prayer, after which she said:

"Kegham loved white pansies very much. After his gravestone was placed, directly at its head I planted a white magnolia tree, which first blooms in spring. Kegham really liked magnolias. I like them too. Somehow, they remind me of Istanbul!"

The engravings on the two tombstones seemed to be summing up the sorrowful and bitter life stories of these two people:

Kegham İşkol
Born: 1924, Istanbul
Died: 1980, Bochum

Vartanush Demirciyan
Born: 1902, Sivas
Died: 1986, Bochum

May things always be as bright as the pansies blooming in the earth over the place where they lay!

"Our religions are different, our God is the same"

Within the silent darkness of the night, Kegham's grave, his gravestone, the inscription, all sparkled brightly in my mind!

In my dreams I traveled from Sivas in 1902 to Bochum in 1986, from Istanbul in 1924 to Bochum in 1980. At one point I saw Miss Kraft... then, the men, women, children and infants sent away and deported.... after that, I heard the cries and wailing of my son.... The Euphrates was flowing red.... Then, I traveled from Kırşehir to Nevşehir.... When? How? With whom?... As we crossed the bridge over the Kızılırmak river at Gülşehir, I saw a child fall into the river... I jumped in to save it... I rescued the child—but I could then see as if the child I had saved was my son!

I held my son's hand.... we marched together... then, we were in Sivas.... in Kangal, my father appeared before me...

"Father, what are you doing here?"

"I came to look for Meline's mother!" he replied. Meline's mother was smiling. She was carrying a book.

"Whose book is that, Aunt Vartanush?" I asked.

"I'm reading a new book that Kegham wrote!" she answered. My father was as happy as always, talkative as always...

"Come now, we're hungry!" he said. "We're about to depart. We can't do that on an empty stomach..."

So we went to the banks of the Kızılırmak and sat down and ate... the waters flowing by sparkled brightly in the sunshine....

"Come, let's head off" my father said. But he didn't say where we were going....

I stood up... I looked at the time: it was the middle of the night, an hour in which the waters should have been tranquil; and I was still under the covers....

Early the next morning, I dialed up Turkey and spoke to my mother in Denizli. I told her all about my dream.... It was as if my father had really been alive... I had spoken with Meline's mother in my dream... we had broken bread together....

"My son," she said, "May all your dreams be blessed! You miss your father. You broke bread together! Meline's mother, your father and Meline's husband were all hungry.... Let's give something to the poor!"

"Should we?"

"Sure! Why not? Armenians and Turks, Muslims and Christians, they're all one... all are the servants of the Lord... Our religions may be different, but our God is the same.... Let's say a really nice blessing... May it reach their spirits!

That afternoon I telephoned Meline and told her about the dream I had....

"Meline, I told my mother about my dream... 'They were hungry, let's give something for the poor!' she said."

"So let's do it, my dear! Let's do it—but where should we do it?"

"We can't do it here, Meline!" I said. "If you're going to give to the poor, you should hold it with those who know its value. I'll cover the expenses from here. My family will hold a feast in our village!"

So, along with my mother, my older sister and Meline we decided to hand out *lokma*.* One sack of flour, two cans of sunflower oil, ten kilos of sugar...

So one Friday, my older sister's family, my uncle's family, neighbors and other relatives all gathered in Honaz at the house of my older brothers İsmet and Ali İhsan and handed out lokma. They went out and gave out loads of lokma to all passers-by, to the neighbors, to those in the market, to those sitting in front of the coffee houses, to children and even to passing animals....

On that day, Honaz became a little more beautiful with the taste and smell of the lokma that was distributed and eaten for the spirits of my father, of Meline's mother Vartanush, of Kegham, and of the countless souls who had died without prayer, without blessing and without even a burial shroud...

The ears of those present were filled with the words, "Peace upon those who say a special prayer for our sakes!"

"My heart laughs with you"

From the very first moment of the professional development course for Turkish teachers in Dortmund, my dear Meline, the flower that I plucked

---

*   . A traditional Turkish sweet; "Turkish delight."

from your glances and placed deep in my heart had taken root and bloomed, and had spread its roots to every corner of my being.

With your love I managed to overcome all the obstacles in the way of getting to know you.... Through your love I was able to understand the prejudices, misconceptions and insensitivities of my own world...

If I hadn't gotten to know you, if I had never spoken with you, if you hadn't trusted me enough to allow me to enter your world, I would only be half-alive.... With you, I managed to take another step in the direction of becoming human.

My dear Meline, whenever I look in your eyes, a turquoise blue water flows out of the songs of Istanbul. From you I was able to hear the hidden sadness of these songs. I saw the tears of yearning in your songs. A glowing ember fell into my heart: it animates the dreams of my subconscious!

From you and from people with whom I spoke in order to understand you, I felt that every Armenian flower is watered with tears.

How many roses have I brought you, Meline? What colors shall I use to paint your universe? But the pain of this frightful wound has not been smothered, even with embroidery, songs or flowers!

Who has picked the unripe fruit from the branch of Ararat? You, I, all of us were the blossoming branches of this land. They destroyed you in broad daylight... They killed you at the dawn of the century.... Who sowed this seed of hatred in the mountains and the rocks?

I am angry at my own silence.

Was this Bosphorus, was this sea really all blue, Meline?

Are you a drop in this ocean of sorrow, Meline? Are you the rose that blooms sevenfold in the scorched earth?

This child, this heart, this seed, this earth, these churches in which no more prayers are read—did they all weep? Did you know them? How alone I am in your loneliness! How deceived I've been, how I've erred, with words, dreams and prejudices...

Meline, you are the indispensable in my soul, the blessing of my earth!

A friendship has been formed with you, a bond of brotherhood established.

You taught us...

You taught us languages, identities; you taught us people, about humanity...

It's good that I loved you...

I loved you… and my world was transformed!
When I understood you, I began to understand myself!
I dedicate my book to you…
My heart rejoices with you!

Extertal, 12 April, 2000

A final note

During the course of preparing this book, I knocked on the doors of a great many Armenians. Not a single one of them knew me beforehand. It was the first time that a Turk had ever asked them about their past; the first time that a Turk had wanted them to dig up their deeply buried but unforgettable memories. These people trusted me enough not only to open their doors to me, but also to open their hearts, their emotions, their thoughts and their consciousness. Some of them did so on the condition that I did not write down anything. Others, that I didn't mention their names. And others said, "Write my name, take my picture, write exactly as I tell you!" And still others said, "I'll tell you, so that you will know and understand, but don't write down these parts…" I have acted in accordance with each of their wishes.

Those whose voices you read in this book have stories similar to those who wished their stories not to appear here, and, no doubt, of those who didn't wish to talk. These people opened themselves, their thoughts and feelings, to a Turk who was willing to listen. But the experiences and the stories that they recounted are not simply their own thoughts and feelings; above all, they are the saga of a family or an entire lineage.

When they spoke, I felt that the people before me were being compelled into remembering their own past. For my part, I was forced to ask questions that would jog their memories, and make them reopen old wounds that had long since healed and scarred over. I observed that every Armenian, when speaking with a Turk—with a Turkish friend—censured their own past somewhat and either consciously or unconsciously repressed certain memories that might make their Turkish friend uncomfortable. In the same way, I also discerned that when a Turk speaks with an Armenian friend, he would skip over the past that was so burdened with sorrow for the person before him, or avoid expressing his true suspicions and thoughts. And much later, when speaking with Meline, I understood that I, too, had made such a mental manoeuvre by not thinking to say to Meline, my Turkish teacher, for two whole years, "You're Armenian. You have your own language, culture and past. Tell us about your own past one time!"

To remember, and to express one's memories, are important functions, both for individuals and for societies. Being able to speak honestly about one's deep memories, prejudices, social and emotional conditioning, fears and taboos—all of those parts of our consciousness that affect our behavior, our reactions, our thought patterns and our identities, this has a calming effect on both individuals and societies. They help people to make peace with themselves. Aren't social peace, or a culture of peace, and the purging and restoration of a healthy social sub-conscious built on the foundation of trust, tolerance, love and respect for differences?

Every Armenian who spoke with me described themselves by calling to attention the logic of Turkish society, its thought patterns, and the widespread notions and understandings within this society. This was because these persons themselves are children of this country, or this society. Similar value judgments and thought patterns simultaneously dominate the life of the society in which these people live and order their own lives, as well.

I saw how those Armenians with whom I met had lived with sorrows and pains that they were unable to describe, even unwilling to describe. When speaking with them, I understood that every Armenian was a single drop in an ocean of pain and sorrow, each one a flower that reemerged and grew on a scorched plain, a heart that had been scarred and wounded.

I didn't submit my questions to anyone in advance. I thought it more appropriate to learn those things that had happened to them face to face, to hear in person the things that passed through their minds and their hearts and to write them down. These persons, whom I had never met before, sometimes recounted the same events; they even used similar words and phrases when doing so! For the repetitions that are found in the text, I request the reader's understanding.

I would like to extend my heartfelt gratitude to those Armenians who were willing to speak to me.

A final note

During the past year, both Vahram Karabent and Kirkor Ceyhan have passed away. May they rest in peace! May they forever reside in the Light! I mention their names here in awe and respect for their memory....

I would also like to thank all of those who helped me or offered their suggestions or ideas as I traveled through Anatolia and as I searched for Armenians who would speak to me in Germany: in Amasya, the master carpenter Ali; in Taşova, the teacher Sedat, Zülfikâr and the grocer Engin; in Erzurum, the teacher Mustafali; in Kars, the police officer from Dinar who showed me the way; in Ani, the soldiers who were serving there; in Germany, the teacher Kemal Uzun; in France, Arsen Ceyhan.

I want to express my thanks and gratitude to my friend and big brother, Doğan Görsev, who went over my manuscript with a fine-toothed comb, correcting my mistakes and offering suggestions.

My hope is that this book will open the way for a greater familiarity with the Armenians with whom we Turks and Kurds have lived for centuries, with their history, culture and national identity, a greater understanding and sensitivity to the sorrows that they bear within themselves, a sounder and unprejudiced reconsideration of our pasts, both shared and separate, and thereby, to the development of heartfelt, warm and friendly relations between us. If this book contributes in any way to the achievement of these things, I will consider myself blessed.

The United Nations General Assembly has passed a decision declaring the year 2000 as The Year of the Culture of Peace. I am publishing this book with the hope that it, too, will contribute to the development of a culture of peace, both in Turkey and in the world at large.

Bochum, 28 September, 2000

Appendix I: Responses to *You Rejoice My Heart*

Venice, 6 April, 2001
Dear Kemal Bey,

As I was leaving the university a few days ago when the concierge gave me a large package that had arrived from Germany. I had no idea who had sent it or what it contained.

When, after arriving home and opening the package I saw the covers of those two large novels, I quickly understood that it was something interesting. But after opening the first novel and reading the dedication, I began to experience strange emotions that I couldn't entirely understand. Perhaps I have to write this letter to you in order to be able to understand them myself. But the fundamental thought that passes through my mind was this:

That the source of hope will grow, that new diamonds will sparkle, and that new horizons will be opened up....

Anything showing Armenians and Turks living side by side is an imminent reality. But I believe that these two nations, who have been "forced" to live side by side, will, sooner or later, discover a way to live together. More correctly, they will be able to "rediscover" a way.

I see your books—in particular, your "You Rejoice My Heart"—as a new harbinger of these hopes and dreams. May your pen never fail!

With love and warmest wishes,

Professor Dr. Levon Zekiyan
Venice University
Department of Armenian Language and Literature

Quebec, Canada, 17 March, 2002
Mr. Kemal Yalçın,

I read the book that you sent me. I thank you and bless you for this great work of yours.

I cried frequently when reading your book. Because the events [that you recount in your book] called to mind the things that my father and mother recounted to me. My father's mother survived the

"Deportation" in Sivas only with great hardship. His father lost his first wife and all of his children at that time. Theirs is a long story. I will save it for another time.

It is necessary for Turks and Armenians to make peace with one another, and they will some day speak of this. I believe that great progress will be made in the next ten or fifteen years. During the last decade a great number of Turkish writers have begun to write on this topic. Taner Akçam, for instance. I have read both his books. I have just given your book to my mother so that she might read it too. My mother is from Zara, my father from Sivas. My sister studied at the Yessayan Armenian Girls' Lycée. I am sure that I know some of the persons mentioned in your book. I was born in Istanbul in 1958. I came to Canada when I was ten. I haven't been able to return to Turkey because of not having done my military service some thirty-three years ago.

In your book, you give a rich and beautifully detailed portrait of Meline, but there's no photograph of her. I'm curious: who is this person? And what are you doing at this time? Please excuse the jumbled nature of this letter. My Turkish is weak. I've simply written down my thoughts. But thank you again. And congratulations for this beautiful book...

With love and greetings,
Noray Gürnagül / Canada

Ankara, 16 January, 2001
My dear friend Kemal,

When we spoke on the phone before the new year, you asked me "Have I received the book?" I did, in fact, receive two books of poetry, but when I arrived at Özgür University during the new year, I understood what you had meant. If only you had mentioned "You Rejoice My Heart"...

As soon as I received this book I began to read it.... It was difficult for me to put it down. In recent years I haven't read a book that has affected me so. I was very moved. I loved it! Upon finishing the book, I said to myself "This is the epic of a tragedy!"

During the years when I was doing my doctorate in Paris, one Christmas I gave my esteemed professor Jean Gabillard Orhan Kemal's novel "Upon Blessed Ground." After returning to the university after the Christmas-New Year's vacation, the first thing he said to me was "There's no dogmatic theory that can explain exploitation so beautifully!" After reading your book I was reminded of these words of my beloved professor. I said to myself "I have read dozens of books about the Armenian tragedy, but nobody had ever been able to explain this question as beautifully and as profoundly as my dear friend and brother Kemal Yalçın!"

I can't praise you enough. I couldn't be more proud of you. You have already become a great writer. Continue your writing from where you left off.... In short, my heart has grown larger because of "You Rejoice My Heart."

Afterward, I thought to myself that nothing can compare with the power of literature.... Send my greetings to Meline if you see her... Convey to her my thanks and gratitude for having been the means for such a book to be written.

I embrace you with love and friendship,

Docent Dr. Fikret Başkaya / Turkey

Kloten, Zürich, 30.10.2002

Most Esteemed Kemal Bey,

I received the books that you sent. I thank you.

I read "You Rejoice My Heart" in entirety, and got more than halfway through "The Security Trousseau." Both of them are extraordinary works. Although I am not one who reads a great number of books, I was unable to put these books down when not absolutely necessary. Above all else, you have managed to express the events which transpired in a fascinating yet truthful manner.

My dear brother Kemal Bey,

I am now seventy-five years old. You may be sure that until now no Muslim Turk has ever called me "brother!" You are the first to ever say such a thing to me. Even in the middle of Europe, there are those who constantly use the word "infidel"—albeit few in number—without any sense of shame or embarrassment. Unfortunately, such feelings don't seem to exist within them.

Again, I thank you for the books and express to you my greatest gratitude. Be well.

Vahan Şişmanoğlu / Switzerland

Bremen, 17 May, 2001

I don't know how I should address you!
Shall I say "Dear Mr. Yalçın? Dear Kemal Bey?
Beloved Friend?
Beloved Brother?
Ah! I know: I will address you as such:

Beloved Friend, Beloved Brother, My Beloved Turkish Brother Kemal Yalçın!

I can't thank you enough! Words cannot explain the joy and happiness I felt, both while reading "You Rejoice My Heart" and afterward.

In your book I rediscovered a hope that I had lost long ago. When reading your book I restored my belief that the people of the world were friends and the different cultures were brothers to one another. In recent years, world developments have shaken my faith in the goodness of people. But the pages of your book are filled with soft language and love; you have treated subjects from which all of us have experienced, whether knowingly or unawares; to read and to learn the manner in which these persons that you have interviewed approach other humans, and their final words, which are full of friendship and humanity; to read and understand the bitterness and injustice of these events of the past—harsh as they may be; to read how they have nursed and attempted to heal their wounds—as deep as any that people have experienced—mournfully and full of sorrow, but without nurturing an enmity or cursing... all of this has renewed my hope.

Yes, you are right. Those who read your book shall look to the future with hope. I feel as if, within me, beautiful ideas like humanity, brotherhood, friendship, trust, peace, reconciliation and love have all gained new meaning.

I want to have many of my friends and acquaintances in Germany, Turkey and in America read your book; in short, I would like all of those who I know, all my friends and enemies throughout the whole world, to read it. But to the extent that I've heard, your book is no longer available for purchase. What a great shame! Naturally, if the book will cause you some hardship you shouldn't put it out for sale. But if they're going to daily stress that "There's democracy in Turkey!", then they shouldn't create problems because of your book, but give it an award!

I congratulate you on your work and research, and wish you endless success.

Brenda Başar

(Armenian by origin, born in Istanbul, now living in Germany)

Frankfurt, 28 December, 2001

Dear Kemal,

I am reading your book "You Rejoice My Heart." At present I'm about half way through it. I love it so much that I couldn't wait to finish it before writing to you to congratulate you. I decided to quickly pen you a few lines.

I congratulate you and bless you with all my heart. You have broached a subject that very few of our own intellectuals have been willing to touch. In your own original way, you have subjected to inquiry the crimes of humanity that some have wished to bury in the dark wells of history. Your writing style is extremely flowing and effortless. You have managed to connect one subject to the next in a most riveting manner.

[... ...] I believe that the bleeding wound of the genocide will finally be acknowledged by our country due to the efforts of Kemal Yalçın and its honorable intellectuals like him, in whom are pure hearts, beating with a love of humanity and beauty, sparkling intellects and who represent bridges—which are albeit sometimes blocked by enmity and hatred—of friendship between the nations. The dignity of humanity, which has been trampled under foot ever since April 24, 1915, will be redeemed through their efforts. Those who can show this human duty, who can simply humble themselves to learn from the Melines of the world, shall ultimately succeed.

[....]

I send my most sincere regards and greetings to you and your family.

I hope that in the new year all things shall be in accordance with your heart.

Ali Ertem / Germany

Bremen, 22 January, 2001
Dear Tankut Gökçe,
Doğan Book Publishers, Director-General of Publications

I sincerely congratulate you for having published Kemal Yalçın's book "You Rejoice My Heart" in 2000, the year which the United Nations declared as "The Year of the Culture of Peace and Against Violence." This means that it has been necessary to wait for eighty years since the Armenian events for a Turkish writer to shed light on these events! Because of this, the publication of "You Rejoice My Heart" is a hopeful development from the viewpoint of efforts to bring peace within our country. Before Kemal Yalçın, there was Taner Akçam, another Turkish writer who touched on these subjects. Yet, on the basis of simply dry documents found in his book, which was published in Germany in 1996 and in Turkey in 1999, high-level persons who were responsible for these publications have been tried and convicted in Istanbul courts.

In "You Rejoice My Heart" there is a truth from real life. In the book, the real victims, meaning those who actually witnessed [these tragic events of the past], their children and grandchildren, while recounting the things they experienced and felt, all extend their hand to Turks—despite their suffering and sorrow—in the hope of reconciliation.

To my great sadness, I was only able to learn about the events at Musa Dagh, which is only some fifteen kilometers from my hometown, not from Turkish history books, but from a foreign author, in a foreign language.

What really bothered me was not just that my grandfather's generation had closed their eyes to these events—certainly, when I inquired, I learned that there were those who helped the Armenians; more than this, it was the continuation of this censorship during the Republican period and the clear intention of keeping our generation in the dark.

I sincerely hope that after these many years of cruel silence and these pointless attempts to hide the truth, Yalçın's book will stimulate a dialogue of peace in our country, and with contribute to the process of democratization in our country.

With hopes for your success and my greatest esteem,

Dr. Tuncer Miski / Germany

Çeltikçi, (near Burdur) Turkey, 30 May, 2002
Dear Author!

I read your letter. Today I am going to read your other writings. In Burdur, people sometimes say to one another: "I'm sick because of you; Come, take me and nourish me!"

So it is with me. My nerves have collapsed because of the things you've written. But as you wouldn't be able to take me and feed me, what's to become of me? Are you laughing? The name of your book shouldn't be "You Rejoice My Heart," it should be "You Ache My Heart." My heart is ablaze! I told myself that I simply have to tell the people around me about it. No one else thought it was that important.... "Whoa, now! Are they belittling us?" they said.

I read a few pages to my son. His eyes grew red. He had a hard time keeping himself from crying.

My dear author, my brother: when I read "You Rejoice My Heart," my head spun. Some of these things I knew already, some of them I had heard... But I'd never heard this much [about these events]! How much longer will we suffer so from the crimes—not of the people, but of the leaders? The things that emerged from us, the things that they concocted... I am heartsick! How could you stand it when you wrote those things? The people around call those to whom they feel close "Our girl" or "Our boy." I accept you as my son. When I read the things you wrote, I became your mother, who gives you her blessing and sends you on your way to the places where you did your research.

I am writing to you, dear friend, to say "Be well!" Send my greetings to those that I love; I kiss you and your wife abundantly, I embrace you ever so tightly. Ha! I almost forgot: Is Meline well? If she is still well, I send her my regards and kiss her a thousand times lovingly. I am curious about the other protagonists in the book.

Write! Write! By all means, don't stop writing! May the hand of one who writes [such works] never falter!

Birnur Şener / Turkey

Bremen, 15 February, 2001
Dear Kemal Yalçın,

In truth, I really don't know where or how to begin. There are so many things I wish to say. With which one should I begin?

First of all, I want to relay to you my sincere congratulations and blessings. I read your book titled "You Rejoice My Heart" because of our Turkish instructor, whose name is İmdat Ulusoy. I read it—and how! With tears flowing from my eyes... In truth, I was very moved and saddened. I didn't have any idea just how bad and difficult the conditions were under which the Armenians in Turkey had to live.

My name is Natilda Büyüker. I was born and raised in Bremen, I'm now a girl of nineteen. I'm Armenian, but what a shame that I can't speak "*Hayeren*" [Armenian]. My mother and father didn't teach me because they thought I would suffer for it. As for me, I thought the exact opposite. For me, it would be an enriching experience to learn my mother tongue, Armenian. One day I'm definitely going to learn it.

I don't know very much about Armenian history. Until now I haven't been able to find many books on the subject. In my opinion, for me to be able to clearly and accurately understand everything, I need to know Turkish history, and that of many other countries, and, most important, to understand it.

What a shame that I have no knowledge whatsoever of Armenian literature. This ignorance is, unfortunately, widespread among the Armenian youth who live here. In Bremen there's been no progress whatever from the viewpoint of cultural activity. Despite a few attempts, we don't even have our own association.

Up to now, everything I've experienced in regard to my identity has not been negative. I've never been insulted in Germany because I was Armenian; I've never experienced any injustice or any evil directed in my direction for it either.

For this reason, it moved me deeply and made me sad to read the stories of Meline, Safiye Güner, Amasyali Ohan Özant, Merzifonlu Vahram Karabent, Master Sarkis of Karaman and others who you recount in your book. The sagas of the lives that are told there have shocked me so much that my eyes fill with tears just to think about it. I would be lying if I told you that I only felt sorrow when reading "You Rejoice My Heart." There were other moments when I felt joy. I saw and became familiar with the things that some good and honest people experienced; and I got to see that such people are still alive today.

I became familiar with those who loved others simply because they were human; with those who ran to the assistance of the oppressed; those who made no distinctions on the basis of religion or language; those who were not prejudiced; those who said the most sacred thing of all is "to approach one another with love." I recognized myself in these people. It was as if these persons had spoken my very feelings, my thoughts.

I have friends from many nations: Turks, Kurds, Azeris, Germans, Arabs and others, and from many different religions and beliefs. I love each one of them because they are good and honest people.

After reading this book, I believe with all my heart that wrong ideas, most of which are based on prejudice, can be changed. For this, I again bless you with all my heart. And I thank you again greatly for having increased my curiosity and interest for what is inside me and for my own past.

And one thing more! A love that has given me goosebumps and enchanted me terribly. The love and friendship between you and Meline are unbelievably bewitching. There are very few friendships like this. How happy you must be to find such friendship! I don't think there's a single sentence that can explain a unique feeling like this. Only those who have experienced it know it....

Now I've thought of something else... I'm studying in the German and Fine Arts Departments of Bremen University. I would like to work as a Turkish teacher in the future. I wish you that your success continues.

With my love and esteem,

Natilda Büyüker / Germany

Cologne, 21 February, 2001
Dear Kemal Yalçın,

Although I received your work titled "You Rejoice My Heart," which you sent almost a month ago, you cannot have greeted positively the fact that—if for no other reason than politeness—I did not even send you a letter of thanks.

The only reason for this is that after reading the lines that you dedicated to me in the first page of the book, I felt myself obliged to read the book in its entirety. First I read half of it on a train journey; the rest I read tonight without sleeping, even though it is now late at night. It is a magnificent work, a monument to history. I bless you with all my heart.

I was truly moved by the awakening of a sense of responsibility within you in response to Meline's answer "But you never asked who I was!", and by your putting yourself through the hardship—and overcoming many obstacles with this awareness—to research who the Armenians were, and especially what a fiery gauntlet they passed through in recent history. It is evidence of just how pure-hearted a person you are, and just how close you feel to people and how much you love humanity.

Be assured that the greatest service possible has been done to the culture of peace through your honest and sincere explanations, expressed in a simple language, of the events in the personal histories of those persons described in your book and of the areas in which they lived, and especially through your introducing them to the average Turk.

By bringing out into the light of day through your eyewitnesses, a question which others have tried to avoid and conceal with phrases like "Let's leave history to the historians!", you are essentially doing a service to humanity. What a shame that historians in Turkey have not done anything but to destroy the ties between these two peoples.

You can probably imagine the spirit in which we would repeat the information regarding "the Armenians enemies" that we received during the history lessons we attended in Turkey.

I recognized exactly who some of those persons were with whom you spoke, and some of the areas in which they lived. I would like to introduce you to one of my own relatives by the name of "Mehmed of Ankara," whom I came across coincidentally in Germany. Although I didn't actually go to the city in which he lives, Mehmet, who is the son of my mother's uncle, was hesitant to introduce me to his family out of fear of being discovered as what he was; nevertheless, he strongly wished to speak with me, as if he wanted to provide some testimony [of his life], and to recount his own sorrowful and bitter memories. If his brother is still alive, he will still be living in Ankara under the name "Halil." While reading the stories of people's lives that were found in your book, I once more experienced the moving sorrows of these relatives of mine.

I bless you again for your civilized courage. I believe that there are yet other enlightened researchers like yourself who can serve the cause of peace between the nations. Apart from Meline, I do not want to forget your mother and siblings among those who encouraged the creation of such a work. Please relay to them my wishes for their happiness and success. Your mother can be proud that she has a son of your quality. And your brothers and sisters should be honored for having a brother like you. Finally, let me state that you have pleased me greatly with your book, and to convey my warmest wishes.

With my esteem,

Archbishop Karekin Bekdjian / Germany

Siegen, 21 October, 2002

Dear Kemal Yalçın,

I read your books "You Rejoice My Heart" and "The Security Trousseau" with great emotion and interest. You are blazing a totally new trail. My prayer and wish is that many other Turkish intellectuals and thinkers will follow the path that you have blazed. The fact that you, as a Turkish writer, have thrown open the door on one of the most important subjects still considered taboo in Turkey will secure a place for you as one of the bright and eternal stars on the pages of this country's history.

I am a seventy-eight year old Greek from Istanbul. I was born in 1924. Ever since I was a child I have had an ever-deepening interest in history and politics. I have heard of the "Armenian Deportation"—and the "Greek Expulsion" which resembles it, more or less—from the mouths of those who experienced these bitter and sorrowful events. My heart has been wrenched with sorrow from a very young age!

I left Turkey when I was twenty years old. I passed my childhood and youth in Turkey. I completed school in Istanbul. I studied Turkish history in the schools. In the history books and the history lessons, there was never any mention of the subjects you've touched upon, such as the "Greek Expulsion" and the "Armenian Deportation." I always asked why they were never mentioned. It's interesting; in those years the school books condemned the Ottoman royal house with the harshest of language, but had nothing to say about the barbarities of the Ottoman Talât and his imbecile cohorts, not even a word of ridicule or contempt.

There is only one reason that the Germans were able to leave behind the barbarity of the Third Reich period and ascend to a brand new liberty and respect, to the stage of a democratic republic: it's because they openly discussed and accepted the past, without any attempt to hide it, every evil and every crime that had occurred in their history; because they opened all of the documentation and archives in their possession in order that these crimes and evils could be fully and honestly explained. Such an honest and courageous revelation of all of the cruelty and oppression of the Hitler regime were a type of therapy and catharsis for the German people. If the Germans had refrained from the tragedies of putting the conscience of the Third Reich up for public review and perusal, or from the brutality of Hitler's regime, you can be sure that we would not be seeing the same Germany today.

I am a theologian. In the Holy Book to which I have devoted years of study, in the Proverbs of Solomon this evident truth is stressed: "He that covereth his sins shall not prosper: but whoso confesseth and forsaketh *them* shall have mercy" (28:13). This Divine principal is the central theme of the Holy Book, which is concerned with both the individual and with society. If the historical truths which many Turkish historians and writers have for years attempted to conceal and the great hardships that were suffered and cruelties that were committed had been exposed to the light of day, the average Turk, and the country of Turkey would have experienced the same spiritual and mental therapeutic benefit as the average German. But until now not only has this not happened, but instead, there has been an attempt to foist the blame for cruelties and oppressions that were committed upon the backs of the victims.

I believe that the path you have newly beaten shall not be grown over with brambles. Perhaps I shall not see it, but I am hopeful that it will be seen: may many more Kemal Yalçıns emerge in Turkey; may the taboos of Turkey, which have been hidden within a locked chest and a sealed book, be brought to the light of day with a civilized courage and humane attitude. In that way, the entire country and its people might reach a place wherein they are able to experience a catharsis and therapeutic release. May the civilized attitude and behavior that you have so munificently shown in this direction be the daily point of reference for Turkish intellectuals and thinkers!

I cannot end my letter without referring to this point one more time: everyone has a number of skeletons in their lives that they must bear; would that it were not so, but it is! Likewise, there are countless injustices and unbecoming incidents to be seen in the history of every nation. In this, the Turkish nation is no different from the others. Turkish historians and writers must be able, without blinking, to openly acknowledge the evils that their nation performed and the injustices that were committed during the eras of earlier administrations. Through such behavior they will find favor with both God and man.

With my most sincere feelings of friendship,

Thomas Cosmades / Germany

Duisburg, 15.12.2001
Autumn Storms

The "Fakir Baykurt Literary Coffee Klatch" is holding its last meeting of 2001 in the Café Orient in Duisburg. Nearly thirty persons attended this final rendezvous of the year. After a round of "Welcome!"s and "Thank you!"s, the participants break up into small groups of two or three persons.

Kemal Yalçın says:

"Mustafa, please open my bag that's beside you and take out the last book I wrote!"

I open his bag. It's an enormous book. It's titled "You Rejoice My Heart." I immediately ask:

"Is it a novel?"

"No, it's reportage," he replies. "This book consists of the detailed reporting that I have been undertaking for two years. Give it here and let me sign it."

I give it to him. He opens it up and signs it:

"To Belgin and Mustafa, with my wishes for days filled with love and joy!"

When I return home, I put the book on the table. A little while later I pass by the table and take the book from the place where it lay and peruse it. It's as if the book is saying, "Read me!" Only the first few pages and it already has me in its grip. Most of the time, I don't read the books I've bought or received right away. First I read the ones that are already on the shelf, waiting. I wait to read the book until I feel the desire from within. When the voice inside me says "Read it!", that's when I read it. But today was different. I reached my hand out for this 426-page "You Rejoice My Heart." I read straight until four o'clock the next morning. The next day I started off at the place where I left off and ignoring everything else in my life, I kept reading until I finished the book.

[....] In a documentary style, and through the testimony of those who have experienced these things, we learn of the history and experiences of the Armenians that have occurred and transpired from the end of the 1800s until our day. I call it "documentary," because upon learning, in the section of your book titled "A Final Word," that Vahram Karabent and

Kirkor Ceyhan both passed away the year before your book was published, we begin to understand better the serious and important nature of the work that has been done....

Yet, Kemal Yalçın doesn't explain these things in the manner of history. We read these events like a novel. The writer even enriches his account by incorporating these things into his own life story.... The author reproduces each account in the words of the witnesses themselves, in the form of narrative sections, and thereby takes the reader on an historical journey. Through his account of each journey he makes to locate and reach the witnesses, the author has enriched and embellished his story.

As a reader, you can see how the truths that have been experienced have left deeper traces than those lives than you have only imagined; deeper than the life portrayed in novels or stories.

You understand once again the human sensitivity, historical consciousness and prejudices in these stories; you perceive that the suffering of the heart does not recognize race or nationality, that the explaining or writing of these realities does not debase a person or society—on the contrary, it makes them more sensitive.

You experience the charitable, humane tendencies of the people of Anatolia, which have been filtered by the lens of history, and you become a guest in the houses of these people. You read all of these things, sometimes in the sparse, direct speech of Kemal Yalçın's explanations, at others in the ambiance of a great epic.

May your hand and your heart remain strong, Kemal Yalçın!

Mustafa Cebe / Germany

Toronto, 3 December, 2002

Most Esteemed Kemal Bey!

As I told you when we spoke on the phone, I received your books from Vahan Şişmanoğlu and I related to you my great respect. But my esteem or criticism are meaningless. What is necessary is the respect and regard of humanity. I just want to say what pops into my head here. I will never forget that poem of my "brother," the late Tevfik Fikret:

"There is a Divine Force / Holy and Sublime / I believed in this with [great] faith / The [good] earth, my homeland; all manner of humanity, my nation / A person is a person: this I have believed upon consideration!"

I ask you: where are these persons? Their fate has overtaken these persons and carried them off. The Tevfik Fikrets, the Aziz Nesins, the Kemal Tahirs, the Nâzim Hikmets: they have all been eliminated struggling, on behalf of humanity and mankind, against a thousand and one deprivations in dungeons or in exile. I'm not a politician. And I'm certainly no professors. I'm simply an artisan, a lathe operator. As for this that they call life, I have already completed eighty percent of the journey. It has taken me through tree- and flower-lined paths. We have snatched up whatever we were able to from these travels, according to our available means.

The entire world knows these truths that I have explained, even Turkey knows this very well from us. But it is a civilized nation that is not working to find a point of resolution for this.

I have read your books. You have labored with the goal of serving humanity, of helping mankind. You have spoken of the injustices that the Armenians and Greeks have suffered. As an Armenian I thank you from my heart.

Nişan Şişmanoğlu / Canada

Appendix II. Destroying Books

The following Turkish documents with our English translations record the destruction of the first Turkish edition of *You Rejoice My Heart* in Istanbul on 21 June 2002. This destruction was due to pressures put on publishers in Turkey.*

---

* *You Rejoyce My Heart* (*Seninle Güler Yüreğim*) was recently reprinted in Turkey by Birzamanlar Yayincilik (Istanbul) in 2006.

Illustration 1

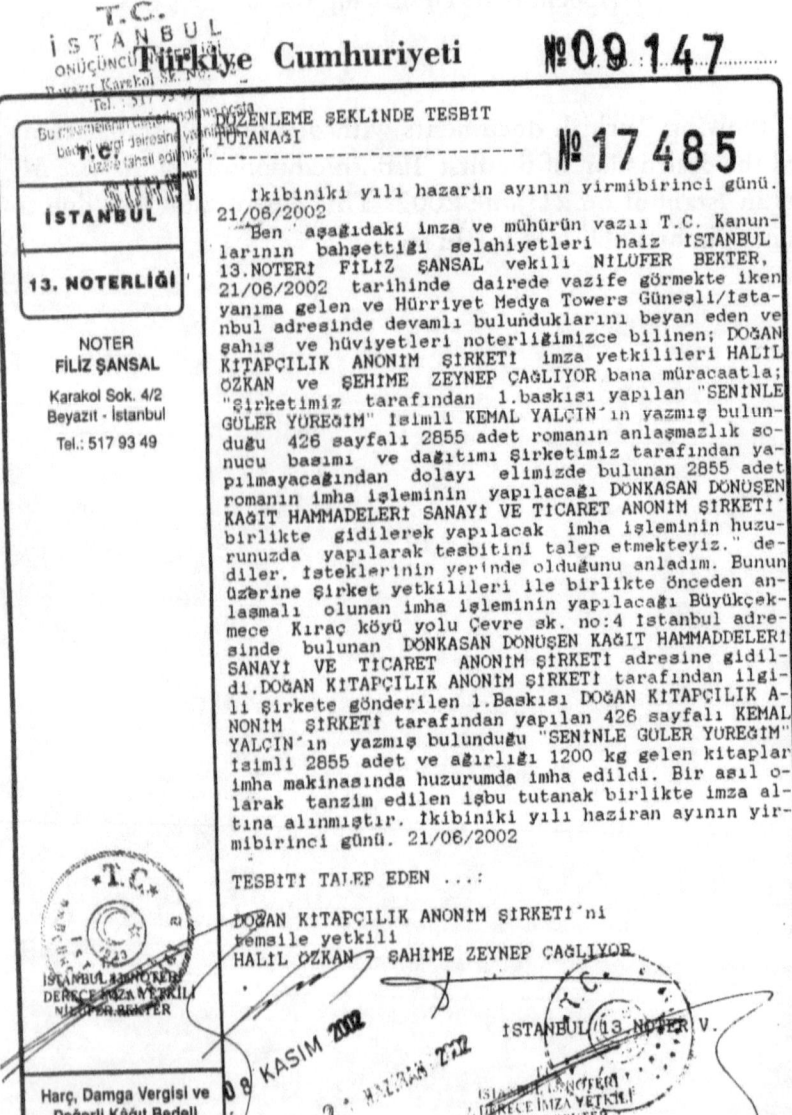

Illustration 1
English translation of main text

Main Turkish text reads:

21/06/2002

HALİL ÖZKAN AND ŞEHIME ZEYNEP ÇADLIYOR, authorized signatories for DOĐAN BOOK PUBLISHING, Ltd., came to me, NİLÜFER BEKTER, the acting representative for FİLİZ ŞANSAL, 13TH NOTARY PUBLIC FOR ISTANBUL, owner of the stamp and signature below and possessing the authorities mentioned by the Laws of the Republic of Turkey, in the course of fulfilling my duties on the date 21/06/2002 within the [aforementioned] offices, declared that their permanent address was Hürriyet Medya Towers, in Güneşli, Istanbul and had their persons and identities verified by our notary's office. They came to me with a request, saying "We request a [notary's] certification by having a destruction operation performed in your presence; together with the DÖNKASAN RECYCLED PAPER MATERIALS INDUSTRY AND SALES COMPANY, LTD., where the destruction of 2855 copies of the 1st printing by our company of the book YOU REJOICE MY HEART, written by KEMAL YALÇIN, is to be carried out by our company due to a misunderstanding regarding the printing and distribution of said novel." I understood that there demands were proper and legitimate. Upon this, I traveled, together with the authorized signatories of the company, to the address of the DÖNKASAN RECYCLED PAPER MATERIALS INDUSTRY AND SALES COMPANY, LTD., which is located at the address Kiraç köyü yolu Çevre St. no. 4, Büyükçekmece, Istanbul, and where it had previously been understood that the destruction was to take place. The 2855 copies of the 1st printing of the book YOU REJOICE MY HEART by KEMAL YALÇIN, weighing 1,200 kilograms and printed by DOĐAN BOOK PUBLISHING, LTD., and which had been sent by DOĐAN BOOK PUBLISHING, Ltd. To the relevant company, were destroyed in my presence in the [book] destroying machine. This document was signed, together with the one which had originally been prepared. The twenty-first day of the month of June, in the year two thousand and two. 21/06/2002

Illustration 2

№ 09147
№ 17485

İMHA TUTANAĞI

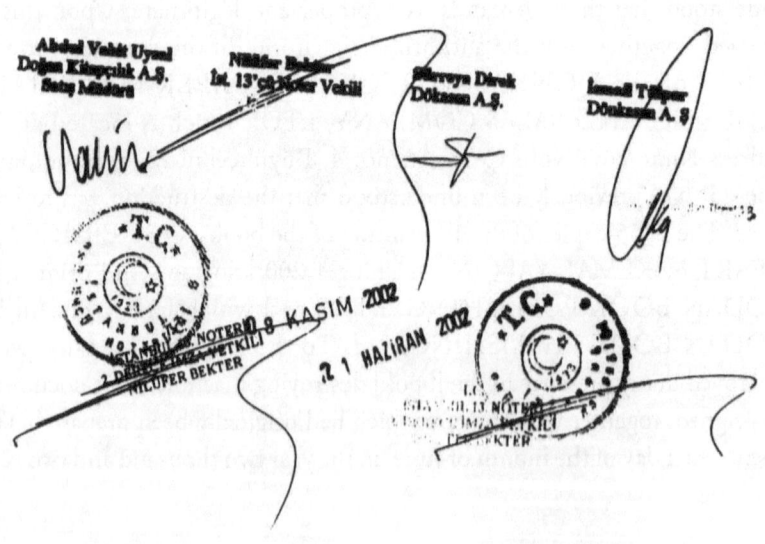

Illustration 2
English translation of main text

2855 copies of the book titled "You Rejoice My Heart," whose author is Kemal Yalçın and which belong to Doğan Book Publishing, Ltd., were destroyed within our company on the date 21.06.2002, in the presence of authorized company representative Abdul Vahit Uysal and Nilüfer Bekter, acting representative of the 13th Notary Public of Istanbul.

Gomidas Institute
42 Blythe Rd.
London W14 0HA
Email: *info@gomidas.org*
Web: *www.gomidas.org*

www.ingramcontent.com/pod-product-compliance
Lightning Source LLC
Chambersburg PA
CBHW021828220426
43663CB00005B/163